PRAISE FOR *THE*

"When I started snowboarding, Craig w
Growing up, I always looked up to him. He inspired me and so many other
riders. I just wish I got to ride with him more."   —Shaun White

"Impressive reporting offers new insight into [Craig] Kelly's final hours, and
the author's empathetic portrayal of Kelly as a purist who 'turned his back
on business deals, high-dollar sponsorship contracts, and . . . prize money'
to return to the 'powdery backcountry that had first drawn him to his calling' will resonate even with those unfamiliar with his legacy. It's a stirring
tribute to a talent gone too soon."   —*Publishers Weekly*

"Eric Blehm took on this biography as I imagine Craig Kelly took on the halfpipe. He studied it, chose his line, and pulled everything off—even tough
parts—with grace and style. It's not just a terrific story of an amazing life, not
just the origin story of an entire sport, but a riveting disaster narrative that
builds tension masterfully. *The Darkest White* grabbed me and didn't let go."
          —Jack Carr, #1 *New York Times* bestselling author of
          the Terminal List series

"Blehm recounts in gripping detail the terrifying disaster, the desperate rescue efforts, and the ensuing investigations into the cause. A stirring adventure narrative and sports bio."   —*Kirkus Reviews*

"*The Darkest White* is a little like riding a magic carpet through a whiteout.
I haven't read a winter saga this good since John Branch's *Snowfall*, which
won the Pulitzer."
          —John Long, adventurer, climber, and award-winning author of
          Gorilla Monsoon, Icarus Syndrome, and *Granite Mariner*

"In *The Darkest White*, Eric Blehm skillfully chronicles the remarkable life
and terrifying demise of legendary snowboarder Craig Kelly, whose journey from youthful shredder to pioneering icon transformed winter sports.
With narrative precision and descriptive beauty, Blehm immerses readers
into the highs and lows of Kelly's career, exploring the captivating world of
snowboarding, its cultural explosion, and the ruthless forces of nature that
ultimately claimed the life of this sensational athlete."
          —Neal Bascomb, author of *Faster* and *The Perfect Mile*

THE
DARKEST
WHITE

A MOUNTAIN LEGEND AND THE
AVALANCHE THAT TOOK HIM

ERIC BLEHM

HARPER  PERENNIAL

NEW YORK • LONDON • TORONTO • SYDNEY • NEW DELHI • AUCKLAND

HARPER ● PERENNIAL

A hardcover edition of this book was published in 2024 by Harper,
an imprint of HarperCollins Publishers.

HarperCollins books may be purchased for educational, business, or
sales promotional use. For information, please email the Special Markets
Department at SPsales@harpercollins.com.

FIRST HARPER PERENNIAL EDITION PUBLISHED 2025.

Designed by Bonni Leon-Berman

Library of Congress Cataloging-in-Publication Data

Names: Blehm, Eric, author.
Title: The darkest white: a mountain legend and the avalanche
that took him / Eric Blehm.
Description: First edition. | New York : HarperCollins Publishers, [2024]
| Includes bibliographical references.
Identifiers: LCCN 2023042741 | ISBN 9780062971401 (print) | ISBN
9780062971425 (digital edition)
Subjects: LCSH: Kelly, Craig Elmer, 1966-2003. | Snowboarders—
United States—Biography. | Avalanches—Accidents—Canada.
Classification: LCC GV857.S57 B54 2024 | DDC 796.939092 B—
dc23/eng/20231023
LC record available at https://lccn.loc.gov/2023042741

ISBN 978-0-06-297141-8 (pbk.)

24 25 26 27 28 LBC 5 4 3 2 1

For Craig

CONTENTS

PART IV: LEGEND

PROLOGUE

Fifty thousand spectators descended upon Aspen, Colorado, in the last week of January 2003 to watch the most "extreme" athletes battle it out in alternative sports' biggest arena: the Winter X Games. Many in the record-breaking crowd came specifically to cheer on a redheaded snowboarding prodigy named Shaun White. Not yet an Olympian, he was well on the road to becoming one of the most famous athletes on the planet—mainly for the manner in which he briefly shot himself into orbit above it, launching off monster jumps and halfpipe walls with the precision of a gymnast and the recklessness of youth.

The Superpipe was mobbed with thousands of fans who hushed as White, only sixteen years old, dropped in for his final run. Cameras from major sports networks and magazines followed his every move, and the crowd roared as he soared above the perfectly shaped halfpipe, spinning and inverting his body and board into history as the first snowboarder to win back-to-back (Slopestyle and Superpipe) X Games gold medals.

Second only to the Olympics as a televised and marketed winter sporting enterprise, the X Games snowboarding scene was electric—a hyped-up, commercialized, energy-drink-sponsored rock concert on snow; a supercharged mutation of the stark, humble, and fiercely independent alpine soul that had birthed the sport decades before. Obscured though it may have been by the glare of stadium lights and the alien neon of plastic-wrapped sugar water, it was a soul that nevertheless still lived in many of the competitors and fans present. It was the soul of the mountain town or surfer and skater kids who'd grown up with boards attached to their feet and ice crystals in their hair. It was even the soul of some of the board sponsors like Burton and Sims who now reaped the financial windfall of a world their founders had created from planks of wood.

But on this day, there was another manifestation of that soul, a silent rider in the form of a sticker displayed by many in the crowd, and worn by Shaun White himself on his chest during his winning run, a rectangular white decal that read in bold black letters:

Craig Kelly Is My CoPilot

Most casual fans didn't even notice the message, but those who did understood that it celebrated the life of a beloved snowboarding legend who had been killed just a week before—on January 20, 2003, by an avalanche in the Selkirk Mountains of British Columbia, Canada. Craig Kelly had been a guiding force to a generation of snowboarders who revered him, a compass pointing the way. Once a fierce competitor himself, Craig was snowboarding's first true professional and four-time world champion. He had stood at the top of the podium more times than anybody who'd ridden a snowboard during the 1980s and into the '90s as the sport burst to life and rapid global influence. His own story was an epic adventure, an alpine odyssey that catapulted Craig—a latchkey kid of divorced parents from small-town Mount Vernon, Washington—around the world multiple times as he helped make snowboarding a worldwide cultural and commercial phenomenon.

Craig's contest results and global rankings made him snowboarding's first international superstar, but when given the choice of more fame and fortune, he followed his heart. He turned his back on business deals, high-dollar sponsorship contracts, and the prize money associated with competition and returned to the powdery backcountry that had first drawn him to his calling. In the process, he inspired people from around the globe to follow him there.

I was one of them.

I FIRST "MET" Craig Kelly in the pages of *International Snowboard Magazine* in the mid-1980s before most of the world even knew what a snowboard was. A subscription to *ISM* in 1985 was like membership to a secret society filled with cool characters who were defining a culture one tweaked air at a time. There was Terry Kidwell, Shaun "Mini Shred" Palmer, Damian Sanders,

Evan Feen, Steve Matthews, Scott "Upside" Downey, Jon "Boy Air" Boyer, Chris Karol, the Achenbach and Coghlan brothers, Tom Burt, Jim Zellers, Bonnie Leary—I remember them all—Mark Heingartner, Dave Alden, Keith Kimmel, Lori Gibbs. Names most people never heard of, even then.

I ended up writing for, and ultimately became the editor of, another magazine I worshipped called *TransWorld SNOWboarding*. It was the best job I could imagine—getting paid to see the world and ride powder with my heroes. During these early years of the sport, one name—"Craig Kelly"—became all but synonymous with snowboarding. And then, suddenly, he disappeared from the public eye and as a perpetual presence in our pages.

There were occasional sightings, rumors that placed him in the fish markets of Ensenada, Mexico, then months later in the jungles of El Salvador, at an internet café in Puerto Montt, Chile. And then again for great stretches of time, there was nothing. Only "historical" rerun photos of him in the mags, cementing his place in the canon of snowboarding's golden age. During his absence, his legend settled comfortably in the hearts and minds of his many fans and drifted into lore—the Obi-Wan Kenobi of snowboarding.

But Craig's story wasn't over; he'd just followed his bliss to an isolated corner of what he called "snowboarding dreamland"—British Columbia—and, much as he always had, was quietly working on what was next.

You can go there, too. Just follow the Big Bend Highway out of the town of Revelstoke, British Columbia. At Carnes Creek, make a hard right and fly (yes, fly—you're in a helicopter) up the drainage into the wild and remote northern Selkirk Mountains. The aircraft will skim treetops and frozen waterfalls until you're so far from the nearest road that you could scream and your voice wouldn't make it halfway to anywhere. Shortly after you ascend above treeline, you'll blast into the white lunar expanse of the alpine. This is the T-intersection at Tumbledown Mountain. You could bank left and fly toward Seven Ravens Knoll or instead bank right, skirt the western flank of Goat Peak, and descend toward a red-roofed chalet perched in absolute solitude on a subalpine knoll with sweeping views of the Selkirks in every direction, their jagged peaks intersected by deep gullies, rock-lined couloirs, cornice-rimmed bowls, and miles upon miles of glaciers.

When Craig landed there on January 18, 2003, a skier he had flown in with said simply, "Welcome to paradise."

Sixteen years later, when I landed at the same spot, I wasn't so sure.

This was, after all, the "paradise" that killed Craig Kelly, who, let's be clear, hadn't even seemed mortal. He was a superhero born from a blizzard on a sleeping volcano. He levitated down mountains, raced avalanches, aired cliffs, and landed on the covers of magazines. "If gods walked the earth," says photographer Gordon Eshom, "Craig was one of them." That's not hyperbole. "We all believed it," says fellow pro rider Jason Ford, "right up to the moment we heard the impossible news of his death."

I had been asked to write a couple of memorial tributes to Craig plus an obituary when he died, but it took me sixteen years to pay my respects at the place of his passing. When I landed on that same knoll and walked into the Durrand Glacier Chalet in the spring of 2019, I knew I was looking for a kind of closure that had eluded many of the friends and family of those who died that day in 2003, as well as some who had managed to survive.

The Durrand Glacier Avalanche, as it came to be known, had been the first of a duo of avalanches in this range that left fourteen people dead and was deemed the "deadliest fortnight" in North American backcountry skiing and snowboarding history. These incidents prompted hard questions about risk management, the ethics of guiding, and accountability. Canada's *National Post* newspaper stated that the Durrand avalanche in particular "changed backcountry culture" forever.

My pilgrimage to the Durrand began when I asked a guide friend if he would mind introducing me to the lead guide in charge—the fiercely proud proprietor of Selkirk Mountain Experience (SME) and its red-roofed outpost, Ruedi Beglinger—the man who had, directly or indirectly, led seven people to their deaths. I asked him to tell Beglinger I was writing Craig's story to honor his life and the lives of all of those who were killed that day; I wanted to tell the entire story of the avalanche, still a controversial and emotionally charged disaster nearly two decades later.

For months my friend told me that Beglinger had not replied, but the truth was he had, with a definitive "no." He had zero interest in talking to me if my questions were about the avalanche.

If I couldn't ask questions, I figured I could at least ride with him. So, I attempted the standard process to book a week at SME, and followed up with a letter that further explained who I was and what I hoped to do. Beglinger needed to understand that Craig was not just some celebrity subject for me. I'd broken trail with him in the Kootenays, shared waves and tequila shots with him in Baja, ridden blower powder with him in Iran. He was my friend. Beglinger and his family also lost friends that day, so I expressed my condolences and wrote, "I have waited sixteen years to visit where Craig took his last turns, and I am wondering if you'll welcome me to at least experience the area. If you wish, I will not ask you a single question about the avalanche. Not one question."

A week later, I received a call from Beglinger's office manager. "We have a cancellation—you're in." A month later, I was one of fifteen guests who were helicoptered in, five at a time, while guests from the previous week were flown out. Beglinger was right there as my group stepped off the skids, welcoming return clients with hugs, and for me—and other first-timers—he pulled off a glove and shook my hand.

The slightly built, sun-and-wind-weathered guide was now sixty-three, but if his grip was any indication, he was as strong today as he had been when he'd first met Craig at this exact spot. "I'm Ruedi," he said in a heavy Swiss accent. "I'm Eric," I returned. "Ya, I know this," he said with a glance down at my soft snowboard boots, the tell among the other guests, who wore hard-shelled ski-touring boots. "You are our only snowboarder this week."

If I felt singled out, it was only for a moment, because for the next seven days I was just a part of the group, having paid my fee to be led through these storied mountains. Each morning, we rose before the sun, packed lunches, ate breakfast, and by eight (if late, you're left behind) were walking, aka touring, away from the chalet in the Nordic tradition: with climbing skins affixed to our ski bases* for uphill traction. We followed guides whose goal was to take us to the mountains' secret places—to share what they knew and revealed—and in the process we learned a little something about ourselves.

After climbing through forests, traversing icefalls, and crossing glaciers for hours, we would ski or ride down for miles—six thousand vertical feet per day, the guides testing the slopes as we went, observing our skills, assessing

---

*   I was using my split snowboard in ski mode.

our fitness, and determining if our group was more suited to roll into a particular run or push farther up the ridge, tiptoe past some exposure, and drop into a hidden, steeper aspect with mandatory air. Each weightless powder turn that followed wasn't just a reward; it was a reminder of what Craig Kelly had considered *the* essence of snowboarding—the freedom of climbing and descending through nature's forces and harnessing them just enough to collaborate with gravity.

Exhausted, we'd return to the chalet single file in the evening, have a sauna, stretch, a snow bath for the brave, followed by a beer, a book, or a nap. At 6:30 p.m., we'd sit down to a meal, shoulder to shoulder with strangers who were becoming friends.

Halfway through the week and shortly after breakfast, I laced up my boots, turned on my avalanche transceiver, and joined the early risers assembling outside. It was snowing lightly and gray and the steep alpine faces that rose up before us were shrouded by the flurries of a gathering storm. We focused on the seemingly impassable Goat Peak, whose ramparts and ridges separated us from our objectives that day. Several of these guests, including a judge and a lumber baron with his family who had been returning here for decades, fielded questions from us first-timers, pointing out runs they'd done in the past while speculating which route or passageway—"Needle Icefall . . . maybe the Ledges"—would take us up, over, or through this daunting quandary of rock, ice, and snow.

As 8 a.m. drew nearer, the wind picked up, and most of this crew leaned on their ski poles, gazing at the routes with a relaxed calm, but I and a few others shuffled about and stomped our skis, anxious in the gate. It was serious business, and there was a pervasive sense of adventure and a giddy, maybe nervous levity just before heading out. I was grateful for the camaraderie and human comfort that somehow manage to make a habitat of nature's extremes.

It *was* paradise.

A minute, maybe two, before 8 a.m., Beglinger rounded the corner of the chalet. Big feathery flakes were drifting down lazily, a gift from the heavens that he marched through with his signature strong, confident gait, not toward the head of the group like he had the past few mornings, but instead, directly to me.

"Eric," he said, pausing briefly, face-to-face. "Maybe later, after we ski, we talk."

PART I

COMPETITOR

CHAPTER 1

ROOTS

IT WAS CHRISTMAS MORNING, 1965, when Sherman Poppen, a thirty-five-year-old businessman in the welding industry, looked at a snow-covered hill across the street from his Muskegon, Michigan, home and had a thought that would change winter sports forever.

His two young daughters, both hyped up on candy canes, had been driving his very pregnant wife just shy of crazy, so he was desperate to keep them outside, but the thin metal runners on the family sled kept getting bogged down in the deep snow, and that got him thinking: that wasn't a hill for sledding; it was a white winter wave. He'd always been fascinated by surfing and, recalling his ten-year-old daughter Wendy's past attempts to stand up on her sled, screwed two of her child-size skis together and fashioned for her a surfboard for the snow. Then, like snowbound Gidgets surfing the point at Malibu, she and her five-year-old sister, Laurie, hiked up and surfed down that dune for hours. Soon all the neighborhood kids were begging Mr. Poppen to make them what his wife, Nancy, called the "Snurfer."

In the weeks that followed, Poppen tinkered—and his girls tested—several design variations. On March 17, 1966, he filed the Snurfer idea and name with the U.S. Patent & Trademark Office, describing his invention as relating "to a snow ski, and more particularly to a surf-type snow ski which is adapted to support both feet of a skier and to be easily maneuvered therefore without foot bindings, thereby providing a new snow sport which incorporates features of certain summer pastimes, namely surfboarding, [and] skateboarding. . . ." Poppen had just foretold the future of an entire subculture of recreationalists, athletes, professionals, and world champions—most of whom hadn't even been born yet.

CRAIG ELMER KELLY came into the world fifteen days after that patent was filed on April 1, 1966—April Fools' Day. He was the first-born child of eighteen-year-old Janet Marie Kelly and twenty-year-old Patrick Lamont Kelly, high school sweethearts who—without their parents' blessings—had gotten married exactly nine months and two weeks earlier in Granite City, Illinois. Pat's mom, Helen Kelly, and Janet's parents, Bob and Gail Moore, had not been too happy about the marriage, but they were thrilled about Craig, whose addition smoothed everything over family-wise.

Janet and Pat spent a few weeks living with Grandma Helen before stacking all their belongings onto a stake-bed trailer that was latched to their '65 Ford Falcon and heading west, to Richland, Washington, where Janet's father had gotten a job at the Hanford Nuclear Complex. They moved in with Bob and Gail, Pat got a job at the post office, and they started saving their pennies, eventually buying a home of their own right across the street from Sacajawea Elementary School.

Just shy of his first birthday Craig was prescribed leg braces—the type with a single flat bar attached between baby-sized shoes—that the doctor said would correct his inward-pointing (pigeon) toes and mitigate the likelihood for surgery. He wore them while he slept, and one time when he tried climbing out of his crib, the brace got hung up on the top rail. "I went in to check on him, and he wasn't crying or struggling," says Janet, "totally comfortable hanging upside down." Several months later, when he was around eighteen months, a loud "clunk!" announced to Janet that nap time was over. Craig was on the ground, his legs splayed out with the bar between his feet, and pushing himself upright using his arms like a tripod. He got to where he could balance there, and propel himself forward by shifting his weight from foot to foot, trying to walk and refusing to be hobbled by the braces, which he stopped wearing shortly after his second birthday, not long before his brother, Brian, was born.

Janet had started a day care business at their home, and Pat worked for a moving company and attended night school, earning credits toward an associate's degree. Around this time, a social worker knocked on their door, looking for prospective foster parents. Soon after completing the application process, Janet became pregnant for a third time.

Craig's sister Gillian was born in the summer of 1973. The same social worker circled back soon thereafter, telling Janet she was having a hard time placing "two little black girls we'd sure like to keep together." A few days later, seven-year-old Imogene and her four-year-old sister, Johnny, joined the Kelly family.

That fall, Pat coached Little League, putting seven-year-old Craig on the mound and Imogene on first. "The two of them made all the outs our first game," says Pat. "Struck out at the plate or thrown out at first—they were quite a team." Craig had always shown an aptitude for sports, as well as a strong competitive nature. A few weeks into third grade, he got into a fistfight on the playground, "a dispute over dodgeball, or basketball, or marbles, or something" says Pat. "He got a swat from the principal for that one."

When another fight broke out during class a week later, it was Pat who got called into the office, where he faced not only the principal, but Craig's teacher, a strict disciplinarian who rarely wrote the letter A on report cards. Usually her face-to-face meetings were with parents who found her grading too tough. In this case, it was the opposite. "Mr. Kelly," she said, "I believe Craig is getting into fights because he's bored." She then told Pat this was the first time in nearly thirty years of teaching that she recommended a third grader be moved up to fourth.

When Pat shared the news with Janet, she instantly recalled Craig's first week in kindergarten, when he'd left his classroom and walked home. When the doorbell rang, she had been shocked to see little Craig standing there with his Evel Knievel lunchbox, announcing he was home because he already knew everything the teacher was teaching. "Finger painting and the ABCs are for babies," he told her. "I'm bored."

Pat and Janet had contemplated moving him up a grade back then, but they'd reasoned that self-confidence on the playground, and in general, was more important at that age than suffering some boredom in the classroom. But now, three years later, they agreed with his teacher, and the next day he was a fourth grader. "That was probably the best decision we ever made together," says Pat. "From then on," says Janet, "Craig was always ahead of the crowd."

The entire family was working hard to get ahead, with Pat still pursuing his associate's degree and Janet supporting them with the daycare business, plus caring for her own three children and two foster kids. They'd earn extra cash buying used lumber from tear-downs: Pat would pick it up in their truck, Janet would unload, and the kids would pitch in and help sort everything, which they then sold for a profit.

In 1975, the family moved west to Bothell, near Seattle, where Pat would finish his bachelor's degree in business administration at the University of Washington. However, as foster children, Imogene and Johnny stayed in the county where their biological parents remained and had visitation rights.

After this emotional uprooting, the Craig Kelly origin story got "complicated." Once the hardworking and mostly happy nuclear family moved to Bothell, nobody—especially the neighbors—could deny that there was some strife in the Kelly residence, and it wasn't the kids who were doing the yelling. What sparked these mostly verbal battles remains a private affair, but they raged for more than a year, during which Craig turned ten. "All he wanted for his birthday," says Pat, "was to go backpacking in the Alpine Lakes Wilderness area he'd learned about in school." Car camping had been affordable entertainment for several years, but this was Craig's first backpacking trip, and the trail he and his father chose took all of their first day to trudge ten hard miles. They made a base camp and survived on pork and beans, sardines, gorp, and oatmeal for nearly a week, doing little more than hiking and exploring by day, and reading paperbacks by the campfire at night.

When asked about his childhood later in life, Craig would say, "I had a varied childhood, happy times and sad times both." A year of trial separations between Pat and Janet only prolonged the inevitable, and following a crescendo of "sad times," Craig and Brian came home from school one day to find a police car in their driveway and a broken living room window. That marked the end of their nuclear family.

It was 1977. Craig was almost eleven, Brian was nine, and Gillian was four. There was no brutal *Kramer vs. Kramer* courtroom battle for custody but "there was plenty of drama," says Brian. The boys went with Pat while Gillian went with Janet and, during the course of the next couple of years, all three attended several different schools and lived in a half-dozen different houses or apartments, enough that the kids stopped memorizing their addresses, because why bother?

Pat's first apartment after the separation was north of Seattle in Lynn-wood, where Craig and Brian went largely unsupervised while Pat was at work, and frequently found trouble, like shooting their neighbors with rubber band–launched paperclips, breaking "stuff," and shoplifting. "It was a pretty big step up from normal mischief," says Brian. "We were revolting—angry, just like, 'oh, no milk for cereal in the fridge, Dad's at work, let's go to the donut shop.'" Brian would follow Craig's lead into the line where they picked out the donuts. "Just smile and act normal," Craig told his little brother. "Act like you already paid." Which is exactly what he did as they mingled in the crowd, passed the cash register, and walked out the door.

Pat recalls that they moved on when the lease ended. Brian recalls the lease not being renewed because he and Craig were the apartment complex's in-house hoodlums. Regardless, "it was a good thing we got out of that neighborhood," says Brian, who recalls that Craig in particular loved the adrenaline rush that came with being bad and had started hanging out with some shady kids who were stealing a lot more than donuts.

They moved on to a more family oriented neighborhood in Mountlake Terrace, which was when Craig first fell in love. He saw her in the shop window of the Lynnwood Bikefactory: a Mongoose BMX bike. Pat couldn't afford the bike, no matter how much he wanted to get it for his son. "I'll tell you what," he told Craig' "If you pay for half, I'll figure out a way to cover the rest."

Craig got himself a paper route and started saving. Once he got that bike, everything was going to be rad: he'd practice and get good like the kids in the BMX mags he flipped through but never bought at the 7-Eleven. There was no extra cash for that, but he'd spend a quarter on a small Slurpee, then park it at the magazine rack and sip it slow while flipping pages. That was smart money, and one of the times you'd catch him smiling—the same as when he and Brian would catch a Sunday matinee with their mom and Gillian, or cram together on the couch with their dad and a pizza on Tuesday nights to watch *Happy Days*.

At first, the boys saw their mom most weekends, though Pat saw Gillian quite a bit less. But as they grew older, Brian spent more time with Janet, while Craig stayed more with Pat, and Gillian didn't see her dad with any regularity—not much more than one weekend a month. That was the state of affairs when Pat and the boys landed at 1015 South Twenty-First Street,

Mount Vernon, Washington, in January 1979, a date that marked the beginning of what Craig would refer to as "my formative years."

THAT SAME JANUARY, but on the other side of the country, a twenty-four-year-old Snurfing fanatic named Jake Burton Carpenter was attempting to enter the eleventh annual "World Snow Snurfing Championships" on Blockhouse Hill in Muskegon, Michigan. It had been thirteen years since Sherman Poppen had licensed the patent-pending Snurfer to Brunswick Corporation in 1966, and since then more than a million Snurfers had been produced and sold to sporting goods and toy stores throughout America.

The Snurfer had inspired a cadre of young entrepreneurs who improved upon the rudimentary design, shaping their own boards and adding bindings, straps, and other improvements. Carpenter was the first rider to show up at this race, armed not with a Snurfer but with his own—deemed nonregulation—Burton board. Organizers created a last-minute "open" division, wherein Carpenter was the sole entrant and winner. While his race time was no better than the top five Snurfer entrants, the addition of a front-foot binding and wider board gave him superior balance and control. Be it evolution or innovation, Carpenter's presence there signaled the beginning of the end of traditional Snurfing and the start of something nobody could yet define.

Snow-surfing, ski boarding, Snurfboarding, Burton boarding, Wintersticking, snowboarding—whatever they called it, they were doing it at golf courses, on backyard hills, wherever they could find an angled slope covered with snow. To fund their addiction, more and more budding entrepreneurs began producing boards in makeshift factories to sell to friends, neighbors, ski shops, surf shops, gas stations close to sledding hills, skateboard shops in the city, and bike shops near the mountains.

This was how five Burton "Backhill" boards—handmade in a barn in Londonderry, Vermont—ended up across the country at Fulton's Schwinn Cyclery in Mount Vernon, Washington, just in time for Christmas 1979. The shop owner's son, nineteen-year-old skateboarder Jeff Fulton, had seen the boards advertised in *Skateboarder* magazine and urged his parents, Phyllis and James, to stock a few for the holidays, even though neither they, nor anybody they knew, had ever heard of snowboarding.

The Fultons' pioneering spirit spoke to the roots of Mount Vernon, a wilderness-encircled town of farmers and industry that had been hacked out of the heavily timbered forest on the banks of the Skagit River in 1870. From its historic red-brick and mortar downtown, row houses sprawled up the hill into cookie-cutter neighborhoods where the town's youth skateboarded and biked to school, hung out at the arcade, and fished for steelhead and salmon running in the river. Located halfway between Seattle, Washington, and Vancouver, British Columbia, Canada, Mount Vernon had become a way station for travelers who need only glance to the northeast, across fields of tulips and beyond forested hills, to see the guardian of the skyline: a snow-covered volcano named Mount Baker. During winter, kids flocked there to ski or slide down sledding hills on silver saucers, inner tubes, and—hopefully—a few of the Burton boards the Fultons displayed next to the new Schwinn Scrambler SX-1000 in their shop's front window.

While four of the boards collected dust in the shop, Fulton rode the heck out of the one he claimed as his own at roadside stashes around Mount Baker. Unbeknownst to him, Bob Barci—the owner of the Bikefactory seventy miles south in Bellevue—and his manager and bike mechanic Tom Raven and Eric Gallison were riding the slopes around Snoqualmie Pass on boards they'd built themselves. They too stocked a few Burton boards and were so amped on snowboarding they were all astonished when neither shop sold a single board that winter or spring, or summer, or fall, or, for that matter, the following Christmas of 1980. In fact, James Fulton was trying to get Burton to take the boards back when Jeff intervened. "Let's rent them out, like gas stations rent inner tubes for sledding," he told his dad. "I'll take some of the shop rats up. If Dano or Craig gets into it, all the kids will want one."

DAN "DANO" DONNELLY and Craig Kelly were among the local teens who rode with the South Twenty-First Street bike gang, a bunch of feral latchkey kids. "There really was no hierarchy in our little neighborhood gang," says Tony Welch, who lived across the street from the Kelly boys, "but Craig was the unofficial leader, pretty much from the minute he moved in." Another neighbor, Marty Brown, recalls Craig's debut, "like a mirage" coming toward him down the middle of the street. "I had to do a double take, to be sure I was seeing what I thought I was seeing," he says. "Was he really riding a wheelie that long? Like almost an entire block before he set it down, all smooth and then, just rode on by."

Brown and a couple other kids sat there on their bikes with their mouths hanging open, and then they followed him.

Trying to be cool, Brown pedaled up beside him and said, "Nice Mongoose." Craig kind of nodded, being cool back. "A couple kids talked smack," says Brown, "like it wasn't skill, it was because he had a Mongoose BMX bike, and the rest of us had cheap, heavy bikes from Kmart or Sears. None of us had that kind of money."

"How'd you get that bike?"

"How do you think? I worked for it."

"How long'd it take you to wheelie that far?"

"That was my first try."

"Bullllllllllshit . . ."

"What's your name?"

"Craig."

A few days later Donnelly did a pedal-by, and Craig was in his front yard just staring, "kind of vibing me," says Donnelly. "I was like, 'What's with this cat?' So I circled back, just looking at him, and his dog comes running out trying to nip at me and I'm like, 'Dude, you gonna call your dog off or what?' He's looking off like he doesn't see me, so I kicked his dog. . . .

"That was a mistake. Out he comes ripping after me on his bike, 'You kick my dog, I'm going to kick your ass!'"

Donnelly threw down a power skid and put his arms up. "Whoa, Jack. Back down," he said. "I'm sorry." He bent down and let the scruffy little mutt smell his hand, then gave him a pat.

"What's his name?"

"Fonzie."

"Sorry, Fonzie," he said. Standing, he reached out his hand. "I'm Dano. Wanna play kick-the-can later?"

"Okay."

And that's how Craig got in with the South Twenty-First Street gang.

..

CRAIG AND BRIAN put down roots officially when the two of them dug a hole and planted their three-foot-tall live Christmas tree in the front yard.

"They did not want to move again," says Pat, "but it was a struggle. I was starting my own moving business, and barely covering the bills, food, and paying child support each month. The boys both knew how to push a broom at the warehouse or mow lawns for extra money. It took Craig almost a year to save up his share of that bike; the other half was his twelfth birthday present.

"For school clothes, we shopped at Sears Roebuck. Craig hated the Roebuck jeans. If he wanted Levi's, I told him, 'You pay the price difference,' and he did."

Pat knew he worked too much, and he tried to make it up to them with movies and ball games, but the reality was the boys were left on their own, "much more than they should have been," says Pat, who admits there were times he'd stop at the Town Pump for a beer after work and lose track of time. More than once, the bartender handed him the phone and he'd hear Brian or Craig asking him when he was coming home and what were they supposed to eat for dinner. Brian didn't like being alone so much and moved in with his mom and Gillian for a while, leaving Craig to fend for himself when Pat was on the road. Pat had drivers working for him, and focused on short hauls, but if the right job came up, or the schedule forced him behind the wheel, he'd be gone sometimes for a week or more—once for nearly a month.

Craig would bike himself to school rain or shine and then roam the neighborhood, bouncing from house to house with pals or—more and more it seemed—with Jeana Clark, the cute tomgirl who lived on Twentieth Street. She liked rock and roll and climbing trees on Little Mountain, and she could hang with the boys on their bikes. "I followed Craig everywhere," she says. "I tore the seat of my jeans following him over a security fence trying to get closer to the stage when we saw Blue Öyster Cult. He felt so bad, he tied his long-sleeved KISS T-shirt around my waist to cover it and then went shirtless for the rest of the concert."

Says Tony Welch, "Craig had the Mongoose, the girlfriend, and made it to expert class [in BMX] before anybody else in the neighborhood."

Jeana Clark was Craig's first love. "He called my mom 'The Enforcer,' because she was so strict," says Clark. "If I came home a minute late, I was grounded."

Once in the front door, she'd stall a bit, eat dinner or whatever, then go to her room and open the window. Craig would be there, sitting on the ground, his back up against the house. "We'd talk for hours," says Clark. "His house was usually empty, and he was lonely. He always said his dad was working. But he loved his dad and his mom. He just sort of understood life, I think earlier than most kids have to, but even with, you know, all that . . . he was so sweet, he'd write me long letters, and if 'Bette Davis Eyes' came on the radio, he'd turn it up because he knew I liked it, and so did he. He said, when he heard it, it reminded him of my eyes. He was tough too—he would jump his bike higher and further than any of them. We were like those kids on *E.T.* Just everywhere we went, we were on our bikes."

Craig got the whole neighborhood into racing BMX. "Pat even built a track in an empty lot down by his warehouse," recalls Welch. "Brian, Gillian, we never made it past intermediate, but Craig, I don't think he ever lost until he made it to expert class. We'd roll up to a race, and there'd be a line of flashy-looking expert-class kids, padded leathers, stickered-up helmets looking like sponsored pros. Then there was Craig, wearing blue jeans, his pant legs pegged with packing tape or tucked in his socks, and a plain white helmet. You'd hear that crackling static over the PA system, just before the start, then: 'Racers ready. Watch the lights.' Red, yellow, green, and bam! The gate would drop, and he still smoked 'em almost every time."

By the time Craig started high school, he practically lived at the Fultons' shop, especially after Jeana Clark moved down to Seattle. That broke his heart. He committed himself to racing, got sponsored by Redline, and retired the Mongoose, and even though he didn't ride a Schwinn, the Fultons still "sponsored" him. This meant they gave him free stickers and discounts, and if Janet or Pat couldn't drive him to a race, he was welcome to pile into the shop van. He also had unlimited use of the repair shop to work on his bike. James Fulton liked Craig because the kid always put the tools back in the right place and swept the floor when he was done.

WHEN CRAIG WAS fifteen, there was a big race at some distant track, and Pat told him, "We're gonna do this right." He borrowed a moving van from work and drove Craig, Welch, and a couple of other buddies to the race the night before. They slept at a rest area, trucker-style, ate breakfast at McDonald's, and got to the track early. When the gate dropped for Craig's first heat, he was ahead of the pack and flying. "Literally flying, like arms flapping off the first jump," says Pat, "but his bike wasn't under him. His front wheel got hung up and launched him. He landed hard right on his rear, jumped on his bike, and finished last."

Incensed by his performance, Craig returned to the van and disassembled then reassembled his entire bike in silence. He cheered on his buddies during their heats, while psyching himself up for redemption on his second heat the next day. They grabbed pizza, then returned to the rest area, where Pat noticed Craig was limping.

"I better take a look," he said.

A massive dark blue and purple bruise had formed on one of Craig's butt cheeks: a hematoma the size of a Frisbee extended below his boxers. "It was a horror show," says Pat. "If I'd had the medical experience, I would have drained some of the fluid to relieve the pressure."

His pals were willing to call it and go home, but Craig refused, and settled down to a fitful night of little sleep.

Come morning, the bruise was black as ink and Craig needed help to stand. He alternated hovering and half-cheeking it above the van seat on the drive to the track, then when the time came, he walked his bike to the start hill, gritting his teeth from the pain.

From the second he got balanced in the starting gate, "he stood on his pedals all the way across the finish line," says Pat. "He didn't make top three, but he didn't take last place either. He'd always been competitive, but that took it to the next level."

WHEN JEFF FULTON had talked his parents into renting out the unsold Burton boards, it had been a strategic move, but not one meant to improve his family's business or with any real awareness that their shop was the first to rent snowboards in the entire Pacific Northwest. His motive was having some extra boards on hand so he could share the stoke, and maybe hook somebody else on this new sport he loved.

He'd spent the previous winter hiking and riding mostly alone because nobody he knew had a snowboard, and his friends—already good skiers—had no interest in the hassles of learning a new sport that wasn't even allowed at the ski area. Who in their right mind would want to trudge through thigh-deep snow off the side of the road just to fall down the mountain?

But Craig and Donnelly were all smiles when they piled in the back of the Fulton shop van after being "selected" by Jeff Fulton to try out this new snow-surfing thing the first weekend in January 1981. They thought that the now-twenty-year-old Fulton, who peeled out of the parking lot, was the epitome of cool. He could drive, rode motocross competitively before a knee injury wrecked his career, still skateboarded, and, unlike their folks, who were all about Fleetwood Mac and the Bee Gees, cranked up Rush, Black Sabbath, and AC/DC on the van's eight-track player.

On this first trip, they were on their very own "Highway to Hell" when the rain turned into what Craig later described as "a wicked blizzard" as they drove higher in the mountains and parked against a snowbank near one of Fulton's spots close to Austin Pass. Craig wore jeans, high-top sneakers, work gloves, and a sweater, and was soaked by the time they hiked to the top of a fairly steep first-timer glade. Winded from the altitude, he shoved his left foot into the board's rudimentary rubber waterski-like binding in front, slid his right foot under the strap at the tail, and gripped the handle on the steering rope the Burton board had at the nose. If Wendy Poppen's first snow-wave in Michigan had been like the point at Malibu, this was like dropping into the Banzai Pipeline for your first wave. "You need some speed to turn," Fulton said. "Otherwise, you're just gonna go slow and straight and that's lame."

Holding on to the rope, Craig leaned forward over the nose to get moving, picked up too much speed, and fell backward. For the next few yards, he pulled up on the rope—like the reins on a horse he didn't want to let run—and got bogged down. "There's a sweet spot," Fulton told him as he glided past doing squiggly S-turns to the bottom, some fifty yards below.

By their second run, Craig and Donnelly weren't turning effortlessly like Fulton, but they weren't falling as much as on their first go either, and by the third run they both made it to the bottom without falling. Fulton knew Craig was on the hook when, on the drive home—soaked to the bone, dethawing his fingers and toes by the van's heater vents—he said, "You think we could do this again next weekend?"

A week later, Fulton recruited his skateboarding and motocross friend, twenty-year-old Eric Swanson, to join them. Craig wore a pair of canvas high-top sneakers he waterproofed with shellac and duct-taped BMX gaiters on top to keep the snow out. They returned to the same slope they'd ridden the week before and, like the "shake to erase" screen on an Etch A Sketch, the interim snowstorms had magically erased their tracks, leaving another white canvas upon which to draw fresh lines. With better balance this time, and more speed, it was easier to turn, but the trees that dotted the hillside kept them from opening up the throttle too much. Once the open glade was tracked out, they headed farther down a snowy logging road to another open slope and did it again. Fulton blew their minds when he railed some slalom turns in and out of the trees, a fan of snow flying off the rails of his board like a surfer throwing spray while turning off the top of a breaking wave. Fulton explained there was a point where—with enough speed—you crossed over a threshold where turning was almost intuitive, and you could feel "that smooth and floaty glide" that was "even better than carving freshly rolled blacktop on a skateboard."

"Once you feel that on snow," says Fulton, "you're done—you're a snowboarder for life."

That happened for Craig on their third day, a few weeks later. They drove up the Mount Baker Highway in the dark—dawn patrol—and arrived at the ski area before the lifts opened. Fulton, Donnelly, and Craig hiked to the top of a wide-open run that was so silky smooth it looked like white velvet. Staring down at the football-field-length pitch, they stepped into their bindings. This wasn't the first time Craig had stood atop a run at Mount Baker. He had tried skiing twice the winter before, but it hadn't gone so well. The plastic boots had hurt, the turning had felt "robotic," and while he'd been determined to improve, he never got into a rhythm.

This morning, the snow was perfect, the board felt slick and fast, and as Craig rolled into the slope, his balance was dialed, and the rope was loose in his hand. "Speed is your friend" was something Fulton had told them. "Don't think about it, just do it, pressure the board like you would on a skateboard."

Craig looked down the mountain instead of down at his feet, trusted the speed, and when the board planed above the powder, he leaned a little into a turn with pressure on his heels and the board arced left, and then he unweighted and the board straightened out, then trended right as he pushed on his toes. With more speed, he felt more control as he pushed with his legs and pressured his feet instead of trying to steer through the snow with the rope. With the wind in his face, the rhythm and ride felt euphoric all the way until gravity ran out. It was like nothing he'd ever experienced. Skiing had felt "disjointed," Craig recalled in an interview, "while snowboarding felt like an extension of my body." He and Fulton turned around to look at their tracks and hooted for Donnelly as he linked his own turns and stopped beside them. "That didn't take long," Fulton said, giving both of his protégés high fives.

They were ready to hurry back up the mountain, but the chairlifts started creaking and a ski patrol ripped up and stopped beside them. He was a cool enough dude, kind of like Ponch from *CHiPs* on a snowmobile instead of a Harley-Davidson, but he was still "the man."

"We're about to open, guys," he said. "You need to clear out."

They obeyed and relocated to a short little slope beside the parking lot, but they'd had a taste of—in surfing vernacular—a long open face, and the day was young. Across the valley, some long steep gullies called out, so they chugged some water at the van, then started hiking. Craig would recall this as his "first backcountry experience."

"I knew nothing about avalanches," he said years later in an interview with Ewan Morrison for *Snowboard Life*. The three of them were post-holing that day, sinking up to their thighs as they climbed higher and higher up the side of the main gully, when they heard something like thunder above them. There was no time to react as "a big rumbler came down beside us," said Craig. "We just thought of it like lightning: 'Oh, we just got so lucky.'"

They just hopped over into the next gully and rode that one down, "because the avalanche messed up all the powder in the main gully," says Fulton. "We were so clueless."

CHAPTER 2

THIS IS
THE YEAR!

DURING THE WINTERS OF 1980 and '81, small tribes of snowboarders started popping up across the country, mostly surfers, skateboarders, and BMXers who, like Poppen, looked at mountains and saw frozen waves, halfpipes, and glorious glassy-smooth powder to ride. It inspired the spirit of exploration as they searched for the perfect slopes to ride or "shred."

Unlike football, baseball, basketball, or, more to the point, skiing, snowboarding had no coaches, no schools, and no rules. There was zero attachment to establishment or the past, and it was something teens could do without some older authoritarian telling them how to do it better. Even the elders in the sport were thirty—tops—and they were figuring it out right alongside the youngsters. The only thing they knew for certain was that it was radical.

Ski areas were the promised land, mythical utopias—where chairlifts were the ticket to ride endless winter waves—but just as skateboarders had been banned from city streets, snowboarders were shunned almost unanimously by ski resort managers who considered them dangerous, a nuisance, and discounted the "activity" as, at best, a fad. So it was a pretty big deal when a little ski area in Colorado called Cooper Hill (now Ski Cooper) hosted what is widely regarded as the first "post-Snurfer era" snowboarding contest in April 1981. Organizer Richard Christiansen, who was the owner of Pacific Shore Surf (and skateboard) Shop in Boulder, sent invitations to the owners or representatives of every brand he could find, including Winterstick (Utah), Burton (Vermont), Flite (Rhode Island), and two brands from California:

A-Team and Sims. Roughly two dozen riders answered the call to compete in three disciplines modeled after skateboarding contests of the era: slalom and downhill races and freestyle (best trick).

Two titanic figures of the young sport fared well: Jake Burton Carpenter, the now-twenty-six-year-old Snurfer-inspired founder of his own Burton Snowboards, took third place overall, while thirty-year-old Tom Sims—a former world champion skateboarder, whose Sims Skateboards had been a bestselling brand in the 1970s, and founder of Sims Ski Boards—placed second. A hot-dog skier turned snowboarder named Scott Jacobson wowed the crowd and took first place overall on his Winterstick board, attempting and sort of landing front- and backflips off the freestyle jump. Left unsettled was what to call this new snow sport. Carpenter called it snowboarding, Jacobson referred to it alternately as snowboarding or "sticking," short for Wintersticking, and Sims dubbed it ski-boarding. "This contest was really good, considering it was the first contest ever," Jacobson told a reporter. "But . . . next year, we're going to do something where it's going to blow minds on *ABC Wide World of Sports.*"

The Ski Cooper contest was also the first time east met west, with Carpenter facing off with Sims. Winterstick's twenty-nine-year-old inventor, Dimitrije Milovich, who was light-years ahead of both Burton and Sims regarding board shapes (offering both swallow- and round-tail boards as early as 1975), material designs, and bindings, was not personally present. Back in Utah, Milovich contemplated if he should enforce a patent he had filed—which arguably both Sims and Burton were encroaching upon—or just let the sport grow.

NONE OF THIS was on Craig's radar in Mount Vernon, Washington. He was still laser-focused on BMX racing, his bedroom walls covered floor to ceiling with brand stickers, race banners, and pullout posters from the center spreads of *BMX Action* and *BMX Plus* magazines. Bike racing heroes he worshipped—"Stompin'" Stu Thomsen, Greg "The Machine" Hill, and Richie "The Avalanche" Anderson—battled with the rock band KISS for remaining wall space.

Craig had been racing BMX seriously for two plus years, accumulating points that determined the number on his race plate. The racers with the best finishes and points worked their way to the number one racer in the state. Shortly after Craig's fifteenth birthday, the April issue of *ABA Action*[*] arrived in the mailbox. Flipping through pages to find his name as he did every month, Craig cross-checked their figures with his own, then pulled out a sheet of lined paper and, with a blue pen in his best cursive, wrote:

> Dear ABA, I am Craig Kelly (Wa-1 #185). I feel that you have incorrectly computed my points for February in your April edition of *ABA Action*. You said that I had 180 points, and I was number 59. I feel that I should have 326 points and should be number 22. I would appreciate it if you would check over my . . . points again. Enclosed is a detailed list of my races and points earned in February. Thank you for your time and help.

The following month, the points had been corrected, and he'd moved up from #59 to #22. Craig was still climbing the ranks when, on November 15, 1981, he won his first national BMX title in the fifteen-year-old expert class at the Canadian Nationals in Langley, British Columbia. That year, in Washington State District 1, fifteen-year-old expert races—he accumulated twenty-six first-place finishes, ten second, eight third, and eight fourth place, earning him the number four plate. He was ranked fourth in Washington, racing against the very best, such as Gary Ellis, who towered physically over Craig and had had facial hair since he was fourteen. Nicknamed "The Lumberjack," Ellis was rivaling the country's best racers in Southern California, the birthplace and epicenter of BMX.

"To be smaller, like Craig was, and successful in BMX, he had to be aggressive, like 'I'm going to kick your ass' angry aggressive," Brian Kelly recalls. "Craig had that inside of him. What came first—the anger or the competitor? He acted out a lot more before that bike, and racing gave him a positive outlet to channel it. If he kicked ass he won. Winning felt good. Bringing home a trophy felt good."

---

[*] The monthly newsletter of the American Bicycle Association, *ABA Action* printed updated points, standings, and thus the racing-plate numbers of member racers.

But the high never lasted much past breakfast the day after, when Craig would start thinking about the next race—and how he would win it.

"In 1982, every minute was action-packed," says Quinn Thompson, the self-described Mormon kid from Conway, Washington, and honorary South Twenty-First Street gang member. "Friday night, we'd hit some parties, I'd crash at Craig's house—divorced parents, dad was never home. Craig and Brian survived on frozen pizza and chicken pot pies. Next morning, we weren't eating cereal and watching Saturday morning cartoons for long. Craig had something to do, and it wasn't watching *Johnny Quest*. My first time in his room—there's a snowboard in the corner (like 'What in the hell is that thing?'), five hundred BMX trophies lined up, a straight-A report card on the dresser, and Judas Priest, 'Rapid Fire,' spinning on the record player. I knew this cat was going to change the world."

"Something was in the air that winter," says Fulton. "I could feel it when the December 1981 issue of *Action Now* showed up, and there was Tom Sims snowboarding on the cover. Hair flowing, snow flying, great style—he's totally stoked. There's a big cover blurb that asks the question: 'SNOWBOARDING: Is this the year?' But they mixed up the words. It *should* have read: 'This *is* the year!' That's what 1982 was—it was a turning point."

Fulton's Schwinn Cyclery sold out of snowboards a week before Christmas, and when James reordered, he included a letter to Carpenter about his son and the growing number of locals renting the boards. Carpenter filled the order and included a couple of "top-secret" test boards stamped with number codes and the name EXPERIMENTAL PERFORMER. The old Backhill boards had a waterski-type binding for the front foot and a leather strap to wedge your foot under in back. This board had two bindings, so you were locked in.

The Experimentals were like night and day compared to the Backhills. Says Fulton, "These babies turned."

That spring, Craig turned sixteen. He had planned the day carefully. So had his mom. Janet had remarried, and her second husband repaired and sold cars on the side. He'd bought a Subaru at auction and fixed it up. With the thousand-plus Craig had saved, his first small bank loan, and a smoking deal,

Craig celebrated his birthday with wheels—and, from Janet, a cake decorated like a driver's license. Even better, Craig told Quinn Thompson, "I'm establishing my credit with the bank."

"Who thinks of that at sixteen?" says Thompson. "He was just bionically smart. Light-years ahead of the rest of us."

That same April, Fulton contacted Mount Baker Ski Area manager Duncan Howat to ask if he would consider letting them on their chairlifts. Howat had been following the ski area industry news and was well aware of these fledgling brands, with their small pods of riders who were lobbying ski resorts across the country to be allowed on the slopes. But Baker was a serious mountain—with little beginner terrain, and extremely difficult-to-ski deep snow that crusted up and got tracked out. It was tough enough for skiers already. Meanwhile, the few kids Howat had seen hiking up Baker's runs after lifts closed were out of control, and on their asses more than they were on their boards.

Howat's main question to Fulton mimicked the concern circulating within the industry. "Can they turn left and right? Can they stop? And are there brakes, so if they lose a board, it doesn't become a rocket and kill somebody downslope? These are kids doing this, teenagers—they're reckless by nature."

"No, sir," Fulton replied. "I'm twenty-one, and my shop riders, they're younger but very respectful, well-behaved kids. Rule followers."

LATER THAT SPRING, at Mount Vernon High School, Thompson called shotgun, Marty Brown jumped in back, and Craig was behind the wheel of that 1979 blue Subaru station wagon. "Everything was fast like a Ramones concert," says Thompson. "Craig always packed two hours into a half-hour set, which is about how much time we had for lunch. Food was optional. We had just enough time to burn rubber down to the river, spin some donuts, pull a Rockford,[†] and rip back to class.

"After school, he kicks me to the curb. He's got a schedule to keep, heading

---

†   The signature getaway move by private eye Jim Rockford, played by James Garner in NBC's *The Rockford Files* (1974–78). "When you're going straight in reverse at 35 miles per hour, you come off the gas pedal, go hard left, and pull the emergency brake," Garner wrote in his autobiography. "That locks the wheels and throws the front end around. Then you release everything, hit the gas and off you go in the opposite direction."

down to his mom's place in Bellevue, three hours round-trip, to pick up his little sister for the weekend."

Gillian was nine, and Janet, who had shifted her career from child care to elderly care, was running a rest home and working on opening another. Shortly after Craig turned sixteen, Pat gave Craig a gas card, and the deal was that he'd do Pat's driving on the twice-monthly weekends Gillian would come up to Mount Vernon. For Gillian, this meant one and a half hours of heavy metal while Craig told her scary stories. "Usually from a Stephen King book," says Gillian. "He would tell it so well, I wouldn't even have to see the movie." They were rarely age-appropriate, but she loved every minute, even if she couldn't sleep that night.

Turning sixteen was a pivotal moment in a BMX racer's career, and it was no different for Craig. With a car replacing the bike for transportation and expanding the world exponentially, big choices loomed, some of them life-changing.

Craig was at the shop the day Fulton got a call from Duncan Howat at Mount Baker, inviting him to come on up. He'd decided to allow snowboarders on a "trial basis" the last weeks of the season, and their skills and interaction with his skiing clientele would dictate his snowboarding policy for next winter.

Craig and Fulton drove up that weekend and, under Howat's watchful eye, rode the chairlift up with their boards across their laps. "You're going to have to keep the board on your feet somehow," Howat told them. "To keep the line moving."

They were so excited to be riding an actual chairlift—not hiking—up the mountain, all Fulton recalls Craig saying was "Yes, sir," to everything Howat said, knowing he held their future in his hands. "I just kept telling myself, don't fall, don't fall, don't fall," says Fulton. Next chairlift ride, they kept a foot in the front binding and pushed the board like they would a skateboard in line. "We probably got more vertical feet of actual riding that day than an entire winter of hiking," says Fulton. "From your first turns at the top of a run to your last turns at the bottom, you could feel yourself improving. Chairlifts were a game changer."

Howat shadowed and observed roughly a dozen snowboarders that spring, then discussed the prospects with his wife, Gail Howat, who recalls a few of them did pretty well, but most of them could barely get down the mountain without killing themselves.

And then there was Craig. "When Duncan saw what *he* could do on a snowboard, it changed his whole outlook," says Gail. "Craig's grace and style showed us all where the sport could go."

CHAPTER 3

MOUNT BAKER HARD CORE

When September rolled around and Craig began his senior year, it wasn't a photo of Greg Hill or Stompin' Stu Thompson, but rather of Jake Burton Carpenter slashing some powder that he taped to his Pee-Chee school folder. Whether Craig realized the significance or not, his BMX days were numbered. The mountains were calling, and not because there was anything to win up there or anything to prove. No trophies. Nobody to beat. Mount Baker hadn't even announced if they would let them on the lifts. He just couldn't stop thinking about snowboarding. And it hadn't even snowed yet.

When the first winter storms did roll in off the Pacific and paint the Cascades white, Craig and Fulton hopped in his Subaru and drove into some of the ugliest weather nature can throw at you. They stopped briefly in the little town of Glacier for supplies and the last actual toilet they would see, which was at Graham's, a one-stop shopping experience with general-store essentials, a bar, a restaurant, and a video arcade. Signs at the front door read: "Danger! Slippery Walk"; "Ice"; "Wet Floors"; "Microwave in Use"; and "Cigarette smoke welcome, loose floorboards guaranteed, enter at your own risk!"

"Crack kills, but so do these mountains." Or "You're in God's Country, but that doesn't mean you want to meet him." These were the signs you read while exiting. The Cascades in winter are no joke, even if you did just stock up with provisions like a can of Pringles, two Slim Jims, and a sixer of Mountain Dew.

These daylong sojourns were tire-spinning, corner-drifting adventures in the Subaru. Bigger storms meant deeper snow, and deeper snow meant more fun. The ski area had not yet opened, so they took turns breaking trail, knowing the longer the hike up, the longer the run down. But it was hard work—the chairlift had definitely spoiled them.

When Baker swung open the gate to snowboarders officially, just after Thanksgiving, Craig had intended to keep racing BMX. But that was before he'd experienced the addictive high of chairlift-serviced powder and realized that this little ski area in his backyard was a virtual snow factory, consistently scoring the highest annual snowfall of all North American ski areas. Every weekend there was a race; there was also fresh "pow" on the mountain, which was only open on weekends. The first chairlift up, the snow was so deep, skiers and snowboarders alike would get stuck after disembarking, bogged down in the deep trenches they'd create while heading away from the lift ramps toward the steeps. "It was Craig who figured out it was better to hang back and take the third or fourth chair," says Fulton. "We'd strap our feet into the bindings on the ride up and then follow in the tracks cut by the skiers—kinda like drafting on a road bike—getting enough speed to swoop around them and score first tracks."

Even without such strategic positioning, snowboards floated better and glided faster than the skinny skis of the era. And in the heavier snow, common in the Pacific Northwest, riders worked less, and seemed "more stoked," than many of the skiers, recalls chair 6 lift operator Carter Turk, who along with fellow liftie Eric Janko took studious note of the shredders who were consistently lapping their brethren two-plankers. Intrigued, Turk asked where they got their boards, and Fulton piped up, "Bike shop called Fulton's Schwinn Cyclery in Mount Vernon rents 'em."

Not long after, Janko and Turk were bombing runs on boards of their own and were welcomed into this little tribe of dedicated riders who made the drive up from Mount Vernon no matter how fierce the storm. If the lifts were running, they were riding. One particularly gnarly morning, Fulton and Swanson were—aside from the lift operators—the only people crazy enough to be on the mountain, and crazier still, challenged each other to a race down one of the mountain's steepest runs off chair 5. Squatting low, they were flying downhill, both in their own versions of an aerodynamic speed tuck, when a mighty gust of wind hit them head-on.

Their boards were pointing downhill, but the wind was howling so hard up the mountain, their descent was slowed to a near stop, as if they were being held in place by an invisible hand. Fulton looked over at Swanson, who yelled above the gale, "Man, this is hard-core!"

"Yeah!" Fulton shouted back. "Mount Baker Hard Core!"

That night, Fulton wrote the initials of their new gang, "M-B-H-C," in permanent ink on the white logo below the nose of his new Sims 1500FE swallowtail.

Like shops everywhere, Fulton's Schwinn had expanded its snowboard line to include Burton and Sims—the two most recognized brands—and Flite Snowboards, which, like Winterstick, had been manufacturing boards well before Burton and Sims but now couldn't touch the leaders that were jockeying to achieve dominance. This rivalry was evident in the first (and only) issue of the sport's first magazine, *Snowboarder*,[*] which was published in fall of 1982. The Sims back cover advertisement read "Tom Sims invented snowboarding and still leads the world with his new 82/83 models," while Burton's ad on the inside front cover read, "When you choose a snowboard to ride this winter, go with the leader. Burton Snowboards are the favorite of virtually every rider from the ambitious beginner to the current National Champion."

"Tom saw claims like that and said, 'Well that's bullshit, *virtually every rider,* my ass,'" says Dave Weaver, Sims's right-hand man during the early 1980s. Carpenter was equally peeved by Sims's ongoing claim that he (Sims, himself) had invented the first snowboard as a school wood shop project in 1963. "Was the Snurfer the first snowboard?" editor Bob Denike had asked Carpenter for the issue's featured interview. "Yes, it was," Carpenter replied, "contrary to what *others* think."

Shots had been fired between Sims and Burton. Both men knew that the consumer would ultimately decide which brand prevailed, based upon a combination of the quality of products, effectiveness of sales and marketing, scope of distribution, and—as in any sport—which had the best and most marketable athletes riding and competing on their namesake boards.

---

[*]   A thin, glossy, twenty-four-page black-and-white "zine" published by Michael George, whose family owned Gremic skateboard (and snowboard) shop in Los Gatos, California, *Snowboarder* was produced and edited by skateboarder/snowboarder Bob Denike, with pro skateboarder Steve Caballero catching big air on the cover.

The burgeoning competitive snowboard circuit of the early eighties was a homegrown affair, in which the owners of the biggest brands were often the organizers, competitors, team captains, course makers, and rule makers who dreamed up the best ways to measure the skill levels of riders in an undefined sport.

Held at Vermont's Suicide Six ski area, the 1982 National Snowboarding Championships consisted of a downhill race and a giant slalom race organized by former Snurfer world champion Paul Graves. Graves sold his licensing rights to Burton, who moved the event to Snow Valley, Vermont, in 1983.

Out on the West Coast that same year, Sims organized his own World Snowboarding Championships with the help of Mike Chantry, a skateboarder turned snowboarder. Chantry lobbied the mom-and-pop ski area Soda Springs, located in California near Lake Tahoe, to host a downhill race, slalom race, and—inspired by a tribe of Tahoe snowboarders who, armed with shovels, shaped a gully at the town dump to resemble a skateboarding halfpipe—the first competition snowboard halfpipe.

Unlike racing, halfpipe runs weren't about speed; they were about style—freestyle.

A nineteen-year-old skateboarder from San Francisco named Tom Hsieh (pronounced Shay) showed up at the second annual World Snowboarding Championships the following year. Henceforth, "the Worlds" was described by Hsieh as "a collision of hard-core snowboarders and every snowboard brand you knew and didn't know existed. The Big Two [Burton and Sims] plus Avalanche, Barfoot, Flite, SnowTech, Glacier, A-Team, Prop Snowboards. The vibe was more skate contest than ski race; punk rock haircuts, bright-colored suits, and skunky ganja was wafting from team vans. And those were the pros."

Sims wore all the hats—contest organizer, celebrity athlete, and company owner. "He collected entry fees, then set up the slalom race by pre-running the course and placing the gates at each of his own natural turns, giving him a clear advantage when he ran the course himself," says Hsieh. "He literally drilled the holes for the bamboo gates himself. Why not? It was his contest, and there was no playbook for setting slalom courses for snowboarders."

Those who were there more for the party than for the competition laughed it off, but there was a growing seriousness to the event—including several

Burton riders who called "bullshit" on the course setting. It wasn't just bragging rights and trophies; there was also $2,000 in prize money, up a thousand since 1983, which equaled $200 for first place, $125 for second, and $75 for third place in each discipline, plus an overall purse for the riders with the best combined score. The pro women received about 50 percent less than the men, reportedly because of the lopsided number of female competitors who showed up and paid entry fees. According to Chantry, "Tom would say, once numbers evened out so would the prize money. He didn't think a guy who competed against, say, twenty other guys should get the same prize money as a woman who competed against two other women."

In the men's division, Burton rider Andy Coghlan dominated the races, taking first place in both slalom and downhill, while Sims rider Terry Kidwell took first in the halfpipe. Coghlan won the overall and walked away with $600, in addition to $1,000 he'd pocketed two weeks earlier when he won the slalom and downhill at the National Snowboarding Championships in Vermont, making Andy "The Dog" Coghlan the richest and fastest man in snowboarding that year.

While Hsieh was blown away by the on-snow talent, it was the antics at the awards ceremony that changed his life. He was sitting among the crowd of maybe two hundred (including Jeff Fulton and Eric Swanson, down from Baker) when Sims called up the third-place finisher for the halfpipe event, a nineteen-year-old Canadian named Ken Achenbach. Some guy seated beside him told Hsieh that Achenbach had opened the world's first snowboard-only shop in his family's garage in Calgary, Alberta. Hsieh watched Sims hand Achenbach a trophy. He then started to hand over the $130 third-place check, then jerked it back. "You know what, Ken?" said Sims, loud and clear, over the mic. "Your shop still owes me for shipping on some boards, so you're not getting the prize money."

The crowd went silent.

"Dude," Achenbach said, "this isn't business, this is a contest. You pay the fucking prize money. You said there's prize money. We came for it, I won it, so cough it up."

He reached for the check, and Sims stepped back.

"Nope."

"Fuck you then!" Achenbach said. "If you're not going to give me my prize money, keep your fucking trophy too." He shoved the trophy into Sims's chest, turned and walked away, flipping Sims off over his shoulder as he went.

Hsieh couldn't quite believe what he was witnessing, but he knew good entertainment when he saw it. *Holy shit*, he thought. *Somebody should be documenting this.*

CRAIG HAD GRADUATED from high school in 1983, having maintained a 4.0 GPA with a full schedule of advanced chemistry, fifth-year math, German, American government, physics, and computer science, and was accepted into the University of Washington's chemical engineering program. That summer he drove a twenty-eight-foot moving truck up and down the West Coast for Valley Moving & Storage and tested out of first-year English, math, and science, and he started his freshman year at the academic level of a sophomore.

Actively recruited by fraternities, Craig ended up pledging Delta Upsilon after meeting a long-haired, head-banging upperclassman named Mark Thomas, who toured him around campus on his skateboard. Thomas described DU as an "intelligent house that parties hard and rocks hard." Case in point, "Hell Half Hour" was a nightly pressure-release ritual when loud music was mandatory, studying was forbidden, and if there was a Frisbee in your room, it had better be airborne and flying down the halls. Craig was seventeen years old when he started college and was soon known as the house snowboarder who cranked up Judas Priest, the Scorpions, or Ted Nugent and Wango-Tangoed his ass off while jumping around and spinning 360s on his bed with his snowboard strapped to his feet.

The half hour ended, he'd settle down at his desk, dripping in sweat, and study. He earned a 4.0 GPA that first year, as well as the respect of his frat brothers for spontaneous adventures such as the time he suggested an overnight winter campout . . . during a blizzard. "It was miserable weather and Craig knew exactly what to do," recounted Brian McClure. "He engineered a snow cave, did most of the digging, and while we were all shivering, wet, and huddled together inside, he said something really profound for a seventeen-year-old kid: 'Remember this moment when we're sitting in class next week. We will probably forget that class, but we will always remember this.'"

Another time, Craig told Thomas he needed to learn to surf, and within twenty-four hours, he'd borrowed a seven-foot surfboard, strapped it to his Subaru racks, recruited a carload of volunteers, and was driving to Short Sand Beach on the Oregon coast. "The water was freezing," says Thomas. "We had a short wet suit to share, or maybe it was a diving jacket—no full suit or booties—and nobody could last more than fifteen minutes. But Craig was determined to catch waves. He stayed out the absolute longest and came in just blue, saying, 'I've got to figure this surfing thing out.'"

He'd warm up by a fire they'd build from driftwood and zone out of the conversation, timing the swells, mesmerized by the surf. Then he'd spend hours at the university library researching the mechanics of waves—the depth of water required for a wave to peak, curl, and break; how the ocean bottom or the curve of the coastline affected the shape or speed of the wave. "The books would just pile up on his desk," says Thomas. "I've never known anybody who was so driven to learn and improve."

Once winter arrived, Craig was back on snow, riding the ski areas near campus two or three times a week, usually with his friend Jeff Krueger—a fellow Delta Upsilon brother and (aerospace) engineering major who Craig had heard was a "Wildman" and converted from skiing to snowboarding on an impromptu hike up Mount Rainier. Or Steve Shipsey, a UW student Craig befriended on chair 5 at Mount Baker, where Craig continued to ride on the twice-monthly weekends Gillian would spend in Mount Vernon. After class on those Fridays, he'd have dinner in Bellevue with his mom, then hit the road with Gillian. She was eleven now, and harder to scare with stories alone, so he'd get creative. One time he took a short detour and ended up on the dark and winding dirt road up Little Mountain, which he knew like the back of his hand. He talked about Bigfoot sightings, what they would do if the engine died, and when that didn't do the trick, he popped in Iron Maiden, *The Number of the Beast*. When the spooky intro began, he turned up the volume, stepped on the gas, flipped off the headlights, and like a good big brother listened to Gillian scream all the way to the summit.

Most trips though, when he wasn't trying to terrify his little sister, he'd drive straight home, throw a load of laundry in the washer, raid the freezer, catch up with Brian and his dad if they were home, and then hit the sack. He'd be at the Mount Baker parking lot before the lifts opened and slide in with the MBHC as though not a minute had passed. They'd rib him for riding the ski areas near Seattle, saying, "You can't ride Ski Acres and claim Mount Baker Hard Core." Then they'd get down to business, ripping top-to-bottoms at full throttle, downshifting only to drop a cliff or enter a chute—all the while trying to put each other in "the white room," which involved throwing snow off the edge of a board while turning hard and fast either beside or above the target and thus blanketing him with a wall of snow.

More often than not, it was Craig who put the other Hard Cores in the white room. Fulton, for one, had never gotten him. "It was hard to get in range," says Fulton, "and Craig rarely fell. You learned not to fall riding with this crew, because if you did, there was no mercy. You'd get destroyed."

Back at school, if Craig couldn't find anybody to ride with midweek, he'd go alone as he did one "shitty, icy, and windy Wednesday night at Ski Acres," recalls Mike Ranquet, who was fourteen years old and teaching himself how to snowboard with his friend Gil. Nearing the bottom of one run, he slid to a stop and looked over toward a big bumped-out mogul field beneath the chairlift. "If I was on skis," he said, "I could rip right down that mogul field. I don't think that's even possible on a snowboard."

At that moment, "a snowboarder, all backlit from the lights, ripped right down the center of the moguls and flew past us," says Ranquet. "Me and Gil looked at each other like, 'What the fuck?'"

On autopilot, Ranquet took off after him, thinking, *I'll just follow him. I'll just do what he's doing.*

"I slid right up behind Craig at the lift line. He was the only other snowboarder on the mountain, only other person really—it was an awful night. And I said, 'Single?' He looked at me, and then looked around and said, 'I'm the only one here, dude.'

"I jumped on the lift with him and we talked all the way up, like 'How long you been riding. Where you from?' That's how it was back then. Even though I was a kook, we were all snowboarders, so we were practically family," says Ranquet. "I was an angry kid, my older sister had cancer, and all I wanted to do was drop out of school so I could skateboard more. I'm sure I told him all of that because Craig was easy to talk to, and I was always talking shit, and acting like I didn't give a fuck."

By the end of the night, Craig had invited them to ride Baker, and if their parents were cool with it, he said he'd take them that weekend. "Either way, you should stay in school," said Craig. "It's important to get an education." They exchanged phone numbers. Two days later, Ranquet's fifty-five-year-old mom, Laurane, pulled up to the Delta Upsilon house. After talking with Craig for ten minutes or so, she pulled away, leaving Ranquet there on the sidewalk grinning with a duffel and his snowboard.

"Leaving me alone with Craig after one short meeting shows what a great judge of character my mom was," says Ranquet. "But it also shows how much of a little shit I was. She honestly felt I'd be safer and get in less trouble snowboarding with a twenty-year-old frat boy I met on a chairlift two days earlier than I would have been skateboarding around the city all weekend."

KEN ACHENBACH was walking down the lodge steps at Sunshine Village in Banff, Alberta, on New Year's Day 1985 when he saw "some dude" near the Standish chairlift wearing white Sorel boots, jeans, a ski sweater, and carrying a black Sims 1500FE. *Holy shit, there's another snowboarder,* he thought as he jogged over.

"Holy, eh?" he said, slapping his Barfoot snowboard down beside Craig's board. "That's a thing of beauty right there—two snowboards in one lift line. You single?"

Craig introduced Achenbach to his fraternity brother Mark Thomas, who had just skied up then invited him to ride with them. On the chairlift, Craig told Achenbach how they'd road-tripped up from Washington because, one, Sunshine Village allowed snowboarding, and two, they could legally drink.

For the rest of the day, the three stuck together, sharing intel on ski areas that had "opened up" to snowboarding, such as Achenbach's original haunt, Fortress Mountain in Alberta, and Craig's own Mount Baker. "Oh yeah?" said Achenbach. "Never heard of it. How is it?"

"Lots of pow, only open three-day weekends," replied Craig. "It's deep on Fridays. You should come ride with us. There's a contest in a couple weeks."

Achenbach, who'd grown up in the ultracompetitive Calgary ski racing scene, loved the instant camaraderie among riders. "I switched from hand-tuned Team Atomic race skis to a piece of painted plywood with no edges, P-tex, or bindings and had more fun and made more friends than I ever did ski racing," he says. "And the best thing about it, snowboarding was totally useless, and that made it very pure. You did it because you loved it. Contests were like family reunions, where we pushed each other, and tried to outdo each other's tricks. If somebody pulled a huge air in the pipe, you weren't thinking, *Oh shit, he's going to score better than me*, you were screaming your head off saying, 'Go bigger!'"

Three weeks later, as the Miami Dolphins squared off against the San Francisco 49ers on the noteworthy date of Sunday, January 20, 1985—aka Super Bowl XIX—Craig Kelly raced in his first-ever snowboarding contest at Mount Baker. Duncan Howat had agreed to host the Sims Open "banked slalom," but only if they scheduled it on the least busy day of the year, with fewer skiers on the mountain who might be bothered by hordes of out-of-town shredders. The "banked slalom" idea—combining a halfpipe and slalom into a single event—had been conceived by Jeff Fulton and Eric Swanson during the 1984 "Worlds" at Soda Springs. They shared their idea to utilize the natural gullies at Baker as the venue with Bob Barci, who recruited Sims as sponsor, and here they were.

The serpentine downhill track was dictated by twelve flagged gates, set on opposing walls of a natural gully that descended roughly 500 feet (nearly two football-field lengths) of twists and banked turns that ended with a short, hard-right traverse and a 100-foot-long edge-catching, speed-robbing dash to the finish line.

First up was Sims, who set the time to beat at 23.86 seconds, then hiked back up the side of the course to where Dave Weaver (Sims's snowboards VP) and a dozen other spectators were watching the action near the start. Says Weaver, "Tom was always on the hunt for new talent. A lot of riders were fast—some too fast, and blew out—but only a few could power through turns gracefully, with a surfing style."

Craig launched himself out of the starting gate like he was going for the holeshot[†] in a BMX race, then immediately got low. "He just flowed fast and smooth," says Weaver, "like the Sultan of Speed."[‡]

"Hey, what's that kid's name, any of you know him?" Sims asked the

---

[†]   A BMX holeshot describes the first racer out of the starting gate and into and through the first turn, ahead of the other racers.

[‡]   Terry Fitzgerald, a 1970s surfer whose stylish turns and ability to accelerate through critical sections of the wave earned him the nickname "The Sultan of Speed."

bystanders. "That's my neighbor," replied Tony Welch, there to cheer on Craig and Donnelly. "His name is Craig Kelly."

"Thanks, bro," Sims replied, then turned to Weaver. "That kid has the best style so far."

By the end of the day, the 49ers had captured their second Super Bowl title, and nineteen of the twenty-eight snowboarders in the Sims Open had made it through the course without missing any of the gates. Sims took first place, followed closely by his fastest, and most stylish, team rider, twenty-two-year-old Tahoe local Terry Kidwell, in second. Ken Achenbach made the drive down from Calgary and took third on his Barfoot, and Craig—riding a Sims, but unsponsored—took fourth just 1.6 seconds behind Sims, who introduced himself to Craig after the awards ceremony.

"You're fast and you've got good style," he said, handing Craig a business card. "You should come down to Tahoe and enter these contests." Weaver was beside him and gave Craig fliers for the Sierra Snowboarding Championships on February 9, and the World Snowboarding Championships on March 29—both at Soda Springs Ski Area.

"I will," said Craig, shaking both of their hands. "Thanks."

"Cool, man," said Sims, throwing up a shaka. "We'll see you there."

"To fully appreciate the magnitude of the compliment Sims paid to Craig," says Fulton, "you've got to understand Tom Sims was a living legend, an icon in both skateboarding *and* snowboarding. He was thirty-five and still winning most races. He had the best carving style on hardpack, the surfiest style in powder, and he had handpicked, maybe not the fastest, but the coolest team peppered with skateboard pros and freestylers like Allen Arnbrister, Keith Kimmel, and nobody could touch Terry Kidwell's style in the halfpipe, plus Kidwell could race, so he was a threat for the overall titles. So Tom Sims—this microcosm of everything cool—took Craig aside and basically said, 'You rip. I want to see you ride again. I want to give you a second look.'"

CHAPTER 4

TEAM RIDER

WHETHER IT WAS THE ADRENALINE of competition again (it had been years since he'd raced BMX) or Sims's accolades that lit the fire, Craig spent the following weekends hitting jumps on frontside and backside gully walls as practice for what would be his first halfpipe competition in three weeks.

Some fifty competitors—and three feet of snow overnight—dropped in for the Sierra Snowboarding Championships at Soda Springs on February 9. Craig almost missed a gate on the slalom race but took third place in his first halfpipe comp, narrowly losing to Sims but getting solidly beat by first-place finisher Kidwell, whose bag of tricks included tweaked-out method airs, frontside nose-rolls, backside alley-oops, and a handplant thrown in. "Kidwell set the bar so high," says eighties Burton pro Bob Klein, "everybody else was hoping for second or third. His only competition was Mini Shred, but he was in the junior's division."

Shaun "Mini Shred" Palmer was the young and scrappy junior division champ, and the newest member of Team Sims, having been recruited at Mount Rose a few weeks earlier. "I smoked a bowl of weed and Tom Sims was on the chairlift with me," recalls Palmer. "We didn't even shake hands, he just said, 'You want to ride for me and travel the world?' and I said 'Fuck yeah,' and that was it."

After his poor finish in the slalom, Craig didn't expect any such offer when Sims approached him just before the awards ceremony with a new candy-apple-red 1500FE board, T-shirt, stack of stickers, and an outreached hand. "Shake, and you're on Team Sims," he said. Craig reached out, and Sims said, "Right on," as they did the bro shake. "Welcome to the team. Come to the Worlds next month, and I'll cover your gas and entry fee."

"I already registered, and paid in advance," said Craig.

"Right on," said Sims. "I'll reimburse you when you show up."

Craig returned to Soda Springs a month later with his dad in tow and his new board under his arm. He'd shoved a pair of Lange XLR ski boot liners into his Sorels and wrapped them with duct tape to stiffen them up for better turning and edge control. Equipment modifications were secret weapons, and he was feeling good about the slalom while rocking the same boot liners Olympian slalom skiers Phil and Steve Mahre had worn when they won gold and silver at Sarajevo in '84. Then he walked around the corner of the lodge and saw weird-looking plastic "Hy-Bak" or "high-back" bindings* on virtually every Burton board lined up against the wall—as well as different renditions on Flite, and other brands—and quickly understood their purpose. Surprisingly, Sims boards were not rocking this binding modification, but Terry Kidwell was "wearing" his own version of a high-back support covertly between his boot cuff and boot liner. The unveiling of this brand-new invention revealed the secret to heelside response and turning power, which was a great advance for the sport, but devastating for Craig, who thought to himself, *I'm screwed*.

There was a beehive of activity near the lodge entrance, where a teenager—dressed in green army wool surplus pants, Sorels, and an REI jacket—was passing out a stack of tabloid-sized newspapers.

One year after he had watched Sims's confrontation with Ken Achenbach and seen a good story, nineteen-year-old Thomas Hsieh Jr. was proudly handing out the freshly inked, premiere "VOL 1 No. 1" issue of *Absolutely Radical Snowboard Magazine*.

He handed out all five hundred copies in less than a half hour, then stood there and smiled as dozens of riders and skiers alike stopped in their tracks—many setting down their board or skis so they could use both hands to read—totally immersed. Feedback was instantaneous. "Rad, dude." "No way!" "Cool." "Whoa."

Carpenter was there thumbing through pages in silence. He had never

---

* One of snowboarding's most critical inventions, with credit given to both Jeff Grell and Louis "Lofo" Fournier. Fournier is usually credited with being first to make a folding high-back, while Grell eventually earned the first patent—both are heroes in the history of snowboarding.

returned Hsieh's phone calls or responded to his letters offering free advertising in the first issue to any snowboard shop or brand that supplied him
with camera-ready art and agreed to distribute three hundred copies to their
mailing lists. Sims had been the first to respond and scored the prime back-
cover ad. Ten advertisers, including Sessions, Glacier, and Barfoot, distributed
some three thousand copies to snowboarders around the country—seeding
the snowboarding revolution. Only thirty-nine ski areas in the U.S. allowed
snowboarding, and Hsieh rewarded them with inclusion in his magazine's
snowboarding directory.

When Carpenter closed the mag, he said, "We'll be in touch," recalls
Hsieh. "He never told me why he hadn't returned my calls, but it was pretty
clear he regretted it."

"The Burton team walked past in matching uniforms like a regiment of
British soldiers," says Pat, "and Craig fell in with the motley-looking Sims
team led by Sims, who was decked out head to toe in an all-white wet suit. He
was the celebrity, Jake looked more like the coach, and then there's all these
independent groups doing their own thing." In the words of Barfoot team
rider Evan Feen: "Burton had the skier jocks, Sims had the snow skaters, and
the rest of us . . . we were the freaks." Inside the lodge, Pat grabbed a cup of
coffee and looked through Hsieh's zine, learning what he could about this pro
snowboarding circus his son had joined. He settled on pages 14 and 15—a
feature story that covered the Sierra Snowboarding Championships a month
before—and smiled and tucked it inside his jacket. This was a keeper.

After Craig took second in the halfpipe, fifth in slalom, and eleventh in
the downhill, Pat saw something in Craig's eyes that he'd never seen at the
nationals and other big BMX races, and that was "confidence." As well, his
combined score gave him more than just a third place overall title; it earned
him three hundred bucks, which wasn't chump change to a college student
whose Subaru needed four new tires.

During the drive home, Craig finally looked through the smudge-inked
zine his dad had saved for him and said aloud what so many thought that
day: "This is so awesome. Snowboarding *finally* has a magazine," not even
mentioning that he was in it, "blasting through the gates" on page 14 and
demonstrating a "tabletop air" in the halfpipe on page 15. Fulton remembers
Craig being "excited, but humble" about the photos.

What Craig was most fired up about was that Sims had offered to pay his expenses and entry fee for the next contest, the North American Snowboarding Championships, organized by his pal Ken Achenbach, who was touting it as "the richest snowboarding purse ever!"

Rad.

EIGHT WEEKS AFTER the 1985 Worlds, snowboarding exploded into popular culture when the James Bond movie *A View to a Kill* opened with Roger Moore wearing an all-white ski suit outrunning Russian ski troops and an attack helicopter on what the movie presents as a makeshift snowboard Bond improvises from the wreckage of a snowmobile. This iconic scene introduced millions around the world to the coolest new way to get down the mountain. The timing couldn't have been better for the industry, and especially for Sims, who, along with his team rider Steve Link, was Moore's stunt double.

The film's "board" bore no Sims logos, making 007 the sport's unofficial (yet highly visible) team rider, and both ski area acceptance and retail shop orders more than doubled the following season. The distribution of high-back bindings made it easier to learn the sport, and subscription orders and letters steadily increased at the downtown San Francisco office for the newly named *International Snowboard Magazine* (*ISM*). After conferring with advertisers, Tom Hsieh had decided that his magazine's original title wasn't going to help break down the walls at ski resorts like Vail, Killington, Park City, Aspen, and Squaw Valley, because, according to Carpenter, "Those resort managers don't want anything *Absolutely Radical* on their slopes."

"Absolutely radical" was just business as usual at Mount Baker, where Mike Ranquet determinedly followed the MBHC around the mountain. Before he'd met Craig the previous winter, Ranquet had been chased, caught, and ticketed by cops several times for skateboarding on private property and was "on the verge of becoming a local weed dealer," says Ranquet. "That was the direction I was heading when Craig came in like this fucking guardian angel and said, 'Let's go snowboarding.'"

Ranquet had also been a serial school ditcher and regularly in trouble with the principal, so when Craig rang every other Monday or Tuesday, the conversation usually went something like:

"Hey, Mikey, it's Craig. You want to go snowboarding this weekend?"

"Totally! But I don't know, man, I kinda got busted. Let me check with my mom though." Pause, footsteps, pause, more footsteps running this time. "She says I can go! I just can't miss any more school this week."

"Cool, I'll pick you up Friday after class."

"Rad, thanks!"

Ranquet recalls that the only thing he rode with Craig his first day at Baker was the chairlift. Once they'd gotten to the top of the mountain, Craig pointed him down one misty, tree-lined run and said, "I'd take that one." Then he delivered the same brief but effective three-word tutorial he imparted to all of his closest friends and even Brian and Gillian when they learned to snowboard.

"See you later."

The message was clear—*the sooner you figure it out, the sooner you won't ride alone.*

Ranquet was soon hot on the heels of the MBHC, and, toward the end of that first winter, he cut a hard heelside turn during one magical run, burst through the curtain of snow he'd created, and *Holy shit!* There was nobody in front of him. For the first time, he was leading, not following, which sort of qualified him for "official" membership to the MBHC tribe.

Ranquet's experience as a skateboarder served him well. Where runs converged, he saw hips, corners, and kickers that—depending on trajectory or angle of approach—lent themselves better for certain tricks, all of which were rooted in skateboarding. Craig had only been a casual skateboarder as a kid and found in the much younger Ranquet an accidental mentor for skate-influenced riding on snow.

All members of the MBHC fed off of and learned from each other. For example, Carter Turk studied the terrain and pioneered ridable lines down Baker's steepest, rockiest faces, inspiring Craig to explore and find his own line, but most important, to "commit." Eric Swanson, aka Swannie, was famous for charging, and was of the opinion that it's better to air over something than pick your way down it. Craig said Swannie didn't ride the mountain—he "devoured it." As a whole, the Hard Cores heeded the wisdom of local mountain man George Dobis, whose table they often gathered around, either at his official address in the town of Glacier or at a bootleg cabin he'd built in adjacent Mount Baker National Forest. Fulton recalls that he and Craig first encountered Dobis on a logging road at the base of a little bowl they'd been riding. He was on his snowmobile but stopped and shut off the engine, lifted his goggles, and eyed the boot trail up and serpentine tracks down.

"You walk here from the road?" he asked in a heavy Slavic accent.

Craig, thinking maybe they were trespassing, asked if this was his property. Dobis replied with a grin that revealed gold upper teeth. "Nobody owns this forest," he said. "Hop on, one of you. I take you up."

That afternoon, they sat at his table in Glacier and learned that in 1968, Dobis had come to the United States after escaping communist Czechoslovakia with his wife, Bobbi, and infant daughter, Marcella, by eluding border guards and swimming a river while towing the baby in an inner tube. He'd gone on to earn his citizenship by serving in the military, including a tour in Vietnam. He drank Coors, preached self-reliance, and denounced communism or any government overreach when it came to personal freedoms—especially in the wilds, where he soon was mentoring this tribe of snowboarders as though they were his own sons, passing along the knowledge he'd gained from early rambles in the High Tatra Mountains around his village, to later climbing in Russia, Alaska, and all the major peaks of the Cascades. He was not a snowboarder, but mountaineering and summiting peaks had been both entertainment and religion during his difficult childhood.

"You go up into the mountains empty," Dobis would tell them, "even with no lunch, you come home full."

To THE VAST majority of Americans, January 26, 1986, meant Super Bowl Sunday, with Mike Ditka's Chicago Bears up against the New England Patriots. Thanks to James Bond, however, dozens of cars were jockeying for parking spaces at Mount Baker Ski Area because the second annual Sims Open Banked Slalom was on.

Competitors had more than doubled to seventy-five racers. And there were just as many spectators, some of whom had heard that a local boy had given Sims—world champion racer and 007 stand-in—a run for his money the year before. One of the riders was Jeff Galbraith, an eighteen-year-old skateboarder from South Snohomish County who made his first snowboard from a scrap of marine plywood two years earlier but was now walking through the lodge with a Sims 1500FE under his arm that he'd bought used from a dude who rode for Bikeworks in Everett. He wrote for his school newspaper, wore out issues of *ISM* and *Thrasher* with rabid consumption, and stopped in his tracks when his friend pointed across the room: "That's him. That's Craig Kelly . . . He's going to win it all."

Years later, Galbraith would remember the moment, and admit his memory of it was a little dramatic, but the point was, even without "winning it all"— Craig took third place, one place better than the previous year—people (strangers) were starting to recognize him, and remember his name. Terry Kidwell took second and Shaun—no longer in the junior's division, but still known as "Mini Shred"—Palmer took first. According to *ISM*'s news and gossip column, "CRUD," Palmer celebrated the win by trashing his hotel room, and Sims "paid accordingly" for the damages. In other news, Craig finished the day with a $150 prize and a commitment that Sims would fly him to Vermont the first weekend of March to compete in the U.S. Open. The only caveat was that he needed to sign the team rider contract that Sims told him was in the mail.

A week later Craig was back at Mount Baker riding chair 6 when a new liftie smiled at him and said, "You're Craig Kelly."

"Yeah," he said, "that's me."

He took a lap and when he got back to the top, she said it again. "You're Craig Kelly."

"Yeah, we cleared that up last time," he replied.

At day's end, Craig was hanging out at the base area bar, the Tap Room, when he felt a shoulder against his. "Craig Kelly," said the cute liftie with the wind-chapped cheeks and a confident, knowing smile, "I'm Kelly Jo. We should get married, then I'd be Kelly Jo Kelly."

"Nah," Craig replied. "Too symmetrical."

JUGGLING A PROFESSIONAL snowboarding "hobby" and maintaining a high GPA as a full-time engineering student was "like speed metal on steroids," says Mark Thomas, recalling Craig's calendar the winter and spring quarters of his junior year in 1986. Every weekend when there wasn't a competition, he was at Baker riding chair 6 and getting to know Kelly Jo Legaz, who was taking classes at a local college and working weekends at Baker. Their "snowboarding" first date was probably the first time Craig didn't say "See you later" to somebody slower than him. Not much slower: this girl could ride.

The U.S. Open was just a month away when Craig hit up the race departments at Ski Acres, and another little ski area called Hyak Mountain—telling them he was a student at the university and trying to compete as a pro snowboarder. "Any chance I could use a few of your bamboo trail markers and set a slalom course to hike on the side of a run? I could really use the practice," he added. "I'll return everything; you won't even know I was here." They both let him do it. Ski Acres was open nights, so "probably three days a week," said Craig in the December 1988 issue of *TransWorld*, "I would go up in the evening, set bamboo gate courses completely on my own, and spend three, four sometimes five hours under the lights hitting the gates."

Hyak was closed on Mondays, which became the day he'd set a course, and maintenance workers and other employees on the mountain watched him hiking ten, twenty times, sometimes thirty runs for fitness, figuring out the mechanics of his turns, as well as the personalities of his two boards—the sleeker and stiffer 1500FE versus Terry Kidwell's new signature pro model. The latter had a rounded nose and tail that were great for powder and freestyle but turns tended to wash out on hard snow.

Craig's training wasn't enough to beat the Burton riders down their home mountain at the U.S. Open. He ended up taking seventh in slalom and seventeenth in the downhill, which didn't put him in the place he hoped to be when he sat down with Sims and his VP, Dave Weaver, to discuss his as-yet-unsigned contract while at the airport, awaiting their flights back to the West Coast. Originally, Sims had offered him a five-year contract with a five-year option to renew, but Craig had been uncomfortable being locked in for that long.[†] In the current rider agreement, Sims proposed a term of three years with an option to extend three additional years, which seemed reasonable to Craig, as were other terms they discussed and Weaver handwrote in the margins.

In exchange for riding on and endorsing Sims Snowboarding equipment, Craig would be provided the following: Year one (1985–86 season)—two

---

[†] All contractual and legal discussions have been excerpted from the original contracts and sworn statements and or testimony.

free boards (with bindings) and two additional at wholesale price, travel expenses to contests, and a season pass to the mountain of his choice. Year two (1986–87 season)—the same deal, plus Sims would start matching half his prize money as well. Year three (1987–88)—the same again, plus Sims would match 100 percent of his prize money.

In addition, Craig told Sims, he wanted to be further compensated if he performed, and helped Sims grow. As well, he hoped to design his own pro model that merged the turning and edging qualities of a race board with the softer, more forgiving flex of a freestyle board, something built for what he and the MBHC had been calling *freeriding*.[‡] Sims told Craig if he pulled off a win at the Worlds or U.S. Open, "hell yes" he'd write an addendum and give him a pro model, a promise Weaver was surprised to hear. Sims had just recently declared no more pro models added to the line because he did not want snowboarding to go the same route that skateboarding had.[§]

"Tom dangled the 'pro model' carrot in front of Craig as incentive to sign the contract," says Weaver, "but at that point Tom had no plans to design a board with him. His focus was on Shaun Palmer and Terry Kidwell, who were full-time riders already making names for themselves. Craig was still in school." Craig took the contract with him and signed it without legal counsel in his bedroom at the Delta Upsilon house on May 10, 1986. Sims saw it as the beginning of a long and prosperous relationship, envisioning college kid Craig shifting from athlete to marketing director, maybe even CEO, down the road.

For now, Sims had bigger, more pressing concerns. In his words, he was "very much in debt" and searching for a solution that would enable him to both fund and produce all the orders that were stacking up.

WHEN CRAIG INVITED Ranquet to come practice on his slalom course, Ranquet told him he considered racing in and out of gates "disrespectful use of a snowboard," whose true raison d'être was a skateboard for the snow. "If I

[‡]   Nobody is certain who first used the word *freeriding* to describe what is essentially "all-mountain" snowboarding. It became a common reference in the mid-1980s.

[§]   Paying skateboarders royalties for their pro-model skateboards had, in Sims's mind, been a big part of "the cause of death" of his predecessor company, Sims Skateboards, which had been the world's largest skateboard manufacturer in the late 1970s before several of his best team riders were, according to Sims, "lured away" to ride for another company.

wanted to race," said Ranquet, "I'd still be skiing. If you're going to practice, practice for the halfpipe."

"There are no halfpipes," Craig said, which was a fact. Of the roughly five hundred ski areas in the U.S., only about fifty allowed snowboarding in 1986, and none of them maintained a pipe. When the odd halfpipe did get built, it was just before a contest, and then it got flattened a few days later because of liability concerns.

Ranquet kept ribbing him: "Don't you have any self-respect? Why would you spend hours wiggling your ass back and forth down the mountain like a skier?"

"Because I'm going to win the Worlds," Craig replied matter-of-factly. "I'm training."

"All right," said Ranquet. "Whatever."

Shortly after that conversation, Craig entered a banked slalom that Bob Barci organized at Hyak on the Saturday after winter quarter classes ended on March 14. He won and celebrated his first victory by studying for a week of final exams, which began the next morning. Immediately following his last exam, on Friday, March 21, he flew from Seattle to Aspen for an invitational downhill at Buttermilk Mountain, a much tougher affair. "The sheer gnarliness of the run immediately went to work on people's nerves," reported Tom Hsieh in *ISM*. "Some riders decided not to risk their boards and bones on the course at all."

The fear was justified. Top riders from the U.S. and Europe were clocked at speeds up to 70 miles per hour, and while nobody got hauled off on a stretcher, several rag-dolled down the "waterfall" section of the course. In the end, Shaun Palmer won, and Craig took second. Thrilled to watch his riders kicking ass on such a sketchy course, Sims treated them to dinner in downtown Aspen. "Don't trash your room!" he told Palmer.

The following Monday, Craig pulled into the near-empty lot at Hyak and was ready to set a course when he saw a legit slalom course was already set up with real gates. As he started to hike, someone from the race department pulled up on a snowmobile. "Rumor has it you're training for the world championships," he said. "Hop on. You've been hiking long enough."

Craig climbed on the back and felt like royalty, being chauffeured to the top so many times, he lost count. By the end of the day, he was ready to take on the "Worlds."

CHAPTER 5

WORLD CHAMPION

AFTER THREE YEARS AT SODA Springs, the Worlds was moving to one of the biggest ski resorts in the country—Breckenridge, Colorado—now open to snowboarders, thanks to a fifty-year-old skier named Paul Alden. Alden, whose son David was sponsored by Burton, worked for a company that assisted in the installation of chairlift towers at several ski areas in Colorado and Utah. Paul Alden met Carpenter and started chatting in terms of business and sports. "Jake, you've got great footballs," he said, "but you don't have any fields to play on. I may be able to do something about that." They struck a deal whereby Paul and David would be compensated for their help expanding Burton's distribution in Colorado in exchange for Paul's efforts to get the state's biggest resorts to allow snowboarding.

Paul Alden was as comfortable in a pinstripe suit as he was in a boardroom, and spoke to the corporate ranks (and insurance providers) of the resorts from the perspective of a growing number of skier parents with snowboarder kids facing the dilemma of where to plan their family vacation. He spoke candidly of revenue they could gain or continue to lose. And of the enduring benefits of pioneering instruction and rentals for riders. Breckenridge was an old mining town, and he played off that when he said, "Stake your claim. Make Breckenridge Colorado's premier snowboarding destination."

Once they were on the hook, Alden suggested they host a big contest "that will really put Breckenridge on the map." He'd done his homework and learned Sims was "done" running contests, and proposed moving the Worlds to Colorado, a more central location for the ongoing East Coast versus West Coast rivalry, and since Sims was ready to let it go, there was no need to deal with licensing transfers. Just rename it. Another deal was struck, and almost overnight, the World Snowboarding Championships became the World Snowboard Classic.

A date was set, letters were sent to past competitors, press releases were faxed to the media, and with Swatch named as the title sponsor, the eyes of everyone in the world of snowboarding were trained on Breckenridge, including Craig. He was as confident as he'd ever been to hit the road and win this thing, when his beloved Subaru suffered engine failure and was stuck in a shop on life support. Ranquet's mom saved the day when she handed Craig the keys to their family van. Craig, Ranquet, Fulton, and Shipsey piled in and headed east to Breckenridge, via the southern route through Lake Tahoe—because a five-hundred-mile detour totally made sense—in order to ride one of the only half-pipes in the country, freshly shoveled and shaped at Slide Peak for a local contest circuit. They got in two days of practice and were finally heading east when Craig announced he had to stop at the Reno airport to "pick something up."

That "something" was Kelly Jo, who called shotgun faster than Ranquet could say, "What the fuck?" With Craig behind the wheel and the Scorpions' *Love at First Sting* in the cassette player, they Rocked It Like a Hurricane through the night to get to Breckenridge, where by the following morning two hundred of the "World's" best snowboarders were amped to compete in giant slalom and slalom. But "the real attraction to snowboarding," said Channel 7 sports anchor John Keating, "is known as half piping [sic]. It's skateboarding without the skates, and it's packed with phrases such as 'Rip it up, dude.'"

That night, they crashed on couches and the floor of the Team Sims condo. "I knew Craig had his shit together," says Sims, "when I asked if he needed a wake-up call, and he said he brought his own alarm clock."

Craig was first on the mountain but placed tenth in the giant slalom (Kidwell won); then on day two, he was a half second faster than Burton's Andy Coghlan. This made him the fastest slalom racer at the Worlds, and thus the "world" champion, which left Ranquet dumbfounded but proud, thinking, "This random dude I met on a chairlift is the world champion, just like he said he was going to be."

Craig ended up taking fourth in the halfpipe but watched closely the runs of the top three finishers, especially Terry Kidwell, who took first in the halfpipe and whose cumulative scores from all three disciplines made him—no surprise—the overall "Worlds" champion, aka the best snowboarder in the world, for the third year in a row.

The "world" title was considered "totally legit," says Ranquet, because riders from Switzerland, Austria, France, Japan, and Australia had crossed oceans to be at this American-made sport's biggest global arena, where the most anticipated score was to see who got closest to Kidwell. And at the 1986 Worlds that rider was Craig Kelly.

"It didn't matter which contest, or what discipline, if Terry Kidwell or Shaun Palmer were on the start list, I expected them to win," says early Colorado ripper cum snowboarding historian Dave Alden. "But at the '86 Worlds, people took notice—Craig was special, and he rode with a very special group of riders. There was a toughness about the Mount Baker Hard Core and their spawn that nobody could fuck with because they rode the most unforgiving mountain. Craig distilled that toughness and the lessons that Baker taught them and applied it to contests. Nobody could fuck with that. Not even Kidwell."

Ranquet's van limped and was eventually towed back to Washington, having provided its passengers a trip of a lifetime. Everybody returned with respectable finishes, offers for sponsorship, and newfound friendships, and having earned the respect of their rider brothers and sisters in what felt, at the time, like one big dysfunctional family.

Sims returned to Santa Barbara, California, stoked that Denver's Channel 7 news had recapped the event and introduced him as the "recognized . . . inventor of the snowboard, having come up with the idea twenty-three years ago at the age of thirteen," which was more frustrating to Carpenter than it was seeing Sims riders continue to dominate in the halfpipe. Still, he couldn't disagree with the prediction Sims made on the news that snowboarding "will become the mainstream winter sport for teenagers . . . within five years," in contrast to that made by the news anchor, whose last words were spoken with authority: "No one's going to get rich snowboarding."

AFTER A FIRST kiss in the Ranquet's van, Craig and Kelly Jo were a couple, and moved into a two-bedroom apartment in Seattle with Mark Thomas. Craig took on a full-time job packing and moving houses for the summer, but still couldn't quite top, in three months of backbreaking labor, what he'd made one winter snowboarding. Once he started his senior year, he researched the salary he might expect (upon graduation) as a chemical engineer: around $27,000 ($71,000 today).

That was a boatload of money, but he'd made almost a fifth of that much snowboarding without training seriously.* Prize money was getting better, and with Sims set to match half his winnings, and willing to send him to Europe to compete, Craig realized he could make almost as much snowboarding as he would sitting behind a desk—and have a lot more fun doing it. Plus there was Sims's promise of his own pro model, which meant exponentially more cash via royalties as early as the following season. If they got moving on his design ideas now, he could have a board in production by summer.

"I'm thinking of dropping out," he told Thomas, who recommended that Craig just finish his degree and go for it full-time in a year. After all, he only had two quarters to go. Jeff Krueger had a different take. His aerospace-engineering mindset considered the quandary in terms of performance, longevity, and timing. "The competition is just going to get tougher; your knees and back are going to get weaker," he told Craig. "I say go for it now while your body is strong. You can always go back to school."

Over Thanksgiving break, Craig invited his dad for dinner at the apartment and after a couple beers, told him his plan to put college on hold after that quarter ended. "The timing is right," Craig said. "I really think I can make it as a pro snowboarder."

Pat was nodding, before he'd even swallowed his beer. "I think you should go for it," he said. "I'll help you all I can."

CRAIG'S FINAL EXAM for the fall quarter took place on December 18, 1986, and was followed by separate Christmas celebrations, as was customary for Craig, Brian, and Gillian, who spent one day with Pat, and another day with Janet, her husband, and their five-month-old daughter, Jessica. Janet was known for surprises, but a new baby sister was one gift none of the Kelly kids had expected.

After the holiday, Craig was off to the Rocky Mountains, where he and

---

* Craig's prize money at the 1986 Worlds totaled $1,500. His season total was almost $5,000 (roughly $12,000 today).

Kelly Jo rented an apartment in Frisco, Colorado, that served as base camp for his first winter as a full-time pro. While Kelly Jo worked a part-time job at a ski shop near Keystone and rode four days a week, Craig trained in some aspect of snowboarding every day. He rode moguls at Arapahoe Basin; raced the modified giant slalom NASTAR courses at both Copper Mountain and Breckenridge; and spent hours hiking and hitting two (one frontside, one backside) quarterpipes he built off the side of the road on the way up to Loveland Pass in order to learn and master tricks.

When Craig was fifteen, he'd told his dad that repetition was the key to "incremental improvement" on the BMX track.

"Craig did a lot of reading for knowledge rather than for escape," says Pat. "He was always curious and interested in self-improvement. When he was younger, and played baseball, out of the blue, he started doing a lot of sit-ups—hundreds at a time—and push-ups, lifting weights, because that was what Nolan Ryan did, and I asked him, 'How'd you learn that?' and he said, 'I read his book.'"

Craig created his own regimen, focusing on individual tricks in order to perfect entire halfpipe runs. Once he could land a trick clean three times in a row, he'd add a tweak, hold the grab longer, whatever flourish would give it more "style." Once he landed the trick clean and "with style" three times in a row, he would move on to the next trick. Then he'd string them together in an actual halfpipe if he could find one.

He used the same repetitive actions to improve his times on a racecourse, concentrating on "a certain muscle group or perfecting a particular technique," he told Wiley Asher, *ISM*'s first staff writer. "If my riding doesn't feel technically perfect, I concentrate on the problem. If I chatter out on a heel turn, I think, 'Why did that happen? Okay, next time, put more weight on your rear foot.'" Then he would focus only on that for several runs. In all cases, the goal was to be faster, and there were three simple rules he'd follow to better his times: Use the terrain to your advantage. Brake less going into your turns; accelerate more coming out of your turns. Less braking, faster time, incremental improvement.

He added up his hours on snow and found he was now getting as much riding in ten days as he used to in a month back home, and his body could feel it. He'd always warmed up before he rode, and stretched some, but now it was a mandatory twenty minutes per day, plus core exercises.

The first contest of the season, organized by the Southwest Snow Surfers Association, was at Wolf Creek, Colorado, and as was common, he and a third of the competitors showed up a couple days early, not to practice, but to help build the halfpipe. Armed with shovels, they constructed massive walls for the era, with some sections topping eight feet. During warm-ups Craig, Kidwell, and Palmer were boosting bigger airs than anybody had ever seen at a contest venue, which made the men's pro finals "by far the raddist halfpipe session seen to date," reported Jim Sechrest in *ISM*.

Kidwell injured his shoulder during practice and didn't compete, which left an opening for Palmer, a new Sims Team rider named Tim Windell, and the rest of a rowdy Colorado-based crew, all of whom Craig beat. After claiming that first halfpipe victory, he crossed the Atlantic to compete in the 1987 World Snowboarding Championships, the European copycat of the event that had been running in the United States since 1983.

Like the Americans, Canadians, and Japanese, the Europeans were doing their best to organize competition that both identified the best riders and legitimized the sport. The fact that both the U.S. and Europe were hosting "World" championships revealed the need for an international governing body—like skiing's Fédération Internationale de Ski (FIS).

Jose Fernandes had competed in the 1985 American "Worlds" at Soda Springs and was the driving force behind the European version. After all, he'd seen that, if you named your event the World Snowboarding Championship and won, you could call yourself the "world" champion.

The international legitimacy of those early—1983 to 1986—"World" titles born in America are open for debate, but it's a fair bet that the riders who earned them were indeed the best in the "world of snowboarding" at that time. And many of those champions were at the European Worlds to prove it. They included Andy Coghlan, Mark Heingartner, Chris Karol, Terry Kidwell, and Ken Achenbach, riding against Euro champs such as Germany's Peter Bauer, Frenchmen Jean-Paul Garcia and Jean Nerva, and Switzerland's Antoine Massy and Jose Fernandes, all of whom would be attending the American Worlds at Breckenridge later that winter. As such, 1987 was the first year that legitimate world champions in various disciplines might be named if they could win *both* the American and European world championships.

Just being there in the "old country," sipping a cappuccino while walking to the lifts on the cobblestone streets of Livigno, Italy—where the freestyles events were held—was a victory in itself for Craig. Still, his focus was on the competition, not the culture. The alpine racing events were held at St. Moritz, Switzerland, where throngs of brightly dressed snowboarders mingled with skiers. In an *ISM* interview in 1985, Jose Fernandes had predicted that snowboarding growth in Europe would outpace America "because in Europe," said Fernandes, "snowboarding never sleeps." Craig learned snowboarding was welcomed at virtually every ski area in Europe, and rider training camps were held year-round on glaciers. Fernandes himself was a national hero in Switzerland, an inspiring spokesperson for the sport and self-marketeer who Craig noted was "a real professional." Still, he lost to Craig, who won the mogul competition, took second in the halfpipe, fifth in both slalom and downhill races, and nineteenth in the giant slalom.

When the scores from all the disciplines were tallied, Craig was named the 1987 Overall World Champion on European soil.

BUT HE DIDN'T stop there. Back home Craig traveled east to the U.S. Open at Stratton Mountain, Vermont, and defeated hometown Burton heroes Heingartner, Karol, and Coghlan for the overall U.S. Open title. "Beating the fastest racers in the world at their home mountain was like knocking out Mike Tyson," says Tom Hsieh.

Two weeks later, at the Grand Prix of Snowboarding in Aspen, Craig swept the field, winning the slalom, super G, and halfpipe. Then he returned to Breckenridge for the Swatch World Snowboarding Classic, where a reported two hundred fifty men and nearly a hundred women from around the world were there to compete, including Craig—determined to defend the world title he'd earned in Europe—and Fernandes, who vowed to take a world title back to Switzerland.[†] An estimated two thousand spectators converged at the halfpipe for the finals. During practice runs, the top competitors were regularly stopped for a sound bite by such media types as Kevin Kinnear, the former editor of the SoCal surf magazine *Breakout*, who had

---

[†]   Those who came to see Terry Kidwell rip the pipe were disappointed to hear that his jacked shoulder would keep him from competing.

been hired by Larry Balma and Peggy Cozens, the publishers of *TransWorld SKATEboarding* magazine, to start up a new snowboarding magazine.

Although Kinnear, thirty-six, was a cool older surfer dude (think the purely saltwater version of Sims), on snow he was admittedly a "kook," as was veteran surf photographer Guy Motil, whom he'd recruited to come along. The trip to the Worlds was a crash course, literally, in snowboarding immersion. Their assignment: learn to snowboard and collect content for their premiere issue.

"I'm Kevin Kinnear, the editor of *TransWorld SNOWboarding* magazine," he introduced himself to riders as they hiked past him on the side of the halfpipe. "You mind if I ask you about the first time you went snowboarding?"

"No fucking way!?" was the spirited response he got from a rider with big curly hair and an even bigger smile. "TransWorld is doing a snowboard mag? Rad! Yeah, I'll talk to you. I'm Ken Achenbach, I run the North American Snowboarding Championships at Sunshine Village," he said, handing Kinnear a business card. "It's Canada's biggest contest. You should cover it. Call me, you can crash at my place. You already missed this year's Banked Slalom at Mount Baker, so you basically missed snowboarding's Pipeline Masters. That's Amy Howat right there. Her dad runs Mount Baker, she rides for GNU, and she rips. That kid with the spikey hair is Damian Sanders. Rock star. His brother and sister-in-law Chris and Bev own Avalanche snowboards. If you're shooting tight [looking at Motil], point your camera about five feet higher than everybody else, Damian goes huge. That's Shaun Palmer. We used to call him Mini Shred, but that's starting to piss him off; he goes bigger than anybody else here aside from Damian. That's Dave Dowd, local Coloradan, George Pappas, Kerri Hannon, Gayle Guerin—Terry Kidwell is here somewhere—he's Tom Sims's Golden Boy. There's Kelly Jo Legaz with her boyfriend, Craig Kelly. Celebrity romance. That's your story: she rips and he's winning everything this year—they're from Baker too; that place breeds talent."

Achenbach rattled on and on, and just like that, Kinnear was on the inside—and Tom Hsieh had some competition.

Another newcomer at the pipe that morning was Bert LaMar, a former skateboarding prodigy—sponsored by Sims Skateboards when he was eleven years old—from the sidewalk-surfing boom of the 1970s. "He quit skating and showed up a decade later in the Breckenridge halfpipe," says Achenbach, who took note of his flashy repertoire of handplants and cocky attitude. Word got around that this twenty-four-year-old skateboarder from Los Angeles had walked up to both Sims and Carpenter before the contest even started and said, "Do you want to sponsor me? It'll be cheaper now than it will be after I win."

Nobody took him seriously.

Until he won . . . edging out Craig, who was not happy about his number two position in the pipe. In the races, Craig took second in giant slalom (behind Jose Fernandes), and won the slalom. His combined scores from all disciplines made him the best all-around snowboarder in the world, having defended his Overall World Champion title in both Europe and North America.

While being interviewed about his win after the awards ceremony, Craig heard LaMar telling a reporter, "I just started snowboarding a couple months ago—this was my first major contest."

Craig didn't believe it. No way. You don't just roll up to a halfpipe and win your first event after a few weeks of practice.

Regardless, getting beat by this skateboarder from LA was sort of a gift. It was a stinging reminder of how young this sport was, and how new talent could show up at any moment and smoke you. Craig even reverted, for a split second, back to that kid who threw elbows on the BMX track when he gave LaMar an extra-long stare after the awards ceremony and told him, as he was shaking his hand, "You got lucky."

IMMEDIATELY FOLLOWING THE awards ceremony, LaMar headed to a private meeting with an entourage from Burton, while Craig and other members of Team Sims met with Brad Dorfman (aka The Solution), whom Sims had licensed[‡]—in essence, sold—his namesake brand to. Not only was Dorfman the founder of the world's biggest skateboard and skateboarding apparel

---

[‡]   In exchange for a signing payment, plus royalty payments for each product sold, Sims gave Dorfman exclusive rights to manufacture, market, and distribute the Sims Snowboards brand around the world. Sims remained on salary as a brand consultant. Team rider contracts, and in most cases, handshake deals, were transferred to the licensee, Dorfman, who was now the boss at Sims Snowboards Inc.

brands—Vision Skateboards and Vision Street Wear—he was the man Sims believed would take Sims Snowboards to the next level, enabling them to compete head-to-head with Burton on the world market.

Dorfman congratulated the team on various wins—including those by Craig, who had doubled down and proved he was the Overall World Champion on both sides of the Atlantic. "We are in a room full of champions" is what Sims team manager, Lori Gibbs, recalls Dorfman saying. "We are going to kick ass in business, just like you guys are kicking ass on the snow." He said things were going to change in a big way with a new international distribution network, sales, marketing, and "No more sleeping on couches or in cars at contests." He said he was there to support them. "If anyone is unhappy," Gibbs recalls Dorfman saying, "come and talk with me and we'll try to work things out."

Craig recalled the same invitation from Dorfman. As well, Gibbs told Craig after this meeting that Dorfman had recently told her that Craig's and other team riders' agreements were unclear, and that "as far as he [Dorfman] was concerned these old contracts drawn up by Tom Sims weren't legal."[§] Craig, who was still awaiting matched prize money and long-overdue travel reimbursements, met with Dorfman that summer at the Sims Snowboards Inc. corporate office in Costa Mesa, California, to discuss and negotiate the terms of a new contract.

According to Craig, upon leaving that meeting in Costa Mesa, Dorfman shook his hand and said, "A contract doesn't mean anything to me; a handshake does. Our lawyers can get us out of this agreement [referencing original contract with Tom Sims] anytime; it's just a matter of spending the money."[¶]

NOT LONG AFTER Craig walked out of Dorfman's office, Bert LaMar walked in.

LaMar had visited Burton headquarters in Manchester, Vermont, and had

---

[§]   Dorfman had a very different recollection of the validity of this contract, which would later become the subject of a lawsuit. This quote is from Gibbs's testimony, during which she recalled the conversation "distinctly."

[¶]   Dorfman also had a very different recollection. This quote is from Craig's witness statement, which he confirmed during testimony as well.

with him a contract—signed by Carpenter—that inked the deal they'd discussed in Manchester. "But I never signed anything," says LaMar, who recalls Burton's offer had been very fair, and gave him salary, incentives, a pro model, and, in the offices of Sims Snowboards Inc., irrefutable leverage. "I knew my market value," says LaMar, "and I knew the snowboarding industry was underpaying its best athletes, if they were paying them at all."

Snowboarding's biggest name, Terry Kidwell, had only recently negotiated a $300-a-month salary, plus a $3-per-board royalty for his signature pro model. Before that, Kidwell's only income—like Shaun Palmer, Craig, and nearly all other pro riders—had come from prize money, matched prize money, and incentives. "If you could clear $15,000 in 1987," says Palmer, "pretty sure you would have been the richest pro in snowboarding."

Sims Snowboards Inc. more than doubled that when Dorfman agreed to pay LaMar a $3,000-per-month salary for one year—$36,000, or in today's money, roughly $100,000. It was by all accounts the most lucrative snowboarding contract to date.

WHILE LAMAR WAS signing on the dotted line at Sims Snowboards in Costa Mesa, Craig was on the Palmer Glacier at Mount Hood, Oregon, testing the final—preproduction—prototypes for the following winter's Sims board line, including a newly constructed, lighter-weight Kidwell pro model, racing Blade, and freestyle Switchblade. Then he was off with Kelly Jo to Switzerland. They bounced from glacier to glacier across Europe, learning all they could about the summer snowboard training camps Fernandes had told him about, where "campers" paid for all-inclusive (coaching, room, and board) sessions, much like the ones ski racers attended. While Kelly Jo learned the business, Craig "guest coached" and trained at the halfpipes and slalom courses. His plan—in addition to starting his own camp—was to be in top shape come winter to not only defend his overall world title, but to crush LaMar the first chance he got. It seemed a solid strategy, until he discovered LaMar was on the same program.

In fact, Craig and Kelly Jo traveled with LaMar between a couple of camps (they were, after all, teammates now) and while LaMar had been told not to share details of his contract with other riders, he did share with Craig some of his history with Sims—specifically that he had been sponsored by Sims Skateboards when he was eleven years old, got his first pro-model deck at twelve, and a couple of years later discovered his pro model had been selling like hotcakes in Europe, yet he had never received a single payment for European sales. LaMar's mom drove him to the Sims office, where they confronted Tom. His mom told Sims if those royalty payments didn't show up quick, the next visit he got would be from their attorney. Sims had been his hero, so it had been a hard but valuable lesson for LaMar—and cautionary insight for Craig—who realized, "Wow, this guy isn't one hundred percent looking out for me."

When he and Craig parted ways that summer, they were still archrivals in the pipe, but a few parting words from LaMar stuck with Craig and Kelly Jo: "Make sure they pay you what you're worth."

CHAPTER 6

CHANGING TEAMS

CRAIG'S LAST STOP IN EUROPE was Jose Fernandes's camp on Austria's Stubai Glacier, where some of the participants were passing around the most recent issue of *ISM* that had a back-cover Sims advertisement featuring Craig lofting a huge method air at the Wolf Creek halfpipe event he'd won seven months earlier. He still hadn't been reimbursed for expenses from that contest and several others the previous winter, so he called his dad to see if any checks had arrived from Sims Snowboards Inc.

"Nothing," said Pat.

A couple of days later, Craig saw a familiar face at the Stubai halfpipe: Jake Burton Carpenter's wife, Donna Carpenter, who was there with members of the Burton team. He sat down beside her and said, "Hey, Donna, if I ever wanted to ride for Burton would you guys be interested in talking?"

"It was one of those moments where inside you're screaming, 'Yes! Yes!'" recalls Carpenter, who played it cool and handed him a card. "If you're not riding for Sims," she told Craig, "you should talk to Jake. Here's his number, give him a call."

WITH CARPENTER'S CARD in his pocket, Craig returned home in August to find the September 1987 issue of *ISM* and the premiere issue of *TransWorld SNOWboarding* in his mailbox. The timing couldn't be better. These were the first mags for the coming 1987–88 season, and there he was—blurred background, white speed suit, on a red Sims blade—on the cover of *ISM*, with his name in big bold yellow font: "Kelly Steals the U.S. Open." Inside, "Kelly had determination written in his eyes as he flew down the course bashing every gate in his path," wrote Hsieh. "Kelly doesn't glide over snow, he coerces it . . . a supernatural combo of talent."

With that kind of killer coverage, plus several shots of him in *TransWorld*, Craig hit the library to learn all he could about sports contracts, negotiating tactics, and deal making. Two weeks later, he'd fine-tuned and faxed his proposal to both Dorfman and Sims, asking for a salary of $2,000 per month, plus expenses and incentives; medical insurance; and a "set of 36 breakaway racing gates and portable battery-operated power drill with an ice bit for training."

Sims was first to respond a few days later, informing Craig that he was asking for way too much. He predicted that Dorfman "would not swallow it," saying that "this is our entire budget for an entire year." For two weeks there was radio silence, then new Sims team manager, Debbie Hendrickson, phoned Craig to relay that Dorfman had declined the proposal. It took Craig several tries before he was able to reach Dorfman, who—according to Craig—told him during the call, "If you've got someone else to give you this offer, you should probably go ahead and do it."*

On October 21, 1987, Carpenter showed Craig around Burton Snowboards' impressive new Manchester Center, Vermont, manufacturing facility. Craig shared with Carpenter his engineering background and how he and his buddy (Jeff Krueger) would loiter at ski shops and totally nerd out on ski construction: sidecut, radius, camber, shape, flex, materials. He didn't give away specs for the dream board he hoped to build, but emphasized it would combine characteristics of race boards and freestyle boards and would "revolutionize" performance.

Craig had pitched the same board to Sims and Dorfman, both of whom brushed him off. Carpenter, however, leaned in and listened to every word. "Let's do it. Whatever you're thinking, we'll build it right here. We've got the technology—we can turn around a prototype in three days."

---

* This quote is from Craig's witness statement, and was further discussed during testimony in the lawsuit *Sims Snowboards Inc. vs. Craig Kelly and The Burton Corporation*, December 28, 1987. Dorfman would have a very different recollection of this telephone conversation. He maintained that he never released Craig from his contractual duties.

"Jake was really excited after that first meeting with Craig," says Donna Carpenter. "He was exactly what we were looking for. West Coast, free styler, competitive as fuck. Getting an engineer was a totally unexpected bonus."

Craig flew from Burlington, Vermont, to St. Louis, where his dad had tickets for game five of the World Series. Pat's team, the Cardinals, were at home playing the Minnesota Twins, and just before the opening pitch, Craig reached into his jacket and pulled out two cans of beer. Taking one, Pat said, "How the hell did you sneak those in here?"

"Dad, I've been going to concerts since I was fifteen years old. I've got a whole six-pack."

Between batters and innings, Craig told him all about his visit to Burton, and two days later they were driving to Colorado to meet Paul Alden at his home in Denver.

Carpenter hired Alden after he'd convinced Breckenridge to allow snow-boarding. Since then, Alden had continued to open up ski areas across the country while simultaneously brokering deals that made Burton the exclusive on-mountain brand used in rental shops and by the resorts' snowboarding instructors, growing the sport and increasing Burton's footprint one resort at a time.

Alden had proven himself a savvy businessman who delivered, which was why Carpenter was confident he would "deliver" Craig Kelly to the Burton team. Craig had assured both Carpenter and Alden that he was no longer under contract with Sims; he believed that his old contract Sims had signed wasn't worth the paper it was written on. Nobody at Burton Snowboards contacted Sims Snowboards Inc. to confirm any of this.

When Alden began formal negotiations with Craig, he "anticipated spend-ing a few hours," says Alden, "maybe a few days, but I quickly realized Craig wasn't just a world champion snowboarder—he was a world-class negotiator."

Craig proposed a three-year contract structured with a "salary escalator," similar to the one Olympian skiers Phil and Steve Mahre had used and described in their joint autobiography, *No Hill Too Fast*. "The harder I work, the more contests I win," Craig said in describing his incentive-based contract. "The more I win, the more money I earn, but Burton wins too with publicity and titles and sales. It's a win-win." Craig ultimately agreed to a first-year base salary of $24,000 ($2,000 a month) plus a victory schedule with bonuses for top five finishes, and when he appeared in videos, television, magazines, newspapers. Whatever he ended up making in total for year one would become the new base salary for year two; the total from year two would become the base salary for year three. In addition, he would receive a $15 royalty for each sale of his future pro model, medical insurance, those breakaway training gates, and a power drill. He also worked in a contract for Kelly Jo in which Burton would match prize money and pay incentives, plus medical insurance and travel expenses. "We're a package deal," he said to Burton.

There was just one remaining caveat: "If I sign with you, you need to promise you'll listen to me."

Carpenter replied, "I will. You've got my word."

The same day he signed the contract, Craig got to work on his first pro model. Shortly thereafter he was testing it in Austria, where Jake and Donna Carpenter had invited the pro team for Thanksgiving and a week of snowboarding. After the first day of riding, Craig thanked them, and acknowledged the camaraderie was great, but said they were missing a big opportunity. "You've got everybody here," he said. "What a perfect time to sit down and talk about product and share ideas."

The following night they had what would become a yearly "Rider Roundtable." "Everybody else showed up with a beer," says Donna, "and Craig showed up with a notebook and a folder full of ideas, sketches, and notes." Some of the riders present said it was a little awkward, if not intimidating, because Craig was so cerebral and driven, but it was soon evident he wasn't trying to show anybody up. "He had more questions than answers," says Donna. "And that opened up the floodgates, for discussion. We always had great input from guys like Andy [Coghlan] and Mark [Heingartner], but witnessing that synergy, with all of them together . . . definitely nudged Jake to let Burton evolve into a *rider-driven* company."

When they returned to the States, Craig and Kelly Jo rented a house on Baltimore Avenue in Bend, Oregon, with Ranquet (now sponsored by GNU Snowboards) and Craig's pal from UW Steve Shipsey, who "was sponsored by Craig." On Monday morning, December 14, they were walking out the door to train at nearby Mount Bachelor for a mandatory qualifying event at

Copper Mountain, Colorado, for the newly sanctioned World Cup circuit[†] when a sheriff's deputy pulled up and served Craig with a court summons for "breach of contract" and a temporary restraining order prohibiting him from using any snowboard other than the Sims brand. Simultaneously, Burton was served with a summons for "tortious interference with a contract."

Kelly Jo remembers Craig taking off his gloves and throwing them to the ground. "Guess I'm not training today," he said, before picking up the phone.

"Hey, Dad, I think I need a lawyer."

THIS WAS THE beginning of the industry's first big legal battle, a "John Grisham thriller meets snowboarding clusterfuck," says Kelly Jo, "with Craig in the middle of the two biggest brands who already hated each other. It wasn't 'Let's figure this out.' It was 'Either ride on a Sims board or kill your career. Make a decision. World Cup qualifying starts in four days.'"

At an emergency hearing the day before the contest, a judge ruled that Craig was only entitled to compete on a snowboard (or any equipment or apparel) that had either Sims logos or no logos at all and to continue on such a board until the case was ruled upon, which, the judge noted, could take a very long time.

Craig qualified for the World Cup riding a logo-less all-black board that Burton produced and rushed to him just in time for him to take second place at Copper Mountain. At the same time, attorneys for Sims contacted the snowboarding media and strongly requested they not run photographs they might have of Craig riding Burton equipment.

Two months later, Tom Hsieh ignored the request and featured Craig on the cover of the March 1988 issue of *ISM* carving a Burton Safari race board. A prominent Burton logo above the knuckles of his forearm-length black-and-neon gate-bashing gloves was as bold as the cover blurb that read

---

†   A newly formed North American Snowboard Association (NASBA) met with the Snowboard European Association (SEA) and created the first-ever unified World Cup of Snowboarding with two events in January (Zürs, Austria, and Bormio, Italy) and two events in March (Stratton, Vermont, and Breckenridge, Colorado).

"Kelly: A Federal Judge Orders Him to Ride Board Without Graphics." Inside, a six-page story featured photos of Craig on both Sims and Burton boards and reported, "Kelly competed in two World Cup events on a board with no graphics. His sponsorship is currently up in the air . . . testimony shows he believes he had been released by the Sims Corporation, but Tom Sims and Sims Snowboards Inc. claim Kelly's contract had never been invalidated. . . . After the World Cup races in Europe, he will sacrifice important training time to sit in court while the judge hears more evidence for a final decision . . . which will determine who he'll be riding for, or whether he'll be riding at all."

For its part, *TWS* only ran photos of Craig on the "mysterious" black board, but the mag's "Yellow Sno" gossip column confirmed the "nasty legal battle" and reported Craig Kelly would "rather go back to school than switch back to Sims." Word got around: Craig was up against "the man" and fighting for the rights of all pro riders.

Despite heavy pressure from the legal battle that would continue to rage for months—Sims Snowboards Inc. was suing him and Burton for $5 million in damages—Craig continued to compete, pulling off second-place finishes (behind Kidwell and LaMar) at the first World Cup halfpipe events in Austria and Italy, and with strong finishes in all other disciplines. He returned from Europe tied for first place overall.

Before the American leg of the World Cup began, Craig entered the fourth annual Mount Baker Banked Slalom. At his first-ever contest in 1985, he'd taken fourth place; in 1986, it was third; and in 1987, second. But 1988 was the year he finally took top prize on his home turf, and while it had been a long time coming, slipping away from the noise—the incessant questions about the lawsuit—and the crowd to sneak in some runs with Fulton was the greatest reward.

They headed to a special spot Craig had discovered, off the top of chair 5. "There's a nice big open face, and super-steep gully on the way there," Fulton says, keeping it vague. "Some pretty heavy cliff exposure, some finger chutes—Craig was just exploring when he found it. You have to ease into it around these trees, it's a little weird, you've got to know what you're doing. If you fall, you might not die, but you're definitely going to get hurt. So that's the vibe getting there, snow is blowing, powder is stacking up, it's wild—it's always deep. But once you drop, the way Craig described it, I'll never forget. He was like, 'Once you're in there, in that little pocket—it's quiet, there's no wind—it's like you're in the womb. And then you come shooting out.'"

Says Fulton, "We've called that line 'The Womb' ever since."

After clearing his head, reborn—if you will—during that short sabbatical at Mount Baker, Craig took first or second place in every discipline (except one race) at five national contests, before returning to the World Cup circuit for event number three at Stratton, Vermont. There he took second place in moguls, third in halfpipe (behind Kidwell and LaMar again), and first place overall. But it was at the fourth and final World Cup—still "the Worlds"—at Breckenridge that he most wanted to redeem himself from the previous year's loss to the cocky newcomer LaMar, and he did, taking first in the halfpipe and a respectable seventh in the slalom.

Once the scores were tallied from all four World Cup events, Craig was named the 1988 Freestyle World Champion and Overall World Champion for the second year in a row. He was the best of the best, a point he punctuated when he won every discipline at the Snoboard Shop North American Snowboarding Championships.

Not everyone was celebrating the burgeoning growth of the sport. According to *Time* magazine, snowboarding was the "Worst New Sport" of 1988. "To traditionalists, the breezy fad is a clumsy intrusion on the sleek precision of downhill skiing, but to some 100,000 enthusiasts, many of them adolescent males, it is the coolest snow sport of the season. . . . Of course, there are holdouts. Complains veteran Vermont skier Mary Simons: 'Snowboarding is not about grace and style but about raging hormones.'"

Parade magazine reprinted the article with an endnote. "Remember when they just took cold showers?"

CHAPTER 7

THE MYSTERY AIR

IN FULL COMPLIANCE WITH THE court order, Craig had won the 1988 freestyle and overall world titles—riding, testing, and competing on all-black prototype boards sans any Burton logos. Simultaneously, the Burton sales team had marketed an all-black freestyle board called the Mystery Air. Playing up the mystique, they transported the board to and from trade shows in a padlocked coffinlike wooden crate with TOP SECRET stenciled on top. Even though his name wasn't on the crate, everybody knew the "mystery" was Craig Kelly's signature pro model, which he had designed and been riding all year long, and orders were going through the roof.

Now a two-time Overall World Champion, Craig returned to Vermont at season's end and privately informed Carpenter that he was going to concentrate his training on the halfpipe for the upcoming year. At the time, professional snowboarders did not specialize in one discipline; they did it all—slalom, moguls, downhill, giant slalom, halfpipe—and the rankings showed that nobody did it all better than Craig. But, as he confided to Burton, Craig's heart wasn't into racing anymore: racing had become, if not exactly antithetical, at least not the essence of the experience he felt on a board.

"We're snowboarders, not skiers," he told Carpenter. "We look at the mountain and ride the mountain differently; our competitions should reflect that." He rationalized that the halfpipe and banked slalom were the disciplines that most closely emulated "freeriding," which Craig defined as "riding the entire mountain," freestyle, carving, airs, bumps, jumps, powder. Everything. "That's why I fell in love with snowboarding," he said. "Not bashing gates."

"Are you sure?" Carpenter asked. "Racing is what got you the overall world title."

"I'll train for downhill," Craig replied, "but my focus is freestyle—nobody is going to train harder than me in the pipe."

CRAIG HAD SAVED up enough that winter to, as he put it, "never pay somebody else's mortgage again," in other words, stop paying rent. He made a down payment on a small three-bedroom, two-bath in Mount Vernon, no doubt the first home in America to be purchased with funds earned solely from riding a snowboard.

The first "furniture" Craig bought was a trampoline for the yard, and his training began: a daily regimen that consisted of twenty minutes of stretching; in-line skating sprints (low impact/high cardio) up a nearby long, gradual hill; mountain biking; core exercises by the hundreds; and a half hour of flips, spins, and corkscrews on the tramp. He called it "air awareness" training and theorized that once he was back on snow, he'd be relaxed while airborne and inverted, and thus able to focus on style.

He combined this regimen with summer training on the glaciers at Mount Hood as well as a trip to New Zealand to film a segment for Warren Miller's next ski movie, *White Magic*. A few days later, Craig was climbing aboard a helicopter with Carpenter and Burton teammates Jean Nerva, Peter Bauer, Tara Eberhardt, and Mike Jacoby for his first-ever heli experience.

"You're going to have to forget you ever did this," Carpenter told Craig. "Otherwise you'll never be able to ride at a ski resort again."

It might have been a joke, but Carpenter was right. After riding untracked powder for days using a helicopter as a chairlift, Craig never looked at a ski area the same.

LIKE CLOCKWORK, THE Cascades started turning white in late October, and while Craig was excited for winter, the change of seasons reminded him it had been almost a year since the quagmire of his legal battle had begun and that no end was in sight. He was by then both bitter and disillusioned by the legal system for numerous reasons, including how his character had been questioned and attacked, not by the opposition, but by the judge. In his December 31, 1987, Opinion and Order, the honorable James Burns had said, "Kelly as a witness has a memory which, to put it as charitably as I can, is convenient. Despite his youth, he is bright and intelligent. Unfortunately, he is also crafty and evasive."

Craig obsessed over those words, and while they'd fueled his fire to train and continue to win, he also just wanted the entire thing to be over. The United States Court of Appeals for the Ninth Circuit, however, was a slow-moving machine, but finally, the case was scheduled to be heard and reviewed by three circuit judges—James R. Browning, Thomas Tang, and Jerome Farris—on November 2, 1988, roughly two months before the first of five World Cup contests (two in the U.S. and three in Europe) would begin on January 12, 1989.

While he awaited the ruling, Craig spent some time with his dad, mom, and siblings, including his new baby brother, Joshua (Janet's second baby with her second husband). Janet had not seen Craig compete, nor was she fully aware of his celebrity status until she joined him, Gillian, and Tony Welch at the Seattle premiere of Warren Miller's *White Magic*. Craig was the local guest of honor "but still as frugal as ever," says Welch, who recalls Craig dropped them at the theater, then parked on his own because he didn't want to spend three bucks for valet.

Warren Miller himself was onstage reminiscing about his forty magical years making ski films around the world when he introduced Craig. "The applause was just deafening," says Janet. "That was the first time I realized how famous Craig had become, but it never changed him. He'd come over and play with Jessica or hold Josh and even when he traveled, he was so good about staying in touch with family, his grandma Gale, aunt Trudy, siblings, all of us got postcards."

The lights dimmed, and when Craig, Carpenter, Jacoby, Eberhardt, Nerva, and Bauer arced beautiful turns down the sparkling powder-covered slopes of New Zealand's Southern Alps, Janet was so enchanted she didn't hear a word of Miller's classic narration. "I always felt I failed Craig," she says. "So many things I would have done different, but that movie—all the movies and the magazines and the stories—all those wonderful experiences might not have happened if his life and past had been different. He made all that happen on his own, and that made me very proud.

On December 6, 1988, Judge Farris, on behalf of the Ninth Circuit Court of Appeals, "reversed and remanded" the lower court's ruling, based upon an obscure statute Craig's attorney Michael Hanlon and his paralegal found while combing law library archives and included in the appeal at the last minute. In short, California law (the state the court found had the most significant relationship to the parties) prohibited the use of an injunction—stopping Craig from promoting Burton—in a case such as this. Craig was now free to ride on Burton boards until the case was ruled upon in the California court system, but he was not free from the tens of thousands of dollars of legal fees he'd already spent ($50,000) or would continue to spend (cost unknown) as Sims Snowboards Inc. continued to seek $5 million in damages from both Burton and Craig.

For the moment, however, it was a win, and publicized as such with full-page advertisements Burton sent out to all the snowboarding magazines that featured Craig pulling his signature method air at twilight beneath a full moon under the title "FREE AT LAST." The copy read: "When Craig Kelly decided to join the Burton Design Team last season and compete on Burton, some people didn't like the idea. In fact, Craig was forced through a court order to take the graphics off all of his Burton equipment. Craig went ahead and won the Overall World Championships despite the hassle, and now in another classic Kelly victory, the court order has been overturned. Craig is now free to put graphics on the board he has been riding on and winning on for the last two seasons.

"When you start riding Burton, be prepared to win."

IN JANUARY 1989, Craig was finally able to ride the "Mystery Air" with full Burton graphics in public at the winter's first big stateside event, the OP Pro of Snowboarding, sponsored by surfing apparel giant Ocean Pacific at June Mountain in California's High Sierra. ESPN hired Olympic gymnast Bart Conner to provide commentary for what he called "the world's fastest-growing sport."

Exactly one month after the temporary restraining order was lifted, Craig, now twenty-two years old, won the halfpipe and took second in giant slalom and fourth in the new discipline "obstacle course," earning him the overall OP Pro champion title and $2,000 in prize money. All hyped up after the awards ceremony, Craig noticed his old pal Ken Achenbach—and a handful of "pow pigs"—surreptitiously ducking under the ropes of a closed powder run below the sloped roof of the midmountain lodge.

Not wanting "Ach" to get all that powder to himself, Craig climbed up onto the snow-covered lodge roof to one-up his pal. He wasn't going to duck under the rope, he was going to air over it.

Following Craig onto the roof was Keith "Duckboy" Wallace, an eighteen-year-old ripper from Idaho who'd joined the Burton team that summer. "Craig was to snowboarding what Bruce Lee was to martial arts: he was my sensei," recalls Wallace. "I took my training very seriously, stretched every day for twenty minutes, air awareness drills on the tramp, I was disciplined. I'd follow him anywhere, including up onto that roof."

A crowd of bystanders saw them on the peak of the roof, where they sat strapping into their bindings, and started chanting, "Go, go, go!" They were joined shortly thereafter by either a ski patrol or mountain manager who looked right at them and yelled.

"I heard it loud and clear," says Wallace. "'If you jump, you will be arrested!'"

One of the earliest lessons Craig had taught Wallace was the importance of committing fully to whatever he was trying to accomplish: a trick, a cliff drop, talking to a cute girl in the lift line. "You've got to commit," Craig said as he stood, solidly strapped into his bindings.

"That was it," says Wallace. "We dropped in side by side and flew off the roof, landed on the closed run, and linked figure eights all the way down one thousand, two thousand vertical feet to the parking lot." Achenbach's crew was long gone, but a Mono County sheriff's deputy cruiser pulled up and the deputy offered them a seat in back. "Jake is not going to be happy about this," Craig said, while Wallace remained silent, thinking, *I'm a dead man. I'm off the team for sure. I'm done.*

Craig refused to identify any of the other perpetrators and was ultimately ticketed and released. Then he "walked straight to a pay phone and called

Jalo," according to Wallace. "I don't remember exactly what he said, but he smoothed everything out, apologized up and down, and sort of spun it like an accidental PR stunt, which wasn't so bad, right? It was always Palmer, the Sims or Barfoot riders, or Ranquet getting all the bad-boy props. Like, spread some of that shit around."

ISM went on to report: "Overall World Champion and overall winner of the OP Pro, Craig Kelly, and fellow Burton team member Keith Wallace disregarded warnings from the mountain management and jumped from the roof of the lodge onto a closed trail [and] were arrested." The article quoted mountain manager Candy McCoy: "'I feel that snowboards are absolutely wonderful . . . I just think the competitors have a long way to go. . . . They better take a long hard look at themselves and how much they like the sport, because they will be the downfall . . . if they don't do something about themselves.' Bonnie Crail of OP echoed Mrs. McCoy's sentiments: 'I hope that future events make the sport look good instead of making it look like *Animal House*. With the cream of the crop [Craig Kelly] not welcomed at a mountain that put thousands of dollars into an event for snowboarders, it's no wonder that snowboarding is having a slow time being accepted as a legitimate sport.'"

Ouch.

Craig wrote letters of apology to McCoy, Crail, the sheriff of Mono County, and both OP and June Mountain employees before hopping on a plane to Austria for the first event in the European leg of the World Cup. The contest kicked off with an extravagant welcome dinner for nearly two hundred competitors at a swanky hotel in Lech, but that affair went sideways when Palmer and Kelly Jo redistributed fistfuls of the "one beer per competitor" tickets to all the Americans, who were hammered by the time the entertainment arrived. Mark Heingartner (known as one of the nicest all-American-boy-next-door racers on the circuit) joined in with the lederhosen-clad folk dancers, which was apparently disrespectful. In response, an Austrian racer threw his beer in Heingartner's face, yelled "USA sucks!" then took a swing at him with the empty stein in his hand.

Heingartner "ducked, balled up his fist, and dropped him so freaking hard," says Kelly Jo, who was close enough to get sprayed with beer. "One minute later it was the Wild West one-hundred-person bar fight, total mayhem, then sirens and police are coming in. I'm bolting toward the door and see some huge dude has Fulton on the ground and is wailing on him. Duckboy, who's like ninety-eight pounds, dives on this guy's back, and he's holding on while this guy pops up, it's like a chimpanzee on Godzilla, he just tosses Duckboy like a rag doll."

With Duckboy running interference, Fulton bolted out the front. He caught up to Kelly Jo running down the street, out of breath and concerned. "Where's Craig?!" he asked.

"Where he always is the night before a contest," she said. "Up in our room, working on his bindings."

The next morning, while most of the Americans were nursing hangovers or still snoring, Craig was heading up the mountain to inspect the slalom course. The weather was uncharacteristically warm, and by noon the course was "just a mess," says Dave Alden.

"Dan Donnelly and I were complaining back and forth," says Alden, "half-joking, half-serious about everything from the warm weather to the 'injustice' that the women got to go first. There were blown-out ruts with cross chatter and unconsolidated slop between every gate."

"There is no way any of us are going to have a clean run," Alden scoffed. "What a fucking joke."

Craig, who had been standing silently nearby studying the course, walked over and, with what Alden describes as "uncharacteristic use of profanity," said "Shut the fuck up!"

"Then he told us the course was in absolutely perfect condition," says Alden, "and that he couldn't wait for his turn to ride such a perfect course, and that he was absolutely going to have the best run of his life on that very course."

Donnelly and Alden stood silent and mortified. "He seemed genuinely pissed-off that our idle chatter was polluting his highly curated mental state that allowed him to visualize something altogether different than what we were seeing," says Alden. "I was just hoping to make it across the finish line, and he had already envisioned himself winning. A few minutes later, he dropped in and rode the ruts wide and high and pumped his way out of every turn. He made that ugly course beautiful and yeah, he won."

Craig rode his Mystery Air to victory in each of the remaining four contests, taking no less than top ten in the World Cup races. As for freestyle, he outscored LaMar, Palmer, and Kidwell and was named Halfpipe World Champion—a first for a Burton rider. This cemented, for the third year in a row, that Craig Kelly was the Overall World Champion.

The final event of the 1989 North American season was the U.S. Open at Stratton, where he took first in both the halfpipe and downhill and won the overall title. At the awards ceremony, Craig stepped up to the mic and was thanking his sponsors, the event sponsors, and everybody at Burton when he pointed toward the Sims Snowboards Inc. contingent in the back. "And thanks again to Debbie Hendrickson and Brad Dorfman from Sims for giving me the motivation to try harder this year, and thanks to the Ninth District Court of Appeals for making it all worth my while."

He lifted his just-released mustard-yellow, ketchup-red, and black Craig Kelly Air signature pro model over his head. And the crowd—especially the riders—cheered.

Watching Craig sweep the U.S. Open and take the overall and halfpipe world titles in 1989 was, no doubt, a bitter pill to swallow for Sims, who had predicted in court fifteen months earlier that his namesake brand would never recover if Craig was allowed to ride for Burton.

There would be "irreparable damage to . . . every aspect of the business," Sims had testified. "It would be just unbelievable." Meanwhile, the scandalous $5 million legal battle continued as Burton ran double, and sometimes triple, shifts to pump out Mystery Airs by the thousands.

CHAPTER 8

THE SMOOTH GROOVE

LIKE MOST OF GENERATION X, Craig had grown up watching both *The Undersea World of Jacques Cousteau* and the Pink Panther movies—the comedic misadventures of the inept French inspector Jacques Clouseau. So when the phone rang one rainy spring day in 1989 and a man with a French accent said, "Hello, Craig? This is Jacques Russo," Craig thought it was a prank.

"Is this Craig Kelly—the world champion snowboarder?"

"Yeah, this is Craig Kelly, world champion snowboarder here," Craig replied in his best French accent.

"Ahhh, very nice to speak with you, Craig. I would like to meet at your convenience to discuss an idea I have to make a movie about you. I believe that . . ." As Russo continued with his spirited pitch, Craig quickly realized he was both legit and absolutely serious about making what he described as "a biographic documentary" (snowboarding's first), which they began filming a couple of months later in Craig's backyard—trampoline and weathered wooden fence as backdrop. "He was a natural," recalls Russo, "just chatting with the camera like it wasn't there." The resulting monologue conveyed an articulate and unassuming journey of a boy next door who stumbled upon a new sport and became a world champion.

Interviews were interspersed with action footage of Craig and his sidekick Duckboy, ripping up the halfpipe at his newest venture—the Craig Kelly

World Snowboard Camp*—on the Horstman Glacier at Blackcomb in Whistler, British Columbia; race training on the Palmer Glacier at Mount Hood; freeriding Mount Baker; and more dreamy powder turns from that trip to New Zealand. "No matter the terrain, the snow, or the type of riding," says Kevin Kinnear, "Craig was beautiful to watch."

The Smooth Groove[†] premiered in fall 1989 and triggered a trove of media coverage in high-circulation mainstream mags such as *National Geographic*, *Sports Illustrated*, and *Rolling Stone*, whose editors profiled Craig and posed to tens of millions of readers the question, "Want to shred like a pro? Check out the Smooth Groove." Tom Hsieh's *ISM*—the trusted voice among snowboarders—proclaimed that Craig was "one of the only snowboarders [with] the versatility and talent to single-handedly carry a thirty-five-minute video . . . a complete picture of Craig Kelly as a person, not just a snowboarder."

Just weeks after *The Smooth Groove* premiere, Craig headlined Burton's new promotional movie *Chill*. And in *TransWorld SNOWboarding*'s first feature interview ever, managing editor Lee Crane presented Craig as a humble and introspective competitor who set "an example for future snowboarding professionals." A month later Wiley Asher gave *ISM* readers a glimpse into Craig's childhood, describing him as "a Dennis the Menace kind of kid who rode his bike around town leaving a trail of destruction." When Asher asked about the more recent "roof jumping incident" at the OP Pro, Craig replied, "I'm really sorry for the whole deal. I learned my lesson there for sure and I won't do anything like that again; it's not my style to go around breaking rules anymore."

"As a kid, Craig Kelly was a hellion," wrote Asher. "Now he's famous around the snowboarding world with four World Championship titles under his belt. . . . A paradox of personality? No, because like snowboarding, Craig has grown from adolescence to maturity."

In one decade, snowboarders in North America alone had jumped from

---

* Craig was head coach and camp director, Kelly Jo was camp coordinator, and campers (mostly teens into their early twenties) spent weeklong sessions riding with and being coached by the pros. Future Olympians, including nine-year-old Shaun White, seventeen-year-old Ross Rebagliati, and eighteen-year-old Shannon Dunn, were among some of the earliest attendees.
† Thus titled because "smooth" was the one word that always came up when Russo asked people to describe Craig's flowing style of riding.

a few thousand in 1980 to almost two million in the early 1990s, accounting for roughly 20 percent of lift ticket sales. Board sales were still almost doubling each season. In response, a third magazine called *SNOWBOARDER* had launched in 1988, competing with *TransWorld SNOWboarding* and *International Snowboard Magazine* ("The First Mag. The Last Word.") for advertising dollars from this rapidly growing industry.

By 1990, nearly all five-hundred-plus ski areas in America allowed snowboarding, so *ISM* stopped running "where to ride" directories, while *TransWorld* started running "blacklists" to scorn the contemptuous few that still banned riders: Colorado's Keystone; Utah's Alta, Deer Valley, Sundance, and Park City; California's Alpine Meadows and Sierra Ski Ranch; New Mexico's Taos; and a little ski area in Vermont that was so tough, it had its own bumper sticker—MAD RIVER GLEN: SKI IT IF YOU CAN. Local rider Greg Saladino's parody—"Mad River Glen, I'd Ride It If I Could"—answered the claim in kind.

On the opposite coast, Craig's small but mighty home mountain that *had* embraced riders early was known around the world as a riding mecca, in equal parts for the consistently deep snow, world-famous Mount Baker Banked Slalom, the Mount Baker Hard Core in general, and Craig Kelly in particular.

As a founding member of the MBHC, competitor, ambassador, professional, champion, and celebrity, it's difficult to overstate how central, how synonymous to snowboarding Craig Kelly became. Says early Burton pro and snowboarding industry insider Bob Klein, "He was the voice of all of us. He was an incredible inspiration to a generation that truly shaped the world with attitude, fashion, and style. Craig was a calm and focused light, in a scene filled with nervous energy and blurry lines. He innovated product, schooled the competition in speed and style, was a diplomat when needed and a rebel when he wanted to be. We could not have had a better example of a snowboarder to show the world."

CRAIG WAS IN Oslo, Norway, in the summer of 1989, on a shop tour promoting his just-released Mystery Air, when Elling Balhald, Burton's northern Europe distributor, invited him to meet Norwegian snowboarding pioneer

Harald Rishovd, as well as some riders from Rishovd's snowboarding club, on the Juvass Glacier. Rishovd, who was also a photographer, planned to write a "World Champ Rides with Local Kids"–type article for Norway's *Skateboard* magazine but had no idea he was witnessing history when the youngest rider walked up to Craig and quietly said, "Hello, I am Terje Haakonsen."

Or as Rishovd describes it, "The best snowboarder in the world meeting the one who would be the next champion."

Craig grabbed a shovel to help shape a shoulder-high mound of snow into something resembling a crude quarterpipe, and for several hours, "fourteen-year-old Terje followed his idol like a shadow," says Rishovd, "and copied every trick Craig did on his snowboard."

The next evening, Craig was at his hotel room in Stryn when he returned a call from Carpenter, who'd heard that he had ridden with the Norwegian kid everyone was talking about. Was he really as good as they were saying? Could he hold his own at the Worlds or the U.S. Open? Should they fly him out?

"What do *you* think?"

The next call Craig made was to Kelly Jo, who remembers distinctly him saying, "That kid's the future."

NOT LONG AFTER Craig returned home from Norway on October 2, 1989, the $5 million lawsuit Sims Snowboards Inc. had filed against Craig Kelly and Burton Snowboards disappeared without a trace. The top-secret, behind-closed-doors "compromise settlement" was not, "in any respect . . . deemed or construed to be any admission or concession of any liability whatsoever . . ." by either party. The two-year "period of confidentiality" stretched into decades, and it was never published that the Burton Corporation paid Sims Snowboards Inc.

. . . a total of One Hundred and Fifty Thousand Dollars ($150,000) as follows:

Upon execution of this Agreement:	$50,000
Six months after execution of this Agreement:	$50,000
Twelve months after execution of this Agreement:	$50,000

In the final analysis, the entire lawsuit—including Craig's attorney fees and half the settlement—cost Craig roughly $150,000, much of which Burton covered up front and allowed Craig to pay back over time, interest-free.

Nearly six months after he'd signed the settlement agreement, Craig, wearing his signature bright yellow pants, was hiking up the banner-topped deck of the halfpipe at the 1990 TDK Snowboarding World Championships at Breckenridge, Colorado.‡ Just a few steps behind him, also wearing yellow pants, was his "shadow," Terje Haakonsen, making his American debut at both the Worlds and the U.S. Open.

Competition was still king in the mags, and if you look closely at published photos of the crowd lining the rider's left-side wall, you might spot Craig's aunt Trudy pointing a video camera upslope to where Craig sat, seconds before his final run, adjusting, and then micro-adjusting, then adjusting again, his binding straps—a ritual that both the crowd and fellow competitors had come to expect from the champ.

One hundred and twenty riders from ten countries were competing for $20,000, and Craig was putting more pressure on himself than ever before, he recalled in Jacques Russo's next movie, *Board with the World*: "I was thinking: *Okay, Craig, you've had a title for four years in a row . . . this is your last shot at maintaining the world title.*"

Everyone knew what the stakes were for this next run, including veteran shred photographer Bud Fawcett, who knelt on the upper deck of the half-pipe wall opposite Craig's first backside hit, anticipating a big method air and trying to decide if he'd shoot it vertical for a cover or horizontal for a center spread as the commentator pumped up the crowd like a prize fight ring announcer: "He just finished off the 1990 season in North America as the overall champion. He's also the halfpipe champion. He is also the defending overall world champion, from Mount Vernon, Washington, riding for Burton Snowboards. This is the number one snowboarder in the world, folks! Craaaaig Kelleeeey . . ."

Craig dropped in and shot across the flat bottom, crouching low and building speed as he ascended the backside wall and sprang off the top and soared

---

‡   Another name change, but riders still called it "the Worlds."

higher and higher above the crowd. His left hand found his heelside edge and steadied the flight while guiding the board to the apex of the jump. There, just as gravity started to tug him back to earth, he pulled the snowboard higher still toward the sky, gaining another foot of altitude while kicking the tail of his board stylishly toward the spectators. He held the grab—back arched, board tweaked and stalled—six, seven feet out. Camera shutters clicked, motor drives whirred, and the crowd erupted.

As Craig landed on transition and pumped powerfully toward his next trick on the opposite wall, Shaun Palmer slid into position at the top of the pipe, thinking, *That was big, but I can go bigger.* Even without watching the rest of his run, Palmer knew Craig's combination of tricks was more technical than his own. "It was the same old story," says Palmer. "I was always playing catch-up to Craig's tricks. The problem was he did it all—he went big, he went technical, and he was so fucking consistent. You couldn't rattle him. My only hope was to hang it out there and go bigger than anybody had gone all day."

None of the pipe riders wore helmets, but Palmer adjusted his signature American flag bandana and proceeded to go, not just big, but huge. The judges saw it that way too. Palmer was so jacked up on adrenaline when he climbed on the first-place podium that he didn't even remember Keith Wallace (third) and Craig (second) grabbing his arms and raising them up in victory. He was still in a fog when commentator Lee Crane held up a mic and said, "Shaun, you've been waiting for this one for a while, what do you have to say?"

In the eyes of the public, Craig and Palmer were two of snowboarding's greatest halfpipe rivals, and both of them hated to lose. And since Palmer was, well, Palmer—snowboarding's original hypercompetitive bad boy, whose "shithead alky dad" (Palmer's description) had left him and his mom when he was born—the crowd expected him to, even *wanted* him to, roast the champ with a smart-ass Palmer-esque quip, something like "I came, I saw, I kicked his ass all the way back to Mount Vernon."

But the thought never crossed his mind. "We all looked up to Craig," says Palmer. "He was kind of a father figure in a sense. That's how important he was to me and to our sport."

So to the mob, gathered there in the snow, Palmer spoke from the heart.

"It was close," he said. "To beat Craig, I just had to bust out the best run of my life."

In the spring of 1991, Craig—who had been called "The most valuable snowboarder in the world" in *ISM*—was on his first-generation Macintosh SE computer at home in Mount Vernon, adding his most recent halfpipe victory to his stacked career resume: four-time world champion (including seven World Cup individual titles in freestyle/halfpipe, moguls, slalom, and overall) and four-time national champion (including six national individual titles in free-style/halfpipe, super G, slalom, and overall). He'd won the first contest of the year—the Professional Snowboard Tour of America–sanctioned Banked Slalom ($8,000)—and this last one, the PSTA Championships at A-Basin, which was his biggest prize purse to date, $10,000, an amount matched by Burton. Prize money was finally getting legit, the sport was blowing up, the Olympics were on the horizon, and Craig was traveling the world with film crews and photographers always in tow. He had three movies in the can,[§] having filmed segments between major competitions, and was still winning—not all, but most of the halfpipe contests he entered, consistently in the top two.

But what would the "most valuable snowboarder in the world"—sponsored by Burton Snowboards, Oakley, and Croakies—make that year? Many believed that Burton sold hundreds of thousands, if not millions of Craig's boards, earning him millions of dollars each year.

When the $5 million lawsuit disappeared, a common, albeit erroneous, speculation had been that Burton paid millions to make it go away, and they could afford it because they were selling boatloads of Craig's boards.

In reality, Craig made a little over $100,000 in gross earnings his first year with Burton, roughly doubled that his second year, on to about $400,000 his third year. His contest winnings and other incentives (per his salary escalator) continued to raise his base salary each year to match his previous year's total. In the calendar year—1991—he would earn about $500,000 ($1.1 million today). Nearly a quarter of that had come from contest winnings.

---

§   Jacques Russo and AdventureScope Productions' *Board with the World*; AdventureScope's *Fear of a Flat Planet*; as well as Burton's new promotional movie *Scream of Consciousness*.

"And he was still winning, still on top of his game," recalls Donna Carpenter, "a dream come true for any company." So, it came as a shock when he returned to Burton for his annual end-of-season recap in spring of 1991 and told first Jake and Donna, and then marketing director, Dennis Jensen, "I'm not going to compete anymore; I just want to freeride and get filmed. That's where snowboarding is going. That's how I can best serve Burton."

"At the time, our team riders were paid to compete," says Donna. "They were incentivized to compete, and Craig was still winning titles, and making good money."

Craig explained that he'd thrived on competing and loved the titles, but while filming between contests these past winters, he was reminded how much he loved, and missed, freeriding and especially powder. "Competition is good for titles, but freeriding is good for your soul" was a tagline Craig proposed but was never used as a Burton advertisement. However, it wasn't just marketing to Craig; it was a calling. He believed in his heart that the *feeling* you got while freeriding was what made snowboarding truly special, and he wanted to spread the gospel.

Jake and Donna weren't sold at first. "I was cynical," says Donna. "Like, 'Okay, Craig wants us to pay for his heli time? Cool, but titles still matter.'"

Once alone, Donna asked Jake, "What are you thinking? What are we going to do?"

"I promised him I'd listen," he replied. "Let's hear him out."

Carpenter did just that in subsequent meetings, as did the sales, research and development, and especially the marketing department, whose head, Jensen, recalls how very much alike Carpenter and Craig were. Outwardly they were very easygoing, but inside, they were crazy competitive personalities with a constantly engaged inner drive and hyper, almost maniacal focus— the gears were always turning, looking ahead. "What do I need to do today, tomorrow, next month, next year, to get to where we're trying to go."

Says Jensen, "While Jake was twelve years older, I always thought of Craig as an older, and in some ways wiser, soul. I vividly remember him saying, 'I don't want to be one of those athletes who hangs on for too long and ends up getting all banged up. The guy who everyone says, That guy used to be the best, he was the world champion. . . every time he gets beat.'"

Craig had been mulling it over as early as 1988, when Wiley Asher, freelancing for *Snow Country* magazine, wrote about snowboarding's then-speculative debut in the 1994 Winter Olympics. "Kelly though, expects to be retired," wrote Asher in the October 1988 issue. "It's not that I don't think I'll be able to handle the competition," said Craig in the article. "It's more of a quit-while-you're-winning thing."

He'd kept his eye on the rearview mirror and "knew what was coming up," says Jensen. "His own protégés, kids he had helped train, were starting to beat him—Keith Wallace, Brushie. Not that Craig liked it."

Says team manager, Chris Copley, "It was Craig who said, 'Bring that Terje kid over, sign him up,' which was like inviting a vampire into your house. Craig knew that kid was a prodigy, but what I love about Craig is he didn't block anybody. He opened the door, and said come on in. But did Terje ever beat Craig in the halfpipe? I don't think so. Craig hated to lose. When Terje started destroying everybody, where was Craig? I'm pretty sure he was out freeriding, and if I'm not mistaken, he was still getting paid pretty well to do it."

In the end, Jake and Donna trusted Craig's intuition and did not amend his contract, meaning no cut in salary for *not* competing, but the incentives remained if he *did*.

There was no formal announcement that Craig was leaving the pro circuit, but he didn't hide it either. When Hiroyuki Nitta, editor of Japan's *SNOWing* magazine, learned of Craig's plans, he asked Craig what had prompted him to retire from the pro tour, and what was in store for the future. Craig's published response:

> Snowboarding is something that I think should be done on your own terms as much as possible. Society is full of rules, and I use the time I spend in the mountains as an opportunity to free myself of all constraints. During this past winter I decided that competing on the World Tour restricted the freedom that I found from snowboarding in the first place, so I decided to try a year with very little competing. Now that I have recaptured the feeling that made snowboarding special to me, I am not about to give it up. This is not retirement. I am simply revolving my snowboarding professionalism around freeriding rather than competing. It sure feels right.

PART II

FREERIDER

CHAPTER 9

WILD SNOW

As Craig turned away from the podium, the public eye, and the confines of contests, he was also pushing out from the controlled resort settings where things were getting crowded. Even the hard-to-get-to lines he'd considered sacred at Mount Baker were getting tracked out faster and faster.

Just a few steps away from the bustling resorts with their noisy lifts, commerce, competitions, and crowds existed the wild and uncontrolled backcountry. But within that white-carpeted—utterly perfect for freeriding—untracked sanctuary lurked a danger that has terrorized all those who have ventured into the mountains since time immemorial.

The avalanche—whose power rivals that of earthquakes, hurricanes, and tornadoes—has been documented by humans as early as 218 BC. Greek and Roman historians Polybius and Livy suggest that snowy torrents were responsible for the 18,000 men, 2,000 horses, and several elephants that perished during Hannibal's disastrous crossing of the Alps, an idea that was supported by the epic poem the *Punica*, by Silius Italicus (25–101 AD): "There where the path is intercepted by the glistening slope, he [Hannibal] pierces the resistant ice with his lance. Detached snow drags the men into the abyss and snow falling rapidly from the high summits engulfs the living squadrons."

Each century and every mountainous region in the world has its own accounts of death and destruction caused by snow avalanches. In 1518, a torrent of snow and ice swept into the village of Leukerbad, Switzerland, flattening dozens of buildings and killing sixty-one people. Two hundred years later, disaster again hit Leukerbad (as noted by resident Stephen Matter) after it had snowed nonstop for ten days into late December, followed by a reprieve until January 16, when it snowed again and then rained. The next evening the steep slopes above the village rumbled and let loose a thunderous tidal wave of snow. One couple was killed praying in the chapel as it was engulfed, and their nearby home was shattered by the blast, killing three of their four children inside. The youngest daughter "was found dead in a meadow some distance away, tucked up in her bed as if by human hands," writes Colin Fraser, an English skier who in the early 1960s took up residence at the Federal Institute for Snow and Avalanche Research in Davos, Switzerland, where he studied and lived with "the beast," publishing his findings in *The Avalanche Enigma.*

Fraser's research included a series of avalanches in Austria that bombarded the Montafon Valley in 1689, killing three hundred. "While a priest was taking the sacrament to the dying [amid the rubble], he was buried by one avalanche, and then promptly unburied by a second," wrote Fraser, who also documented local beliefs that evil spirits were at play, in fact riding atop the torrents, steering them "with a tree as a rudder," sparing some homes, while destroying others. "Considering the devastation caused by avalanches in the Middle Ages, and the number of lives they took," Fraser writes, "it is not surprising that superstitions and strange beliefs grew up around them. People thought avalanches omnipotent and incontestable. At best, therefore, they were believed to be acts of God as He worked His divine, albeit abstruse purpose for the world; but more usually they were thought to be the diabolical weapons of the powers of darkness."

Fraser also discovered in the institute's archives the writings of Austrian skiing pioneer Matthias Zdarsky, who taught his countrymen how to ski in order to defend the mountainous Tyrol border between Austria and Italy during World War I. Zdarsky became an expert on avalanches, writing in his own book: "The mountains in winter were more dangerous than the Italians." Zdarsky's records included a forty-eight-hour cycle of avalanches that killed three thousand Austrian troops and at least as many Italians; his conservative estimate was that forty thousand were killed—suffocated by "the white strangler"—during the course of the war. In W. Schmidkunz's book *Der Kampf über den Gletschern* (Battle over the Glaciers, translated by Fraser), a surviving Austrian soldier was quoted as saying, "The White Death, thirsting for blood, claimed countless victims. Whole barracks filled with happy men, dashing patrols and marching columns were buried in the raging avalanches that followed the blizzards. Here and there some were quickly rescued, while others remained for a terror-filled day with both feet in the grave. But these were rare. . . . The snowy torrents are like the deep sea; they seldom return their victims alive. It is no glorious death at the hands of the enemy; I have seen the corpses."

The Avalanche Enigma also documents the arrival of tourists into mountain regions, which correlates with the golden age of mountaineering in the Alps. Climbing for recreation or to conquer a peak was a foreign—if not preposterous—idea to most of the locals living in the mountain valleys who did everything possible to avoid venturing or, God forbid, standing atop a summit where resided demons who did the bidding of the devil himself.

These superstitions were tempered over time by earthly treasure, as lowlanders seeking shelter happily paid for room and board. Shepherds became innkeepers, and the mountaineers supported their families and funded their own expeditions by becoming guides for hire. Those who had the highest success rates in summiting, and whose teammates or clients suffered the fewest incidents of death or injury, rose in stature. In his book, Fraser designated Alexander Burgener as the greatest of the early Swiss mountaineering guides, "the high priest among them," he wrote, having led groups up "some of the most terrible climbs in the Alps, the Caucasus, and the Andes . . . He was a legend in his own time, a man whose daring and exuberance, agility and strength took him up places others thought impossible . . . his snowcraft was exceptional."

On July 8, 1910, Burgener—well known, at sixty-six years of age, as one of the wisest and safest guides in the Alps—was leading eight strong climbers in the Bernese Oberland. The group was within sight of the hut that was their objective when an avalanche broke beneath their feet and "with a monstrous roar, it carried away the whole party," killing Burgener and six others, including one of his two sons; his other son survived but lost an eye during the violent descent. Shortly after Burgener's death, the *Swiss Alpine Journal* ran an article that read in part, "If any party of mountaineers can be safe his ought to have been. One can only call it fate—when in a perfectly easy spot, in one mad, surging rush—hurled the great guide and his companions to their doom." Fraser regarded "the accident as an illustration of the essential unpredictability of avalanches, even for guides of vast experience."

Or, as in the words of Zdarsky, "Snow is not a wolf in sheep's clothing, it is a tiger in lamb's clothing."

IN THE SUMMER of 1992, with Mount Shuksan as a backdrop and the skirl of bagpipes bouncing off the Cascades, Kelly Jo Legaz went symmetrical. She was married to Craig Elmer Kelly before family and friends at Artist Point. This trailhead was a breathtaking viewpoint not far from the top of chair 6, where they'd first met almost seven years earlier, and also not far from Glacier, where they had been building their first home Craig Kelly–style—nice but nothing extravagant—on the wooded quarter-acre lot that cost the exact amount Craig had won at the 1991 Banked Slalom: $8,000.

The Kellys moved into the 1,700-square-foot home in 1993 and started building a cottage on another quarter acre Craig owned on the stretch of rugged and wild Oregon Coast where he'd learned to surf a decade before. Although Kelly Jo had always been happy with their adventurous life of travel, she was content to sink roots in Glacier, where she opened a restaurant, El Pavo Real, just down the street from a little snowboard shop that Bobi and George Dobis—the MBHC's Czechoslovakian mountaineering mentor—had opened with their daughter Marcela in 1988.

The Mount Baker Snowboard Shop had become an institution for local riders, as well as a destination for wandering rippers whose board needed a sharpen and wax before hitting mecca up the road. Sometimes Craig would stop by for a Coors at five and still be there after midnight—working through a debate or dilemma that required six-plus cans to solve. But more often than not, he sped into the parking lot, ran in to grab a bar of hot wax to go, then spun his wheels when he left. "Craig, dude," Dobis would say, "you get nowhere in life, driving so fast."

And that was Craig: perpetually in motion, up and down the Mount Baker Highway or chasing storms around the world. His hair had grown long, which only amplified his persona as Burton's freeriding guru who channeled his style and engineering mindset into every board, boot, and binding he helped design. That might sound like spiel written by Burton copywriters, but in actuality, Craig's riding had always done the talking. It had spoken volumes to Duncan Howat in 1981, Sims in '85, and fellow Pacific Northwest riders Jeff Galbraith and his buddies in '86. "Before he ever won a thing," said Galbraith, "we knew."

Galbraith was the kid who'd made his first board from a scrap of marine plywood pulled from his dad's woodpile, wrote for his school paper, and had shown up at the Banked Slalom with a Sims 1500 under his arm. A decade and a degree in journalism later, he'd been a contributing writer for *ISM** and would have stayed on the masthead there had it not been for the perfect financial shit storm of a recession and bank crisis that broadsided Tom Hsieh in the early 1990s.

Publishing is a tough racket anyway, and running *ISM* as a sole proprietor since he was nineteen had taken a toll on Hsieh, who had kept the mag afloat another year until several stress-induced medical issues landed him in the hospital with two potential remedies: keep control and shut down *ISM* in an orderly fashion or be forced out of business and maybe into an early grave. He chose control, and closed up shop upon completion of *ISM*'s final issue in May 1991: volume 6, number 8.

Hsieh was sad but proud that his magazine had, for a time, been the conduit that kept snowboarders connected to their world, documenting the progression of the sport and tracking the careers and lives of the heroes who resided between the mag's glossy covers and were the influencers of the day.

Around the world, snowboarding magazines had become neatly stacked ink and paper treasures—the history books of the sport—stored on top shelves, safe from spills or the reach of younger siblings who might desecrate an entire issue by carelessly bending a corner or wrinkling a center spread. There they sat, at the ready for researching a trick or reminiscing on the past; they also had the power to conjure adventures and inspire the futures of those who flipped through their pages.

Galbraith subsequently spent a summer as an Angry Intern at *TransWorld SNOWboarding*, but ultimately landed as managing editor of *Snowboarder*.

---

* Some might recall his first feature in "The Dark Lord of Launches" in January 1991, which detailed the christening of the Mount Baker Road gap, a rock outcropping on the way to Baker's upper lot that "wild man" Shawn Farmer used to launch himself over fifty feet of blacktop.

Almost ten years after he and his buddies had first seen Craig ride and knew he was "the one," Galbraith interviewed Craig for a future "Evolution"-themed issue that would highlight "People Who Made a Difference" in snowboarding. Craig "got to where he is through shrewd decisions and hard work," wrote Galbraith. "And ultimately that ethereal, sublime style. In terms of economy of motion, of every minute movement being directed into a perfect, unbroken dance—he is still the one. You can say that he quit while he was ahead . . . but on a deeper level he never really quit anything . . . [He] simply took a left on the road less traveled and redefined progression: The ideal of solitude and powder and 'moments of simplicity.' Whatever he's done is not nearly as significant as what he continues to do."

In the last week of March 1995, Craig flew from Seattle to Tokyo and from there to the Russian industrial city of Khabarovsk. There he, along with Scott Schmidt, the "extreme skiing" poster boy of the era—arguably of all time—and ski filmmaker extraordinaire Greg Stump and his crew, took a van full of gear and film equipment outside the smokestacks and sprawl of the riverside city, across Arctic tundra to a brand-new Siberian helicopter skiing operation that Stump had discovered. Its base of operations was a Soviet military base/helicopter graveyard, which appeared deserted except for a couple of people loitering around a fuel truck and a massive helicopter with a roof streaked black from oil and exhaust and sagging rotor blades. Accustomed to the sleek, meticulously maintained workhorses of Canadian heli-ski operations, Craig and crew took in the sheer girth of the retired-military Sikorsky while loading gear into its cavernous hull.

A second van lurched to a stop nearby, and four stern-faced, cigarette-smoking men—two pilots and two crew—climbed aboard without so much as kicking a tire. Sans the preflight check and safety demo that were mandatory back home, they were soon flying across an endless flat sea of white and gray tundra beneath a hazy chromatic sky.

"This," Craig said to Schmidt, "is living."

Craig and Schmidt had been handpicked by a Japanese production company as the most popular snowboarder and skier in Japan, in order to disprove a popular Japanese narrative that skiers and snowboarders did not, would not, and could not get along. Says Schmidt, "Craig and I were meant to showcase the fact that skiers and snowboarders can coexist." The subplot was promoting this new heli operation whose partners seemed to be Japanese, Korean, Chinese, Mongolian, and Russian.

An hour later, the engine changed pitch, laboring as it climbed in altitude to follow a densely forested river valley into the peaks and ridges of the Badzhal Mountains, then spiraled down toward a lake, landing in a meadow that contained three rustic cabins, two outhouses, and a traditional Russian sauna. As they disembarked, both pilots lit cigarettes and told Craig through a translator that they only had two hours combined of mountain flying under their belts, and that they had never actually landed on a peak or upper elevation.

"Tomorrow," one of them said, "we will see how that goes."

The partners who ran this hunting lodge in the summer months had decided to expand into winter. Along with their wives and children, they fetched water from a hole cut in the lake, heated the cabins with firewood from the surrounding forest, and cranked up the generator come nightfall. They crowded into the small dining room to feast on a hearty stew of root vegetables, potatoes, and rabbit. Pierogi were piled high, and vodka flowed like water as Craig and crew pored over maps with Kim, their Mongolian/Korean host. He informed them there was no resident ski guide, no established landing zones, and no scouted runs. Says Schmidt, "It was a reconnaissance mission."

The following morning was gray when the helicopter lumbered into the stark surrounding mountains, aiming for a long, sloping ridgeline where they could assess the snow—and the pilot's mettle as he climbed, circled back, descended, and brought the machine in at a horizontal line to the ridge. The engine shook and rattled the hull, and they could feel the sway when the pilot locked into the rhythm of the updraft and tried to hold it steady. Though there was plenty of width on this long sloping ridge, the pilot refused to land, giving the crewmen a sharp directive in Russian that the passengers interpreted as "Get the fuck out!" So out the door they went, one after the next, holding their skis and snowboards tightly and horizontally while the machine bobbed up and down.

Those first to hit the snow watched the blur of the fore rotors pulsing dangerously close to the slope while the pilot fought the ridgeline's updraft. "You could feel the static electricity in the air," says Stump. The second they were all off the aircraft, the helicopter leaned more than banked, and drifted down and away while a spontaneous cheer rose up from their huddled mass. They'd survived the landing.

The closest thing they had to a ski guide in their group was Schmidt, who pulled a shovel from his pack and dug a pit to assess the snow conditions. Every member of the group carried probes and shovels and wore avalanche transceivers that emitted an electronic signal—something required by every heli operation back home and in Canada. Here they did so of their own accord.

Schmidt found three unstable layers of snow on top of "rotten" sugary snow that went all the way to dirt and rock, which was a textbook snowpack for "climax" avalanches that break away at ground level. Because of the dangerous conditions, they stayed on the ridge—avoiding the open bowls on either side—and worked their way carefully down toward the valley. As they approached the treeline lower on the ridge, their sound man ventured near the edge and set off an avalanche that nearly dragged him down the mountain.

The following day they flew to a different elevation on a different windblown ridge, where Craig volunteered to recon. He tied a rope around his waist in old-school-mountaineering style and was belayed several yards below a more northerly facing slope, then dug down and found the snow more compact. There was also a good runout with no cliffs or trees below if it did avalanche.

They rode and skied this slope "gently," cold, smoky Siberian powder hanging behind their turns, but that was it because every other aspect they poked around in was sugary, hollow "death snow." Craig spent the rest of the afternoon on the wooded slopes nearest the lodge, teaching Kim how to ride a snowboard. For Kim, after a lifetime of trudging up and down these hills on snowshoes, it was fantastically foreign and fun.

Back to work the next day, they found another less sketchy, partially wooded face and kept close to a line of trees that they could slip into if the slope ripped out beneath them. Craig's run went fine. So were Schmidt's first turns—and then the mountain broke apart around him. He was able to angle down and right, away from the huge avalanche that came to life and left large trees trembling in the following silence.

Skiing back across the debris field, Schmidt was feeling the adrenaline when he joined Craig and the camera crew, who had kept the cameras rolling from a safe distance. "Somebody's going to get hurt," he said. "We gotta get out of here." There was no argument on this point, but they needed someplace to complete the project. "Island Lake Lodge," suggested Craig, who was met by blank looks.

None of them had heard of this cat-skiing operation nestled in the Lizard Range near the town of Fernie, British Columbia, which photographer Mark Gallup had introduced Craig to earlier that season. Snowcats are a cheaper, albeit slower, alternative to helicopters for wilderness access—the people-moving (twelve to fourteen in a heated cabin) version of the fully tracked vehicles that groom ski area slopes. They build their own snow roads—like the "cat tracks" at ski areas—through forests and up ridgelines toward the highest peaks, and, unlike helicopters, they can keep driving through any storm.

A week and a half after Craig and crew had bid the Badzhals goodbye (and gifted a new snowboard and boots to Kim), they were in Canada with cameras ready, two angles trained on Craig as he hiked away from a lone snowcat perched like a toy on a snowy ridgeline. He traversed along a rocky face, then headed up toward a small notch that was just big enough to accommodate his board as he strapped into his bindings and prepared to drop in. Watching his every move, Schmidt recalled Craig's words from when Stump had interviewed them both in Siberia.

"I haven't had very many experiences that were truly frightening while snowboarding," Craig had said. "Very, very few times I've been scared snowboarding, but it's usually from hiking around on a ridge, especially because in soft snowboarding boots, you're there to snowboard. I'm not up there to be a mountaineer. . . . Walking on some kind of ridge, and you have to deal with ice and a cornice and possibility of an avalanche over here, a lot of wind, and you're at a very high elevation. Your heart's beating because you're hiking. That really adds up, and with these heights and looking over a cliff, that scares me a lot. But as soon as I put my snowboard on and I start riding, very, very rarely, if ever, am I scared. I think the main reason for that is because I don't even attempt to go on a snowboarding run unless I think it's really within my limits to ride it safely."

Says Schmidt, "Siberia, we couldn't do anything big or steep but here,

Craig was facing those fears, just billy-goating up in the crags and climbing high into the tight stuff. I was thinking, *Wow, that's pretty ballsy going up there, a little scary. I don't know if I'm going to do that, I'm going to watch him first,* you know?"

What he—and the cameras—saw next was Craig going airborne off a fifteen-foot cliff right out of the gate, his shoulders forward, arms calm. He lands, transitioning smoothly into a turn that propels him toward the camera, then he takes flight again, stylish in the air, grabbing method, his landing absorbed and speed-checked by another turn that carries him into a gully. Like the back of a wave, snow sprays off the top with each backside turn until he drops out of view—then bursts back into frame, another turn flowing him into another lane where he arcs onto a frontside vertical wall of snow.

Craig pushes the tail of his board deep into powder, gouging a cutback that triggers the surface around him to life. He looks back at the avalanche, then snaps his head forward, riding the slide as snow billows up around him—in it, then just ahead of it, racing for the open slope that fans out below.

"He rode it out masterfully," says Stump, "so calm and composed when all hell was breaking loose around him, like a surfer in the pit of a tubing wave." The surfy "all-encompassing" line became the final segment in Stump's next movie, *P-Tex, Lies, and Duct Tape.*

Watching the film, surfing legend Gerry Lopez—Mr. Pipeline himself—says, was the first time he'd ever seen anybody cut back on a bank of snow exactly how a surfer does in the water. Says Lopez, "Such powerful grace and effortless style on such a critical section of the mountain *while* it's avalanching. Zen master—next level."

At the end of the film, Stump calls it simply "the avalanche save of a lifetime."

BUT IT WASN'T just luck. Before riding any line, Craig would study the slope and envision how gravity's natural pull, speed, and trajectory would affect an imaginary ball that was rolled down it. And how said ball would react to natural features—channeling into a low point, rebounding off an embankment, airing off a cornice or cliff—thus helping Craig find the safest lines that also flowed and looked best on film. "I try to ride the funnest line," he told Galbraith in the *Snowboarder* interview. "Not necessarily the hardest one, or most dangerous one, or the toughest trick, but the one that feels the best."

The rolling-ball exercise also helped Craig anticipate where the snow would go from the surface slough that came down a steep slope or if he kicked off an avalanche. In any terrain, his escape route was high ground—the top of a ridge or spine—or away from the natural fall-line descent of the free-falling or sliding snow. It was a puzzle because hazards might exist—cliffs, terrain traps, rocks, trees—on your line or escape route, plus everything looked different when you were on top looking down.

Therefore, although Craig's line was tight and had ultimately triggered an avalanche, he had made sure the features beneath funneled him away from potentially deadly trees and rocks. He had also been wearing his avalanche transceiver and there were two guides and a film crew on high alert at the bottom, so in Craig's mind the risk had been normal, not mortal.

Says Schmidt, "Craig was bold but he wasn't reckless. Like me, he'd learned by watching the guides he worked with, and was just starting to take an interest in snow science—getting up early to listen in at the guide meetings and watching them do their snow studies. In Siberia, we were making decisions for ourselves, and before we'd dug a pit or had that first avy or anything, we were just walking on that ridge and he said, 'Feels hollow.' Right away, I knew he was tuned in and thinking. That comes with experience."

One experience Schmidt himself had that Craig had not was unbridled terror at the hands of the mountains. As he'd described it to Craig and Stump during their interviews, Schmidt was skiing a big—couple thousand vertical feet—and steep hourglass couloir in Verbier, Switzerland, ten years before. The powder was so great he'd already gone twice, but on the first turn of his third lap, the entire slope fractured. In the snap of a finger Schmidt was half-sitting-on, half-skiing "these gigantic blocks, just accelerating like crazy," he says. "When the snow reached the [neck of the] hourglass, it just engulfed me . . . like a big wave; [it] felt like [I] was going sixty, seventy miles an hour, and the sound and the force . . . was just incredible. I was completely buried and just flying in the snow.

"I saw my life flash before my eyes. I saw scenes of my family and childhood."

Then as quickly as he'd been picked up and hurled down the mountain, he was spit out of the maelstrom, upright and humbled. "It didn't leave any scars," says Schmidt, "but I gained a lot more appreciation for the mountains and forces of nature."

While at Island Lake Lodge, Craig learned that its owner, Dan McDonald, had the option to buy the land he'd been leasing from Shell Canada and was looking for partners; otherwise, it would be sold on the open market. Craig, Schmidt, and Mark Gallup joined a growing alliance of investors who hoped to come up with enough cash to preserve this corner of frontier they had all fallen in love with.

Craig had also gotten to test-drive Schmidt's four-wheel-drive Sportsmobile van and decided that it was exactly the type of vehicle he needed for "La Mision del Camino Real." Since 1989, when Craig had first tested boards in the Chilean Andes, he'd dreamed of driving (and surfing his way down) the 30,000-mile, thirteen-country El Camino Real from Alaska to the tip of South America. For her part Kelly Jo had "no interest" in living out of a van in third-world countries for at least a year. In short, *his* dream was not her dream, just as her idea of fun wasn't always his. "And there were bigger issues," says Brian Kelly. "But the root of it—and they both agreed—was that instead of growing closer together after they got married, they started to grow apart." With plans to remain friends, and not let an eventual divorce get ugly, they separated during the summer of 1996.

CHAPTER 10

GETTING SCHOOLED

WHILE SOME PROS WERE STILL rocking Day-Glo in the early 1990s, it had all but disappeared by 1995, overwhelmed by a contingent of "counter" culture jibbers* who were going dark, baggy, and grungy and exemplified how snowboarding was still finding its way. This new generation of flannel-wearing, short-board-riding snow skaters was sliding the same logs and bonking (tapping or rebounding off) the same fences and lift towers that had been scarred by the metal edges of others before them, but with a shifty spinning style that was refining the art of riding on anything but snow. This urban skateboard influx into the mountains, known as jibbing, ushered in the "new school" style of riding that Mike Ranquet would tell you "is the same old shit we've been doing at Baker for years, and we were doing it fakie."†

If the snowboarding jib and terrain parks being built at ski areas were for the "new school," freeriding—particularly in the backcountry—was decidedly "old school," and that was just fine as far as Craig was concerned. Natural terrain was his preferred "park" and the mountains in general had been his playground for well over a decade, but he had come to realize more and more that they were also his classroom. Because of his inquisitive nature, Craig wanted to understand the mechanics of the mountains, the engineering

---

*   The term originated in the mid to late 1980s. A "jibber" is a snowboarder who is generally influenced by skateboarding, partaking in "jibbing," or the act of riding, sliding, grinding, jumping onto, or bouncing—aka bonking—off any natural (log, stump) or man-made (picnic table, handrail, lift tower) object not covered by much, if any, snow. Jib can be used as a noun (e.g., "Hit that jib") or as a verb (e.g., "Jib that stump").
†   "Fakie" is riding your board backward, which is more difficult and makes any trick performed "fakie" more technical.

of avalanches, and the science of snow. He'd learned how the oceans manu-factured waves so he could find the best surf; now he wanted to better under-stand avalanches, but with the ultimate goal being to avoid them.

On December 15, 1995, Craig wandered into the dining room at Island Lake Lodge, of which he was now officially a shareholder, and stood at the back of an avalanche class being taken by snowboarders Shawn Farmer, Pat Abramson, Doug Lundgren, and Jim Hale; a young snowboarder from the Yukon Territory named John Klein; and the youngest participant, Dan Mc-Donald's sixteen-year-old daughter, Jen. Craig wasn't enrolled in the class, but he'd asked the instructors if he could listen in—aka "shadow" the course—and had arrived just in time to hear park warden Mark Ledwidge say, "Every storm has a story to tell if you dig deep enough."

I was there too, on assignment for *TransWorld SNOWboarding* (I was man-aging editor and had in fact assigned myself to take the course). Officially it was titled Level 1 Avalanche Course for Ski Operations, but the seventeen of us who signed up for this weeklong Canadian Avalanche Association inten-sive called it avalanche boot camp.

For nearly all of us, this was our first formal introduction to studying snow at the granular level—the foundation upon which avalanche forecast-ing is built. There are no shortcuts. The only way to fully understand the history of the snowpack and make an informed decision in any given area is to dig down to the dirt. It's called snow science, but with all the shovel work and careful excavation, I liken it to the buried layers of time found in archaeology.

"Your shovel is going to be your best friend this week," we were told. Led-widge used a layered cake as a metaphor to illustrate how each winter storm leaves behind a unique layer of snow that records the event's temperature gradients, duration, wind, and precipitation, be it rain, hail, graupel, snow—a laundry list of factors, terms, and characteristics that started to make sense when we went outside and started digging.

By this point, two of my friends had been caught in—and barely survived—an avalanche on an out-of-bounds run at Breckenridge that I had ridden so many times, I'd lost count.

More and more riders were getting caught in avalanches, which was attributed to the predominantly youthful and male demographic of snowboarders at the time, as well as a quick learning curve and ability to ride steep and technical terrain without much experience. And of course, the addiction to riding fresh powder, which is always best during or right after a storm, which was also the period of time most fatal avalanches occur. Until my friends were nearly killed, I'd never even thought about it. Fresh snow was awesome snow; the deeper the better. My only concern was getting to it before somebody else did.

That week, Craig told me he had just seen our current December 1995 issue with "The Killing Season" feature highlighted in big red letters on a black framed cover. It was dark and foreboding, and Craig said he liked it because it drove home the point. The feature was a compilation of avalanche survival and fatality stories, including the account of Whistler-based Mountain Heli Sport (MHS) guide Brian Ebert, aka Bert. Bert had been leading two pro snowboarders, Brian Savard and Alex Warburton, along a ridge. He was being cautious, hiking from rock to rock some twelve feet back from the edge, when the snow collapsed under him—a moment of horror for Savard and Warburton, who were too far away to help as Bert attempted to self-arrest before disappearing off a cliff.

The owner of MHS provided the final lines to the story: "Here's a guy who knew more than anyone in Whistler, and he still got in trouble. That shows how dangerous it is—people don't realize how fucking dangerous it can be out there. He was such a wonderful person. It would be Bert's legacy if people learned from his death. That would be the only good in this."

Not only had Craig known Bert, just weeks before the guide's tragic fall Craig had been hiking toward a line at MHS "between an overhanging cornice and a four-hundred-foot cliff," when he got spooked. "You had to thread the needle and then get through the tube," he recalled in a *Snowboarder* interview. "I just turned around and said, 'No, I can't do this . . . I can't even get out there.'"

Craig ended up shadowing three of our seven days at "avalanche bootcamp." On his last evening he told me he needed a new book. "You ever read John Long?" he asked, holding up a copy of *Gorilla Monsoon*. "He's good—you'll blow through it." I'd just finished *The Avalanche Enigma*, so we cruised up to my room to swap. "What in the hell is that?" said Craig, as he got his first momentous, if not fateful look, at the odd-looking snowboard leaned up against the wall,

I told him what the Nitro rep had told me: that this "Nitro Tour"—what would come to be known as a splitboard—was a regular snowboard cut in half lengthwise to form two touring skis. To walk uphill, you attached adhesive-backed "climbing skins[‡]" to the ski bases that provided traction on snow. Once on top of a run, you removed the "skins" and connected the two skis with special clips, transforming it back into a snowboard. The bindings—on sliding track systems—shifted from forward to a sideways stance for snowboarding downhill.

The hybrid system—though heavier than a traditional snowboard—was meant to be more efficient than carrying a board on your back while slogging uphill wearing snowshoes that then needed to be strapped onto your back for the ride down.

Intrigued, Craig asked if he could "check it out," which entailed flexing the board, taking it apart, and flexing the individual skis. He snapped a pair of hardboots into the plate-style bindings after inspecting them part by part. He transitioned the two skis back into a single board then flexed it some more, twisting it, trying to make it separate. He held it in front of him with both hands and shook it violently, I recall. The parts rattled like something was loose.

Then after what must have been a half hour, he leaned it back up against the wall and looked at it for several seconds.

"I gotta be honest," he said. "You couldn't pay me enough to ride this thing."

THE FOLLOWING DECEMBER, Craig took that same seven-day, Level 1 avalanche course he'd shadowed beside us the year before, in part to self-test

---

‡   A synthetic version of the animal skins used by various ethnic groups in ancient times. Originally strips of horse skin with hair still attached, they were cut to match the length and width of the ski. When stretched tightly and attached to the bottom of the ski—usually with a loop at the tip and a hook at the tail—the skins allowed the ski to glide forward, but not backward when weighted and taking steps.

and see what he already knew from eight-plus years working with certified guides. Beyond personal safety, he hoped to better understand the teaching process.

He recognized the influence that he and other pros had on the youthful masses who watched them ripping up backcountry powder with little to no context or understanding of the safety measures they took or the guides they employed while filming. He decided if he was going to spread the gospel of freeriding, he would also preach the wisdom of avalanche safety along the way.

Japanese riders had never gone off-piste in the birch forests flanking the resorts in Japan until pros from Europe and North America started filming in them, hence introducing the magic of the backcountry to the locals. As Craig said in one interview, for the Japanese it was like "living on a beach and never being allowed to get into the water, until all of a sudden, you're an adult, and you want to go surfing, but you don't even know how to swim."

Instead of performing publicity stunts during his promotional tours in Japan, Craig started organizing avalanche safety courses to educate and hopefully save a few lives. "It's braver and more honorable to turn back than to forge forward into uncertain terrain," he told a group of snowboarders in one such course he led in Hokkaido. "Snowboarding is about living, not about dying."

CHAPTER 11

FOLLOW YOUR BLISS

AFTER CRAIG AND KELLY Jo split up, the house at Seaside became the base camp from which he followed his bliss, surfing and snowboarding around the world. Africa to Iran, Iran to Turkey, Turkey to Greenland. "Paradise always seems like it's just around the corner," said Craig while hanging out on a couch at British Columbia's Tyax Lodge in the spring of 1998. "Like the next trip I'm going to take, the next run I'm going to make, maybe even the next turn I'm going to make in the powder. I never really feel like I'm completely there. I guess that's just within myself to figure out."

December, Craig was invited to join photographer Jeff Curtes, his brother Joe Curtes, and Burton pro Dave Downing at North Cascade Heli Skiing for some early season Pacific Northwest pow. They were flown into the backcountry and dropped off at a yurt with a week's worth of food, and the helicopter would be their taxi, flying in every morning to take them wherever they wanted to go. But then it started dumping snow, and kept dumping, and dumping, grounding the aircraft. Craig and Joe had snowshoes but Downing had brought along a prototype splitboard that Craig eyed suspiciously at first. Even though it was made by Burton and Downing had been riding it, even in big mountain conditions, for a year, Craig didn't trust it any more than he'd trusted that Nitro Tour I'd shown him three years earlier. It was ugly, heavy; and the flex pattern had to be horrible. But after three days of snowshoe slogging up a wooded ridgeline, with no end to the storm in sight, Downing was taking two sometimes three runs to every one of his.

That was when Downing pulled out a second splitboard, and encouraged Craig to give it a test run. The bindings were made for Craig's soft boots, so he strapped in, started walking, and was amazed by the uphill efficiency.

And the ride down was fine. It wasn't symphonic, like the powder board he was designing, but it wasn't bongo drums either.

"This is life-changing," he told Downing. "I'm never going to use snowshoes again."

THE SPLITBOARD PROJECT at Burton soon became Craig's new product mission in life—it was like the Swiss Army knife of snowboards that he would strap to his snowmobile while ripping into the backcountry, and when he hit the end of a logging road, it was just the beginning. No longer did he have to posthole through powder; he glided over it. The splitboard provided the mobility of cross-country skis for crossing flats and climbing ridgelines, and it was so simple at the top to clip the skis together, remove the climbing skins, and slip the bindings back down to his sideways stance. Then he was surfing.

In fact, the system was clunky, the transition from skis to board and back was slow, but with Downing and the "mad scientists" at Burton, they'd figure it out. The flex wasn't so bad after all; it all just needed refining. Once they got it dialed, Craig told Downing it would be "the backcountry powder tool of all powder tools—the future of freeriding."

Kurt Hoy, the senior editor of TransWorld's newest publication, a freeriding magazine called *Snowboard Life*, invited Craig and a big-mountain rider from Canada named Karleen Jeffery to be the guest editors of its first-ever backcountry issue. Craig accepted the job but had a couple of provisos: that he could pay homage to some of the people in his life who helped him during his snowboarding career, and he could interview one snowboarder of his choice, which was a big deal because magazine interviews helped make a pro's career. He also took the editorship as an opportunity to offer tribute to the mountains, to the average rider, anybody who just loved to ride and wasn't one of the current superstars of the sport.

Indeed, his letter from the editor began with "Backcountry. Ahhh, just writing the word picks my mood up a notch. Immediately, thoughts of freedom, purity, and powder pour into my head. While the rewards offer me even more today than ever, there's nothing new about the venue. . . . What you do once you're beyond the confines of your local lift service can be as limitless as the mountains themselves. While I will always have the utmost respect for the superhuman out-of-bounds freestyle extreme stunts that seem to continually progress beyond our imaginable limits, my highest appreciation goes out to the simple rider who's just out there for the experience. Taking in the mountains rates even higher to me than the mark we make on them, and the people who do that the best are the ones I most wish to emulate."

For the interview of his choice, Craig didn't pick a pro rider or big-mountain hero. Rather, he went with someone off the beaten path: John Buffery, a local guide from Nelson, British Columbia, who had been guiding snowboarders on a makeshift splitboard for seven years.

Craig had first met Buffery shortly before his own conversion to splitboards when Buffery served as a safety consultant on a snowboard movie Craig was filming in the Yukon. On a wet "down day" when the helicopter couldn't fly, Craig noticed Buffery sorting ropes out in the parking lot of their hotel and joined him in the rain. He started asking questions: about ropes and knots and building anchors and how they could pull his buddy Tex (Mike Davenport)—a big guy—out of a crevasse on the off-chance he fell into one.

So Buffery showed him. ". . . Then you run it up here, you do a turnaround, you add a prusik here, that compounds the mechanical advantages, that now gives you a two-to-one pulling on the rope, up a three to one, gives you a six to one. This one is the anchor point; it's got to be a bomber. And if it's not, then it has to have two, and you have to equalize it."

"You split the forces," said Craig. "Okay, I get it. I understand."

In Buffery's experience, no one ever "got it" that fast, but then Craig demonstrated that he indeed had. They messed around with knots and ropes for a couple more hours, during which Buffery divulged that he also guided telemark skiers and the occasional snowboarder on a homemade splitboard he had fashioned—coincidentally—from a Craig Kelly Air in 1992. He'd MacGyvered his own bindings, rigged his own connectors, and "sawed the board right down the center," said Buffery. "I cut it right down the center," Buffery said.

"How does it ride?" Craig asked.

"Like a dream.

"Where do you guide?"

"Canadian Rockies, little fly-in touring operation called Mistaya Lodge."

"What's it like?"

"Heaven on Earth."

In his interview with Buffery, Craig would say he "probably puts in more true backcountry days on a snowboard than anyone I know." And Craig *did* know, because he himself had put in more miles due to Buffery, whom he considered his splitboarding mentor and personal guide.

The issue Craig guest-edited also happened to include a feature about a helicopter-accessed lodge in the Selkirk Mountains that was welcoming snowboarders and especially splitboarders to come and earn their turns. Selkirk Mountain Experience was "a snowboard/ski-mountaineering mecca for those who relish hardcore touring," wrote Mike Harrelson. "Our guide . . . Ruedi Beglinger hikes somewhere in the neighborhood of a million vertical feet a year. In 1998, he did the first snowboard descent of the Yukon Territory's 19,540-foot Mt. Logan, North America's second highest peak and reputedly the coldest spot on the continent. Hanging with a maniacal mountain guide like this, it's virtually guaranteed you'll be sandbagged—pushed to your physical limits—then pushed a bit further."

After approving the article, Craig forwarded Beglinger's name to Chris Mask—who was heading the "hush-hush" splitboard design program at Burton in 1999—as someone who might help.

IT WAS BUFFERY who first shared with Craig some amazing terrain close to his hometown of Nelson. There, Buffery's friend Jeff Pensiero, a former snowboard sales rep, was on the quest to open a snowboarder-friendly cat-boarding operation, the working title of which was Baldface Lodge.

Craig was as drawn to Baldface as he had been five years earlier to Island Lake Lodge. He was also happy to add his name to the shareholders—per contractual terms, of course, all of which were handwritten and signed on Buffery's kitchen table. While touring around the as-yet-undeveloped tenure with local photographer and friend Matt Scholl, Craig looked out over the acreage and said: "Remember how it is right now, because in a few years, this place is going to be huge. Cat tracks everywhere, the first lodge will become a second, then a third. I've seen it happen." Then the cell phone—still fairly new technology—in his pocket rang.

"Hey, check it out, we've got coverage up here," Craig said and picked it up, like he often did, using the Japanese greeting "Moshi moshi?"

The woman calling was a massage therapist named Savina Findlay.

Craig had met Savina shortly before the millennium when he had driven Buffery to a massage appointment in Nelson. Recalls Buffery, "I introduced them and it was like they were both stuck," he says, "like they couldn't move toward each other, but couldn't take their eyes off each other either. They were complete strangers and broke into this spontaneous discussion that was instantly quite fast and intense. I just stood back, and watched thinking, *Holy shit, so this is what they call sparks.*" They exchanged phone numbers, and, says Buffery, "From then out, they were inseparable."

Savina was studying traditional Chinese medicine at a university in Nelson. She also waited tables at the Rice Bowl, "which," recalls Buffery, "suddenly became Craig's favorite restaurant." In short order, Craig learned she'd grown up outside of Toronto, had done a lot of traveling after high school, and was one year into her four-year degree program.

She was also a skier, but after Craig got her to try snowboarding, she was "quite amazed what it did to my state of mind while looking at terrain," says Savina. "Following Craig and the way he looked at mountains opened them up even further. I mean, how do you open something up more, when it already seems endless? Well, that's Craig."

It wasn't long before Savina realized this free-spirited snowboarder was famous. Random individuals approached him on the street for an autograph, or to share something like "Hey! Craig Kelly! My first board was your board," or to shake his hand and say thank you. He always took the time to share a few words, pose for a photo, or reciprocate a hug or high five: "Oh my God, Craig Kelly just high-fived me—legend."

Even with those moments of celebrity, it took Savina a long time to understand all that he had done, and how many people's lives he had affected. "I just remember one time he said he was glad we met when we did," says Savina.

"He told me, 'I don't know if you would have liked the guy I was not too many years ago'"

"Don't worry, I wasn't an ax murderer or anything," he said. "I was just too serious."

"Too serious about what?" she asked.

"About everything."

SAVINA COULDN'T REMEMBER when Craig brought up his idea to drive to the tip of South America, but she recalls telling him both "I'm in" and "How many years are you thinking of taking?"

That spring of 2000, Craig found a tenant to rent his Seaside home. Pat met him there to help pack up, and "He couldn't stop talking about Savina," recalls Pat, who said to Craig, "Sounds like she's the one." Craig, who never answered anything without pause and reflection, responded instantly. "Yeah, she's the one."

"Well," said Pat, "this trip is going to be a pretty good test."

If this journey was a test of compatibility, it would also test his love for the mountains and snow. Some wondered if this grand coastal adventure was reconnaissance for a pivot to the sea. "I half-expected Craig would find some mysto break on that long drive and put down roots close to the sand," says Scott Rowley, his Kiwi surfing mentor from Seaside. "I'd get a postcard with an address in Nicaragua, or El Salvador, maybe mainland Mex that said, 'Come visit sometime.'"

The trip began in Haines, Alaska, where Savina and Craig met up with their travel partners, Brett Livingston and his girlfriend, Patty Segar. Craig had first encountered Livingston back in 1996, napping on the job in the chair 5 liftie shack at Baker. Not long thereafter, he gifted Craig a tattered copy of *Jonathan Livingston Seagull*—"no relation"—and they'd been deviating from the flock, and adventuring ever since.

In Livingston's truck "The Patty Wagon" and Craig's van "Chitty," they surfed their way down the Baja peninsula, crossed over to mainland Mexico, and rubber-tramped through central American countries reportedly fraught with bands of guerrillas bent on revolution. They camped atop ocean bluffs and on desolate beaches, the unwritten rule being if there were waves, they stayed; if the horizon went flat, they'd pack up and continue south.

In a village near Punta Las Flores, El Salvador, that saw few travelers because of the political climate, Craig and Savina stayed behind to surf mostly empty waves while Livingston and Segar forged ahead, the plan being for the couples to reunite in Ecuador. It was here that Savina confirmed at a local clinic that she was pregnant.

After learning from some fishermen that waves were firing at a remote point known to be a beach where banditos targeted gringos, Craig, now "hypervigilant" for Savina's safety, hired a guard as he surfed. And so she sat comfortably on a bluff overlooking the cobalt blue water; behind her, mangos hung plentifully from branches that jutted out of the jungle over a white sand beach strewn with black lava rock. And then, as if it couldn't get any more picturesque, the horizon blurred with millions of dragonflies on their yearly migration. This image remained clear in Savina's memory, as did the two Salvadorian guards flanking her: the twelve-year-old son of one of the fishermen armed with a 9mm handgun, to her right, and his younger cousin, to her left.

It was September and they'd been on the road for nearly six months. By their estimates, she'd conceived somewhere in mainland Mexico, and would continue the pregnancy with drive-by prenatal visits in clinics they'd seek out in towns and cities they passed through. It never ceased to amaze Craig how "powerful" Savina was as they continued south. Both the pregnancy and peregrination were uncharted territories—and she was figuring it all out on the fly, while living out of a van in third-world countries.

Now and again their thoughts spun the compass and their minds—maybe their hearts—drifted north. Some nights, as they lay dozing in the back of the van—listening to Johnny Cash, clothes smelling of campfire, hair salty from an ocean bath, geckos chirping in the darkness—they'd muse about how and where they'd raise this little being growing inside of her. Perhaps once back in Nelson, they would find a perfect patch of wilderness and open a splitboard touring lodge. Nothing too fancy; just cozy and warm with a crackling fire and hearty, healthy meals to fuel the vertical they'd climb and mountains they'd ride. They'd build a business and create a life that would provide their family both the stability of a home and the adventure they craved.

"Savina was the one to do it," says Livingston. "Craig had met his match, his partner for life, his soulmate."

Having met back up with Livingston and Segar in Ecuador, Craig and Savina explored Panama, Peru, and Chile until Savina was well into her third trimester. In Puerto Montt, they waved goodbye to their travel partners and rented a casita that was within walking distance to an internet café. It was also a short drive down narrow streets to the hospital where, just a few weeks later, on April 15, 2001, their daughter, Olivia Maria Kelly, was born.

The following day, while Savina recovered from the birth, Craig made several phone calls—Savina's family, his siblings, mom, dad, and grandparents—with the news. He'd been away a full year, the longest he'd ever gone without seeing his family, and he missed them, and loved them, and couldn't wait to introduce them to Olivia. While Savina slept, he looked out from the hospital room window over the expansive blue of the ocean, and when Olivia stirred in the crib, he picked her up and settled into the recliner beside the bed. He knew Momma needed the rest, so he quietly kicked off his shoes and propped his feet up on the side of the bed, resting them gently beside Savina. Olivia faded back to sleep in his lap, and in the near silence of the room, he opened his diary.

It was a good time to write.

CRAIG AND SAVINA drove away from the hospital with "Oli" two days later, giggling and holding hands—in the giddy fog of new-parent shock, and also feeling like they were getting away with the greatest treasure in the world.

The South American winter came in June, some fourteen months after they began the trip in Alaska. They'd experienced less than two months of parenthood when they pulled out long-stored snowboards and reunited with the snow and winter in the nearby Chilean Andes. To be back on snow and making turns was like being reunited with an old friend. Olivia was only seven weeks old when he took her snowboarding for the first time. He wanted her to feel the sensation of the turns, so he tucked her into his jacket while riding mellow groomed runs. A liftie would, at times, notice the bulge and ask what he had under his jacket, to which Craig would reply. "No te preocupes, es nada . . ." If they asked him to unzip it, he'd just smile and nod, maybe a wink and a wave of his hand, like "these are not the droids you're looking for," to which the liftie, every time, would let them pass.

Savina rode beside them, listening to Craig narrate as they carved down the mountain, "toe turn, heel turn, toe turn, heel turn." Olivia was facing Craig, wearing tiny booties on her feet. Savina noted Olivia's right foot was thus downhill, opposite of Craig's regular-foot, left-foot-forward stance.

"You realize," she told Craig, "she's going to be a goofy foot."

CHAPTER 12

THE PLAN

SIXTEEN MONTHS AFTER THEY HAD left, Craig and Savina drove back to the mountains where they'd met and then moved in with the man who had introduced them. Buffery was tickled to have them back in town and to meet Olivia, whom Craig introduced as "our souvenir from South America."

They'd returned to Nelson in order for Savina to complete her degree program, but it didn't take long for them to fall in love with the community, and it was Craig who decided to make it more permanent. "It was no longer just about his freedom, it was about the future of his family," says Buffery, who was impressed by the ease with which the two travelers had embraced parenthood and how willing they were to put down roots. He likened Craig's return to that of Santiago in Paulo Coehlo's novel *The Alchemist*—the story of a shepherd boy who follows his heart and travels the world in search of treasure, only to find it where the journey began, but now with an entirely new outlook, clarity, and purpose.

Reflecting back, everything Craig had done in life seemed to lead him here to this island of mountains, as some describe the Selkirks, an island because they're encircled by the Columbia River and its tributary, the Kootenay River. Craig called the whole of BC a snowboarding "dreamland" and he couldn't wait to settle in and explore, find that perfect piece of land to pioneer. But personally, he wanted more than just the challenges of wilderness entrepreneurship. If they were going to do this right—build a splitboarding lodge, raise their children, and ride the wild snow with like-minded souls—it was time to take the next step.

Craig would become a mountain guide.

It wasn't just about his part in the business he foresaw; it was because he knew he wanted to be challenged, and there was no better avocation in the mountains than guiding to provide what he needed physically, spiritually, and intellectually. "I need to find growth, especially as a person and as a snowboarder . . ." he told a friend. "Areas for learning; newness." There was much to learn before he'd feel confident enough to lead clients, guests, friends, or his family safely into these majestic mountains he was committed to calling home.

As excited as they were, Craig and Savina kept their splitboard-lodge idea close to their chests, not wanting the pressure or questions that would inevitably come if they shared their plans. Instead it remained a comforting and inspiring objective still hazy on the horizon, their "together dream" to research and build. There were no delusions: establishing a touring business in the Canadian wilderness would be hard work. But neither of them was deterred.

They hadn't been in Nelson for more than a few days before Craig asked Buffery what he thought about his prospects for becoming a guide. Buffery knew it was a massive undertaking, the mountain equivalent of obtaining a master's and then a doctorate. For most aspirants, it was a six- to eight-year commitment, "a quest, really," says Buffery, "loaded with challenges, rites of passage, pitfalls, and tests.

"A huge percentage, maybe eighty percent of those who begin the process, wash out," he adds. Some lose interest, fail the exam, and of course there are the occasional few who die in the process.

Canadian mountain guides are a hearty lot, with a storied past. Like the special operations communities in the military, they are the top 10 percent of mountain explorers and travelers. In fact, the Canadian military employs mountain guides to train its elite forces in such areas as ski mountaineering, rock and ice climbing, and general movement through some of the most remote and treacherous landscapes on the continent. But even with that lineage of training hardened warriors, the core of their purpose—for most of them anyway—isn't to conquer the mountains, but to share them.

Buffery encouraged Craig wholeheartedly, not just because of the unconditional love he knew Craig held for the mountains, but because he already possessed numerous attributes of a great guide, the first being mileage. "He'd spent the better part of his adult life in mountains around the world," says Buffery, "and during the times I was with him, he was always thoughtful regarding terrain, group dynamics, and always keen to learn. He was humble, and that was probably the one trait that made me feel good about encouraging him. Arrogance kills more people in the mountains than anything, and I couldn't imagine Craig ever being arrogant, no matter how much he knew, or how much he learned."

Buffery told Craig that there were two paths forward, either the Association of Canadian Mountain Guides (ACMG) or the Canadian Ski Guide Association (CSGA). Buffery had gone the ACMG route because it offered full alpine mountain guide (ski touring, rock and ice climbing) certification, and was also recognized by the International Federation of Mountain Guides Associations (IFMGA), considered the gold standard for guide certification worldwide. The CSGA, on the other hand, trained guides to work at mechanized (heli and cat) operations, which was downhill guiding, not uphill or climbing or touring, and it was not recognized internationally by the IFMGA. Both Craig and Buffery thought the ACMG was the way to go, but when Craig requested an application and a list of prerequisites, "It was déjà vu back to the 1980s," says Buffery. "He was denied before he was even able to apply." Just as ski resorts had once banned snowboarders from their slopes, the ACMG still did not allow snowboarders in their program. Period.

Buffery was then a twelve-year veteran ACMG-certified guide with almost twenty years as an avalanche forecaster, safety consultant, and examiner for the Canadian Avalanche Association (CAA). He'd gone through his guide certification process using skis, because at the time splitboards didn't exist. Once certified, he was able to use whatever "tool" he deemed appropriate for the situation at hand. For nearly a decade that "tool" had been his homemade splitboard. Now, he saw no reason Craig couldn't attempt the actual course using a splitboard. Colin Zacharias, the technical director of the ACMG, told him that the official reason Craig was denied was that the association simply did not have a program in place to evaluate snowboarders.

"I think they're reaching for reasons to deny you," Buffery told Craig.

"One, the old guard doesn't like change, and two, I don't think they can wrap their minds around a snowboarder being able to do everything in the course that they can do on skis."

Craig had heard that same line too many times in the 1980s. His response to Buffery wasn't anger toward the ACMG, but rather a simple "Okay, thanks. It's too late to apply for this year anyway—but I'm going to keep pushing forward on the application. I'm going to do this."

Buffery hadn't known Craig during the competitive phase of his life, but through that refusal to accept no as an answer, he got a glimpse of what had made him unstoppable. "I'm going to do this" came off not as flippant or cocky to Buffery, but as a sheer statement of fact.

Like the time he was driving to Breckenridge in 1986 and told Mike Ranquet, "I'm going to win this thing." Or to Steve Matthews in 1987: "I'm going to be the overall world champion this year." Or to Mark Gallup: "I'm going to drive from Alaska to the tip of South America."

His brother Brian speculates, "Maybe putting it out there to somebody he was close to and respected was part of his own accountability game."

At any rate, Craig had just given Buffery—and perhaps himself—notice. *The ACMG was going to let him in. He was going to become a mountain guide.*

"All right then," Buffery responded. "I'll do all I can to help."

Craig first requested a course catalog from what was then the University College of the Cariboo (now Thompson Rivers University) Adventure Studies Department, which worked in partnership with the ACMG. To be accepted into the coveted "ski guide" certification program, Craig needed to pass the "assistant ski guide" course, then work as an assistant ski guide for a period of time before being invited to enter the full ski guide program. According to the course description:

> Ski guides specialize in ski touring, ski mountaineering, and helicopter/snowcat ski guiding including ascents of non-technical peaks. . . . *You* will be required to show that you are capable of guiding clients in alpine terrain including glaciers, snow and ice, and simple-short roping showing confident and efficient movement. You must be capable of guiding clients on skis showing efficient and confident movement while linking appropriate turns in variable backcountry snow. Your

personal skiing standard must demonstrate smoothly linked turns in all terrain, , , ,

If he could have changed the word *ski* to *snowboard* he would have been good to go, but, as it was, the course description taken literally was a deal breaker.

There was another option. He could learn to ski, take the course as a skier, and then—like Buffery—use his splitboard as *one* of the tools in his guide's toolbox. Of course, it would take even him years to gain the skills required to ski confidently in the uncontrolled, wild snow of the backcountry. Beyond that it would be a kind of betrayal to himself and snowboarders who he knew were capable of performing everything required of the job on a splitboard.

Next Craig reviewed the extensive assistant ski guide course prerequisites, including: Proof of completion—

CAA Level 1 Avalanche Course and First Aid Course (80 hour); letters of reference; Personal skills resume including the following—15 one-to-two-day tours in high alpine or glaciated terrain, 2 five-day or longer tours (not hut based) in remote, glaciated terrain, 5 three-to five-day or longer tours in remote, glaciated terrain (may be hut based), 5 peaks requiring mountaineering skills, climbed during ski tours, a summary of relevant summer mountaineering experiences, a logbook documenting at least 50 days of recorded snowpack and weather observations, and a total of 3 or more years of experience in a variety of snow climates.

The course requirements alone gave Craig a new level of respect for the guides he had worked with over the years and illustrated why so few make it through the entire program or into the program at all. How could the average skier (or snowboarder) possibly complete all of that just to get into the course? It was the unwritten prerequisite of "total dedication" to the craft, and the hard truth: the ACMG wasn't interested in wasting time and resources on "average" candidates. The association sought aspirants who were already self-motivated mountain experts capable of doing themselves what they hoped to share with others as guides. The prerequisites were a sort of pop quiz that tested an applicant's desire and commitment to zip up their parka, pull down their goggles, and face the storm.

CRAIG DOVE IN with a pad of paper and began listing experiences he'd had that might qualify as a prerequisite. There was his CAA Level 1 certification he took at Island Lake Lodge back in 1996. Check. Three or more years of experience in a variety of snow climates. Check. He had roughly fifteen of the fifty required days of recorded snowpack and weather observations; several shorter one-to-two-day tours in the bag; one seven-day tour based out of Mistaya Lodge; five days snowed-in at that yurt with Jeff and Joe Curtes, and Dave Downing in the Cascades. His expedition to climb and ride Mount Kenya in Africa qualified. Seventy-plus days in Alaska (heli access, but many lessons learned hiking to lines), a week in Greenland, hiking for turns in the Caucasus Mountains in Soviet Georgia, as well as all over Western Europe. He'd splitboarded in Iran, Chile, Japan, and both the coastal and continental ranges of the United States and Canada, including the Yukon. Countless day tours out of Island Lake Lodge, countless lift-serviced hiking days in Japan, New Zealand, and nearly every mountainous state in America, from California's High Sierra to Tuckerman Ravine in the White Mountains of New Hampshire to his home mountains, the Cascades in and around Mount Baker. All told, thousands of days on six of the seven continents.

He had extensive experience, but there was much work to be done, including the first-aid course; three multiday, tent-based tours; one five-day tour in glaciated terrain; climb three peaks requiring mountaineering skills; summer climbing experiences; log an additional thirty-five days of snowpack and weather observations. To get all that done and write a bulletproof application with references by the following September deadline, one year away, "would be logistically nearly impossible even for a single person without a family," says Buffery. "But Craig thought it was 'doable' and I didn't doubt him, because, well . . . this was Craig Kelly."

Craig could expect stiff competition against eighty to one hundred other applicants, only twenty-four of whom would be accepted. If he was accepted, the course's on-snow and classroom instruction would eat up the entire 2002–2003 season. If he passed, he would be eligible to take the final assistant ski guide exam in the spring of 2003. If successful, he could theoretically be an ACMG-certified assistant ski guide in exactly one and a half years.

Passing the assistant ski guide exam would trigger the ability to apply for the full ski guide course, which was another highly competitive process that would take another application and, if accepted, another year. If up to that point, Craig amassed fifty days of work experience or thirty days of guiding apprenticeship working under a certified guide—who agreed to write a favorable letter of recommendation—he could then complete that course and pass the final full ski guide exam the following March, in 2004. If all the stars aligned, he could be a fully certified ACMG ski guide in three and a half years, during which he and Savina would find the perfect acreage and apply for tenure and be on track to build their dream lodge, the home base from which they would guide their splitboarding guests into the surrounding mountains.

CRAIG ADDED A "Guide Course" file to his nomad office: a cardboard box where he kept his Burton, financial, family, and other papers in order. The first items filed included his Canadian Avalanche Association Level 1 certificate; two snow and avalanche observation field books he'd sporadically updated since he'd taken that course in December 1996; and all the literature he'd just received concerning the ACMG Mountain Guide Training and Certification Program. Over the next year the file would be filled with hundreds of pages.

At some point, he added a couple of magazines as well as an article torn from a 1998 issue of *Couloir*, which he kept paper-clipped to his certificates of achievement. "The Backside of Beyond" was an essay written by an American mountain guide named Allan "Bardini" Bard. As the only article in the file perhaps it conveyed some of the thoughts and feelings that had drawn Craig toward this next phase of life. Bard wrote:

> In my job as a backcountry ski guide, I see people arrive at my doorstep from . . . busy lives in the city, ready to leave all the stress and schedules and meetings and freeway traffic. . . . They need time to recreate, to recharge the old batteries, to think of nothing and reflect on everything. . . . Mostly they need to go skiing on the high and distant

horizons. But skiing and mountains are only the medium for this revitalization, not the message. The message we receive is the importance of a quiet mind and a satisfied soul.

Suddenly my job description is so much more than an expert skier, tireless trail breaker, beast of burden, clever navigator . . . and avalanche forecaster. In addition, I become confidant, confessor, entertainer, friend, and perhaps even the Right Reverend Bardini–First Church of the Open Slopes. It is a job with great responsibility and not just those related to hazard and risk management.

As a ski guide I have the pleasure of bringing benefit to both. I notice that when people have been touched by the wild lands they are forever changed, forever more aware. They will never again see snow and mountain peaks and wind-sculpted tree trunks, without being affected inside, differently than before they knew of such things, and they will return time and again to get in touch, and be touched. . . .

COME SEPTEMBER, CRAIG and Savina were still living with Buffery. Their plan was for Craig to go through guide training and for Savina to finish school. "I had two years remaining," says Savina, "so that was the timeline we gave ourselves; two years to line everything up, find the right tenure, and be ready to get something off the ground."

After Labor Day, Savina started classes, continuing the four-year degree program in traditional Chinese medicine she'd put on hold during their drive south, and Craig became the main caregiver to six-month-old Olivia. While Savina learned the more technical elements of acupuncture, clinical massage, and Western pathology, Craig focused on Olivia, playing, changing diapers, and exploring the world outside—but whenever she slept he used that time to research everything he could about applying for tenure in BC's vast wilderness and the guiding profession.

Buffery's well-curated bookshelf held several titles not only from the recommended reading lists of the Association of Canadian Mountain Guides and Canadian Avalanche Association, but also word-of-mouth titles passed on from the fraternity of wilderness academics, including climbers, skiers, and guides. Craig devoured titles like Rob Wood's *Towards the Unknown*

Mountains: An Autobiography from the Canadian Wilderness Frontier and *The ABCs of Avalanche Safety* by E. R. LaChapelle and Sue Ferguson. But it was the history chapter in the 1999 edition of the *ACMG Technical Manual* that sent Craig down a rabbit hole into Canadian mountain guiding's past.

It was the summer of 1886 when the Canadian Pacific Railway finally connected the country's eastern and western rails over the Canadian Rockies, an engineering marvel that linked the town of Golden, British Columbia, on the east side to Revelstoke on the west over Rogers Pass, providing easy access for the first time for adventurous tourists to the high alpine terrain of the newly opened Glacier National Park. The railway recruited Swiss mountain guides in 1889 to work in the Rockies, promoting the Canadian frontier as a destination for adventure and natural beauty, and reasoning that individuals who were led by properly trained guides were less apt to get themselves killed (which wouldn't be good for attracting further tourists), thus increasing passenger traffic—and revenue for the railroad.

According to the technical manual, "By 1888 amateur climbers from the U.S. and Europe began arriving in the so-called Canadian Alps and by 1890 mountaineering in Canada was established . . . centered in the Selkirk Mountains surrounding Rogers Pass where the CPR hotel, Glacier House, provided a base for activities and a point of entry to the mountains."

When these early passengers disembarked from the train at Glacier House depot, their necks craned upward, drawn to the spectacular peaks that rose up out of the wilderness beckoning them to explore. Prominently placed signs greeted these tourists as they entered the hotel or dining hall, calling them to partake in "The Challenge of the Mountains." There were horseback adventures to the "Great [Illecillewaet] Glacier" for one dollar, farther still to the Asulkan Glacier for two dollars, or deeper still into the surrounding peaks to Baloo Pass via Cougar Valley for five dollars. Each sign included the following notation: "Swiss Guides are stationed at the hotel and are available for the service of tourists for the fee of $5 per day. The guides provide rope, ice axes, etc and visitors intending to climb should be equipped with stout boots, well-nailed."

These men were professionally trained and held certificates which the Swiss government renewed annually. They had served apprenticeships by training as porters and working under the supervision of qualified guides, eventually obtaining full guide status.

It was fascinating reading, especially because Craig and Savina were living where it had all begun roughly a century before. Craig shared bits and pieces of what he learned with Savina, who sometimes found it difficult to focus on her coursework. Her mind wandered into the past and to that future they planned in these mountains.

IN CHASING THAT future and loading himself up with all of the work required for it, Craig's biggest concern—which he confided to Buffery—was balancing these early years with Olivia. He knew he was setting himself up to be nearly as busy as he'd ever been, and he didn't want to look back and have any regrets, like he did about some of those years as a pro, when "life was going by really fast for me," he'd told reporter Ewan Morrison. "I could have remembered better if I had taken it a little bit slower."

Savina knew he could do it, reminding him that you can lead a goal-oriented life and not be overwhelmed by the objective if you remain conscious of the daily journey. They weren't just working toward a new adventure; the journey itself *was* an adventure, in great part because they weren't quite sure how they'd pull it off. That "unknown" wasn't stressful to Craig, it was exciting. And "it felt right," says Savina.

In anticipation of the crazy year to come they picked up an all-weather, super-tech, full-lumbar-supported baby backpack. Just like those days of riding the lifts with a bump in his jacket or the sled crib they'd rigged while splitboard-touring the Andes, Olivia was coming along for the ride.

CHAPTER 13

BREAKING DOWN THE WALLS

In early October 2001, Buffery had what he describes as "several encouraging conversations" with Colin Zacharias, the forty-two-year-old technical director of the ACMG, about Craig's mission to become a guide.

Both Buffery and Zacharias were at similar places in their careers. Both had worked in avalanche control since the early 1980s, were instructors or examiners for both the CAA and ACMG, and were fully certified alpine and ski guides. Buffery sensed that Zacharias was receptive to the idea of integrating snowboarding guides into the ACMG program, but also knew there was skepticism and resistance within the association's members.

The first snowboarder who had encountered this intense resistance was probably Lyle Fast, a rider from Vancouver Island who, during the winter of 1987, had decided his life's mission was to become a mountain guide. While taking the mandatory Level 1 avalanche course, he asked the instructor if the ACMG would consider letting a snowboarder in. The instructor laughed heartily at what he thought was a joke. Reading the writing on the wall, Fast dusted off his old telemark skis and ticked off the prerequisite mountaineering summits, tours, and overnighters. His application was accepted a couple of years later, and he dutifully passed each necessary phase on skis. Then, when it came time for the crux of the course, "I wore an old Look sweatshirt that boldly stated SNOWBOARDING IS NOT A CRIME for the entire final ski guides exam," he says. "This was 1992, and when the old Swiss examiner saw my sweatshirt, he said, 'Snowboarding looks like fun but I can't see any future in it.' I replied with a very polite 'fuck you' smile and when I passed the exam, I didn't ski again for eight years. I guided snowboarders almost exclusively. Using snowshoes for hiking up, we carried our boards on our backs. For the ride down, we strapped our snowshoes to our pack. This was before splitboards caught on, but snowshoes did the trick—they were the perfect tool in my toolbox."

Johann Slam is another pioneering snowboarder who hit the ACMG wall, pivoted, and became the first snowshoeing shredder to pass the Canadian Avalanche Association's Level 1 in '93; took his Level 2 on a Voile split in '97; and became a CARDA* (not to be confused with CARCA†) certified avalanche rescue dog handler in '98. That was when he started to notice that large numbers of snowboarders were hiring ACMG guides to lead them into the backcountry. Still, some of the old guard remained not just skeptical but outright cynical about a snowboarder's aptitude for guiding while using a splitboard. "I don't care what kind of board they're using. Bringing a snowboard to an ACMG course would be like bringing a knife to a gunfight," one such guide said to Buffery. "Not a chance—you're not gonna make it."

Others suggested that snowboarders should stick to downhill guiding at mechanized operations that used helicopters or snowcats to ferry clients up the mountains. "Send him down to the CSGA" was something Buffery heard more than once. In fact, there had been a few snowboarders who had tried to apply to the ACMG in recent years and ended up doing exactly that, including Scott Newsome, an early splitboarder who had knocked on the ACMG's door in 2000 and found "zero room for discussion," he says. "Walk up with a splitboard under your arm, and the door was shut. Come back with a set of skis on your shoulder, and the door swings open—you're welcome to try."

Buffery was determined to get Craig's foot in the door so that he could show the technical committee and other naysayer members of the association what a modern-day splitboarder was capable of. Like a broken record, Zacharias reiterated that the technical committee had "no formal policies to screen a snowboarder's skills." Recalls Zacharias, "if we were going to certify

---

*   Canadian Avalanche Rescue Dog Association.
†   Canadian Avalanche Rescue Cat Association. . . . Look it up, it's a thing.

somebody, thus telling the world the ACMG recognizes this individual has earned our accreditation, we needed to be able to stand behind that statement. The truth was, we just did not have a system in place."

Buffery suggested there *was* a system in place, one that screened any candidate's ability to *move* through the mountains and perform the duties of a guide. Said Buffery, "It should not matter what's on his feet if he can perform the job."

"Mobility," and specifically how a snowboarder's was "limited," was a point of contention. How could a snowboarder move up and down terrain efficiently with both feet attached to one board? How to traverse, ski-cut a slope, negotiate rolling terrain, and still assist skiing clientele quickly, effectively, and safely? How about long approaches or subtly inclined benches and other flat areas encountered during descents? Skiers can pole or skate across, while a snowboarder is rendered immobile without unstrapping.

With his knowledge of splitboarding, Buffery rebuked nearly every scenario Zacharias threw at him. "Just as a ski guide can avoid creeks and other obstacles, a snowboarder can avoid the flats on a downhill, and for uphill you split your board and you're skiing," he told Zacharias. "It's all about route planning and execution. Once you see Craig ride, you'll understand."

It was friendly banter, and they began debating scenarios. "Let's say Craig ends up in steep terrain with a skier that is over his or her head—maybe they aren't as good as they thought they were—and needs to get down the mountain," said Zacharias. "They're on skis, Craig is on a snowboard. How is a snowboard guide going to *demonstrate* skiing skills to a skier client trying to survive getting down the hill?"

Buffery flipped it. "Okay, what if you're a ski guide and you need to *demonstrate* survival turns to a *snowboarder*. How are you going to do that on skis?"

It was a great point given that snowboarders were now hiring ACMG guides. Still, Zacharias couldn't promise anything. It wasn't his decision to make unilaterally, but he agreed to put the topic up for meaningful discussion with the president of the association, the technical committee, and the guiding community at large—a positive step forward that sounded fair to Buffery.

..

MEANWHILE CRAIG, SAVINA, and Oli found a little hundred-year-old house on the hillside overlooking the lake in Nelson. After living as nomads, the roughly nine hundred square feet felt palatial compared to the van, like "what are we going to do with all this space?" recalls Savina, who likened the first several months to camping inside. "We had beds, of course, a crib, a desk, and a little table off the kitchen, folding camp chairs—furniture wasn't a priority." The first holiday in their new place was Halloween. Oli, just a little over six months old, was a snuggly bunny with big floppy ears. She alternated between Craig's and Savina's arms as they walked the spookily decked-out streets of Nelson.

By mid-November the house was feeling like home, with a photograph of that cute little bunny on the mantel, a teakettle on the stove, and books on a shelf. They were in walking distance from town; had a yard with fruit trees and a shed for mountain bikes, boards, and gear. They had friends with babies, and there was snow in the mountains.

The only thing Craig didn't have was a commitment, or any word at all, from the ACMG, so come Thanksgiving, he started considering backup plans. Buffery suggested he reach out to Bob Sayer, an old friend Craig knew as the lead guide at Mike Wiegele Helicopter Skiing, based in Blue River, British Columbia. "Bob can tell you more about the CSGA than anybody," said Buffery. "He wrote the original curriculum."

"Craig called and told me his dilemma," says Sayer. "He wanted to know about the CSGA, its guiding philosophy, what made our program different than the ACMG, history, everything."

It was knowledge Sayer had shared many times. The ACMG had been first, forming in 1963, just a couple of years before an Austrian guide named Hans Gmoser pioneered and commercialized helicopter skiing in Canada. Gmoser's Canadian Mountain Holidays grew into the world's largest heli-ski operation, followed by Mike Wiegele, who opened his namesake business in 1970.

Both heli- and cat-skiing business boomed in the years that followed, and by the mid-1980s the ACMG wasn't "producing" guides fast enough to supply the demand, so Wiegele and other mechanized operations recruited guides predominantly from Switzerland, Austria, and France. "The stereotypical European mountain guide was very versed in mountain skills, but when it came to helping a low-level skier down a run that is maybe out of their league, they had little patience for it," says Sayer. "Customer service wasn't part of their training."

Wiegele, an Austrian himself, looked to local Canadian ski instructors as guide candidates, his philosophy being, "It's much easier to train a ski instructor in mountain skills, than it is to turn a mountain guide into a ski instructor with people skills." With this revelation, Wiegele and other members of the BC Heli Skiing and Snowcat Operators Association issued a mandate in 1988 to form their own guide training organization, their stated rationale being "a shortage of qualified guides with the skills necessary for the mechanized ski industry." Wiegele hired Sayer, his most senior guide, to spend the next two years observing guide courses in both North America and Europe in order to develop a guide training program specific to helicopter and snowcat—aka "mechanized"—accessed backcountry skiing.

The Canadian Ski Guide Association kicked off in 1990, and from the start there was big competition between the two groups. "The ACMG was first, and then we came along," says Sayer. "They would claim our guides couldn't climb, and we'd claim their guides couldn't ski." Both comments, flourished with various colorful adjectives, had some truth to them. "Not all our guides were rock climbers, and most of their ski guides came from alpine guiding, in other words rock-climbing backgrounds, and, in many cases, couldn't ski as well as the clients they were guiding."

Toward the end of their conversation Sayer made it clear that, while he'd love to have Craig on board as a guide at Mike Wiegele Helicopter Skiing, he knew that Craig's aspiration was to learn how to guide (not fly) clients up the mountains. "I told him that ACMG was the best fit," says Sayer. "And I told him he should talk to Schwarty."

ACTUALLY, DON SCHWARTZ was someone Craig already knew. "Schwarty" was one of the pioneers of Canadian snowboarding and an early competitor of Craig's. He was also a survivor of snowboarding's first disaster, a horrific helicopter crash that had occurred twelve years before, during the Powder 8 World Championships at Mike Wiegele Helicopter Skiing.

On April 12, 1990, a Bell 212 helicopter took off with fourteen passengers, lost power shortly after liftoff, spun, crashed, rolled onto its side, and burst into flames. Wiegele's wife and daughter, along with snowboarding pioneers Schwartz, Doug Lundgren, Drew Hicken, Karl Achenbach, Patty Petrone, Neil Daffern, Danny LeBlanc, and five others, were trapped. A handful of onlookers rushed in and helped free several passengers who were hanging sideways, locked in by seat belts that would not readily release while bearing weight. Flames separated Schwartz, Petrone, Daffern, and LeBlanc from the remaining exits. As the fire spread, Schwartz broke free from the seat belt and dove through the flames into the cockpit, where he was the last to escape, his face and hands severely burned. The other three were unable to free themselves, and died in the fire.

For several years, Schwartz was a living memorial to that tragedy as he continued riding with a specially fitted plastic face mask designed to protect his skin while he underwent ongoing reconstructive surgeries. Three years after the crash, he entered the CSGA program, which—he clarified to Craig when they spoke—had also required him to set aside his snowboard for skis. Furthermore, the CSGA actually mandated certification by the Canadian Ski Instructors Alliance, something that was only "strongly recommended" at the ACMG.

Schwartz and fellow survivor Doug Lundgren became the first and second snowboarders to pass the CSGA, which then allowed them the flexibility to use either a traditional snowboard or skis while guiding. Generally, they'd make their choice based on their clients on any given day.

Schwartz told Craig that he had gone the CSGA route because he hadn't been as interested in the ski-touring (uphill skiing and traversing) aspect of guiding taught by the ACMG. "But that wasn't the only reason," says Schwartz. "I was pretty blunt, and there was no shame in telling Craig that I had lacked the confidence to go out and knock off all the prerequisites you had to show the ACMG just to get into the course. . . . A lot of people were doing a lot of solo ski touring and big routes to get their experience, and I just decided, 'I'm not going to do that. I don't know enough about what I'm doing.'"

Unlike the ACMG, "the CSGA had a mentorship program built in," says Schwartz, "where I could train underneath somebody so I wouldn't go out there and kill myself in my first week of training. I liked how I was always under the supervision of another more experienced guide keeping an eyeball on you. . . . It's thrashed upon you. Every day you go out . . . that lead guide is always looking over his shoulder making sure you're where you're supposed to be and doing what you're supposed to be doing. Helping you out, teaching you and just yeah, it's a full mentorship program to get you through it. I needed that, but Craig—he was way ahead with his experiences, and he had John Buffery looking after him, and he was a dad, so the timing was kind of perfect . . . cautious, quiet, nothing to prove, just pure focus, kind of like you imagine somebody who goes back to school, they're like in their thirties or forties, sitting in the back of the class at university. You know they'd done something else; you can see that life experience in their eyes, but now they *really* know what they want to do, and you just know they're going to crush it.

"That's kind of what it felt like the last time I saw Craig."

ON DECEMBER 3, some fifteen years after he'd dropped out of the University of Washington—fifteen credits shy of a degree in chemical engineering— Craig found himself back in a classroom, taking the Occupational First Aid Level 3 course. This was a requisite course for acceptance into the ACMG program, his first choice, but also for the CSGA, if that became his only option.

He was thirty-five years old, and while he'd witnessed plenty of stunts that could have required acute, critical lifesaving care, he'd never had to administer anything more than moral support, like "No, your ass is not broken, you'll be fine." There *was* the time Duckboy jumped a crevasse and landed so hard, the impact drove his knees up into his face. He blacked out, and when Craig called in the helicopter, Duckboy couldn't remember having ever flown in a helicopter before—and that was his fourth flight of the day. Craig had recognized the concussion and got him to a hospital.

Lots of bumps, bruises, blood, and knocked-out teeth, plenty of adrenaline-pumping close calls, but he'd never witnessed a fatality, and he hoped he'd never have to. If something bad did happen, the eighty intense hours of classroom study required to pass the course would teach him how to stabilize a patient and hopefully keep them alive. The course began on the bunny slope of injuries, like a blister on the heel, but progressed quickly to more serious scenarios, like sprains and broken bones. Soon he was learning how to perform CPR, stop arterial bleeding, recognize and stabilize a patient with head and/or nervous system injuries, and deal with unconsciousness (spontaneous or as a result of trauma), shock, asphyxiation, and cardiac arrest.

Passing the course allowed Craig to check another box for both applications and qualified him to work as a tailguide at Baldface Lodge, the new cat-boarding operation that Jeff Pensiero was just getting off the ground. Luckily, Buffery was a shareholder, lead guide, and would be Craig's boss and mentor. Most aspiring guides cut their teeth as a tailguide, which in the simplest of terms is the person who brings up the rear at cat-skiing, heli-ski, and touring operations. Usually they earn a wage, but sometimes they're volunteers who get paid in powder while logging hours in their own quest to guiding certification. The full guide's job and ultimate responsibility is to assess the snow, choose the routes, and lead the group down the mountain. The tailguide's, aka tailgunner's, job is to make sure the clients are spread out, stay on course, and regroup at the proper location. In this way, they are sometimes derided as glorified babysitters and cheerleaders. But if a guest ends up lost in the trees or headfirst in a tree well, it's the tailguide's job to be Johnny-on-the-spot and get them up and riding.

Most operations require their tailguides to take a Level 1 avalanche course and advanced first aid, and go through a training process, and while they aren't ultimately responsible for the group, they're still second in command in a business where all can be fun and powder one second and chaos the next. They monitor the lead guide—who is first to cut the slope, thus most likely to trigger an avalanche—and guests as they descend, listening for snow settlements and watching for telltale cracks in the snow, ready to alert the lead guide via radio if a slope avalanches. If that happens, and the leading guide is injured or buried, the tailguide takes command and leads the rescue. There's a lot of responsibility, and it isn't without risk. While the lead guide is more apt to trigger a slide, the tailguide gets caught in avalanches more often than you'd think, sometimes because they're helping a struggling client in exposed terrain.

"How was it?" Savina asked Craig after his first day of work. "Honestly?" he said. "It sucked. Everybody else went first."

He'd always been the movie star who got first tracks, and now he was the workhorse—digging head-deep snow pits and logging snow profiles at the bequest of the lead guide before the day even began. Then it was all about riding chopped-up, tracked-out snow, rarely flowing an entire line top to bottom without stopping to pick someone up who had fallen along the way. He was paying his dues.

Aside from that tongue-in-cheek response, Craig embraced the suck and rarely, if ever, grumbled. "I think he was too excited to complain," says Savina. "It was never 'I had to do this today.' It was 'I got to do this' or 'I learned this today.'" He'd share stories, one about a guest who had been struggling in the morning, kind of freaking out, but with just a little bit of encouragement and instruction, he saw her break through that barrier. By the end of the day she was ripping.

Tailguiding is "a gut check as much as it is a job or apprenticeship," says Buffery, who remembers a guest who kept falling, going over the front of his nose in the deeper snow. "Craig saw what was happening and on the next ride up the mountain, there he was in the back of the cat, this guy's snowboard on his lap, with a screwdriver, moving his bindings back on the board, a simple correction that helped the nose float, not dive in the powder. The next run, top to bottom, the guy didn't fall once—had the best day of his life."

"I was never into teaching snowboarding," Craig said in an interview. "I was too selfish . . . snowboarding was such a special thing . . . it just had to be on my terms, totally self-centered . . . but now I've come to realize that the beauty of helping and taking care of other people is something that comes with parenthood. I really like sharing snowboarding now, and this totally opened my future up to guiding. Now that I really understand the beauty of sharing your knowledge and experience with other people, and how much more rewarding those experiences become through doing that—I'm super thankful that Olivia has opened me up to that."[‡]

When he wasn't guiding or training, Craig was with his daughter. When she napped, he'd cozy up beside her or barricade his sides with pillows and she'd crash right on his chest. A firm believer in the rejuvenating effects of siesta, he'd catch a few Z's himself, "the best naps of my life," Craig told a friend.

Olivia spent many hours of her first year bundled up in the pack on her

---

[‡] Craig's quotes about Olivia, here and to follow, are all from *Frequency: The Snowboarder's Journal* vol. 2, no. 2.

dad's back, listening to his singsongy narration: "We're walking down the trail . . . mosquitos in the air, this is a lodgepole, a Doug fir over there. . . ." Stopping, he'd pull a few needles from a low-hanging limb, smash them between his fingers, and watch her reaction as she smelled that magical piney scent of the forest. Once the trails were buried with snow, he shifted to mellow splitboard tours, and on the descents, "toeside turn, heelside turn, toeside turn, heelside," he'd sing her way down the mountain and sometimes right to sleep. Other days, Craig would wade them into the warm waters of the community pool, making good on the promise he and Savina had made that Olivia would also be a water baby. It wasn't unusual to see him sitting comfortably on the ground in the children's section of a local bookstore, with Olivia in his lap, reading to her long before she could understand the words. "On a much deeper and personal level, I find so much peace being with her and devoting the times of my life with her, which isn't nearly enough. You always have the feeling you want to spend more time with your child. Being with her are the times that I feel the best, in the history of my life."

Olivia, of course, had no idea she was riding, literally, on the shoulders of a giant when the occasional stranger stopped them on the streets of Nelson for a photo or an autograph. Nor did she understand that the steady stream of people who showed up at their house pointing cameras and mini-cassette recorders at them were filmmakers, photographers, and writers—friends he'd met over the years who'd heard Craig was back from his trip and wanted to catch up and meet "the souvenir." Most of them were just passing through, but some were on assignment for magazine editors whose worldwide readership wondered what had happened to their favorite snow-surfing soul rider who'd dropped off the map the season before. Some, especially the die-hard old-schoolers who'd grown up on regular doses of Craig Kelly in the videos and mags, wondered if the Obi-Wan Kenobi of freeriding had retired.

According to the interview, they were missing the point. "If you kind of track the inside history of my snowboarding since 1991," said Craig, "every single year there's a major shift, or major direction change in the consciousness of what I'm doing. Really, every time I do something, it's not so much a shift away from pro snowboarding, but just a way to continue it." A way to make a living doing what he loved, and at the same time progressing the professional "career" opportunities for snowboarders as a whole.

Craig would carefully avoid disclosing his and Savina's plans during these interviews, but their closest friends could read between the lines when he said things like splitboarding "really puts you in touch with the flow of the mountain; you're able to glide and walk and actually . . . get to see the mountain on the way up. . . . It's of course easier to ride the snowmobile, take a helicopter, or ride a lift. But if you're into working hard, and you have some experience, the challenges—and beautiful rewards for the challenges—are just endless for me. There's more mountains and lines than I could possibly do in a lifetime. The more I learn . . . the more I'm able to do; it's kind of a nice circular feeding frenzy."

WHILE CRAIG CONTINUED onward and upward toward that future, several in the snowboarding industry were contemplating how they might honor him for his past. In anticipation for the publication of *TransWorld SNOWboarding*'s one hundredth issue, then-editor Andy Blumberg assigned one of the magazine's Angry Interns to painstakingly thumb through fifteen years' worth of magazines, tabulating every editorial photo (advertisements not included). It turned out that of the 1,055 snowboarders who had photos in the mag, Craig had been featured more than any other rider with two covers, two full feature interviews, and 103 photographs. And he was one of only a handful of pros who had continued to evolve.

He was so ingrained in the hearts and minds of riders around the world that even with his one-year hiatus drive to the tip of South America, Craig's image never faded. "It was that smooth, effortless style that belied how hard he worked for every inch of success," recalls Tom Hsieh. "And he was still working, still progressing the sport and defining the image of who or what a snowboarder can be."

Beginning in the early '90s, TransWorld hosted "industry conferences" each winter, during which manufacturers came together to discuss the issues of both business and sport. The highlight of each five-day conference, aside from full days of snowboarding, was the bestowing of a lifetime achievement award to individuals who had, in some very significant way, impacted snowboarding. The sports version of the Oscar, TransWorld's "Tranny Award" was first awarded to Sherman Poppen, whom many considered the grandfather of the sport. In following years, the award focused on recognizing industry pioneers like Jake Burton Carpenter, Tom Sims, and Craig's original mentor, the father of freestyle, Terry Kidwell.

When the one hundredth issue came out with Craig named the most photographed snowboarder in the history of TransWorld, group publisher Tim Wrisley passed along the news to Carpenter, who told Wrisley about Craig's plans with the ACMG. *Still breaking ground after all these years*, thought Wrisley when he nominated Craig as either "The Father of Professional Snowboarding" or "The Father of Freeriding." There were other names up for consideration, and as always, the winner would be decided by secret ballot.

CHAPTER 14

TAILGUNNER

ON JANUARY 24, 2002, THE avalanche danger was rated "high" in the southern Columbia Mountains—the Purcells, Cariboos, Monashees, and Selkirks—at all elevations. Craig was Buffery's tailguide for another week at Baldface. Guests and guides were there for the five-star powder, and they were getting it. It had been snowing steadily for days, roughly two and a half feet since January 21, and another two feet had come down before beginning to ease up on the evening of the 27th.

Warming temperatures and strong winds during the storm created some dense wind slabs* over the colder and weaker snow surface beneath, leading to widespread natural and human-triggered avalanches, several of which Craig had observed up close and personal and recorded in his field book. One size 3 avalanche (enough to bury and destroy a car, damage a truck, destroy a wood-frame house, or break a few trees), triggered remotely by the vibrations of their snowcat as it traversed beneath a run called Moss Garden, had stopped just thirty meters† short of the cat road. Several size 1 (relatively harmless to people) to size 2 (could bury, injure, or kill a person) avalanches in the days that followed spoke volumes to Buffery, who dialed back the risk-versus-reward meter, keeping his groups in forested slopes where the snow was more anchored and less apt to slide.

---

* Wind slabs form when blowing snow creates a dense "stiff" wind-compacted layer (or layers) of snow over a weaker (loosely packed) layer of snow.

† Craig used and encountered a mix of metric and U.S. customary (imperial) units of measurements throughout his globe-trotting career. In his notes, letters, guidebooks, and discussions, elevations were sometimes in feet, other times in meters. Snow depth was measured in centimeters or inches. He almost always used Fahrenheit instead of Celsius. This book uses both systems of measurement, with zero consistency, to reflect Craig's experience and documentation.

The season had started off with a bang, with more than 120 centimeters of snow measured on November 1 at the Mount Fidelity weather station near Rogers Pass. This doubled the average snow levels for that time of year, setting a healthy base. As winter progressed, however, some high-pressure warm fronts brought a couple of significant pulses of rain to the higher mountains in mid-November and then again in early January, each of which was followed by cold snaps that left behind two different frozen crust layers that were buried shortly thereafter by subsequent storms and, in Buffery's words, "had to heal."

Craig knew that "healing" meant bonding, and/or "stabilizing," which would come with time, when the weight of new snow sitting atop those frozen crust layers compressed and/or broke down. These decomposing crystals would either bond together or remain loose, sugary snow, depending on a number of variables that included temperature, moisture content, and wind before, during, and after each phase of weather. Like a layer cake, the frozen layer—the frosting—could act as an adhesion between the two layers, or it could resist bonding and act like a slide on which the snow (cake) on top could eventually slip, especially on steeper slopes. This was exactly what Craig had been observing at least once a day since he'd arrived at Baldface. Back at Baker, George Dobis would say of days like this, "The mountains are showing their teeth."

Each avalanche they observed, either on distant peaks, or sometimes occurring during their snowboard descents, was used by Buffery as a teaching moment at end-of-day debriefs, when the guides and tailgunners would discuss the who, what, when, where, and why the avalanche likely occurred. Further, they would explore the reasoning by extrapolating data from the snow profiles they'd dug and the weather they'd observed.

The storm dissipated overnight on January 27, and the next morning dawned cold and clear—the first blue sky in more than a week. The air was calm—not a whisper of wind—and the branches of evergreens were laden with snow. The hoots of guests getting their first clear look at the terrain echoed off surrounding peaks. Everywhere, smooth, sparkling powdery slopes beckoned like sirens, calling them to dive into the deep.

Craig knew well the alluring buzz and infectious "stoke" of such epic mornings from photo and film shoots, when the weather window was narrow, the risks were wide, and the camera crew was ready to roll. Few images can capture the essence of snowboarding better than a single serpentine line tracking a rider's descent of a pristine open slope. Add to that a high-speed slashing turn off the top of a corniced ridge with an explosion of feather-light powder hanging like white smoke against a bluebird sky, and these are the days when magazine cover shots are born.

Craig could feel the excitement like static among the guests as they climbed aboard the snowcat, but he tempered their expectations, having already discussed the options for the day with Buffery, who resisted the seductive calm with steadfast prudence and patience. "Too many bad decisions are made right now," he told Craig that morning. "It's the 'blue-sky factor.' People want to charge when a storm has passed, but the dangers are still there. We're sticking to the trees."

Buffery had seen death by avalanche, most recently as an incident commander and first responder. "It's as horrible and ugly as you can imagine," he says. "Digging out a body—a fellow human being who's all geared up just like you—is a kick-in-the-face reality check you just can't teach. Now you've got a perspective that you wouldn't wish on anybody, but as a guide—I think you're better for it because . . . you know, there's nothing hypothetical about it."

That evening, as their clients relaxed in the post-dinner haze of an IPA buzz and reveled on shaky legs from the twenty thousand vertical feet of powder they'd ridden on Baldface's forested slopes, the radio sprang to life. Buffery quietly stepped away and learned there'd been an avalanche, "a wreck," in the parlance of guides, with multiple burials. Details were sketchy, but as the evening progressed, he heard through the grapevine that the avalanche had occurred near Mount Carlyle, roughly twenty-five miles north of Baldface, just beyond Kokanee Glacier Provincial Park. One fatality in a group of self-guided skiers was reported; two others were missing and being searched for in the dark by determined survivors in a slide path still threatened by additional avalanches two hours later. Although a live recovery was unlikely, helicopter and rescue personnel remained on standby.

By 10 p.m. Buffery learned that the other two skiers had been killed too.

A later investigation outlined how eight American backcountry skiers had been helicoptered in to a remote lodge for a weeklong holiday. They were experienced in the backcountry, had all the safety equipment (transceivers, probes, shovels), and had been warned of existing dangers and avalanches observed by the lodge's custodian. They'd also refused the services of a local guide.

They'd started the day in the trees, but at lunchtime the group split up, three of them heading in one direction while the remainder ventured up into the higher, steeper subalpine terrain that the custodian had recommended they avoid. As a safety measure, they dug a two-meter-deep snow profile and performed a rutschblock stability test[‡] and scored five on a scale of seven, indicating that the dangerous layers were not reacting to the pressures of human movement at that location. The conclusion: it was safe to continue down.

One at a time, the skiers dropped into the 32- to 36-degree slope, the first three descending well into the treeline, where they regrouped among the lodgepole binding each side of the narrow treeless avalanche path that ran to the valley floor a couple thousand vertical feet below. The fourth skier was two turns into his run when the entire upper mountain broke loose, sucking him downward and leaving the fifth skier standing just above the crown. Somehow the fourth skier managed to escape the torrent while high on the slope, as the remaining three skiers below disappeared into the wall of snow. The fourth and the fifth skiers turned on their transceivers and immediately descended into the slide path to search for their companions who were buried in the rubble of snow, ice, and broken trees toward the bottom of the valley.

It took them two hours to locate and dig out the first deceased skier. He had carried the radio, which enabled them to call for help around 5 p.m. and start the exchange of information with the outside world. It took another two hours to locate the second victim, well after dark, and the third an hour later. One had died of asphyxia; the other two succumbed to traumatic injuries.

[‡]   Reportedly first used by the Swiss Army in the 1960s to simulate a mini slab avalanche, the rutschblock—"sliding block"— involves applying the weight of a person in increments to a large column of snow dug into the side of a slope, with the column's sides fully exposed. If the column fractures while it's being dug and a slab layer slides downhill, this indicates extreme instability and scores R1. If the column slides while a skier or rider approaches from above and stands atop it, the test scores R2. If the person weights the slope with bent knees, it's R3; first jump, R4; second jump, R5. If the person moves to the center of the block and jumps in a deep knee bend, R6. If the column does not slide, it scores R7. Any block fail before R5 indicates signs of instability. At R5 and above, there is a low chance of a human triggering nearby slopes with same snow depth, angle, and aspect.

The investigation revealed that the fatal avalanche had "released in a layer of faceted snow crystals above the 7 January rain crust. While this rain crust was generally buried under 70 to 100 cm of snow in the southern Selkirk Mountains, the fracture line profile showed that this weakness was only covered by 35 to 40 cm of snow. This can be attributed to the strong westerly winds during the storm period prior to the accident, which must have scoured the starting zones. In the more sheltered sections on the lee side of the tree bands, the slab was between 1 and 1.5 m thick."

There were lessons here: the skiers had ventured into steep terrain less than twenty-four hours after a storm (warning number 1); the storm had been accompanied by significant wind (warning 2); local knowledge reported naturally occurring avalanches in the area (warning 3); multiple skiers had been exposed in the fall line of a clearly defined avalanche path (warning 4).

The most compelling lesson, however, was that these skiers were experienced. They'd skied onto the sparsely treed upper section of the slope they intended to ski, dug a two-meter-deep snow profile, and performed a fairly involved stability test, all of which must have taken twenty, maybe thirty minutes during which they enjoyed the view, contemplated their descent, and ultimately decided to go for it.

This was a group on holiday. They had a short one-week window to ski, and the snow gods had bestowed upon them fresh powder and high visibility on a stellar blue-sky day. Had the results of the test outweighed the other four mistakes? If they had dug their test pit five, ten, maybe twenty meters away, where that problem layer was in a shallower patch, would the results of the test been a 2 or 3? Would that have given the skiers pause enough to move away, to ski another line, to live another day?

These were the types of questions Craig pondered while talking with Buffery and other guides. "He wasn't quick to judge," says Lee Usher, the second-most-senior guide at Baldface. "I think he had empathy for people who got into trouble, because he had so much experience in different scenarios around the world. He could envision himself right there beside them faced with similar choices and wanted to learn. He was very much a student of the mountains. Super keen on the science and digging the pits and looking at the snow and really analyzing it, but the guiding community, and avalanche professionals were just starting to shift focus to the concept of human factors in decision-making and reading terrain versus studying snowpack and crystals. Digging a good pit and knowing the snow at the granular level was still a critical component, it was your baseline for decisions, but it was starting to become secondary to how and why you're making decisions."

BACK IN NELSON the following week, Craig continued his studies with a phone call to Paul Norrie, the operations and safety manager at Island Lake Lodge as well as an independent guide who loved touring with clients in challenging terrain.

In the course of their conversation, it became clear that Craig needed multiday touring experience, and Norrie could use some help on a five-day trip he had planned with a dozen "super-keen, strong clients" at Rogers Pass on March 19–23. He invited Craig to join him as his apprentice/tailguide. Combined with what Craig had already lined up in April and May, those five days of touring would help him complete his requirements, really round out his training as recommended in a variety of terrain, and allow Norrie, an ACMG guide, the opportunity to observe his skills and perhaps provide Craig with a letter of reference.

Truth be told, Norrie wasn't totally sold on splitboarders in 2001, mainly because he'd yet to encounter one who could keep pace with telemarkers or skiers using alpine touring equipment. It wasn't their fitness levels or downhill abilities, but more their ability to transition back and forth from snowboard to skis in order to keep pace in varied, sometimes flat sections of terrain. "Back then, we were constantly waiting for them," says Norrie, "partially because the splitboarding equipment just wasn't dialed yet."

Still, he'd seen Craig ride at Island Lake Lodge. "If the Wayne Gretzky of snowboarding was all in with this splitboarding thing, I figured it was only a matter of time before everybody else caught on," says Norrie. "You know, skate to where the puck will be, not where it's already been."

CRAIG MET NORRIE the evening of March 18 in the Glacier Park Lodge at the summit of Rogers Pass. Since 1962, the lodge had been the only refuge for motorists stranded at the summit due to avalanches or blizzards and a favorite among backcountry skiers due to its affordable rates, dining room, and access—literally across the parking lot—into the high alpine. There was an always-stoked fire and cozy bar, which is where Craig and Norrie sat with a topo map spread out between them on a rustic table. The tentative plan, to be tweaked according to weather and avalanche conditions, was the Bostock Creek trail and surrounding peaks on day one; Terminal Peak on two; Mount Rogers/Rogers Glacier on three; Bonney Glacier and Bonney Trees on four; and, on the final day, they'd tackle the long haul to Asulkan Pass, which Norrie called "the Asulkan 500."

"It's a fantastic big alpine tour up the Asulkan valley," says Norrie, "but you've got several kilometers in and out, very gradual uphill then back down, lots of bumps and side-hilling, which is a splitboarder's nightmare. It's one of the longest, bumpiest exits of any long day tour, and I'd never seen a snowboarder who wasn't cursing, carrying his snowboard, and walking to get out."

By the third day, Craig had proven his abilities tailguiding groups of nine to fourteen skiers in all types of terrain; from steep semitechnical pitches to gradual but tricky glacial slogs, he was as calm, cool, and helpful as any assistant guide Norrie had worked with. On day four, while descending in the Bonney Glacier zone, several of Norrie's clients wanted to ski a different route. Norrie called Craig to the front, spent a couple of minutes looking over a map, and then split the group, with Craig leading a handful of skiers on a slight detour through the Bonney Trees. As far as dangers went this route had low consequences, but there was a real probability for getting lost. Says Norrie, "I'd observed him for several days at that point, and it was the perfect opportunity to sort of give him a little leash which he was ready for, kind of like a pilot instructor telling the student 'you've got the controls' for a few minutes."

Craig navigated the topography perfectly and converged with Norrie's group some fifteen or twenty minutes later at exactly the X on the map where he'd told Craig to meet up. But the crux of the trip for Craig remained—as far as Norrie was concerned—the Asulkan 500. Norrie's concern about how Craig would handle that nightmare of an exit at the end of a long leg-burning day after an ambitious five days of touring was short-lived, as he "never had to wait for him once, the steeper terrain, side-hilling, traversing was no problem, clients loved him, and on the way out that last day—which was the big test—he pumped the terrain like a skateboarder and just coasted out," says

Norrie. "Keeping momentum on long stretches, kilometers of nearly flat, mixed-up, low-incline terrain is kind of like walking on water for a snowboarder. I'd never seen anything like it."

Each evening, Craig and Norrie debriefed before dinner—discussing the conditions they'd encountered that day, comparing notes, cleaning up the observations they'd jotted in their field books, and if Craig had any questions, he'd ask them. After dinner with the clients, they'd wander into the lodge's bar for a nightcap.

That was when Craig asked Norrie who his mentors had been. "He was a sponge for information and exploring his options," says Norrie, who told him he had two: Rudi Kranabitter and Ruedi Beglinger.

KRANABITTER WAS AN Austrian from the Stubai Valley who had climbed the north face of the Eiger at age sixteen, earned his guiding certification two years later, immigrated to Canada to guide heli-skiers in 1973, and had been instrumental in developing the ski guide portion of the ACMG's guide training. He had been the technical director for the ACMG for ten years, and had remained the association's most senior examiner.

Lynn Martel described Kranabitter in her book *Seizing the Sharp End: 50 Years of the ACMG* as:

> an all-mountain master who moved swiftly, efficiently and intuitively on snow, vertical ice, or rock . . . and became both revered and feared for his blunt frequently intimidating examining styles. One version of a favorite story relates how Kranabitter (nick-named "Krampon biter") while examining a hotshot sport climber hesitantly leading a 5.10 traditional rock climbing pitch . . . soloed up beside the candidate and asked, "Are you afraid? Do you want to call your mother? I'll give you a quarter."

He was tough on candidates because Canada's mountains were much more remote than the European ranges and, in winter, avalanche forecasting systems weren't as refined as at, say, the Arlberg or the Alps. As such, Martel quotes Kranabitter as saying the Canadian ski guides' "winter component needed to be better than their European counterparts. . . . If you can guide in Canada, you can guide anywhere . . . If you want to be in this profession, there's a lot of risk involved. The training demands more of you than if you were guiding."

Paul Norrie had originally met Kranabitter as a young skier in and around Banff, was ultimately inspired by him on several trips as a tailguide, and then challenged by him as an instructor once Norrie had been accepted into the ACMG training course. After Norrie passed the assistant ski guide course in the early nineties, the next step was to complete a "practicum"§ at an unfamiliar location or operation with an unfamiliar guide. Norrie of course asked Kranabitter for a recommendation.

"And he told me," Norrie recalls, "'you should go work for Ruedi Beglinger. There's no other operation where day after day, you ski in complex terrain like he has. You're going to get your butt worked off and you're going to get some hard debriefs, but you're going to learn more there than anywhere else.'"

CRAIG HAD NEVER met Kranabitter or Beglinger, but he was familiar with their reputations. Beglinger held a special appeal. He was the rare mountaineering guide, a skier who not only embraced snowboarding, but did it himself while guiding snowboarders. In fact, Craig had been invited to join a trip with Beglinger's operation—Selkirk Mountain Experience (SME)—in spring of 1996 when it was one of the first touring operations to actively market to snowboarders in its brochures and advertisements.

In the mid to late nineties, with splitboarding still in its infancy, the enterprising Beglinger offered guests the use of Miller "approach skis" that were shorter and wider than traditional touring skis, but more efficient than snowshoes for touring purposes. If you didn't have a splitboard, you could carry your snowboard on your backpack while climbing up, then you'd strap the short skis to your pack and ride down on your board.

The 1996 trip Craig had declined ended up including two of the sport's

---

§ *Practicum* is the commonly used term in Canada versus apprenticeship, more common in the U.S. Both mean the same thing.

most celebrated snow-surfing mountaineers—Bonnie Zellers and John Griber—as well as a World Cup racer turned freerider named Jeremy Jones, who had never been "touring" before in his life. The group climbed around five thousand vertical feet a day, Zellers, Griber, and Beglinger on splitboards while Jones used approach skis and carried his board. In seven days, they summited fourteen peaks, rode miles and miles of virgin snow, and never once crossed another track.

Jones, who had spent his fair share of time heli-boarding, said that week of camaraderie in the solitude of the high alpine had been life-changing for him: "They were the hardest-earned but most rewarding turns of my life." The adventure was documented by photographer Eric Berger and writer Greg Daniells in the October 1996 issue of *TransWorld SNOWboarding* in an article called "The Thrill of Powder and the Agony of Da Feet."

Craig had read that story, as well as the *Snowboard Life* feature in the issue he had guest-edited. There was also a 1997 issue of *Couloir* magazine with Beglinger on the cover riding a splitboard (likely the first splitboarder to grace the cover of any magazine) and profiled as "Guide for the Hard-core." So it wasn't without context that Craig listened to Norrie's stories about the two and a half winters he had worked at SME as well as several private guiding trips to Europe that Beglinger had brought him on after SME closed for the winter.

"He climbs around a million vertical feet per season," Norrie told Craig. "He's a machine, and SME is a unique learning environment because of the complexity of the terrain, the fact that you don't shy away from it just because the light is bad. I spent my entire first winter at SME setting track [for clients] up the summits in whiteouts. At the beginning, I was like, 'Whoa, what are we doing out here in this?' but then, a year or two later the pea soup came down on me while I was guiding the Haute Route[¶] in Europe, and I was like, 'no problem.' You deal with it. You know it, and you're confident. Ruedi prepared me for that. As Ruedi says, 'What are you going to do if the weather comes in and you've only practiced in sunshine. Let's get good at this.'

[¶]   The Haute Route (High Route) is a classic six-day hut-to-hut hiking or ski-touring traverse of the glaciers, peaks, and passes between Mont Blanc in Chamonix, France, and the Matterhorn in Zermatt, Switzerland.

"He'll challenge you, and he won't coddle you. No. He's not that guy and everybody knows it. But does he care? Does he want to teach? With a passion. And does he have more consistent energy than anybody I ever worked with, other than maybe Rudi Kranabitter? Absolutely. And did he demand pretty much perfection? Yeah, he did, and some people get tired of that. If you can't handle that, don't work for Ruedi. He's not going to feather your ego, but I didn't take anything personal and here's why: One of my fondest memories of my early guiding career was when Kranabitter came up to work at SME for a week. This was a big deal. I'm watching my two mentors, Rudi Kranabitter, who I've known since I was a kid, and my boss Ruedi Beglinger, two guides who in my mind, at that stage in my career, can do no wrong. Kranabitter, who doesn't travel this terrain every day, comes in and sets an exceptionally nice uptrack to the top of one of the summits, with one kick turn, and at the guides' meeting that night, Beglinger was giving Kranabitter shit for the kick turn. And I thought, *You know what? I am never, ever going to sulk again.* Because it doesn't matter who you are. It's not a personal attack. If Rudi Kranabitter is not immune from it . . . it's nothing personal, because there was nothing but mutual respect between those two at the time.

"I'd had times, more than once, where Ruedi didn't mince words with me. He was direct, told me one time, 'That track is lousy. That wasn't up to the standard that somebody who's paying should receive. You're a professional, make a nicer track next time.' Would he then sit down and explain to me how to do that? No, but you watch him and you learn. And you fail sometimes, and he'll tell you when you do, and it might be with a four-letter word for emphasis.

"When I was set to leave for my final certification exam with the ACMG, I was nervous but ready, and Ruedi gave me a hug and a smile, and in his Swiss accent said, 'You're going to be fine. You failed with me a hundred times. You're ready for this.' That sums up Ruedi perfectly in my mind. His goal was not to make me feel good as much as it was to teach me, and had I failed a hundred times? Yeah, probably at least, but he never let me actually get into trouble. He watched me like a hawk."

When Craig asked Norrie if he recommended he do his practicum with Beglinger, Norrie told him exactly what Kranabitter had told him years before: "There's no better person or place to have an apprenticeship." Even some of Norrie's guests that week were able to echo his sentiments because they too had skied with Beglinger.

"Hey, yeah, good luck there, buddy," they told Craig. "Get on your leather underwear. Better eat your Wheaties."

In 1892, Scottish mountaineer William W. Naismith developed a method that assessed the time a fit individual requires to walk a proposed route according to its distance (horizontal) and (vertical) elevation gain. Fast-forward to March 31, 2002, and Craig had used "Naismith's Rule" to calculate a two-day traverse into Kokanee Glacier Provincial Park with ascents and descents of several summits. These included Grays Peak, the park's most famous landmark not only because it's the tallest, most dramatic peak viewable from downtown Nelson, but also because, well, everybody should want to stand atop the mountain featured on the label of the easy-drinking local lager, Kokanee Glacier Beer.

Buffery was helping Craig tick off another prerequisite "multiday tour" but at the same time he had tasked Craig with this exercise to give him a feel for both in-depth trip planning and what he might expect in his future ski guide exam (assuming he was accepted into the program), during which candidates lead examiners through complex unfamiliar terrain in an allotted period of time, a full-day tour or a multiday epic. The candidate must convey everything from travel time to food and water breaks to the gear necessary to lead a client safely to and from the objective in a reasonably close timeframe as estimated beforehand. The rule of thumb, as taught by the ACMG, is to plan for the slowest member of your group, and to pad your schedule for unforeseen circumstances such as weather. "The only thing more unpredictable than the mountains are people in the mountains," Buffery told Craig. "The only way to master it is to practice it in different mountains with different people."

The Kokanee adventure began with a quick morning heli-flight to the summit of Sitkum Peak near the southern boundary of the park, where Buffery, Craig, Heath Lockhurst, and skiing pal Jaye-Jay Berggren donned heavy packs and strapped into their boards to begin the traverse with a descent. This isn't the standard way to start a tour; usually you're on split skis, climbing skins on, and traveling out or up into the wilderness. With this in mind,

Buffery threw out a casual reminder. "Make sure you've got your skins in your pack," he said. "Don't want to get to the bottom and realize you left them up top or at home." They descended the north face of Sitkum Peak at 8:30, and when gravity gave way to the valley floor, they skinned up and headed toward West Kokanee Peak, then repeated the process again to the top of Outlook Peak, then down and across the eastern shore of Kaslo Lake to their objective, a wooded hollow near the Slocan Chief cabin. It took them roughly seven hours to travel ten horizontal miles, during which they ascended about 3,800 feet and descended 4,000 vertical feet. Craig had allotted 8.4 hours, but since everything went smoothly, they'd arrived one hour ahead of schedule, pitched their tents, ate some dinner, and then wandered over to the historical miner's cabin, which had been renovated and rented out by a skiing club. A modern hut was scheduled to be built, and Craig wanted to check it out. Seeing smoke rising from the chimney, Craig knocked, and when the door opened, he said, "Good evening. We don't want to intrude—we're camped nearby—but do you mind if we just take a peek inside?"

"Holy shit, eh," someone bellowed. "You're Craig Kelly, right? C'mon in, all of you, join us for a drink."

The 4:30 a.m. wake-up the next morning came with a headache, and not from the altitude. After breakfast and a snow profile, they were packed and gliding onward and upward toward their waypoints—the Giant's Kneecap to Kokanee Peak, where they rode down to a saddle that led to Grays. Here they split their boards and ski-toured across this broad col, stopping just shy of the knoblike summit of Grays Peak. They dropped their packs, transitioned their skis back to snowboards, kicked steps up the short but steep couloir, and reached the 9,000-plus-foot summit at 10:45 a.m., again one hour ahead of Craig's planned schedule.

"It was a glorious day," says Buffery, "views forever into the Purcells, the Valhallas, over to the Monashees, all the way up to the northern Selkirks. It was spectacular." Capitalizing on their elevation, they put eyes on the next leg of their route, especially the 30-plus-degree east-facing bowl, with some tricky cliff bands they would navigate around in order to get to their waypoint, Rosehip Lake. This is where they planned to melt snow, rehydrate, and fill their water bottles to sustain them through the second half of what they calculated would be a fourteen-hour day.

Craig was first to drop down off the summit, making tight turns in the steep couloir adjacent the boot-pack line. A few minutes later, the others had joined him at their packs and were peering over the edge, contemplating the open slope below. There had been recent snowfall, maybe ten centimeters a few days before, and it sat on top of a crust they could feel another ten centimeters down while probing with upturned ski poles. To the untrained eye, the fall-line slope looked solid, and wide open for turns, but the lake was some three thousand vertical feet below and to their right, "around the corner" over a ridge, a circuitous route that would take them to a different slope with a different aspect. Getting to that aspect was a little tricky because they had to traverse the upper section of the open slope below them, gain the ridge, which was an island of safety, and then continue on traversing. A fall in that zone, or an avalanche, would expose them to a band of cliffs a thousand feet below. There was another option, and that was straight down a couple thousand vertical feet, then tour back along the bottom of a very big open slope. Totally doable, fun even, but sketchy. Buffery dangled the carrot, thrusting his chin toward the gut of this tempting bowl below them: "So, what do you think, guys? Fall line?"

"Looks fun," responded Craig, "but the bottom, that's a sketchy long traverse. Maybe better to cut the slope." He motioned toward the ridge Buffery had identified as an island of safety. "Drop here, around this rocky bluff, and stay high and fast across there, see if it holds."

That was good intuition, and the right answer. On a nonconsequential slope Buffery might have asked Craig to make the cut, but because of those cliff bands he felt better doing it himself. He dropped in—angling down and across the slope—drawing the perfect line to keep speed in order to ride to the side if anything did go. He made the ridge, then Berggren went, and then it was Craig's turn. "I wouldn't have been very comfortable going across this big, really open, steep convexy, rolly, exposed terrain," says Lockhurst, who was bringing up the rear. "But with Buff and Craig. . . it's hard to explain, but it was very peaceful, it was a very safe feeling. Then I watched Craig roll into the first pitch, made the turn that locked him into Buff's track, and just before I was going to drop in to follow, he kicked off a size two avalanche." It ripped like a zipper, just behind the tail of Craig's board as he flew across the slope toward the ridge where he stopped, at the safety "island" exactly as planned if the slope slid. Craig and Lockhurst watched the surface slab break apart and cascade off the cliffs far below.

Lockhurst followed, taking care to set a solid edge on the now hard, crusty surface upon which the avalanche had run. A slip here could have been a slide-for-life, off the cliffs. His heart was pumping when he joined Craig, who looked him in the eye and said casually, "How do you like that?"

"Holy jeez," replied Lockhurst. "I don't know, man."

They looked ahead and saw that Buff's traverse took them across another pretty steep and sporty section. "We had a bit of a laugh," says Lockhurst. "I was like, 'Oh man!' and Craig gave me this look, like 'walk in the park, no big deal' and then he went, not giving me much time to think about it. If I was with somebody else, other than Craig, it would've been far more nail-biting than it was. I was right on his ass, 'cause I didn't want to get too far away from him. I wanted to be where he was because I knew that chances were I was generally safe."

They regrouped with Buffery and Berggren, and then leapfrogged to another ridge, cut another slope, and then could finally open it up and make some turns to the frozen lake—cotton-mouthed and thirsty—an hour after they'd stood on the summit. As he pulled a stove, pot, and fuel canister from his pack to melt snow for drinking water, Buffery realized his climbing skins weren't in there.

A bonehead move for a rookie, this was unforgivable as the mentor and lead guide. "I'm boiling water, thinking I must have left them on the col," says Buffery. "I'm trying to keep it together because we have like five hours and a few thousand more vertical feet to climb to get out of there, and shit, I'm supposed to be the one that's kind of showing these guys how to guide, right?" With a steep climb to reach the east col of Silvertip Mountain, their next waypoint, a kilometer away, he realized he was basically screwed. His only option was to use the rescue cord in his pack—a couple of five-meter pieces—to fashion snowshoes, macraméing knots every couple of inches on the bottom of his split skis to hopefully provide enough friction to walk.

Lockhurst was first to notice, and asked Buff what he was doing.

"Ugh, you guys, I think I left my skins up on the col," Buff admitted. "I can't believe it . . . maybe the wind blew them out or . . ."

"No wind up there, Buff," Craig said, shaking his head.

"Yeah, so, I'm going to do this, thread this cordelette together, some knots."

"Is that going to work?" Lockhurst asked.

"That's really going to slow us down," Craig said.

Head down, Buffery continued tying knots and feeling "really stupid" while the other guys put on their climbing skins and ate some food, not saying a word. "They really were just letting me suffer," says Buffery, "when Craig said, out of the blue, 'Hey, what day is it today?'"

Glancing at his watch, Buffery realized it was April 1, Craig's thirty-sixth birthday. "We all knew Craig—and April first is a memorable day—and we had all forgotten, so I said, 'Oh geez, man, I'm sorry . . . Happy birthday, Craig. I completely forgot."

"No worries, Buff. But hey, what time is it?" Buffery was thinking by this point it was time for Craig to get a watch, but he dutifully pulled up his sleeve and reported it to be 11:45.

"Nope," said Craig, standing twenty feet away and dangling Buffery's climbing skins, one in each hand. "It's April Fools' . . ."

Buff jumped up and took Craig out in a full-speed tackle. "I washed his face with snow and we all had a good chuckle," says Buffery. "The other guys had no idea. He'd dropped off the summit and dipped into my pack and grabbed them in those few minutes before I got down with Heath and Jaye-Jay. But that was Craig's alter ego Elmer,** pranks to the nth degree."

Beyond the pranks and the route-finding, Craig was also—unbeknownst to the others—scoping potential territory for their lodge. Grays Peak had provided him a supreme overview of the landscape, including various drainages he'd been exploring on maps and while flying overhead in the helicopter. But the only real way to get a feeling for the terrain is to travel through it.

One of the zones he had been looking at was Coffee Creek, which was just a ridgeline over from Rosehip Lake. It backed up against the park boundaries, so if tenure was available nobody could come in behind them. As for riding, it was mostly below treeline, but that might suit a small operation. The right site on a wooded knoll could provide front-door touring access to myriad ridgelines loaded with gullies, glades, and fun shreddable descents.

** Elmer was Craig's middle name—passed down from his grandfather on his dad's side—but his closest friends say "Elmer" was Craig's mischievous alter ego. Elmer was famous for filling gloves with warm oatmeal, swiping windshield wipers during snowstorms, and instigating the occasional food fight, though he rarely got caught.

What really interested Craig, though, was the backdoor pipeline—aka the creek—access into the park where an enterprising guide, with the proper permits, could lead small groups into the serious alpine. He had no intentions to swoop in and, in surfer vernacular, "crowd the lineup." But from what he'd learned thus far, there was room for what they had in mind. This was literally at the exploratory stage, "still at the dream level," according to Savina, but it had piqued Craig's interest enough to see if tenure was even a possibility.

Several times, during their tour out of Rosehip Lake, Craig paused at certain vistas to study his surroundings more than you'd expect from somebody who was just passing through.

CHAPTER 15

CHECKING ALL
THE BOXES

CRAIG HAD ONLY BEEN HOME from the Kokanee Glacier trip for a couple days when he, Savina, and Olivia hopped on a plane and flew north on April 5, 2002, to attend the twelfth annual *TransWorld SNOWboarding* industry conference at the Alyeska Resort in Girdwood, Alaska. In Anchorage they rented a car and headed to the resort, with Craig pointing out the Chugach Mountains, peaks he had explored years before.

The next morning, while Savina rented cross-country skis to tour around the town's network of tracks with Olivia on her back, Craig, Jake Burton Carpenter, and a couple friends from the snowboard industry took off heli-boarding. They hooted and hollered their way through some thirty thousand vertical feet of untracked Alaska powder. That evening, Scotch on the rocks in hand, cheeks wind-burned, and still buzzing from the vertical, they ambled into the Columbia Ballroom at what was then known as the Alyeska Prince Hotel, where Craig would be presented with that year's coveted Tranny Award.

While the snowboarding industry did glitz things up with bling and black-tie parties in Vegas and prom nights in Southern California, the Tranny Awards was still a low-key affair. Craig sported a button-down flannel and a Baldface Lodge baseball cap while Carpenter wore jeans and a sweater over a T-shirt. Their peers—a boisterous cast of pros, hopeful entrepreneurs, and youthful execs mingling with their older, wiser contemporaries—filed in and filled the room with raucous claims and friendly jeers, but all eyes were on Craig as he and Carpenter found their way to reserved seats near the podium.

The lights dimmed, and a slide show of Craig ripping deep powder around the world lit up the room, accompanied by the audience soundtrack of "oohs" and "ahhhs." This was followed by Carpenter's presentation of the award: "I don't know about you," he said, speaking into the microphone, "but watching Craig ride never gets old. If you've ever had the pleasure to ride with him in person, like I got to today, it's pretty special and humbling. . . .

"You know the story of my life is listening to Craig. And when I finally figured out how to do that, is when my company and our industry took off. And it wasn't just me, it was the magazines, and everybody else. When Craig started, when he got into it, it was all about overall competing. To be successful you had to ride gates, you had to do moguls, halfpipe, everything. And he kicked ass, and he won overall world championship after world championship.

"And then he said, 'I just want to focus on the halfpipe.' And all of us thought he was kind of crazy, like 'Man, you're going to give up your overall title? That's so special.' And sure enough, the whole industry followed him. Halfpipe and freestyle blew up. He was right.

"And then after dominating that scene for a few years, he decided, 'I just want to freeride.' Everybody was taken aback. 'Stop competing? This is what it's all about.' And he's like, 'No, I just want to freeride.' Sure enough, he became more influential and did more for the sport than anybody ever had. He got us all focused on what the sport is about. He just reduced it to its purest form.

"And then, most recently he decided to become a guide. I mean, this guy understands the soul of this sport better than any of us. And what he did for the sport and for me personally and Burton, I think we'll all be forever in debt. So, Craig, I'm honored to present to you this Tranny Award, for your lifetime of achievement in snowboarding."

Once upon a time, Craig would have raised his board or trophy over his head in triumph, the ultra-competitor, but now he just held the Tranny close to his chest, sort of shrugged his shoulders, and thanked the crowd until the applause trailed off. Looking over at his longtime sponsor and friend, Carpenter, he said, "You know, today was the first time I rode with Jake in almost four years, and it was just so good to be on snow riding with him today, and now to be here with all of you tonight. Some of you know, I took about a year and a half off from riding, and during those months I came to the realization of how much I love snowboarding. It feels good to be back, and on a new path with guiding. So thank you all, and I'd like to thank my partner, Savina, and my daughter, Olivia, who are right there, and have helped me realize what's most important in life."

While attendees mingled after the awards, the editorial director of *TransWorld SNOWboarding Business*, John Stouffer, combed the crowd for Sherman Poppen. Camera in hand, Stouffer dragged him over to Craig and Carpenter for a once-in-a-lifetime photo op of these legends—the grandfather of snowboarding; the pioneer of professional snowboarding and father of freeriding; and the founder of the world's most influential snowboard brand—together.

"I was in the presence of greatness for a few minutes that night," Poppen recalls, "and it just never ceased to amaze me, how everybody in that room came together because of their love of snowboarding. I heard a lot of stories that night. Jake said if the Olympics had come around a few years earlier, Craig would have brought home the gold. I heard about Craig the prankster, Craig the hellion, Craig the engineer, but the man I met was a soft-spoken gentleman and a proud father. A real class act. After we took that photo, he shook my hand. It was pretty loud in there, but he leaned in and told me, 'It's an honor to meet you, sir. You started all this. . . . You gave me and all these people one hell of a life.'"

BACK IN NELSON, Craig set the Tranny on a shelf beside the desk where his laptop was framed by stacks of books on one side and neatly arranged piles of papers on the other. If he needed more space to spread out he'd move to the dining table where locals with appetites for adventure often found a seat. Buffery had helped him tap into the Kootenay backcountry scene, and on any given day Lockhurst, Joel McBurney, Joe Pavelich, Matt Scholl, Demian Whitley, Kevin Arcuri, Greg Johnson, or other backcountry types, most with aspirations of mountain guiding, were there, leaned in over a topo map, pointing out the location of a hideaway cabin or planning a route. Together they formed a network of reliable partners and mentors whose growing brotherhood was not unlike the earliest days of the Mount Baker Hard Core.

In mid-April, local skier Mark Karlstrom was brought to the table by Buffery. Though six years younger than Craig, he was a year ahead as an aspirant guide, having already been accepted into the assistant ski guide program and having taken the mountain skills course earlier in the winter. As was common, however, he had not been invited to move forward to take the final exam. The recommendation he'd gotten from one of the instructors, none other than Rudi "Crampon-biter" Kranabitter, was "You need to take some more time and go practice."

That had led Karlstrom to Baldface, where Buffery took him under his wing and soon realized that he and Craig could benefit from their respective stations in the ACMG. Karlstrom was a hard-charging skier (indeed, he'd been featured in ski mags and videos, ripping heavy lines and dropping big cliffs) with an impressive ski mountaineering background. He'd also climbed and skied North America's second-highest peak, Mount Logan; winter-camped twenty-three days straight on one self-supported epic; done various big traverses; and rappelled into more couloirs than he could remember.

Neither man had seen each other ski or ride, and they had only met once before hatching a plan that would check off another box for Craig's prerequisites, based on Buffery's intuition that their fitness and skills were compatible. Their objective was the Horseshoe Glacier in the Purcell Mountains, where they would establish a base camp and climb six surrounding peaks in four days, starting with a warm-up on the smallest of the list, Toad Mountain, then on to Quibble Peak, Truce Mountain, Cauldron Mountain, Covenant Mountain, and ending with Ochre Peak.

A week before the trip, Craig recruited Mark Fawcett, a two-time Canadian Olympian snowboard racer who, after the 2002 Games in Salt Lake City, decided to retire his hardboots for softies and do some tailguiding at Baldface. "It was kind of a backcountry first date for those three," Buffery says. "Karlstrom had all the skills but could use more experience leading; and after the Kokanee trip, Craig was ready for a mini expedition to bag some peaks he needed. Fawcett was the wild card—never winter-camped, but he was keen for the adventure and strong as an ox."

"In hindsight," Fawcett says, "Craig set himself up for the ideal training scenario. He had Karlstrom, who was way more experienced than him, and then he had me. I'd had lots of experience with my beacon, shovel, probe, but with all the survival stuff, I was super green, which for Craig was perfect. He had a mentor and a guinea pig client all on the same trip. Just like a client, he gave me a list of everything I needed and told me, 'All you have to do is show up.' And then, a few days later, he said, 'By the way, bring a snowmobile too.'"

On April 17, 2002, they were checking gear—rope, harness, Prusiks, food, tent, stove, backup stove, fuel, sleeping bags—spread out on a tarp at Craig's house. The one item Fawcett hadn't begged or borrowed was crampons, which Craig wasn't certain they'd need, but said they'd sure be nice to have along if they did. Once they'd divvied up the weight, Fawcett was astonished his pack was pushing seventy pounds, which helped him make up his mind *not* to pick up another couple of pounds of plastic, alloy, and pointy stainless-steel spikes at the mountaineering shop.

They hit the road early the next morning, and a few hours later were snowmobiling up a drainage on an old logging road, past summer campsites and into the snowy, desolate Canadian wild. When they shut down their engines at 11 a.m. Craig hushed them with a "Hear that?" Fawcett swung his head around, on the lookout for danger: perhaps a bear that had awoken early from hibernation. "I can't hear a thing," Fawcett replied. Craig just nodded and smiled . . . *exactly*.

The elevation was 5,720 feet, temperature 39 degrees Fahrenheit with overcast skies when they stripped down to base-layer tops and vented pants and climbed away from their machines. Two and a half hours of breaking trail through the forest brought them into a drainage and the toe of the glacier, where they roped up. This was Fawcett's first crack at glacial travel that didn't involve flying downhill at 50 miles per hour, so he got the quick-and-dirty primer with Fawcett tied in and about twenty feet of rope between Karlstrom up front and Craig in the rear. They headed through a steep jumble of seracs, around little ice caves, and eventually onto the glacier where Karlstrom probed the surface—two, maybe three times—ahead of each step, feeling for hidden crevasses and navigating across snow bridges, while Craig, with map and compass, knocked off landmarks and kept them on route. It was slow, tedious, and "holy shit, it was a mission getting up there," remembers Fawcett. Seven and a half hours after they'd left the snowmobiles, they finally slogged up over a rise and onto a great white semi-flat expanse, elevation 9,860 feet, with a light snowfall shrouding the peaks. After gliding forward another hundred meters, Craig said, "This is it," the icefield between Quibble Peak and Toad Mountain. Dropping their packs, they probed and stamped the camp perimeter with their split skis, and then collapsed.

"Craig threw up," says Fawcett, "then he pulled out his field book and made some notes."

It was 6:40 p.m. and snowing a centimeter per hour. Stepping down into the fresh snow outside the camp perimeter, Craig measured the depth of his boot penetration at 25 centimeters. The wind was light, and the temperature had dropped to 16 degrees. They'd started the day in spring conditions, but up here it was still winter. Weather observations complete, Craig pocketed the book, pulled a shovel from his pack, and asked Karlstrom, "So how high should we make these snow walls around the camp?"

"It was game on," Fawcett says. "This wasn't a holiday. Craig was here to learn—he was in training mode." When Fawcett and Karlstrom surrendered the warmth of their sleeping bags and crawled out of their tent at 6:30 the next morning, it was just in time to see Craig making turns down Toad Mountain, the smallest of the six they planned to summit. This safe, mellow ascent was just a few hundred feet above camp, but nonetheless Craig had scored the first peak of the day while the other two were still sleeping. The first words he said when he glided into camp were, "Oh. I guess you guys are only doing five?"

After breakfast, they toured over to Truce Mountain, dug a full snow profile, and began ascending. It was a beautiful day, and Craig suggested, "Maybe we can get four in today," confirming for Fawcett that all the stories he'd heard over the years were true. For Karlstrom, well, "I'd never met somebody with that much drive and determination," he says. "I was like, 'Ahhhh, this is how somebody becomes a champion,' and bear in mind, I hadn't even seen him snowboard yet."

They gained the wind-scoured, firm high ridge to the summit of Truce around 11 a.m., took the climbing skins off, and Fawcett and Craig connected their splitboards. They were walking from here, carrying their skis and boards and boot-packing to the summit, but with each step, the winds got gustier, the ridgetop got narrower, the incline got steeper, and the snow harder—so much so that it was impossible for Craig and Fawcett to kick their own steps. So they followed the little indentations that Karlstrom's hard-toed ski boots made until even those became micro divots. When it got to the point that they would have to get on their hands and knees and use their boards as horizontal ice axes to pull themselves up, they stopped. Sitting across their boards and skis to prevent them from sliding away in the wind, Karlstrom and Craig dug into their packs.

"Sure am glad I lugged these up here," said Craig, holding the crampons he'd helped Burton design. While strapping them on his boots, he told Fawcett, "If it gets any more sketchy, we'll send you a rope."

Meanwhile, Karlstrom had donned his crampons and continued up the pitch to the summit. He turned to watch Craig, his snowboard strapped to his pack and catching the wind like a sail, sort of bucking him around a little. It was steep, and Craig put his hands forward on the slope to steady himself as he moved slowly and deliberately upward, kicking in his crampon points, testing them, and then pausing to take the next step.

"It was quite high and steep," says Karlstrom, "but I was still surprised to see him moving really slow, kind of timid and careful, and I realized this was probably scary for him—for both of them. Reading his body language, I thought, *Oh, he's still pretty new to this.*"

Karlstrom's intuition had vectored in on that "I'm not up there to be a mountaineer" mentality Craig had mentioned in various interviews, a fear he generally experienced only while ascending a peak, climbing a couloir, or hiking a ridge to get to a line.

So he knew that about himself, but the ACMG selection process didn't excuse anyone from their fears. Craig had no plans to guide future clients on technical mountaineering routes, and the ski guide course examiners weren't going to test him on such, but he would "be required to show that [he] is capable of guiding clients in alpine terrain including glaciers, snow and ice, and simple short-roping showing confident and efficient movement."

Craig clambered up the final twenty yards onto the icy 10,702-foot summit of Truce Mountain at 11:40 a.m., sat down, and took a sip of Scotch from a flask he pulled from his pocket, then handed the flask to Karlstrom, who offered him the rope.

Meanwhile, Fawcett had attempted to gain a few more feet on the slick upper ridge. He'd bruised his toenails trying to punch even a couple of millimeters of his soft boots into the rock-hard snow, and when that failed, he tried to get the edge of his snowboard, held horizontally, to hold so he could pull himself up, but it kept slipping down like a giant ice scraper. Tossing him the rope, Craig told Fawcett to clip in and then pulled him up, hand over hand. They each took a pull from the flask to celebrate the summit while scoping out Cauldron Mountain, their next objective, but first things first: there was an entire northeast face, a couple thousand vertical feet of untracked powder, begging for turns.

"All right, skier," Craig said. "Let's see it."

Karlstrom obliged, making glorious tracks down the blank canvas, some surface slough pouring down beside him, as he covered hundreds of vertical feet in a matter of seconds before arcing a long sweeping turn to the right and easing to a stop. He turned just in time to see Craig "taking this gnarly line through the rocks, just flying," says Karlstrom. "And then Fawcett caught air off the top and power-carved into this insanely steep space, huge powder sprays that just hung there. I was like, 'Holy crap, these guys rip.'"

An hour and fifty minutes later, they summited 10,700-foot Cauldron Mountain at 2:12 p.m., rode its most northern aspect down, then toured over and summited the 10,400-foot Covenant Mountain at 3:30. More turns down before skinning up the 10,450-foot Quibble Peak ten minutes shy of 5:00 p.m. By 5:30 they were bundled up in puffy down jackets and sipping hot cocoa at base camp. The surrounding summits were aglow in soft alpine light, which accentuated the serpentine tracks etched on their faces. As Craig once said, "There are really very few places in life where you can look back and see a track that registers what you did."

That day, they did good. Craig got in some short roping, Karlstrom some lead time, and for Fawcett—what an introduction to the full backcountry experience. He was a world-class athlete, an Olympian who'd trained for years to hold his country's flag and walk into a stadium filled with thousands of screaming fans. But this moment here, the three of them tiny specks of color in an amphitheater of peaks that seemed to stretch outward forever, rivaled even that. He was just grateful Craig had invited him and couldn't stop thinking, *How lucky am I?*

All day long, Fawcett had been the silent observer as Karlstrom and Craig "talked shop," and now, as night covered their tracks in darkness, Craig was still in training mode, contemplating the day's routes in his mind and bouncing alternatives off Karlstrom. "He would reverse-engineer things, come in through the middle," Karlstrom says. "Like with crevasse rescue, he would make up new scenarios, trying to anticipate how an examiner would try to trip him up. He was so incredibly cerebral and thorough that . . . honestly, I didn't have answers to half his questions."

On day four, a misty fog moved in while they were breaking camp and got thicker by the minute. "By the time we reached the lower glacier, I could barely see my outstretched hand," says Fawcett, who was roped in at the rear. "It was one of those whiteouts where you lose all perspective. Just standing still, you'd get that falling sensation and have to catch yourself." This surreal, panic-inducing vertigo was made exponentially worse because they were on a steep 38-degree pitch riddled with crevasses. "We were literally inching down the slope, side-slipping a few inches at a time," recalls Fawcett. "I could hear them—Karlstrom was probing ahead, and feeling for air pockets—I knew what the situation was, but could not see shit. The rope just disappeared into the misty white, and at some point, Craig says, 'So, ummm, we've got some low visibility here,' like, ridiculous understatement, and 'We're gonna camp out here for a few minutes and assess the situation.' Totally pro, totally calm."

They sat there for a half hour—Craig timed it—and right about when they thought camping out was a real possibility, the fog thinned, and the slope materialized just enough to reveal the dips and dents of the crevasse field. They picked a line and descended safely to and then off the toe of the glacier.

CRAIG TOLD BUFFERY about the whiteout the following week. "Those are the moments you dread in an exam," says Buffery. "But examiners welcome them, even hope for them, so they can test your mettle in a stressful situation." In essence, the mountains had dished out a pop quiz, and Craig had passed. Buffery agreed with Craig when he told him the lesson he'd learned was that sometimes the best thing you can do is nothing. You had to bottle the energy of fear, the impulse to do *something*, and learn to suffer a near-total loss of control.

Buffery had news as well, that word of Craig's crusade had cycled through the guiding community and people were finally getting back to Zacharias. Even Rudi Kranabitter had reportedly said something along the lines of "As long as he can keep up, maybe we give this snowboarder guy a shot. If not, we'll send him home to his mother."

Craig asked what it all meant, and Buffery replied, "I think it means you better start polishing that application."

Craig emailed Zacharias who confirmed that—as long as he had fulfilled all the prerequisites—the technical committee and board of directors welcomed him to apply as a splitboarder. This meant his application would be added to an unknown number of prospects, of which the top twenty-four would be selected and screened. If he was one of those twenty-four, and his snowboarding, split-skiing, and various mountain skills were up to par, he could then enter the course.

"By the way," Zacharias told him, "I'm retiring as the technical director. I'll still be instructing, and helping with the transition, but the new technical director is Dwayne Congdon. You'll be submitting your application to him."

This was still the era of dial-up internet and rudimentary search engines. You couldn't just type in a name and get a biographical profile in ten seconds or less. But a couple of phone calls revealed that Congdon was a high-altitude climber who'd summited several peaks, including Mount Everest. In fact, he and Sharon Wood had been the third and fourth Canadians (Woods was in fact the first North American woman) to reach the summit of Everest sixteen years earlier. Notably, it was a self-supported "light expedition" (no porters) via the notorious West Ridge and Hornbein Couloir, details that meant little to Craig but were soon simplified in terms he could understand. "He's a badass," Buffery told him. "Full alpine guide—climber first, and skier second."

"Any chance he snowboards?" Craig asked.

"Possible," replied Buffery. "But, unlikely . . ."

CHAPTER 16

A LETTER FROM THE ACMG

THE DWAYNE CONGDON DEVELOPMENT SHONE a light on something Buffery had emphasized to Craig throughout the winter. "You need to do some technical snow and rock climbing," he said. "They'll be sniffing out the weak links like bloodhounds, and if you're fumbling around with your ropes and gear, you're done. You need to get on some granite to legitimize yourself in *their* world."

Though he'd ridden all the lines off the Mount Shuksan's Arm, and most chutes, glades, and gullies spilling off the surrounding peaks, Craig had never climbed and ridden down from the summits of Mounts Baker or Shuksan. Both of these he knocked off on June 1 and June 3, respectively: Baker via Heliotrope Ridge, where he camped for the summit assault the next morning, and then Shuksan's spire-like summit pyramid via the Sulfide Glacier route.

Accomplishing these two objectives satisfied two more prerequisites, but it was also a full-circle journey for Craig, who'd brought along one of his new riding buddies. Twenty-eight-year-old snow-science academic Greg Johnson was surprised when Craig told him he'd never "done" either of these peaks, despite their dominance over the ski area that Craig and the MBHC had made famous. Jeff Fulton couldn't recall anybody snowboarding either peak, "not from the summit," says Fulton. "Not back then. Too technical for us, even when we thought we were invincible."

Indeed, Mount Shuksan—especially the south-side summit pyramid—looks abominably steep and impassable, that is, when it's visible. Usually the summit is locked in winter storms that batter it for weeks, and when it does clear up, it's hard to fathom how snow sticks to such an incline. Much of it comes tumbling down in spindrift and avalanches, but the summit gully remains deep, as it did that June 3, a thousand-vertical-foot artery of snow that Craig and Johnson ascended, kicking toeholds with their crampons and carrying an ice ax for security, like flies on a white wall. They summited the final 50-degree pitch at 1:30 p.m., took in the 360-degree view, and then Craig rolled in with an aggressive first carve, immediately linking—and indeed air-dropping between—several turns. This impressed upon Johnson Craig's comfort level and ability to read the snow; for his part Johnson side-slipped the summit drop, then cautiously eased into the rhythm of the jump turns. At the bottom, Craig arced a long toeside carve before stopping to face back uphill and watch Johnson ride the bottom third.

Craig's figure was a silhouette against the glacier below him, his arms raised high, shaking his fists in utter stoke. As he got closer, Johnson could see that Craig was smiling, and then both of them were grinning and nodding their heads in both affirmation and disbelief at how freaking good that run had been. Then Johnson noticed Craig had come to a stop right beside their boot-pack: the line that had led them to the top an hour and a half earlier.

Craig unstrapped his snowboard, wiped some slush from the bindings, and didn't give Johnson a choice when he said, "Let's do it again."

A COUPLE OF weeks later, Craig loaded up the family and drove four hours west of Nelson to Skaha Bluffs Provincial Park, near Kelowna, British Columbia, roughly two and a half months shy of the application due date. This trip was just another example of Craig's uncanny ability to . . . "I can't really describe it," says Savina, "the way his brain worked. He could fit everything together in this incredibly efficient, anticipatory, multitask way, and you didn't even realize it's happening."

In this instance, they were meeting up again with Johnson, who, Savina learned, held a master's degree in civil engineering with a focus in avalanche mechanics. While camped on Heliotrope Ridge, he and Craig had discussed the challenges of guiding on a splitboard—identifying solutions for each problem—and decided to coauthor a paper on the subject. Johnson mentioned that he'd been hired by the U.S. National Park Service as a seasonal climbing ranger and was going to be working at either Mount Rainier or Rocky Mountain National Park later in the summer. "Really?" said Craig. "If you want to do some climbing, I could use the practice. I'm basically a beginner, but I'm a fast learner."

On that trip Craig honed his rock climbing by day and, in the evening, discussed and edited the first draft of the paper he and Johnson had titled "Guiding on a Splitboard: Challenges and Solutions." Craig's intent was to pass it along to the ACMG with, or in advance of, his application so that the technical committee could better understand why a splitboard was a viable guiding tool for the winter backcountry.

As for the climbing, Johnson was accustomed to watching and assisting—sometimes rescuing—neophyte climbers with aspirations that exceeded their skills or experience, so he was only mildly surprised when, after just a couple of warm-ups on some sport routes, Craig homed in on, as his first lead climb, a 5.9 trad route (traditional lead climbing, where the climber places his own protection while being belayed from below). Granted, he'd done some bouldering, been to a climbing gym once or twice, and been top-roped several years earlier, so he knew what it felt like to dip his hands into a chalk bag. Just barely.

"Leading a 5.9 trad when you're basically a beginner is pretty heady," Johnson says about that day. "He stared at it for a while, then fired up it right out of the gate. I was belaying him with my mouth open, like 'Damn?!' It showed me a couple things. One, his head space was amazing, and two, so was his strength. I was climbing a ton, fit, and eight years younger than him and I got on it and was like, 'Fuck, this is fucking hard.'"

From Skaha, Craig moved on to bigger routes. "He trained hard in the big granite peaks that summer," says Buffery. "We ripped up the classic 5.9 multi-pitch southeast ridge of Mount Gimli in the Valhallas. Then in typical Craig style, he left the next day with his and Joel McBurney's family into the Bugaboos and climbed the classic southeast ridge of Bugaboo Spire two days later."

By July 15, Craig's hands were cracked, his fingers were swollen, and he could tie a figure-eight knot with his eyes closed. He knew a carabiner from a cam, the latter of which he'd come to think of as a "friend." Was he legit in the climbing world? Probably not. He hadn't slept on a portaledge or pooped into a plastic bag, but metaphorically speaking, if an examiner asked for a wrench he wouldn't hand him the pliers.

And he was ready enough to introduce himself to Dwayne Congdon.

CONGDON WAS NO doubt already receiving a slew of applications, and Craig wanted to be absolutely sure that when his was reviewed, Congdon didn't immediately see that he was a snowboarder and discard it into the circular file. "He had always advocated for himself," Pat Kelly says. "From his BMX days to his snowboarding days, he could write a good letter, not only to communicate but to document. He'd learned in court that phone calls and conversations didn't mean anything. My guess is he wanted proof on paper that they knew he was doing that course on a splitboard and had agreed to it."

Dear Dwayne

My desire is to become an Assistant Ski Guide Candidate and I have been focused on fulfilling all of the prerequisites as well as training hard for the course. Snowboarding and ski touring on a split board has been my means of travel and I have been riding a board since 1981. For the last 16 years I have worked in the snowboard industry, with 12 of them having been very active in the winter backcountry, working in a full variety of terrain on most of the continents in the world.

My interest to become a Guide soared last year as I spent most of the winter working under John Buffery as a tail guide for Baldface Snow Cat Skiing in Nelson, BC. In addition to John, I have also had the pleasure of working or traveling with many other certified guides in the backcountry including Paul Norrie, Reto Keller, Lee Usher, Steve Kuijt and a few Assistant Guides as well. Every one of them has supported my decision to apply for the course and offered to be references for me.

I just wanted to confirm that you would allow me to use a split board for my primary means of travel. Colin Zacharias . . . said as long as an applicant had met the prerequisites there would not be any resistance to allowing him or her to use a split board for the course.

I realize that this is a step forward for the ACMG and that there will be certain issues that will need to be discussed in order for everyone to be comfortable with having a split board on the course. Please let me know if there is anything I can do to help out.

Sincerely,
Craig Kelly

CONGDON RESPONDED TO Craig with a brief email that acknowledged receipt of the letter, noted the deadline was September 11, and said he looked forward to reviewing his application.

On September 7, 2002, Craig dropped off the application in person when he drove through Kamloops on the way to Blue River to attend the CSGA Summer Glacier Skills course: seven days of intense instruction on glacier travel, proper crampon and ice ax usage, rope techniques, protection (aka building anchors), rescue techniques, navigation, route selection, trip preparation. None of this was to beef up his application; that was out of his hands at this point. Taking this course was pure knowledge acquisition and skill refinement to better his odds with the ACMG and add to his mountain mileage.

Following two weeks of uninterrupted family time, Craig and Johnson then attended the International Snow Science Workshop (ISSW), a biannual gathering of snow and avalanche science practitioners and researchers whose motto is "a merging of theory with practice." That year, nearly seven hundred participants from nineteen countries converged on Penticton, British Columbia, to exchange ideas, experiences, and research. These were mountain nerds of the highest order, as savvy on the slopes as they were with a spreadsheet, and for five days, Craig listened intently to presentations with such titles as Heuristic Traps in Recreational Avalanche Accidents; Forecasting Shear Strength and Skier-Triggered Avalanches for Buried Surface Hoar Layers; and A Microstructural Dry Snow Metamorphism Model Applicable to Equitemperature and Temperature Gradient Environments. At one point, Craig leaned over and whispered to Johnson, "A lot of this stuff is going over my head, but I guess I'm learning some of it through osmosis."

After Penticton, they hit Skaha for some climbing. Craig also practiced setting up a rope for glacial travel, prepping one end for the last person he'd tie in, and then quickly and efficiently measuring out seven double-arm-length sections (roughly 21 meters), tying a butterfly loop, and repeating the process for a couple of theoretical clients. Then he'd tie himself in as the lead, neatly looping the remaining rope and draping it across his chest—ready for quick access in the event of a rescue.

"Here it was October, winter had melted away months earlier," recalls Johnson, "yet somehow all summer long, Craig had kept his mind in the snow."

Back home, Craig hung up his ropes, filed several papers he'd collected at the workshop, checked his email and voicemail, then picked up Olivia and strolled out the front door to check the physical mail. Playing "Peekaboo, anything there?" with the mailbox became a daily ritual as he awaited word—any word—from the ACMG.

CRAIG WASN'T THE only one. Some eighty other applicants were living their lives in limbo, anxiously watching the leaves turn as the clock ticked toward fall. This was the time of year that an entire ecosystem of winter-focused guides prickled with excitement for the upcoming season. From first-time candidates like Craig, to those waiting for a second crack at the assistant ski guide exam like Mark Karlstrom, to the newly minted assistant guides like Craig's friend Joel McBurney—who'd passed the exam the previous spring and was now looking for work experience that would move him onward and upward to full ski guide status—everybody had a story.

Take Ken Wylie, an alpine climbing guide and assistant ski guide from Revelstoke who had passed the exam in spring of 1999, a year before some of the requirements and parameters changed. According to the ACMG Training and Certification Program dated July 2000, "To become a [full] ski guide: You must have been an Assistant Ski Guide for no less than one year, and no more than two years." To apply, Wylie needed: "Proof of work experience showing a minimum of 30 days guiding apprenticeship, or 50 days of work experience documented as follows: A letter from a supervising guide, or guide's book photocopy signed by supervising guide, or work-experience resume signed by supervising guide." He also needed a recommendation from an ACMG ski or mountain guide and personal skills resume, updated to include "significant additions" from the version he'd submitted years earlier. It was noted a second time that the applicant "may wait a maximum of 2 years after getting your assistant ski guide certification before you are required to take the [full] Ski Guide Exam."

According to the current standards, Wylie was a year and a half past the deadline, but he wasn't concerned, as the rule was changed after he'd gotten his certificate. With winter just around the corner, he was, however, concerned with putting finishing touches on the house he and his wife, Nancy, were building and narrowing down where he'd be working over the winter. He needed the job both for the income and to accumulate the fifty hours of work experience and a letter from his supervising guide in order to qualify him for the full ski guide exam.

Wylie had gained most of his ski guiding experience at Island Lake Lodge, where he'd worked as a tailguide the season before he passed the assistant ski guide exam, and then for a couple of years after, even guiding Craig a couple times. While he enjoyed Island Lake Lodge, he loved touring and also needed more experience working in the high alpine. He heard that Ruedi Beglinger and Selkirk Mountain Experience was hiring but before applying he did some research—and the portrait he ultimately arrived at of Beglinger was very different from the one Paul Norrie had given Craig.

Unanimously, Wylie's sources agreed that the mountains, the terrain—there was a little bit of everything: tree skiing, glaciers, high alpine summits—the chalet, were all outstanding at SME. But when it came to working there, the overwhelming feedback he got, according to Wylie, was not to go. One of the most vocal was Chic Scott, a pioneer in Canadian ski mountaineering, an honorary life member of the ACMG, and the author of several books, including *Summits & Icefields: Alpine Ski Tours in the Canadian Rockies and Columbia Mountains of Canada*. The cover photo of the first edition published in 1994 was in fact taken by Beglinger, whom Scott had been friendly with at the time. In January 2000, Scott finally took Beglinger up on the offer to spend a week at SME.

Scott considered himself a fair critic, having visited dozens of backcountry lodges and skied with dozens of guides over the years. With that context, he told Wylie that he would never return to Selkirk Mountain Experience, for one reason—Beglinger himself. The sentiment he shared with Wylie reflected the more detailed version he had written in his diary on January 31: "Well I experienced a week at Ruedi Beglinger's boot camp. It was a horrible experience. It seems he went out of his way to make his weaker guests suffer . . . on top of that, I think he is an unsafe guide. I am surprised that he has not had a serious accident."

Despite Scott and others painting a picture of what he might expect working for Beglinger, Wylie applied for the job. "I chose not to listen," says Wylie. "My heart could not go mechanized [heli or cat skiing]; I thought I could be different." Ultimately, he believed he could hold his own. Says Wylie, "It was my ego."

IN THE SECOND week of October, an envelope from the University College of the Cariboo showed up in the Kellys' mailbox.

Dated October 9, 2002, the letter from Congdon read:

Craig:

Congratulations, this letter formally accepts you to the Assistant Ski Guide program.

As a successful applicant, you are registered and scheduled as follows. Guide Training Mechanized: December 6–12, 2002 at Monashee Powder Adventures. Guide Training Touring; February 9–15, 2003 at Rogers Pass. Complete logistic packages will be sent out 4 to 6 weeks in advance of each program.

Please be informed that the Guide Training—Skiing is both a pre-requisite and a screening for the Assistant Ski Guide exam. Upon completion of both Guide Training—Skiing components, you may be requested to wait a year before taking the Assistant Ski Guide exam if your applied skills are not up to the standard as described in the training. The two exam dates are: March 21–29 or March 28–April 5.

Some specific feedback from the Technical Committee, Craig is to continue your touring training in complex alpine and glaciated terrain.

Good luck with your work experience and winter preparations. Again, congratulations and I look forward to seeing you this winter.

> *Yours Sincerely,*
> *Dwayne Congdon,*
> *Technical Director*

According to Buffery, the news was well received by Craig but not cause for celebration—because now the real work began.

WINTER ARRIVED EARLY in 2002, as it often did in the mountains of British Columbia, and by October 15 the peaks were dusted white with the first snowflakes of the season. The delicate crystals stood on top of one another, interlocking and building in depth a few inches from that first storm to more than three feet by mid-November, creating the silky-smooth foundation on which skiers, snowboarders, and mountaineers would explore for months to come.

Buffery watched these storms closely. Soon he would lead hearty adventurers into the untracked backcountry, and the routes that he'd climb, the slopes that he'd give the nod to descend, virtually every decision he'd make in the coming season would be dictated by the nature of these storms and his ability to read the clues they left behind. Throughout the winter he would dig down into the snowpack and examine the layers created by each storm. He would consider the characteristics of the terrain, perform stability tests, and ultimately ascertain the snow's likelihood to hold fast or fold. Buffery had pulled bodies out of these mountains—he knew they would be unforgiving of mistakes.

Winter progressed, the snow settled, the storm layers began to bond, and Buffery started to map out the terrain he would open up first at Baldface. If he could make time, he hoped to independently guide a few trips with return clients, most of whom were professional skiers and snowboarders, film producers, cinematographers; friends who for years had trusted him to get them to "the goods"—and back out alive.

··

CRAIG TOO HAD closely watched the storms. They were creating, literally, the snow science problems he'd be solving as examiners tested his knowledge and challenged his instincts in the coming months.

Craig continued his avalanche training by completing the first part of the Canadian Avalanche Association's Level 2 curriculum. Known as Module 1, the four-day classroom-based course focused heavily on human factors and decision-making and included several exercises designed to help students define their personality types and predispositions for risk. Comparing his past actions as a professional snowboarder with his current temperament in the mountains, he noted in his daily course log, "My attitude toward risk has sure moved in the conservative direction." After taking a hazardous attitude survey, he wrote, "When faced with a risk-taking scenario in the future I will probably have this survey pop into my head. . . . If there is nothing to gain by taking the risk, I have been programming myself to simply not even consider it."

Course instructors discussed everything from team-building desert survival scenarios to avalanche incidents to aviation crashes. Bruce Jamieson, one of Canada's most respected experts in the merging fields of avalanche mechanics, forecasting, and mountain guiding, spent a great deal of time sharing with the class his findings on spatial variability, one of the most complicated, if not wholly unpredictable, problems encountered in the snowpack. In layman's terms, this meant variations in snow depth on any given slope. Since the depth of snow is relevant to the stability of snow, guides are keenly interested in how to best identify where the shallow (weaker) areas are on a slope that appears uniformly smooth. If the snowpack is well consolidated without any weak "problem" layers, the variability of depth isn't as much of an issue. But if there are weak layers, then navigating through terrain gets trickier. You want to aim for the deep (or fat) snow, which is more likely to support weight and not trigger the volatile weak layer.

Think of a foot of snow like a giant sheet of inch-thick plywood. This plywood would not support the weight from one person, but stack together two, three, four sheets (two, three, four feet of snow), and it gets incrementally stronger. Now imagine that underneath those sheets is a layer of crystal glasses. Together they support the sheets (snow) above, but in places where the snowpack is thinner—like one sheet of plywood—a skier's weight is going to flex or break that plywood, shattering the glasses. Then the plywood drops down with a "whumpf!" and, if the slope is steep enough, starts sliding downhill atop all those shattered pieces of glass—everything once stable is now loose and crashing downhill thanks to gravity. It's a slab avalanche, racing down the mountain and taking out anything and everything in its path.

Deep slabs that persist through the winter are harder to trigger, but the amount of snow on top and the depth of the slab make them increasingly more dangerous. Jamieson described this dichotomy as "lower probability, higher consequences."

The mechanics behind an avalanche are fascinating, but devilishly difficult to predict. The odds of avoiding them are increased by sticking to certain types of terrain, avoiding avalanche paths, and limiting numbers—that is, overall weight massed in a concentrated area—as well as limiting exposure across a slope and in avalanche funnels such as couloirs, gullies, and ravines. It all comes back to levels of acceptable risk, which dovetails nicely into the importance of decision-making. This course was designed to help students identify their predispositions to risk and further understand why they tended toward that outcome.

Craig came to the conclusion that, as a guide, "one of my biggest challenges is thinking for the client and operation instead of myself and that has helped me to realize that risk taking is in my control. One thing I do know is that if I spend enough time exposing myself to higher risk situations, I will eventually get caught."

CRAIG RETURNED HOME on November 17 to a large envelope from Dwayne Congdon summarizing the assistant ski guide program. The program was broken into three components: mandatory guide training (mechanized and touring); a voluntary practicum; and the final exam. "Mountain skills are introduced from the perspective of ski guiding including rope work, crevasse rescue, navigation, and snow craft; . . . client care on day and multi-day trips, terrain choice, and transceiver rescue skills . . ."

Breezing through the letter, Craig felt confident he was prepared for everything that was going to be thrown at him—until he got to page 6, which described in detail how his downhill "skiing skills" would be screened in two runs, the first being a "technical run" that demonstrated his "technical knowledge of alpine skiing," with "a variety of turns appropriate to the terrain and conditions" in order to illustrate to a client a basic knowledge and foundation of ski technique. The second was a "terrain run to demonstrate how a skilled skier anticipates the terrain, adjusts the alpine technique to illustrate a dynamic, athletic, and controlled descent . . . of over 400m vertical in tracked or variable snow conditions, using touring/or alpine telemark gear and a light pack. This is not a demonstration run to a client, but an evaluation of the candidate's skiing skills in varied conditions."

Had Craig missed something in his earlier conversations with Zacharias? Had he missed something in Congdon's acceptance letter from October 9? There had been nothing about skiing, and Craig had made it a point to clearly state in all of his correspondence that he would be splitboarding. He'd worked his tail off for an entire year, checked every box, only to get this change-up at the last minute—and if he had to ski downhill there was no way he'd pass the course.

The next day, his worst fear was confirmed via a phone call to Congdon. While the ACMG had accepted him into the course as a splitboarder, this did not change the screening requirements. The technical committee had decided (and had thought Craig understood) that he still had to exhibit both the technical and terrain runs on split skis as part of his mountain skills screening process.

Craig was livid when he sat down to gather his thoughts and formulate his argument for a follow-up conversation he planned to have with Zacharias. It was "fundamentally not correct to make me ski—I guide best on a board and am competent and effective," Craig wrote in his spiral notebook.

Demonstration runs should be done on a board. [It would be] bad for my overall presentation to do full judged run on my skis, [I should be doing] it on guiding gear. I can do a [split]board version of skills and timing of use. If I score lower here on skis than an aspirant on skis who does not pass skills training then it would not be easy to pass me, for his sake.

The [guiding] history/principle [should not be a] determining factor now in 2002. Yes in 1990, but times have changed. It is a new world.

Having to ski to guide is old school mentality, similar to what ski areas, SKI PATROLS, and even Heli Ops once said about guests [who were on snowboards]. Now snowboarders represent, often 40 percent of business. I would be more effective than a skier as liaison/guide to most snowboarders yet still okay for skiers.

Guides I have been with agree I am ready and good to guide. Let's change the hand book to allow snowboarders. I can help write the standards.

Neither Congdon nor Zacharias can recall specifics of Craig's follow-up phone calls. He never lost his cool, but he was "quite concerned about the short timeline to pick up new skills," says Zacharias, who does remember discussing the ski skills screening with Congdon and suggesting a compromise of sorts. "I advocated for participants on a snowboard to be able to complete the terrain run [aka free run] in snowboard mode, but still require them to show that they can ski in split mode as well [the demo run] in intermediate terrain. . . . The technical committee agreed to this."

In the end, whether it was politics, a misunderstanding, or miscommunication, the timing sucked.

To MAKE MATTERS worse, on November 20, a warm front moved in over British Columbia, the type of wet low-pressure system that had interrupted early winters more and more in recent years. For three days, significant amounts of rain fell up to treeline in virtually all of the Canadian mountain ranges, while rain mixed with sleet fell at even the highest elevations, which made for wet, slushy, altogether crappy conditions for Craig to practice downhill skiing in the backcountry. Conditions grew not just miserable but dangerous when temperatures dropped back to freezing on November 23, and the rain and sleet froze into a solid icy crust, upon which acres of vertical hoarfrost formed. Two weeks of cold temperatures with little wind to scour the hardened surface nurtured the frosty formations and allowed them to persist. They shattered with a tinkling sound as Buffery's splitboard skis glided through them during an exploratory tour with Craig.

Stopping among the trees in a windless hollow adjacent to a creek, Buffery crouched down to scrape a patch of the crystals onto a metal card and examined them with a magnifying loupe. When magnified, a single crystal transformed into feathery branches of ice; each feather shot outward from a central stem with twisted, otherworldly splendor. They were perfect specimens, like nothing he'd seen in his two decades of studying snow. He handed the card over to Craig, who squinted into the loupe, mesmerized. "They're beautiful."

"And deceptive," added Buffery.

THESE EARLY SEASON conditions presented a textbook example for Craig of what Buffery believed was a wicked foundation for future avalanches. He anticipated this layer would become a slow-to-heal instability that Craig would encounter as he pushed deeper into the mountains in coming months, forcing him to make the kinds of hard decisions he would have to on his own at some point.

"You'll have to really watch this November 20 layer," Buffery couldn't help himself from punctuating the point. "It's going to have to do a lot of healing."

Craig had heard Buffery say this before, just the previous winter in fact, but the difference between that November and this one was the two weeks of windless cold following the rain and freeze. It was the reality of the mountains. Every year presented its own challenges.

"Once it snows," Buffery added, "I'd be really wary of riding anything very steep—all aspects. Be super conservative in your route-finding, too." He was preaching to the choir. At this stage in Craig's training, Buffery knew he was stating the obvious, but all his instincts told him to be vigilant. He'd encouraged Craig to take on the challenge and responsibilities of guiding, and he was excited for his friend, but at the same time he couldn't deny the quiet worry he felt in the pit of his stomach.

CHAPTER 17

LAYERS

WHITEWATER SKI RESORT, NELSON'S LOCAL ski area, had snow on the ground but the lifts weren't yet running. It was barely light out as Craig separated his splitboard, affixed the climbing skins, strapped into the skis and started climbing with stoic determination all the way to the top . . . of the bunny slope.

"Goggles down, gator pulled up over his face so nobody would recognize him," says Mark Fawcett.

Two sessions going downhill on icy groomers was anything but "the smooth groove" of Craig Kelly lore. With his heels lifting and soft boots flexing, Craig's legs were as rickety as a just-born colt: all of the ambition but none of the control. If he didn't lock down the heels on these bindings, he was doomed.

He called in a four-alarm fire to John "JG" Gerndt and Chris Doyle, his "mad scientist" pals at Burton's research-and-development "lab," alerting them to check the fax machine, which spit out a pile of papers. Their mission was to transform Craig's ideas—sketched out in surprising detail—into a mechanism that would allow him to quickly (without tools) lock the heels of his bindings for downhill (skiing) mode or unlock for uphill (walking) touring mode.

Doyle flipped on the lathe, turned on the mill, pulled down his safety goggles, and got to work shaping and grinding metal into a working prototype he had boxed and at the local FedEx hub in time for their last truck to rush it to the airport.

A truck pulled up in front of Craig's house the following evening and delivered, though not exactly what he had conceived, something that amazingly worked. With his binding heels locked, Craig started thrashing his way down steeper groomed runs at the ski hill. Not knowing what kind of terrain the examiners would choose for his demo runs, he pushed himself into patches of moguls and in and out of trees, skiing as fast and hard as he felt comfortable without risking injury. In little more than a week, he would have to hold his own beside a bunch of guides who could ski, in some cases, as good as he could ride. He felt like an all-star righty batter being told he had to switch-hit for the World Series.

JUST A FEW days before the mechanized course, Craig sat down for the first major interview he'd allowed in his schedule since returning from Chile. It was for *Frequency: The Snowboarder's Journal*, a new magazine launched by four of Craig's friends—former *Snowboarder* editor Jeff Galbraith; photographers Ari Marcopoulos and Chris Brunkhart; and pro snowboarder Jamie Lynn.

Craig told Marcopoulos that he had not been reading the snowboarding mags or watching the videos and had no idea what the latest trends, tricks, or superstars were. "I'm really quite out of it," Craig said, "but I really like some of the smaller backcountry magazines like *Couloir*. I enjoy reading stories about people working so hard, and who've stuck it out with a sense of adventure, not knowing what was going to happen and came through and scored. . . . I'm honestly not that concerned with what's modern, or what's up-to-date, or what's cool, stylish. . . . The smile after a good run, to me, is all I need to know about snowboarding."

Craig had just completed the Module 1 Avalanche course, and spoke for a time about snow science, which prompted Marcopoulos to ask if there was a point beyond science where avalanche "prediction is impossible . . . where nature is beyond that control."

Craig replied yes, there are "limitations to what we do know right now about the snow, because our observation skills are limited. Our ability to see through the snowpack and see what is happening everywhere with the snow in a given month is not possible. It may never be possible. . . . We've reached a point like in quantum mechanics, and molecular or atomic physics, where we can't go any farther by looking at it. Right now, we're at a stage where the variability of the snow, from one little place to another, is the biggest issue for us.

"That may mean there are rocks under the snow, but how deep? You can't tell because it's all smoothed over mid-winter. A thinner snowpack in certain places may mean it's a weaker snowpack in that area because the crystals might be faceting due to a higher temperature gradient. There are so many things we don't know.

"We can't see underneath the snow, so the best thing you can do is feel it with a probe. . . . You dig your pit off to the side but you never know what it's like 20 or 30 feet over. That's a lot of what they teach now; in the high-end coursework they call it, 'spatial variability.' . . . You'll find a lot of papers written on this which basically say the more we study, the less we can rely on our observation skills. We have to be more intuitive. . . ."

A WEEK AFTER that interview, the barometer began to drop, and ever so slightly snow began frosting the mountains of British Columbia with a thin but welcome layer of fluff.

These were the conditions on December 8, 2002, when Craig strapped into his skis, locked down his heels, and waited his turn atop a sparsely wooded bench in the lower reaches of Cottonwood Bowl at Monashee Powder Adventures (MPA). The open slope beneath him was steeper at the top, maybe 27 degrees, that decreased in angle as it descended through some mild rollers before terminating on a cat road a few hundred vertical feet below. Of the more than eighty applicants who had applied for the assistant ski guide course, twenty-four had made the cut but, for reasons now unknown, only nineteen of these actually arrived at the course. Having completed their demonstration run, they were gathered together on the cat road below, waiting to see if this snowboarder could actually ski.

One of the applicants who'd made it through was Jeff Bullock, a twenty-six-year-old snowboarder who had taken up telemarking several years before as a way to better access powder in the backcountry. Bullock considered Craig a childhood hero and couldn't believe it when he saw his name on the course list. On day one in the MPA lodge, he approached Craig. "I was kind of shy and it's an intimidating course, a lot of really skilled athletes, so I just said, 'Hey, how's it going?' and he was really, really nice. He showed me his splitboard and this innovative heel lockdown system. You could tell he's very thoughtful, you could see that in him, right? A lot of these guys in these courses are pretty macho, the egos are a little out of hand, they're ready to take on anything. But with Craig, you could tell he was at a place in life where he didn't have to show that. He seemed very relaxed, super chill. I told him how I was a snowboarder too, and he gave me a little Burton tool and said, 'Put this in your pack, you might need it someday.'"

On the inside, Craig was "very stressed-out about the skiing," says Savina. "He didn't want to blow it, and was still pretty upset he had to do it at all. But he had trained as much as he could . . . was as ready as he could be."

Craig hid the stress well. Zacharias, the course leader, and Congdon, the technical director, were both taken by Craig's relaxed calm—more so after they answered a few of his questions about their expectations for the skiing demonstration. "This would have included setting a downhill track, downhill kick turns, slide turn, wedge turns, and parallel turns, but keeping it slow, as if you're getting a client down lower-angle terrain," recalls Zacharias, who made it clear to Craig that he would not have to ski on the bigger, high-speed terrain run, saying, "That one you can just ride your board." This no doubt helped Craig focus on the transceiver rescue skills, snowpack and weather-gathering skills, basic map and compass skills, and rope-handling skills, all of which he had breezed through during the first two days of the course.

Though competitive, the candidates were not direct competitors with each other. There were not a limited number of seats at the certified guides' round table; all of them had a place if they had the skills. As such, Craig didn't hide the fact he was nervous, and word got around that he had only learned to ski downhill in recent weeks. Still, few noticed when Craig slipped away into the dark and practiced stem christies (aka wedge turns) by headlamp on a chopped-up, chunky, and frozen section of the cat road, preparing for the worst but hoping for the best.

On day three, temperatures were cold, visibility was good, and a few inches of powder atop a firm base squeaked beneath their ski bases as all nineteen candidates lined up across that bench in lower Cottonwood Bowl to be critiqued by Zacharias from the top, and Congdon and another examiner at the bottom. While the run beneath them wasn't technical, the turns needed to be.

Congdon reminded them to "demonstrate it as if you've got a beginner skier behind you, use the technique that you want the client to replicate using a variety of turns appropriate to the terrain and conditions."

One after the next, the candidates showcased their turns and techniques while Craig hung at the back until only he remained, a lone figure against the skyline. Reaching down, he tightened his bindings, then did it again—that same compulsive competition ritual he'd never outgrown. Arms forward, split skis parallel, he dropped into his lane, reaching and planting his poles to initiate his turns. On the steeper upper slope, he tightened the turn radius and opened up the radius as the incline mellowed, which was exactly what the examiners wanted to see—as well his fellow candidates who welcomed him to the bottom with a collective cheer. "I felt like I'd just won the U.S. Open, and my most technical trick was a wedge turn," he later told Buffery. Someone had snapped a picture of his run, which ultimately made it into a course photo album with the caption: "December 8, 2002. Craig styles the split board for Dwayne Congdon @ the first ACMG Mechanized training on the slopes of Monashee Powder Adventure. This guy was not your average Joe."

Next, snowcats shuttled the candidates to the top of Cottonwood Bowl, where steep if not vertical upper walls funneled out into a terrain garden of cliffs, rollers, and wavy, wind-sculpted heaven with ample opportunities for air if a candidate was willing to risk a fall.

"Adjust your technique to illustrate a dynamic [1,500 vertical feet] descent in variable conditions," said Zacharias. "We want athleticism, control, and speed. This is NOT a demonstration run for a client; this is a freerun to show us what you've got."

After two and a half days of exams, everybody let off some steam and ripped. But as the only snowboarder, Craig's line was "unique," recalls Congdon. "He rode it at Mach 5," recalls Zacharias. "Cliff, airs, he hit this big bump midslope and landed way downslope, and then carved up onto another big bump like a wave, a big, arcing stall turn, throwing snow and just showing his mastery, like this wasn't a demonstration, this was pure fun. And I think for everybody there, because of what happened later, we'll always remember that."

CONGDON HAD NEVER heard of Craig before emailing him the previous summer, but he came to admire him, not only for his abilities but because he was "a humble and respectful student," says Congdon. "His participation was as much an education for us—the instructors—as it was for him."

The examiners were so impressed, they invited Craig to conduct a presentation on guiding snowboarders the last night of the course. "We sort of threw it at him at the last moment," says Congdon, "so he didn't have a lot of time to prepare, but it was very well received. He really showed us the way forward in terms of ultimately having a rigorous program that recognized the splitboard as a valid guiding tool, and to help us get to where the best snowboarders are treated as an equal to the skiers. It was an important first step for the ACMG on that journey."

COME CHRISTMAS, THERE was no time for extended holiday travel for Craig, Savina, and Olivia. After a slew of "We love you, we miss you, Merry Christmas" phone calls to each and every member of their family, they saddled up the truck with plans to snowmobile out to a remote cabin in the woods, where they'd light a fire, decorate a tree, and celebrate a little white Christmas—just the three of them. Savina simply remembers the adventure as "classic Craig." On New Year's Eve, they joined their Baldface family up at the lodge. Jeff and Paula Pensiero, Buffery, and a host of locals enjoyed a bar stocked with top-shelf libations and tables topped with a meal fit for royalty. "Happy New Year!" they screamed as the clock struck midnight. They kissed. They raised up their champagne flutes, beer cans, and shot glasses and called out toasts to health, happiness, peace, and lots and lots of powder.

Indeed, it had been storming off and on since December 10, burying that frozen November 20 layer with the first of several feet of snow.

"A dragon," says Buffery, "sleeping under a blanket of powder."

..

THE SNOW GODS delivered again that New Year's Eve, and the entire crew brought in the new year by snowboarding fresh powder on January 1, 2003. This included twenty-month-old Olivia, who found her usual spot in the pack on Craig's back as they rode together as a family down mellow glades and enchanted tree runs. It was probably the first time Olivia experienced floating and gliding through truly deep feather-light powder, a sensation that even her dad had a hard time describing.

For years, people had asked Craig what it was like, and he'd always been stumped until it finally came to him during an interview for *Snowboard Life* in 1999.

"Flying," he said. "That's probably the best I can describe the feeling I get when I'm riding deep powder. It's like flying—playing with gravity on a mountain covered with clouds. I've read a lot about dreams, and some people say, if you dream about flying, you are probably at a good place in life where there aren't any constraints, nothing's holding you down, you feel complete freedom. . . . So, some people dream about flying, I dream about riding powder. There's your answer."

Craig, Savina, Olivia, and Buffery spent that morning and most of the afternoon flying down the mountains together. Years later, Buffery had one word to describe that day—everything from Olivia's rosy cheeks to Craig's joyful smile.

"Magic."

CHAPTER 18

THE DRAGON
STIRRED

THE NEXT PHASES OF CRAIG'S training and certification process would include the Level 2 avalanche course at and around Rogers Pass on January 7 to 14, then the "guide training touring" on February 9 to 15. Upon completion of the guide training touring, examiners would either invite candidates to take the assistant ski guide exam or recommend they get more experience and return the following winter.

The ACMG encouraged candidates to participate in a practicum to prepare them for the exam in March. Craig squeezed his in between the Avy 2 and Touring Course, to better his odds of getting invited to the exam. According to the ACMG, the purpose of the practicum is "to create an opportunity for guide candidates in training to observe realistic guiding situations and balance theory and actual guiding practices. . . . It is recommended that the practicum student observe a business in terrain that he or she is not already familiar."

With all this in mind, Craig reached out to Ruedi Beglinger.

AT THE POINT Craig called him, Beglinger had led clients through the complex glaciated terrain of Selkirk Mountain Experience for eighteen years without a single serious injury or avalanche fatality.

"Craig understood the importance of mentorships and considered many of his friends as mentors," says Savina. "He had this unbelievable way of really seeing people—finding resonance with aspects of them that was really beautiful and admirable, and simply not focusing on aspects that maybe others saw as flaws. Ultimately, Craig understood fallibility and nobody's perfect, right? We're all human. He never let polarizing views color his perspective."

Regardless of the fact that Buffery knew Craig was not a pushover and would form his own opinion, he had advised Craig, "Never feel like you need to acquiesce to a guide with more experience, because you've got a ton of mountain miles yourself. If you find yourself in a place that you don't like or you don't want to be, you owe it to yourself to say something."

Buffery understood SME was loaded with complex, big terrain, and that Beglinger guided with an old-school European my-way-or-the-highway style and pushed it hard. That, combined with the complicated "spooky" snowpack concerned Buffery, who sent Craig off "without really discussing the snowpack or Ruedi's reputation," says Buffery. "I told him, 'You're Craig Kelly, and you are going to get a different experience with a different guide who's not at all like me. Glean what you can, but just stand strong in who you are and what you know.'

"I've gone over that conversation in my mind a million times. . . ."

JUST TWO DAYS into 2003, the sleeping dragon stirred.

Widespread avalanche activity was broadcast on the InfoEx, the Canadian Avalanche Association's private daily exchange of technical snow, weather, and avalanche information. This confidential exchange had begun in 1991 following a fatal avalanche at Canadian Mountain Holidays, where nine out of a group of thirteen heli-skiers were killed on a run called Bay Street. What had originally been the sharing of avalanche reports via telephone calls among neighboring mechanized, ski area, or touring operations was formalized by the InfoEx utilizing cutting-edge technology of the time—aka fax machines. Each evening piles of faxes were collated, compiled, and often retyped by a clerk who redistributed them as a single report that night or the following morning.

The fax evolved to emails, then to a rudimentary website; in 2003 subscribers were just beginning to both submit and read reports via the internet. The CAA describes this private system as a "platform for candid and timely exchange of critical observations and assessments to enhance the decision-making context for subscribers." These include avalanche forecasters who review the widely reported data to distill it for regional distribution to public avalanche bulletins such as those issued by the Canadian Avalanche Association (now known as the Avalanche Canada Foundation) and the Avalanche Control Section of Parks Canada at Rogers Pass.

Thirty-plus years after its inception, the InfoEx data remains closely guarded and unavailable to the public. An eventual investigative report, however, would provide a summary glimpse into the InfoEx reporting from the northern Selkirk region during the early weeks of 2003:

> January 2: Widespread natural and explosive triggered avalanches up to size 2.5 on all aspects: 1 size 2 SR [skier remote: This means the weight of a skier triggered a failure in the snow, and an avalanche released some distance from that trigger point] West [facing slope], 1700 Meters [Elevation]; 1 size 2 SR, Southeast, 2000 meter. January 3: Widespread natural and explosive triggers to size 3.5. January 4: Widespread natural and explosive triggered to size 3; 1 size 2 SR, East, 1500 meters, 1 size 2 SR, West, 2200 meters, 1 size 3 SR, East, 2200 meters. January 5: Widespread SR and HR [helicopter remote, similar to skier remote but triggered by the weight of a helicopter]. This triggered an avalanche up to 500 meters away.

By January 7, more than twenty avalanches in the northern Selkirks had been reported, all of which identified the November 20 rain crust as the "failure plane": the dragon.

A few days into January—and a few days after Craig had reached out to Beglinger via email—he received a response. Like most of the remote touring operations in BC, Selkirk Mountain Experience used either two-way radio or satellite phone to communicate with the outside world. Linking up to the internet via sat phone was slow, expensive, problematic, and sometimes impossible, so Paula Couturier, SME's office manager down in Revelstoke—a small town and tiny pulse of civilization at the base of these remote mountains—would sometimes relay important emails over the phone and Beglinger would then dictate a response.

The short note welcomed Craig to join SME for his practicum either the week beginning January 18 or February 8. January 18 was the only option for Craig since the Guide Training Touring course started February 9. Savina's birthday was January 19, but Craig would find a way to celebrate that before or after the trip.

"He was the most organized, mellow person I ever met," recalls Joe Pavelich, an assistant ski guide at Baldface whom Craig carpooled with on the way to the CAA Level 2 course on January 6, 2003. "I was going to drop him off at the [Halcyon] Hot Springs after the course," says Pavelich. "He'd rented one of those little cabins for Savina's birthday. He had it all planned out. On the way to the course in Golden, we were gonna stop for a quick ski up at Rogers Pass. That was the plan anyway until we hit this straightaway and there's this dude coming at us in his lane, doing donuts, spinning out of control. No time to think, it was just 'holy crap' and with my driving ninja reflexes, I pulled quickly onto the shoulder of our lane, and he slid over, still spinning, and clipped the back end of my pickup. It sent us spinning like a top into the oncoming lane, and there's this big semitruck coming toward us, horn blaring. We slammed into the snowbank, and the truck whipped past us. It would have annihilated us. We looked down the road, and the car was still spinning and suddenly it flipped over the embankment and rolled down into the creek. We ran over, people were getting out of the car and climbing back up the embankment. I was in shock, and we just looked at each other, heart racing, like 'That was so close.'"

Craig and Pavelich didn't talk as much the rest of the drive, focused on the road, life, and the coursework ahead of them.

Scott Rowley, Craig's Kiwi surfing buddy from Seaside, can't remember why he called Craig that evening. "Maybe to share something about a board I was shaping or the surf," he says. "What I do remember clearly was Craig describing that truck flying past a few hours earlier, 'Just inches away,' he said, and how 'in an instant everything could have been different.'" He also recalled talking about how it sucked for Craig being away from "Sav and Oli," but how happy he was to be taking such a technical course, because, as he told Rowley, "I don't want to get blindsided."

"At this time, the Level Two was the pinnacle of avalanche education in Canada," says Mark Vesely, a ski guide who joined Craig on both the Mod 1 and Level 2 courses. "You passed that course and there was almost an assumption that you were a forecaster. That would change over time, but it was as high as you could go in the CAA and everybody approached it differently."

While Vesely had goals to work avalanche safety at a ski area, others aimed for the British Columbia Ministry of Transportation, to protect motorists and keep the highways open. "We'd be talking about a big slope above a road or highway," he says. "Different approaches, like explosives and trigger points, how to protect the road, and Craig would listen and take it all in, then redirect it to 'How do we look at that from a guiding perspective? How would you move a group of people across that slope?'"

For seven days, the class was in the field from 7 a.m. till nearly dark, doing avalanche training—examining recent slides, crown profiles, etc.—in areas ranging from Kicking Horse Mountain Resort to Rogers Pass. "We were just starting to see this deeply buried November layer and another layer—we called it the Christmas layer—starting to react," says Larry Stanier, a course instructor who had also been Craig's Level 1 course instructor in 1996. "It was a very dynamic teaching environment. Case in point, we learned a skier had triggered a big Class Three avalanche up on Rogers Pass, so we went up to investigate."

That skier, a guide from New Zealand, was coincidentally one of Vesely's roommates back in Revelstoke, so Vesely was able to share with the class specific details. The skier had been ascending, breaking trail up onto Bruins Ridge, when the snow changed and got shallower. As he moved onto some wind-scoured crust, he felt a huge settlement and the entire slope cracked five hundred meters across—five football-field lengths—just a few meters below him. Luckily, he and his partner had been above the fracture line. If they'd been on it, or below it, they would have been taken for a ride, injured, buried, or worse.

It took several hours for the class to reach the avalanche site. *Wow, this is huge, definitely a scary place and a scary layer,* Vesely thought at the time. The depth of the crown ranged from 40 centimeters, just below where the skier's track had been, to 100 centimeters deep, and traveled 150 meters downhill. To really understand the mechanism that caused this failure, the class used their shovels to dig a fracture-line profile, a meter-and-a-half pit into undisturbed snow. That can be sketchy on a steep slope, "like going up and tickling the dragon's ass," says Stanier. This slide, however, was three days old, and what was going to come down had come down.

The pit provided a clear picture of the failure mechanism; the ski tracks crossing over a rocky area told the rest of the story. The slide had triggered the more-shallow December 25 Christmas layer, then stepped down to the deeper November 20 layer, and had run on a combination of faceting grains and buried surface hoar. After spreading out and digging some stability tests, the class found that the deeper snow was indeed quite stable, getting moderate to hard results, but shallow areas were hair-trigger, potentially deadly.

At the end of each day, students reviewed their field-book notes, considered their observations, and prepared their own snow stability forecast worksheets. Long columns of checkboxes spoke to the level of detail involved and included current weather observations (sky, precipitation—type, rate, air temperature, wind, snow surface, foot penetration, etc.) and evaluation factors (avalanche activity and testing, snowpack tests, significant weak layers, snowpack structure/slab properties, and snowpack cover—including depth variations, slope use, and compaction).

By the end of the week, Craig produced six forecasts and had, along with his fellow students, probably as good an understanding of the local snowpack as any avalanche professional working in Canada. His forecasts included concise advisories for terrain, as though they would be delivered to the public: "Caution in thin or rocky areas, especially on steep or solar aspects," he wrote. In his field book he'd noted that the upper snowpack seemed to be strengthening with cold temperatures, but his bottom-line terrain travel recommendation for the public was to remain wary: "Still possible to ski trigger avalanches, large propagation potential exists. Use good travel safety techniques and limit exposure to open slopes."

For understandable reasons, the CAA took this course very seriously. As such, not all students passed. Craig did, with "fully satisfactory scores in all field and technical skills." His last forecast, dated January 12, 2003, rated snow stability as fair at all elevation bands (alpine, treeline, and below treeline). It was snowing moderately, and winds were increasing, however, so conditions were "trending toward poor, with new snow and winds. Take extra care in shallow or rocky areas and steep slopes and watch for wind loading and slabs with new snow. Resist temptation to follow tracks into risky terrain."

While all the instructors of both the Mod 1 and Level 2—including veterans in the field Bruce Jamieson, Phil Hein, and James Blench—wrote positive comments regarding Craig's performance, Larry Stanier was perhaps the proudest to see Craig's evolution from the snowshoeing movie star he'd instructed in the 1996 Level 1 course. He recalls that one of Craig's most common questions in 1996 while evaluating terrain had been, "Do you think it's safe to drop that cliff right there?"

"Now you had to listen closely," says Stanier. "His questions about temperature gradients, and how faceting either increased or decreased depending on snow depth, ground cover, they were layered questions, which is like the snow, right? Those types of questions tell us, 'Right on, you're getting it. You've got questions, but you understand what's going on.'"

On the last day of the course, Stanier and Craig went their separate ways with a handshake. He knew Craig was soon heading to Selkirk Mountain Experience. "The northern Selkirks was the dragon's den, just in terms of the snowpack," he says. "Basically I said, 'Well, have a great time up there and keep your eyes open. It's going to be a hell of a learning week.' He was totally prepped and aware. There was no sense of concern, or anything like that. I think he was hoping to get a lot out of it. I mean this is scary and serious, but it's a good time. Holy smokes, this is where the learning is."

It was a far different drive heading back home over Rogers Pass for Pavelich and Craig, both of whom now had a better understanding of what it took to keep this road open. Passing a military truck towing a howitzer artillery cannon reminded them that the Selkirks were ground zero for Canada's longest-running military operation, known as the Snow War.

For more than fifty years, the Department of National Defence had deployed an artillery unit to battle the fierce avalanches that continually roared down the mountainsides with enough force to flatten buildings, clear forests, and take lives. Dubbed Operation PALACI, the armed forces' mission was to stop catastrophic avalanches from occurring naturally, lest they block or destroy the Trans-Canada Highway, a passageway through the mountains that was Canada's only major south-to-north thoroughfare in the region for both freight and ground transportation.

The military was part of a complex apparatus of science, technology, and machinery that sprang into action when forecasters from Parks Canada or the BC Ministry of Transportation attacked sleeping avalanches. Howitzers shot heavy exploding shells at the start zones of notorious avalanche paths, or less-damaging Gazex cannons—three-meter-high vessels filled with propane and oxygen—placed at the start zones ignited with a spark when remotely activated. The explosive percussion of air collapsed weak snow layers and triggered manageable avalanches that either stopped short of the road or were quickly cleared by snowplows on standby.

It's a 24/7 job all winter long in the Selkirks, where the seemingly endless snowfall can be a blessing or a curse, depending on your vantage point. The region is a magnet for tourism and the gateway to the powder capital of Canada. The bulk of these travelers come for lift-serviced terrain at a handful of ski areas, while those with deeper pockets snowboard or ski untracked snow at many of the world's premier helicopter, snowcat, and backcountry touring operations.

Those operations are remote, and accordingly each must function with its own mandated risk management plan in the event of emergencies. Operations have agreements of reciprocity in place with neighboring enterprises that will drop everything and come to their aid: search-and-rescue dog teams, emergency medical technicians, and guides armed with shovels, avalanche probes, and trauma kits, all of which are transported by helicopters flown by expert mountain pilots who, despite their skills, can only fly as visibility allows.

The Selkirk Mountains are geographically spectacular, but it's the depth and quality of the snow that reels in powder hounds from around the world. It's been called a white-gold adrenaline rush, snowboarders and skiers having replaced the original adventurous souls who came to this frontier armed with shovels, pans, and pickaxes to test their luck up the creeks flowing into the Columbia River.

THE BIG BEND Gold Rush of 1865 kicked off after a prospector named William Downie and a crew of miners, including Henry "Hank" Carnes, discovered gold around Carnes Creek.

One hundred and twenty years later, in the early 1980s, Ruedi Beglinger camped in the same area, pondering where he might build his chalet, nestled 6,384 feet high in a floating city of mountains. And while Beglinger had inevitably been called to assist in several emergency search-and-rescue operations over the course of his twenty-two-plus years as a mountain guide, he'd never once, in eighteen years of operating Selkirk Mountain Experience, had to call for help. None of his guests had ever suffered a major injury, nor had there been any avalanche fatalities. For nearly two decades, the snow had been only a pure and joyous blessing, which Beglinger celebrated every time he shared a photograph of his guests skiing or riding deep powder or the quintessential image of his red-roofed, Swiss-style chalet framed between the walls of snow—ten, sometimes twenty feet tall—lining the walkway to the front door.

Carnes and other creeks originated from several glaciers high above the valley floor, which, Beglinger knew from his childhood and teen years spent exploring his native Switzerland, were a sign of consistently deep snows, a cornerstone for long ski seasons. The largest of these glaciers would be the namesake for his Durrand Glacier Chalet.

To describe to prospective customers why the Selkirks in general, and the Durrand Glacier area in particular, get so much snow, Beglinger and his wife, Nicoline, hired meteorologist Matt MacDonald to write for the SME website:

> The Columbia Mountains are the first major barrier to incoming moisture across British Columbia's Interior Plateau. The Northern Columbias which include the Monashees and the Selkirks receive some of Canada's highest annual snowfall.
>
> Located smack dab in the middle of the Northern Selkirks sits the Durrand Glacier. . . . From the Durrand Glacier, several glacial valleys fan out in a variety of orientations including the East to West Carnes Creek, the Southeast to Northwest Downie Creek, and the Northwest to Southeast Woolsey Creek. This medley of drainage orientations promotes convergences for each of the major atmospheric flows which ultimately results in enhanced snowfall. . . . Year after year these factors combine to give the Durrand Glacier some of the highest annual snowfall while many surrounding ranges experience large seasonal variability.

It was hard work running a lodge in this snowbelt, and while the heavy snowfall meant everybody on staff helps shovel, there is only one designated "snow shoveler." This person's main duty is to keep the heli-pad, doorways, decks, and walkways clear, though cleaning the outhouses, unloading groceries from the helicopter, and washing the dishes are also part of the deal. The arrangement includes room, board, and tips from guests, and if you can keep on top of everything, you are welcome to join the guests as they ski.

That sounded like a pretty good deal to an adventurous snowboarder named Dave Finnerty, who had been a paying guest in 2001, and then didn't stop writing letters until the Beglingers hired him for the winter of 2003. He'd been a loader at a grocery warehouse in New Westminster, a city near Vancouver, so the hard work came easy, but it was his kind heart and youthful spirit that earned him the secondary role as nanny to the Beglinger girls, ten-year-old Charlotte and eight-year-old Florina. That was his duty one morning during the second week in January, when he watched Beglinger and assistant guide Ken Wylie—who had accepted the job despite Chic Scott's warning—glide away from the chalet and disappear into the trees with a line of guests trailing behind them.

Finnerty joined Nicoline, the girls, and Wylie's wife, Nancy—hired as a fill-in cook for the week—for breakfast. They were chatting over their meal when Nicoline told Finnerty he'd be having some help shoveling in the next week. "There's a couple ski guide practicum students coming up to work under Ruedi," she said. "One of them is a snowboarder from Nelson . . . Craig Kelly is his name."

"Dave nearly fell off his chair," says Nicoline. "He was wide-eyed and gasping," and literally held on to the edge of the table with both hands.

"THE. Craig. Kelly?!" he said. "There is no way I am letting Craig Kelly do my work for me. Man, that guy is . . . Do you even know who he is?"

That night, Finnerty was so excited he used the chalet's satellite phone to call his girlfriend, Corinna, back in New Westminster to tell her the news. Finnerty had just turned thirty-one that week. What a birthday present!

When Finnerty had scored this job for the winter, he'd packed his bag carefully. Everything had to be transported to the remote lodge via helicopter, and there were weight limits. Aside from his clothing and snowboarding equipment, he'd brought with him some carefully chosen reading material, including a couple of books and two magazines: an issue of *Couloir* and Finnerty's favorite "backcountry" issue of *Snowboard Life*, the one that Craig guest-edited.

It had been one of the last magazines to feature Craig before he had dropped off the map, and now Finnerty felt like he was going to witness a tiny part of history. Craig Kelly was in training to become a mountain guide?

The news might help him to solidify his own plans. Because for Finnerty, this winter wasn't only about shoveling snow in order to snowboard; after shadowing Beglinger for the season, he intended to make a decision. He'd always been a planner and had his life with Corinna all mapped out on paper, a literal chart. But there was a floating question mark branching out at the end of this season, taking him one of two planned routes: firefighter or guide.

Craig was one of Finnerty's heroes, not in the sense that he wanted to emulate him as a snowboarder, but because of the sense of adventure he inspired.

"I'll write you all about it," he told Corinna over the phone. "I love you!"

After they hung up, she envisioned him bursting with excitement, probably unable to sleep, rereading that February 2000 issue of *Snowboard Life* that he'd kept all these years. She knew Finnerty had already gotten Beglinger to sign the copy of *Couloir* that featured him as "Guide for the Hardcore" on the cover; and there was no doubt in her mind he would find some appropriate moment to ask Craig to autograph his prized copy of *Snowboard Life*.

Beglinger conducted his business seven days a week. Every Saturday, roughly eighteen clients were flown in from Revelstoke by helicopter to Beglinger's spectacularly remote lodge adjacent to the Durrand Glacier. It was like a five-star (in wilderness terms) "base camp" from where they would push outward into the surrounding mountains in two guided groups, one guided by Beglinger and the other by an assistant ski guide. The job was to give the customers what they paid for: seven days of fully catered steep, deep, and wild powder snow, what *National Geographic Adventure* had rated in its fall 1999 issue as one of the "25 great adventures" in the world.

At 3:25 p.m. on Thursday, January 16, Beglinger was chest-deep in a snow pit on the 40-degree west face of Goat Peak, throwing shovelfuls of dry powdery snow onto the slope beside him.

Observing from the opposite side of the deepening hole was Ken Wylie, on day six of his first week as an assistant guide. Beglinger worked quickly, both because he and Wylie were exposed on a steep slope and because the seven skiers they guided remained twenty or so meters above them on the summit ridge awaiting instructions. Once Beglinger hit the ground, he set his shovel aside, then examined the wall of snow, looking for layers and probing into the snow—with his finger and the pencil he kept inside his guidebook—to see how compacted the snow was at various depths to the ground.

Down around where the November 20 layer would have been, Beglinger reached into the wall of snow and, according to Wylie, grabbed a gloved "handful of snow," examined the crystals with his naked eye, and then tossed it aside. His findings were noted exactly as follows on page 194 of his logbook for January 16, 2003, 15:25 hours:

Exposure	West
Elevation/Location	7300 ft, Goat Face
Incline	40 degrees
Test/Observation	Check on ground layer, Visual of whole profile
Comment	

[solid faceted crystals] on ground well consolidated to finger and pencil
•No specific layer with any threat

He climbed out of the pit, pushed some of the snow back into the hole, then strapped into his splitboard and began to "cut the slope" with a slight diagonal traverse, weighting the board aggressively, trying to get the surface snow to slough down. All the while he watched for telltale fracture lines, which might travel down into the snowpack and trigger a layer.

Wylie, meanwhile, had on his own initiative sidestepped with his skis a bit higher on the slope so if it did crack, he'd be above it. He zipped up his jacket and was ready to react, already pointing his skis toward his emergency exit route. This was steep terrain. If it did slide and you were caught in it, you'd get pummeled all the way down some 1,500 vertical feet. From this perspective and at this height, there were no trees to either hold on to or slam into. Everything looked white, but Wylie knew there were cliffs below, off to his right; he just didn't know the terrain well enough yet to recall exactly where they were. He trusted Beglinger—he had to trust him. Even though that was the haotioot pit he'd ever witneoocd, copccially knowing about that deeply buried layer, he trusted his local knowledge and expertise.

The snow didn't crack. It didn't even slough. In fact, the ski down was filled with impromptu hoots and hollers from the guests, whom Wylie followed down to a rally point, a bumplike ridge where he handed Beglinger the poles he'd mistakenly left on top before cutting the slope. Even stopping here, midslope, made Wylie nervous—but Beglinger's casual demeanor and the grinning, chatty guests reminded him that this was the type of terrain offered by SME. He'd better get used to it.

Beglinger would record the run as a final note to the day's "snow test/avalanche observations": "With skiing the Goat Face, the conditions proved extremely stable. SF [surface snow] sluffing was not able to fracture any slabs. Skied up to 40-degree incline."

Once at the chalet, as the guests looked back to admire their tracks, Wylie asked Beglinger if skiing that line had made him nervous.

"No," Wylie recalls Beglinger saying. "When I make a call, it's one hundred percent."

Wylie wondered to himself, *Like is he saying he's always right 100 percent of the time or he would only go if he was 100 percent certain it was safe?*[*]

He shrugged it off for the time being. *Maybe he is that good.*

THAT SAME DAY back in Nelson, Craig took Oli swimming at the community pool, which was probably shocking for some of the other parents who watched him wade out into water up to his chest, hold her out in front of him, spin her around to face him, and then let go, keeping his hands hovering close. It was another swim-to-daddy date. "She's okay," he'd tell the onlookers, "she's got this." One of their goals had been to make sure she was water-safe before turning two in mid-April, and already she could half-thrash, half-doggie-paddle to keep her head above the surface. That evening, Craig and Savina

---

[*]   All quotes/thoughts/descriptions from Ken Wylie come from a variety of sources including his book, *Buried* (Victoria, British Columbia: Rocky Mountain Books, 2014); emails and/or interviews with the author; as well as various podcasts. Many of the same topics in the book were discussed, confirmed, and in some cases expanded upon during interviews.

sat down at a table for two at their favorite bistro, the All Seasons Cafe on Herridge Lane in Nelson. With a sitter at home watching Olivia, they raised a glass three days early for Savina's birthday.

Early the next morning of January 17, Craig drove Savina and Oli to the Baldface staging area. "See you later," he said, holding Olivia. Then a hug and a kiss, before they parted ways—Savina and Olivia on the back of a snowmobile heading up to the lodge where she was working weekends as the in-house massage therapist, and for Craig, off to Revelstoke.

He drove his truck west from Nelson and then north up the rural Slocan Valley—a long, narrow wilderness passage through towering peaks—and through the village of Nakusp on the eastern shores of Upper Arrow Lake. Taking advantage of cell phone reception while he had it, he called first Gillian and Brian, his dad, and then his mom, whom he told briefly that he was on his way to do some more guide training, then focused on explaining to her the beautiful scenery he was driving through. Janet had long since stopped worrying about her son, knowing he was as comfortable and savvy in the mountains as most people are walking down the sidewalk in suburbia. "I just wanted to tell you I love you, Mom," he said. "I love you, Craig," she replied, and then the signal was lost.

PART III

THE
AVALANCHE

CHAPTER 19

WELCOME TO PARADISE

THE BIG BEND HIGHWAY WAS still in shadow a couple hundred feet below as the Selkirk Mountain Helicopters A-Star banked right over the Columbia River and began to climb, skimming treetops and frozen waterfalls as it ascended some eleven miles up the Carnes Creek drainage. Several minutes later, the forest began to thin, and suddenly they burst into the white lunar expanse of the alpine. Banking right again, skirting the seemingly vertical western flank of Goat Peak, the helicopter carrying Craig and three other passengers descended toward the red-roofed Durrand Glacier Chalet—perched in absolute solitude on a subalpine knoll with sweeping views of the Selkirks in every direction, their jagged peaks intersected by deep gullies, rock-lined couloirs, cornice-rimmed bowls, and miles upon miles of glaciers.

"Welcome to paradise," announced John Seibert, a fifty-four-year-old skier and return guest, over his headset moments before the helicopter settled onto the landing pad next to the chalet. There was a shuffle of people and gear, with Beglinger saying his goodbyes to the departing guests and hellos to the new ones, including Craig, who, with a big smile, reached out and shook Beglinger's hand as he stepped out onto the skids. The incoming guests dispersed, crouched low beneath the spinning blades, as Ken Wylie quickly unloaded their skis, Craig's splitboard, and duffels and stacked them off to the side. The outgoing guests and their gear were loaded, and then the helicopter lifted off with a flurry of powder to retrace its route down the creek for the next load. In between what would be five total flights in a well-choreographed routine,

Craig helped Wylie—whom he instantly recognized from his stints at Island Lake Lodge—schlep gear to and from the helipad. Also there was Jeff Bullock, the aspirant assistant ski guide Craig had met during his mechanized guide training weeks earlier at Monashee Powder Adventures. They were surprised to see each other, having both independently scheduled practicum weeks at SME, Bullock's taking place the week before. Beglinger had offered him the opportunity to stay on an additional week.

When the final flight of the day was on approach to the chalet, Wylie stood beside the last load of gear, which included the yellow backpack belonging to Nancy. Her week helping Nicoline in the kitchen complete, she was heading back to Revelstoke to work on their nearly finished house. It had been Wylie's idea to move to Revelstoke, and he could feel both the excitement and financial pressures of the life they were building. While chatting about tile and how she too was excited to move into their new home, Nancy's gaze settled on the looming west face of Goat Peak. "It was scary seeing you guys ski Goat Face the other day," she remarked, to which Wylie replied, "I was a little nervous up there in the big terrain myself, but it's all about committing to the guests."

His concerns about working at SME had been a nightly topic of discussion during their week together. Now he told her, "I have this chronic uneasy feeling up here, and I'm not sure whether it's caused by Ruedi . . . or by my fear of the hazards. When I'm around Ruedi, I just get all flustered and confused."*

Their conversation was interrupted by the incoming helicopter, which they loaded—both passengers and gear—together. Nancy was last to board after a goodbye hug in the doorway, then Wylie checked hers and the other passenger's seat belts, shut the door, and crouched just forward right of the nose of the aircraft, where he gave the pilot a thumbs-up. The helicopter lifted off, leaving Wylie alone to reflect on some of Nancy's last words to him: "You be safe up here."

THE GEAR SORTED and guests assigned to their rooms, Wylie chatted with Craig, whose celebrity, he noted, was as indiscernible now as it had been when

---

* Conversation excerpted from Wylie, *Buried*.

he'd guided him at Island Lake Lodge in 1998. There was barely time for a coffee before the staff and guests assembled in the chalet's dining room and Beglinger began that day's rendition of an orientation he'd polished over nearly two decades. First, he introduced himself and the staff, including Nicoline, who managed the chalet; Wylie; Kim Lomas, the chef; "our resident snow shoveler, Dave, and vee haf two practicum guide students with us, that's Jeff and Greg," which was how Beglinger, in his heavy Swiss-German accent, pronounced Craig's name. "Vee don't haf a lot of time for da introductions, I think, you vil all introduce yourselves later, so vee can get skiing, but first da schedule, and Nicoline vil tell you a little bit about the chalet and how vee do tings here."

There was a palpable buzz in the room, recalls Rick Reynolds, a forty-five-year-old contractor from Truckee, California. He was with fellow Sierra Nevada/Tahoe locals Rick Martin, a fifty-one-year-old electrician; Kathleen Kessler, a thirty-nine-year-old realtor; Bruce Stewart, a forty-five-year-old builder; Keith Lindsay, a forty-three-year-old contractor; and Heidi Biber, a forty-two-year-old nurse and three-time return guest who had organized the trip. All six were serious backcountry telemark skiers and fired up to be there. "It's remote," says Reynolds. "No roads, no snowmobiles parked out front, no chairlifts snaking up the mountains. Once the helicopter drops you off, you look around and you know you're in for a wild week with a bunch of . . . if they're here, they're your kind of people. Physically fit, hard-charging expert-level skiers who want to get a lot of vertical. The sooner we could get out of that welcome meeting and hit it the better."

A week at SME was not for the unfit or the faint of heart. "You signed your life away," says Biber, "same as you do at all backcountry ski operations." It's an ironclad legal document with language modeled after the waiver and release of liability contract that guests had signed prior to the 1991 Bay Street avalanche, the same tragedy that had led to the founding of CAA's InfoEx. Nine heli-skiers had been killed that day but the guide survived, and the waiver held up in court, setting the precedent for all cases that followed. If you were going to ski in Canada, you were releasing the operation of any liability, including "negligence on the part of the operators or its guides." Therefore, careless mistakes or even inattention that led to injury or death were forgivable in a court of law. Gross negligence, however—reckless or deliberate disregard for the reasonable treatment or safety of others—was not.

Each guest paid 1,500 Canadian dollars for a seven-day self-propelled powder adventure and accepted a laundry list of risks clearly stated on the waiver, including death. Telemarkers and snowboarders like Craig Kelly and Age Fluitman—a twenty-six-year-old Dutch snowboarder who grew up riding in Chamonix, and had cross-country skied but never splitboarded before this trip—signed an addendum: "NOTICE TO SNOWBOARDERS AND TELEMARK SKIERS—INCREASED RISK. Unlike alpine skiing . . . [telemark and snowboard] . . . boot/binding systems are not designed or intended to release. . . . These factors will increase the risk of not surviving an avalanche."

By the end of the fifteen-minute orientation, guests knew the outhouse was out front and the smaller, red-shuttered chalet upslope from the chalet was the Beglinger residence and guide room. On the path to the left was the sauna, and to the right was a little shop equipped with tools for ski repairs. Around the back of the residence was the weather station, where the guides monitored daily conditions. Beglinger methodically narrated the daily program for the next seven days: wake up at dawn; make lunch; eat breakfast at seven; assemble out front at eight; ski your butt off till three or so; return to the chalet and enjoy refreshments, read a book, have a nap or sauna; and then dinner was served promptly at six-thirty. Basic house rules included don't go in the kitchen, don't wear outside boots inside, and, most important, do *not* touch, start, or feed the fire, lest you receive a "gentle Swiss reminder."

An oft-circulated story from old guests to new was usually prefaced by two points: Beglinger painstakingly built this wooden chalet with very flammable local timber; and two, they don't airlift fire trucks up from Revelstoke. As the story went, back in the mid-1990s a very large Paul Bunyanesque woodsman from Alaska woke up early the first morning of his ski week, ambled downstairs, opened the stove, and stoked the fire—got it burning really hot to take the chill off. He stood up, warmed his hands for a few minutes, spun around to warm his ass, and found himself facing the piercing, steely blue eyes of the five-foot-seven Beglinger, who said, "Don't ever fucking touch that fire again."

That guest never returned to SME—unlike the familiar faces Beglinger saw this morning, some of whom had been returning for more than a decade. In addition to Heidi Biber from the Truckee crew, these returnees included Seibert, a geophysicist from Alaska on his fifth trip (four at SME itself, one doing the Haute Route with Beglinger in Europe); forty-eight-year-old Joe Pojar, on the second week of his eighth trip; twenty-seven-year-old Charles Bieler, a winemaker from New York on his third; twenty-eight-year-old Evan Weselake, a corporate trainer from Calgary on his fourth; Laura Jameson,[†] a travel agent from Seattle on her fourth trip; twenty-five-year-old Naomi Heffler, who had come hiking here with her family fifteen years earlier, and was currently on a gap year after graduating from the University of Calgary; and forty-year-old Jean-Luc Schwendener, a chef from Canmore, whose Swiss-family lineage was ski making. He had skied here several times and, like the other returnees, could mouth Beglinger's mantra: "We ski to the summits. The day's moving fast because you come here to ski and snowboard. There's no time, really, for hanging around much out there. If you want to hang around and relax, you can stay back here at the chalet. We have been doing this eighteen years, and never have we had a serious accident. But what we are doing has hazards, and this morning you all signed a waiver. That means that you understand those risks. We also have accident insurance you can pay in case you need a helicopter to get you out for an injury. That is not included. If you're interested, just see Nicoline. Otherwise, you will all be assigned an avalanche beacon, and we meet out front ready to ski in . . ." He looked at his watch. "Fifteen minutes."

EXACTLY FIFTEEN MINUTES later Beglinger and Wylie stood before sixteen men and four women whose worn and weathered gear announced that they

---

[†]   Laura Jameson is a pseudonym.

weren't weekend warriors, but rather serious skiers with lots of mountain mileage. In addition to the return guests and the Truckee friends of Heidi Biber, there were four other first timers: fifty-year-old Dennis Yates, a ski instructor from the San Bernardino Mountains, near Los Angeles; forty-nine-year-old Vern Lunsford, an aerospace engineer from Colorado; Dan DiMaria, from Aspen; and Erik Brentwood, from Los Angeles. SME office manager Paula Couturier, up from Revelstoke for a week of skiing, joined the group along with Jeff Bullock and Craig. Two-dozen people, many strangers to each other, whose names alone were hard enough to keep straight on paper, without taking into account uphill fitness, downhill skills, and overall demeanor when grouped up and asked to climb and then ski a mountain—or several of them in a row.

First on the agenda was the safety briefing, which took place a few hundred yards south of the chalet in a meadow called the Soccer Field. With avalanche transceiver turned on, thus "transmitting" a signal, each guest passed by Beglinger, who had his transceiver set on receive or "search" mode and stood as gatekeeper to the wilds. When each guest skied past, a loud beep indicated that the transceiver was functioning.

As the guests streamed down the trail, Age Fluitman was still in front of the chalet frantically setting up a brand-new Burton splitboard, bought two days earlier. Wylie was assisting him. "This guy 'Greg' came over and said, 'I got this,'" recalls Fluitman. "He put the skins onto the bottom of the skis, but they had not yet been cut to fit.‡ It was an embarrassing minute."

"Don't worry, I'm pretty fast at this," Craig said as he took out the tiny tool that luckily was still in the packaging. For the first-timer, cutting skins is a half-hour process, but Craig had them sized in about a minute per ski, and they joined the others at the Soccer Field, just as Beglinger began. The mandatory day-one SME Avalanche Beacon School, per his protocol, was to last at least one hour but not longer than one hour and ten minutes—a timeframe he had honed over time to deliver all the required information but not be so long that guests lost interest. He arranged them in a half circle so any sun, wind, or blowing snow was at their backs, then went over

---

‡   Brand-new skins were not pre-cut to fit the varied shapes of skis, and had to be placed on the split ski. The overhanging excess "skin" is cut off.

the Barryvox Opto 3000 digital beacon's functions: on/off, send, receive, volume control, and a built-in safety feature in the event that a secondary avalanche came down and buried a searcher who had turned a transceiver onto receive. A transceiver will revert to transmit after eight minutes on search if no keys are pushed.

Once he'd demonstrated the beacon's features, Beglinger explained how to react to an actual avalanche, the first thing being to yell, "Avalanche!" He then described what to do if an avalanche occurred while skiing up or touring up or across a slope versus while skiing or riding down.

Beglinger tells every group the same thing: "You cannot outski, you cannot outride avalanche. You must fight! With everything you have! To stay on the surface. Swim, kick, fight!" He explains how your adrenaline will be going and it will all happen very fast. But when the avalanche begins to slow down, "this will probably be the first time you realize fear," he says, "because everything has stopped and now you have time to think. But the worst moment comes right now. You will feel pressure onto you, and that is the upper slope coming down. That stuff has to come down too. Eventually you'll feel it crushing onto you, and you need to move!" With his arms in front of him, tight against his body, fists clenched, he demonstrates, wiggling his arms back and forth in front of his chest, "making room for your chest to expand," up with his hands to in front of his face, "to make an air pocket. Try and gain some space and then . . . it will be quiet. It will be dark."

It is an eerie and convincing demonstration to behold.

"There isn't much time," he continues, "and that is why we practice."

The school continues, outlining in meticulous detail all aspects from the search and rescue (if you're on the surface) to survival techniques (if you're buried), to mock rescue drills where guests team up to take turns burying one transceiver a couple feet under the snow in a general direction and practicing the skills they learn in a game of "hide and seek." Then to practice the worst-case scenario of multiple burials, the guests line up as though they were at the edge of avalanche debris and turn their backs. That day, Wylie ran out into the field and buried two transceivers hidden under squares of plywood, twenty to thirty meters out and in different locations. The guests turned back around, and Beglinger hit the stopwatch and said, "Go!"

The group homed in on both transceivers' signals, probed down, hit the plywood squares, and dug out both in about two and a half minutes. "In a real avalanche," Beglinger said, "it will be much harder snow, on a slope, and everything will be different than here, but you will be ready.

"Now," he called out, "we get some turns in!"

CHAPTER 20

SELKIRK MOUNTAIN EXPERIENCE

BEGLINGER DIVIDED HIS GUESTS IN two. He led "Group 1"—including Bullock and Craig—up and away from the soccer field. Breaking trail toward Woolsey Peak, his guests followed single file with a couple meters' spacing between them. Wylie's Group 2 followed fifty to a hundred meters behind.

This tour gave Wylie and Beglinger a preview of their group's overall dynamic and individual fitness, attitude, and personality. Each guest and, in this case, each apprentice guide, had his or her own story. Craig's, of course, came with the burden of celebrity and attendant skepticism.

Beglinger watched him closely. "I have to be honest," he says, "as much as I respected Craig as a driving force in snowboard mountaineering, as a famous person, as a world champion, I still wanted to see how he deals with the mountain, how does he move, can he split the snowboard fast, how helpful he is towards clients. Well, he came out of the helicopter and was right away helping people . . . then after we reached the first summit, Craig got down on his knees and ripped that board apart and put it together very fast. I wasn't even close to finishing my own when he jumped over to a client and helped pull his skins off. That is something young guides, you have to tell, 'Go and help other clients.' Not Craig."

Beglinger told both groups they would ski this bowl—"Boogie Basin"—with three-turn spacing. He dropped in and shredded turns to the bottom, with his group spread out behind him, a chorus of stoke-filled laughter and hoots sweeping down the bowl. The Selkirks had delivered. The snow was champagne-light and blew like feathers as the skiers arced through it. There was nothing but smiles as Group 1 regrouped one thousand vertical feet below, to the left of the descent, out across the flats and away from any sloughs or slides the group above might kick off. "See, this is how I get these," Beglinger said, smiling broadly, pointing at the deep, weathered lines at the corners of his eyes. "This is why we do this. Yes?!"

Ripping his climbing skins from his skis, Bruce Stewart, one of the Truckee crew—none of whom knew who Craig was—turned uphill and watched Craig as he made sweeping, effortless turns, throwing up walls of snow, popping off opportune drifts, never missing a beat while floating, if not levitating, down the mountain. *Whoa, that dude can ride!* Stewart thought to himself as Craig slid to a stop, snow crusted over his beanie, his own grin bursting and dusted with powder. "So good watching you guys rip that up," Craig told the group.

Any preconceptions Beglinger had about Craig's ego were swept away with the powder. "What I saw was a champion-caliber snowboarder, with a human touch. Already I can tell this person has everything he needs to become a very good mountain guide."

BEFORE THE GUIDES' meeting that evening, Craig showed Beglinger the heel lockdown system he'd designed, curious if Beglinger thought it would be a helpful feature to work into the production model. Though he liked the option, especially for traversing, Beglinger was not a fan of softboot bindings. "I have to tell you, Craig, I don't like this kind of binding," Beglinger told him. "The straps, you cannot get out. This is what I keep telling Chris."*

For his part, Beglinger showed Craig a quick-release system he had designed by threading a short length of parachute cord through a hole drilled into a bright orange golf ball and tying off the end with a knot. The other end of the cord was affixed to the toe clip of his plate binding, leaving roughly

---

* Chris Mask headed up the splitboard program at Burton. "Ruedi was adamant about using plate bindings and hardboots," says Mask. "He was a mountaineer and skier so hardboots were natural for him. He definitely said, 'It's about safety—not just style.'"

an inch of cord between it and the ball. He put his boots on, dropped the board to the ground, clipped into the bindings, and demonstrated. "You reach down with both hands, grab the ball, [yank up] and it's gone.

"There's no way you can do this in an avalanche with soft binding or even toe clips. You need something to grab onto quickly." Beglinger went on to explain the other benefits of this hardboot-and-plate binding system for uphill travel. "It's not sloppy, you can side-hill and climb much more efficiently."

Craig was a softboot-binding zealot, but to Beglinger, he seemed genuinely interested, telling him, "I don't know how to explain it to them at Burton, but I'm going to talk to them. I like the idea of plates for those reasons."

When Bullock and Wylie joined them in the guides' room, Beglinger moved on to discussing the runs they'd taken that day on Woolsey (Central) Peak and Elm Peak, and then logged the conditions and rated the avalanche hazard as "good" in the subalpine (treeline), lower alpine (up to 7,000 feet), and higher alpine (to the peaks) with "some partial windslabs of minor sizes." Beglinger rated the surface snow quality as excellent.

During the meeting, Wylie interjected periodically. Regarding quality of the skiing, he had noted some wind-effect snow on Elm Peak and thought it was too crowded with both groups on the same objective. "I think my group should be on a separate objective so it's not too crowded."

Wylie says that Beglinger responded that he was wrong, the skiing was "excellent . . . You don't know bad snow." Regarding the crowding, and his desire to separate, Beglinger told Wylie he didn't know the routes well enough to be off on his own. He also stressed to Wylie that it was "critical" the lower group skied well out of the range of any avalanches the upper group might kick off above.

"You don't want to nuke your whole group," Wylie recalls Beglinger saying.

DAY TWO DAWNED cold (–9.6C/14F) with no new snow and overcast with the cloud ceiling at 10,000 feet. Both groups headed out at 8 a.m. sharp and were soon skiing up the Ledges, a short and steep switchback accent of a nearby ridgeline that led to a narrow passageway into the alpine—and quick access to the Durrand Glacier.

Dennis Yates, the ski instructor from LA, was the only guest who stayed back, to nurse a sore knee; everybody else was gung-ho for a seven-hour loop tour of both the Durrand and Forbidden Glaciers. Six thousand vertical feet of skiing, including a long run from Forbidden Peak all the way down toward Fang Creek, another steep descent from the upper west face of Mount Durrand, ending with a mellow descent of the Durrand Glacier looping back to the Ledges.

Less than half an hour from the chalet, Wylie—leading Group 2—radioed Beglinger and told him guests were already having to wait for Laura Jameson to catch up to them. He suggested now was a good time for Jameson—a return guest whom Beglinger had also guided on the Haute Route—to return to the chalet. According to Wylie, Beglinger said, "No, Ken. You have to guide her. A good guide is able to manage the people he gets in his group."

It's difficult to manage complex group dynamics in real time, and it's this human element that creates the tension of guides who must be at once friendly facilitators, authoritarians, and businesspeople delivering a "product"—six thousand vertical feet of skiing—to paying guests. While the client is just chugging along, the guide is mentally tracking the route, the snow and safety, the client's health, the pace required to achieve a goal—usually a string of goals—and his group's ability to return to the lodge on schedule, while predicting which guests might get a second wind or crash as the day progresses.

Wylie's intuition told him Jameson wouldn't get a second wind. He called for a short break and asked discreetly how she was feeling, adding that she seemed to be struggling some. (If she bowed out here, near the chalet, Finnerty could ski up and escort her back.) Her response was short: "I'm fine." Even the strongest skiers have off days due to altitude, illness, whatever—but in this case, Group 2 was just very fit and quite fast. Their comfortable "go all day" pace was, for Jameson, pushing it hard, which was not an uncommon occurrence at SME. Groups regularly have one or two slower guests—in that case, the guide sets the pace up front for the slower client, which was something Beglinger had explained to Wylie.

Some fifteen minutes behind Group 1 at this point, Group 2 carried on and caught up to Beglinger just as his group had finished a tea break atop Forbidden Peak and was preparing to ski the day's major descent to Forbidden

Glacier, then down the glacier toward Fang Creek, well below treeline. Wylie skied directly over to Beglinger—catching him before he pushed off—to inform him that he didn't believe Jameson had the energy required to ski the distance even *downhill* to the creek, let alone back up.

Beglinger's response, according to Wylie, was "If you are a good guide, you can get her through it."

Nearby, Nicoline, who had joined Group 1 for the day, was listening in as Craig and Age Fluitman, the snowboarder from Holland, were gearing up. She recalls, "A few guests realized who Craig was and would quietly ask, 'Is that *the* Craig Kelly?' But Age had no idea he was famous, *and* probably designed Age's splitboard." She heard Age cursing while showing Craig how his board's top skin was peeling off at the nose. "Now I see why this board was half-price," he told Craig in English. "Shit board."

"No way, you got one of *those* boards?" Craig replied. "You scored. When that topsheet peels all the way off, there's a picture of a naked lady underneath."

"Ya? Seriously?" Fluitman responded, half-believing him.

Chuckling at the exchange, Nicoline pushed off the summit of Forbidden Peak and skied down the ridge behind her husband toward the north headwall, an up-to-40-degrees-steep and wide-open pitch with a big "bump" or rollover. Well above that roll, Beglinger stopped the group, then angled down onto the slope, probing deeply with his upturned ski pole. Feeling no weaknesses, or hollowness, he then skied over the bump, down and across the convexity where it was roughly 35 degrees, the "spicy" spot with the most tension and the least support and where, if there was a weakness, it was most likely to release and avalanche. No cracks appeared as he cut the slope. Says Beglinger, "This was a big slope, but safe to ski cut, good runout, a rollover in terrain. I probed, I skied it, cut it hard, it was perfect—it was a great run, but it also told me a lot."

Nicoline and Group 1 followed, laying beautiful tracks down more than a thousand vertical feet, and then regrouped, one-hundred meters out on the Forbidden Glacier. From the headwall, they trended right, down the vast terrain of the Forbidden Glacier toward the trees. To Evan Weselake, it was near three thousand vertical feet of untracked, pristine perfect powder—a heli-run minus the helicopter. They hit an elevation where a crust had formed, and stopped there for lunch, well above Fang Creek, and fueled up for the trek back up all they had just skied.

After giving his guests a ten-minute break atop Forbidden Peak, Wylie and his Group 2 followed off to the side of Beglinger's tracks, Rick Reynolds from the Truckee crew bringing up the rear. Reynolds watched Jameson fall several times, something he—as a former ski racer and coach—attributed to fatigue rather than lack of skills. They all regrouped at the same spot Beglinger had some fifteen minutes earlier. It was a great run, but when Reynolds saw the other group's serpentine tracks still descending, disappearing down the glacier that took them farther away from the chalet, he shuffled over to Wylie and quietly said, "I don't think Laura's got the gas to get back up this if we go too far down."

Wylie told Reynolds he was aware of the situation and was watching her. They then skied down the glacier, well off to the side of the other groups tracks, and stopped for lunch near the treeline. That's "when we saw Ruedi coming back up," says Reynolds.

Although Wylie's earlier intuition about Jameson's energy level had been spot-on, Beglinger never sent clients back to the chalet—especially just a half hour into the day—when they still had the heart and grit to go on. As he'd done in the past, however, he *would* shorten the entire group's day. At the bottom of Forbidden Glacier, both groups had downhill skied roughly 3,500 vertical feet. The original plan had been for both groups to ski back up Forbidden Glacier, turn left and head back up the headwall to Forbidden Peak, then traverse Mount Durrand's west face to a run called Durrand Gendarme. From there they would angle down and back across the Durrand Glacier over a ridge to Final Run gully that would take them back to the Ledges and the chalet. As was standard, Beglinger radioed his position to the chalet when he stopped for lunch; he remembers checking in with Wylie and telling him to take a lunch break and then ". . . follow my tracks back up Forbidden Glacier, directly to Forbidden Pass, and straight to chalet down Needle Icefall."

This is where I believe a breakdown in communication occurred, unbeknownst to both Wylie and Beglinger at the time. Wylie had heard they were returning to Forbidden Peak, and when he thought to ask Beglinger where they should meet up next—a "collection point"—he heard a low battery signal on the radio and abandoned the effort.

With Beglinger's proposed route, when his group turned left to climb back up adjacent the headwall to Forbidden Peak, Wylie was to continue straight to Forbidden Pass, which would essentially be the end of uphill climbing for Wylie's Group 2 (avoiding the one thousand vertical feet required to summit Forbidden Peak a second time). From Forbidden Pass it was a fairly straightforward ski (some slight downhill, some flat) to the top of Needle Icefall, where Wylie's Group 2 would then have a nice, scenic downhill ski adding another 1,500 vertical to their day. At the bottom of Needle Icefall, there would be a short, 300-vertical-foot climb to the chalet, giving them a respectable, 5,000 vertical of skiing. Wylie had also skied the Needle Icefall route the previous week so Beglinger was aware it was familiar terrain for his new assistant guide that would provide him some independence to set his own track—something Wylie had expressed wanting to do the day before. In fact, Beglinger had sent other new guides on this same diverted route home when ascending Forbidden Glacier as a confidence builder as they learned the routes. It was also the standard, most direct route home for groups with a struggling skier.

The issue was that for whatever reason—radio static, Beglinger's accent, or his abrupt directions—Wylie must have heard "peak" when Beglinger said "pass." So as far as Wylie was concerned, nothing had changed; if anything Beglinger had reiterated the route home after lunch: "Follow my tracks back up Forbidden Glacier, then go directly to Forbidden Peak then to the chalet." Wylie had somehow missed the words "pass" and "Needle Icefall," which, according to David Lussier, who had worked as an SME assistant guide for six years, was likely due to the language barrier between Beglinger and his guides. "If I wasn't absolutely certain what a direction was," says Lussier, "I would ask him to repeat, sometimes a couple times. But when you're a new guide, you might not realize you missed something, or you're flustered and don't feel comfortable asking to repeat, and you just go with it, figure you've got the gist of it and you're following, so you just go. It happens, and sometimes words get lost on the radio. I wasn't there, but it's very likely something got lost in translation or the radio ate a few words. It happens and can lead to a misunderstanding of a situation."

After their lunch break, Nicoline, who was just ahead of Craig on the way back up Forbidden Glacier, passed the time chatting. Craig talked pretty much nonstop about Olivia and asked Nicoline about raising her girls up there, the homeschooling, how much she got to ski. He had seen enough to know that he wanted something like they had. He'd told Nicoline that he couldn't wait to bring Savina up so she could see what they'd built there.

A lot of aspiring guides had come and gone at Selkirk Mountain Experience. The ones who made a life out of it had a certain something beyond just skills and a passion for the mountains. Says Nicoline, "Ruedi gets such a thrill from what might get a little mundane for some people. He gets a thrill taking guests up the same mountain he's skied a thousand times. One of our guests, a grade-two teacher, commented on that and said, 'If you don't like reading *Charlie and the Chocolate Factory* out loud every year and be excited about it, you probably shouldn't be a grade-two teacher.' From what little I saw of Craig's interactions with the guests, he was just calm and happy. Like you could tell nothing is going to rattle this guy—he's in it for all the right reasons."

THEIR PACE WAS strong, 1,200 vertical feet per hour, and less than two and a half hours later Group 1 was back atop Forbidden Peak and traversing the connecting ridge to Mount Durrand and then onto the west face, where Beglinger set a high line above the steep open snowfield located just beneath the summit cliffs. Above a 35-degree run called Durrand Gendarme, they stopped. It was silent but for a slight wind and they were offered a spectacular view of the upper Durrand Glacier all the way back toward Tumbledown Mountain, which was in full sunlight, jutting above a layer of dense clouds.

It was 2:24 p.m. when Craig pulled out his camera and took a photo of Tumbledown Mountain, which appeared small and distant, giving some perspective on how far they'd traveled that day and how far they had to go, because somewhere below those clouds was the chalet. Beglinger checked in with the chalet as he did throughout the day; he reported his position and that they were taking a break.

While waiting for the rest of his group to arrive, Beglinger walked out onto the 35-degree pitch and performed a hand shear test. Using his poles he cut down 120 centimeters into the steep slope, while Craig observed, asked questions, and took a couple more photos. Once Beglinger had isolated the

Sherman Poppen showing off the first Snurfer he made for his daughters on Christmas morning, 1965. Plus two water ski–inspired prototypes he built while drawing up his patent application, which he submitted in March 1966—just two weeks before Craig Elmer Kelly was born on April 1.
(Poppen Family Archives)

Craig leading the pack in the Washington state fifteen-year-old expert class during spring of 1981.
(Kelly Family Archives)

As the Miami Dolphins squared off against the San Francisco 49ers on January 20, 1985—Super Bowl XIX—nineteen-year-old Craig Kelly raced in his first-ever snowboarding contest, the Sims Open "banked slwalom" at Mount Baker, Washington. Thirty-four-year-old Tom Sims won but took note of Craig (in fourth) as the local boy who had the best style.

(Bud Fawcett)

rian, Gillian, and Craig Kelly at his wedding
Kelly Jo, summer 1992.
Kelly Family Archives)

Craig, Shaun Palmer, and Keith Wallace on
the podium moments after Palmer finally
beat Craig in the halfpipe at the TDK
Snowboarding World Championships in
Breckenridge, Colorado, 1990.
(Bud Fawcett)

raig and Kelly Jo Legaz during an ISM board test in Bend, Oregon, December 1987.
ud Fawcett)

Craig had never even seen a halfpipe when he entered his first freestyle event at Soda Springs in February 1985.
(Bud Fawcett)

The world champ at the time was Terry Kidwell, the "father of freestyle" who honed his skills sessioning quarterpipes in the Tahoe backcountry. Craig ultimately beat Kidwell—his mentor and hero—in 1987, then dominated the halfpipe and overall world titles until 1991.
(Bud Fawcett)

Craig boosts a big method air for the era at the TDK "Worlds," Breckenridge, Colorado 1990.
(Bud Fawcett)

Archrivals Jake Burton Carpenter and Tom Sims pose cordially in 1988 just weeks after Craig left Team Sims to ride for Burton Snowboards, sparking the snowboarding industry's first big legal battle.
(Bud Fawcett)

Free at last to ride his Burton Craig Kelly Air in public, Craig styles the cover of the October 1989 *TransWorld SNOWboarding.*
(Rod Walker)

"Craig Kelly . . . a supernatural combination of talent . . . " September 1987, *ISM.*
(Hubert Schriebl)

Drawing a fast, inside giant slalom line at the OP Pro, June Mountain, 1989.
(*Bud Fawcett*)

Halfpipe trickery circa 1990–91: stalling an Andrecht handplant (bottom left), and tweaking a crail to the max (bottom right).
(*Rod Walker/Trevor Graves*)

Craig defines the essence of freeriding natural terrain in one powerful yet soulful turn at 15,000 feet in the Chilean Andes backcountry, 1999.
(Mark Gallup)

This December 1992 *Snowboarder* told the world that freeriding was Craig Kelly's new calling, and he was going to shout it from the mountaintops. Location: Mount Baker.
(Sean Sullivan)

Scott Schmidt and Craig peer through the window of the old
Russian military helicopter that flew them deep into Siberia's
Badzhal Mountains, 1995.
(Ace MacKay-Smith)

This December 1998 trip into the Cascades was the
last time Craig used snowshoes and carried a board
on his back while hoofing it in the backcountry.
Dave Downing—and a seemingly endless storm—
convinced him to try a prototype splitboard a day or
two later. It was life-changing.
(Jeff Curtes)

Craig Kelly portrait,
Hintertux, Austria, 2000.
(Vianney Tisseau)

Craig's dream rig for the road less traveled. (Mark Gallup)

Craig, Olivia, and Savina in Puerto Montt, Chile, shortly before heading home in August 2001. Olivia was splitboarding with her rad dad in the Andes before she could crawl, then back home in the Kootenays before she could walk. (Kelly Family Archives)

Grandma Janet with Olivia, 2001.
(Kelly Family Archives)

Craig in the pit—recording weather and snow profile observations while training for acceptance into the ACMG, winter 2002.
(Matt Scholl)

Craig and Olivia "flying" down the powdery glades at Baldface Lodge on January 1, 2003.
(Matt Scholl)

n Buffery, aka "Buff," with a caption that
ig wrote for *Snowboard Life,* March 2000.
edFoto, IMAX Extreme)

2003 Selkirk Mountain Experience assistant
guide Ken Wylie, shown here at Mount
Revelstoke, 2006.
(Nancy Geismar)

SME owner and
lead guide Ruedi
Beglinger with the
"snow shoveler" Dave
Finnerty, 2003.
*(Finnerty Family
Archives)*

La Traviata West Couloir
January 20, 2003 • 10:45 a.m.

○ Group 1 skiers
● Group 2 skiers

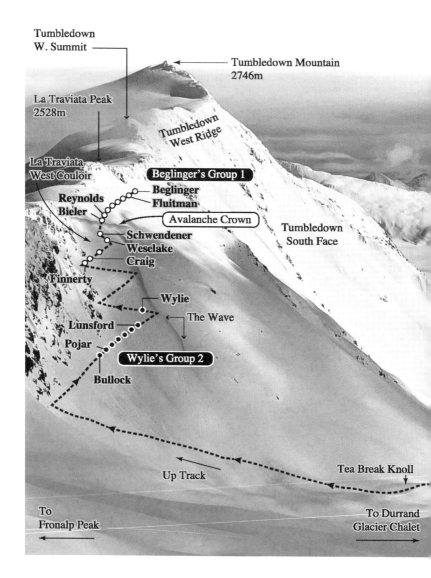

Tumbledown
W. Summit

Tumbledown Mountain
2746m

La Traviata Peak
2528m

Tumbledown
West Ridge

La Traviata
West Couloir

Beglinger's Group 1

Reynolds
Bieler

Beglinger
Fluitman

Avalanche Crown

Schwendener
Weselake
Craig

Tumbledown
South Face

Finnerty

Wylie

The Wave

Lunsford

Pojar

Wylie's Group 2

Bullock

Tea Break Knoll

Up Track

To
Fronalp Peak

To Durrand
Glacier Chalet

La Traviata West Couloir
January 20, 2003 • 10:40 a.m.

(Roughly One Minute After Avalanche.)

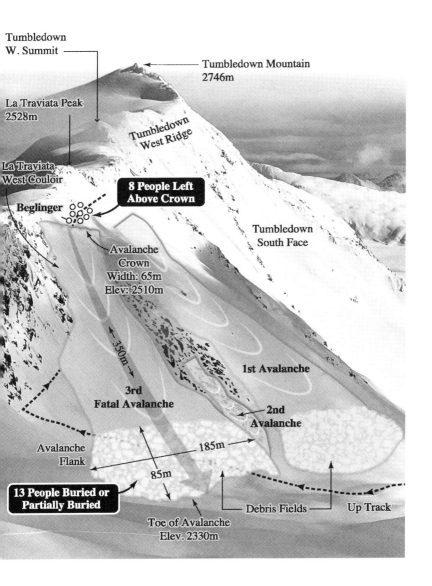

Tumbledown
W. Summit

Tumbledown Mountain
2746m

La Traviata Peak
2528m

Tumbledown
West Ridge

La Traviata
West Couloir

**8 People Left
Above Crown**

Beglinger

Avalanche
Crown
Width: 65m
Elev: 2510m

Tumbledown
South Face

350m

1st Avalanche

3rd
Fatal Avalanche

2nd
Avalanche

Avalanche
Flank

185m

85m

**13 People Buried or
Partially Buried**

Debris Fields

Up Track

Toe of Avalanche
Elev. 2330m

Buffery, Olivia, and Savina, spring 2003.
(*Victoria Jealouse*)

Grandpa Pat with Olivia in 2022.
(*Kelly Family Archives*)

Durrand Glacier Chalet and adjacent helipad (opposite page) deep in the northern Selkirks. "Welcome to paradise."
(*Eric Blehm*)

One of the many mags that honored Craig with cover shots and tribute stories in 2003. *(Matt Scholl)*

Sherman Poppen, Craig, and Jake Burton Carpenter when Craig was awarded the TWS lifetime achievement award, Alaska, 2002. (*John Stouffer*)

Craig, finding his line in harmony with the Coast Range near Whistler, British Columbia, Canada, Mountain Heli Sport, 1995. (*Dano Pendygrasse*)

RIP to all seven "raven

Go to www.Ericblehm.com for more photos and extras.

snow column, he got "no result" from the test. "No layers found," he wrote in his guidebook. "Pole-probing, handle first, no signs of weakness."

During this twenty-minute break, Craig asked a slew of questions about local conditions, the tests Beglinger performed, and especially that November layer as Beglinger had a long-standing perspective on monitoring such weaknesses buried in the snowpack.

"When it comes to rain crusts and weak layers, the question is 'Is it reactive or is it not reactive,'" Beglinger explains. "And if it's only for one or two days, not reactive, I would question the test, but if it hasn't been reactive over seven or eight days, you can start to believe it, and somewhere comes the point where you have to believe it, otherwise you cannot go ski-touring at all anymore."

This layer had not been reactive to his field tests—had not slid, cracked, or showed signs of instability—in over two weeks. Like Beglinger, most guides monitor problem layers throughout the season until, at some point, it's deep enough in the snowpack that it will not react to the weight of a skier, or tests that are meant to mimic the weight of a skier, and guides relax some, and stop worrying about it. Generally, 100 centimeters of snow will easily support the weight of a skier. Beglinger's test had gone to 120 and had not "reacted" to his test.

The problem, which Craig had noted during his avalanche courses, was that difficult-to-predict "spatial variability" where snow depth varies, especially on wind-affected slopes. Staying in the deep or "fat" snow is paramount to safety, as well as spreading out your group and minimizing exposure to your group in avalanche-prone areas. The recent public avalanche bulletin had warned backcountry travelers to avoid the big, open slopes, and to avoid grouping up in areas (the weight of multiple skiers concentrated in a tight group penetrates deeper into the snowpack than skiers who are spread out). Beglinger had chosen this spot to group up, taking into consideration all those factors, and after some twenty minutes, he radioed Wylie to check in.

"Ken, this is Ruedi, I'm at Durrand Gendarme, how is your progress." Beglinger recalls Wylie had responded all was fine, and that he was exiting Forbidden Glacier.

According to Beglinger, there was no indication anything was amiss. He envisioned Group 2 leaving Forbidden Glacier, about to crest Forbidden Pass, and that they would soon be on a slightly descending traverse heading toward Needle Icefall, where they would have a nice downhill descent. "I remember thinking at that point," says Beglinger, that "they will probably beat us back to the chalet."

In reality, Wylie was just leaving Forbidden Glacier and had not left Beglinger's tracks; he was actually following them back up toward Forbidden Peak adjacent the headwall they had skied down earlier. There was increasing mist and some blowing snow, making it hard to follow the tracks, but he kept his eyes on the rocky northeast shoulder of Forbidden Peak, which was a highly visible landmark guiding his trajectory.

After checking in with Wylie, Beglinger turned his focus back to his group gathered around him. They were tired, sore, but ready to drop in and make some more turns before heading back to the chalet. But first, no reason to rush this celestial panorama, with the sun, the clouds, the perfect light. Some recall it was Jean-Luc Schwendener who commented, "You planned this whole day so we could be right here, right now, eh, Ruedi?" Standing beside Nicoline, Beglinger didn't say a word. He just smiled with his guests, all of whom were facing west, their faces bathed in the soft radiance of the slowly setting sun.

Beglinger loved moments like this. He tried to savor them. But he was a guide. And Swiss. So even at the end of a near-perfect today, he was already thinking, *What can I show them tomorrow?*

CHAPTER 21

THE HUMAN FACTOR

RETURNING TO THE CHALET AROUND 3:30 p.m.—a half hour past target—Beglinger was surprised Group 2 was still in the field. Beglinger's Group 1 had skied roughly six thousand vertical feet, plus had at least a twenty-minute break at Durrand Gendarme, which meant Group 2 should have beaten them back.

But with sundown being at 4:23 p.m. and Wylie still not arriving by 4 p.m., Beglinger called him on the radio to ask his location.

When Wylie responded that he was at Goat Lake looking for the entrance to Needle Icefall, Beglinger's response was, according to Wylie, "Fuck." Wylie prickled at the curse.

For his part, Beglinger had no idea what Wylie's group had just been through. During the roughly half hour between Group 1's departure from Durrand Gendarme and Group 2's arrival there, the climb back up the Forbidden Peak had been "heroic," recalls John Seibert, describing Reynolds's efforts to literally push and pull Jameson up the mountain.

About the time Beglinger assumed Group 2 had been approaching the top of the Needle Icefall—close, just one downhill run away from the chalet—they had still been approaching the summit of Forbidden Peak, and once they got there, Wylie continued to follow Beglinger's tracks toward Durrand Gendarme. Bringing up the rear, Reynolds had stayed behind Jameson as a psychological "push" and could not believe how long this day was taking and how "smoked" Jameson was. This was Reynolds's first time at SME, but he knew the direction Wylie was heading in, taking them farther from the chalet, so he skied up to him to reiterate for the second time that "Laura keeps falling and I'm helping her to get up. I'm getting her to eat and drink, but we need to head back to the lodge not away from it." At the same time Reynolds was thinking, *This is foolish; by the time we get Laura out of here it's going to be dark.*

"Ken didn't really make too much of it," says Reynolds. "But I was thinking, *Jesus, it's going to be a long day.*"

Wylie did not realize he had somehow missed Beglinger's new route directions but was doing the best he could to stay upbeat and get his group back to the chalet by following Beglinger's tracks. By the time they'd skied down from Forbidden Peak to Durrand Gendarme and back onto the Durrand Glacier—the final stretch home—visibility was down to at most twenty meters, and Wylie became concerned he could lose a guest in the fog. To follow the route back to the Ledges, he had to angle down and across the glacier, aiming for a little dip in a ridgeline he could not see because of the fog, so he was relying on his altimeter. They started the traverse at roughly 8,694 feet and the dip was on the far side of the glacier at an elevation of 7,874 feet. This dip was a little passage across a ridge that would take them to a gully—appropriately called "Final Run"—that would take them down to the Ledges and then home. Wylie told his ten guests that they would ski down and across the glacier in segments, keeping each other close and in sight. As they descended, Beglinger's tracks came in and out of view through the misty fog, which was accompanied by some blowing snow and biting cold. It was like skiing in a vertigo-inducing cloud that caused several of the guests to fall over while trying to maintain a visual with whoever was in front of them.

During the 1.5-kilometer glacial descent, Wylie attempted to stop every hundred meters or so to regroup. At one point, after checking his altimeter, he realized they were below 7,874 feet, which meant he had missed the passageway over to Mirror Lake and the Ledges. There was no way that Jameson had the energy to put on her skins and climb back up the couple hundred feet needed to get to the passageway so he pulled out his map and chose an alternative. If they continued down the glacier, they'd get to Goat Lake. From there he was confident he could find the entrance to (ironically, given it was where Beglinger had intended him to go in the first place) Needle Icefall, which he recalled was marked by a large boulder he should be able to see even in this foggy whiteout. However, it was all but dark, which complicated matters.

He was somewhere on the south end of Goat Lake, looking for that boulder in the combination of coming darkness and whiteout, when Beglinger's "Fuck" had crackled in over the radio. Using compass and GPS, Beglinger directed him toward the icefall, and the boulder appeared like a beacon in the fog, providing the bearing Wylie needed to get his group to the Needle Icefall and down to the chalet.

It was dark by the time they returned to SME, trudging into the chalet one after another, with those who had brought along headlamps wearing them. Jameson disappeared to her room and still looked exhausted an hour and a half later at dinner. The Truckee crew was more "cold and frustrated" than they were tired, after going half-speed all day. That and skiing along other people's tracks wasn't what they'd paid for.

The endnote for several in Wylie's group was "Tomorrow, we'd better be skiing with Ruedi."

Shortly after Group 2 returned, several guests from Group 1 heard Beglinger "tearing into Ken outside." He was "ripshit," recalled one guest who had walked to the outhouse. "They were up by the residence, but we could hear them all the way down at the chalet with the doors closed."

Reportedly this "eruption" occurred when Wylie told Beglinger that he had deviated from the route because he felt it was the best thing for his guests, one of whom was exhausted. "That was not his decision to make," says Beglinger. Still having no idea that Wylie had gone all the way back to Forbidden Peak, Beglinger thought that he had blatantly "ignored" his directions to go from the Forbidden Glacier straight to Needle Icefall and could not understand how he had been unable to find the boulder. This had likely been further exasperated when one of the Group 2 members told Beglinger that Wylie had been "lost in the fog" while trying to get back to the Ledges.

The ensuing "bit of a shouting match" had both Beglinger and Wylie unable to realize the core of the dispute. Wylie would go to bed that evening believing that Beglinger was angry because he had lost Beglinger's track in the poor visibility and wasn't able to ski back to the chalet via the Ledges, whereas Beglinger was fuming because Wylie had, in his mind, willfully ignored his directions from Forbidden Pass to Needle Icefall, and then gotten lost trying to find the route to the Ledges, which was insubordinate behavior. In the end, Wylie's Group 2 had climbed 300 more vertical feet than Group 1 for a total of 6,300 vertical.

After dinner, a Group 2 guest who had taken the entire day in stride told Beglinger, "It was an adventure. I'm just glad I packed my headlamp." Another guest said, "Ken was pretty turned around up there." These comments, in addition to the first "lost in the fog" comment, plus a request from the Truckee crew to ski with Group 1 the following day further eroded Beglinger's confidence in Wylie. He couldn't trust him to navigate the terrain quite yet, especially in poor visibility. He would, for the time being, have to keep their groups close together.

But if Beglinger had known the truth, that Wylie had simply missed the new directions, how was he at fault for anything except an honest mistake? The problem was that neither of them had identified the original miscommunication—nor would they. Ultimately it was the human factor that was to blame rather than Beglinger or Wylie.

THE ONLY THING Wylie knew for certain at the end of that long and stressful day was that he wanted to crawl into bed, close his eyes, and try to get some sleep. He had a decision to make, but that would come tomorrow.

Craig ended his day on the satellite phone, wishing Savina a happy birthday. She asked him how it was "up there" and there was no hint of drama in his voice, nor any mention of yelling or strife. If he had felt strongly that something was amiss, Savina believes Craig's tone would have revealed the discontent, but on the contrary, his reaction to the days he'd spent thus far seemed positive. "Like he wanted me to go up there and check it out, and see what Ruedi and Nicoline had built," says Savina. "The impression I got was that he was loving it."

CHAPTER 22

JANUARY 20, 2003

THE NEXT MORNING DAWNED SNOWY and gray for the guests at Selkirk Mountain Experience. A centimeter of snow had fallen overnight, winds were light, and the temperature was 20 degrees Fahrenheit—cold, but not too cold, perfect for touring. Walking down the narrow wooden steps from his room, Craig was greeted by the rich aroma of dark-brewed coffee and freshly baked bread wafting up from the kitchen.

In the warmth of the dining room, he ambled over and fell in line with the other early risers hovering around the central table, picking bread from baskets and building a sandwich from plates of meats, cheeses, and veggies. His lunch stashed away in his backpack, he pulled on boots, swung open the front door, and headed up the snowy pathway—no doubt with a spring in his step—to his first stop at the weather station and then to the morning guide meeting. As Larry Stanier had described it, "This is where the learning is!"

The new snow squeaked under his boots as he plodded up to the weather plot and pulled from his chest pocket his field book and the nub of a pencil he kept tucked into the front cover adjacent a photograph of Olivia. It was a wallet-sized black-and-white of her in the bunny suit costume she'd worn their first Halloween in Nelson, right about the time he embarked on this journey to become a guide. He and Savina had taken turns carrying her that night, and she'd fallen asleep with her head on his shoulder, warm and cozy with her long floppy ears draped down over his back. She'd be two years old in three months, and before he knew it, she'd graduate from his backpack to her own toddler-sized snowboard, which he'd get JG or Doyle to split as soon as her legs were strong enough. From the weather station, Craig could see a number of gently sloped hills within view of the chalet, perfect for sledding, shredding, whatever a kid might choose to tire herself out.

Just three days in, this practicum had given Craig so much more than just the learning. It gave him a glimpse of his future.

For KEN WYLIE, the morning hadn't been so idyllic.

He had, for the third night in a row, barely slept, having been tormented by something inside him that kept saying, "This is a bad situation here, we're pushing the envelope." He was scared—fearful of some of the terrain, the conditions, that deeply buried layer of snow. The rational side of him knew, from his evolution as a rock climber and ice climber, that it was important to push through that, to get to the other side of fear, so he could develop and grow as a skier and a guide. Still, he just couldn't shake that feeling, or stop asking himself why he had ignored Chic Scott's warnings and other red flags about working here. What had made him think he'd be like the easygoing guides who *did* enjoy working here? After another night of tossing, turning, and obsessing, he was done—ready to quit. That was his plan at 4:30 a.m. but by the time he'd splashed some cold water on his face, he decided to stick it out until Friday. He'd give notice and then fly out with this group Saturday morning and, just like Chic had said, never come back.

Craig and Wylie had flown into these mountains with very different preconceptions about Beglinger. From the articles Craig had read and overwhelming feedback he'd received, Beglinger was badass. "What do you call the rare combination of unyielding strength and smooth, fluid movement? His parents called him Ruedi Beglinger. We call it Liquid Steel." That was the latest Marmot ad being circulated in the outdoor magazines. Paul Norrie had told Craig exactly what Kranabitter had told him years before: "There's no better person or place to have an apprenticeship. . . ." A message Craig had left for his brother Brian during his drive up the Slocan Valley three days earlier was a good indication of what he felt about Beglinger: "I'm going to do some training with this legend. Super excited."

While Craig most likely considered Beglinger a badass, it's fair to say Wylie considered him a hardass. In nine days, he'd confirmed that the descriptions of Beglinger as "autocratic," "short-fused," and "arrogant" were true.

But "unsafe"—the word of Chic Scott—was the most troubling to Wylie, and none of these were helping his confidence in either Beglinger or himself.

"Ken looked like he was stressed-out to the max," recalls one of the guests who heard the yelling the night before. "I just assumed it was because Ruedi was riding him a bit, but you know, he rides all his guides. There's no denying that. He's notorious for being hard on assistant guides. But he doesn't usually do it in front of guests. Occasionally he does—and it's total bullshit. That's one of Ruedi's flaws. He's got a lot of good points, but he's got his flaws."

AFTER WYLIE HELPED Finnerty do some shoveling, he joined Craig and Bullock at the weather station. It was 6:45 when they recorded the temperature, new snow, wind sky, all the usual details in their respective field books before heading back inside, where Beglinger awaited them in the guides' room. The usual end-of-day guide meeting had been canceled the night before, so he began this meeting with "Let's talk about yesterday."

"You could feel the tension in the room," says Bullock, who had been mentored by Wylie in Alpine Club of Canada climbing courses during previous summers. "Ken just wasn't himself. I felt he was stressed-out because it seemed like every time he tried to speak about the guests or the snow, Ruedi would kind of shut him down."

Rather than comment directly on what he felt was Wylie's insubordination the evening before, Beglinger let it go. But he made a mental note that he could not yet trust Wylie to follow his directions. According to Wylie, Beglinger said, "Why couldn't you just follow my tracks?" Wylie said the tracks had been erased by falling snow combined with wind so he'd had to rely upon his own navigation. On top of that, visibility had been nil, a whiteout that Wylie compared to being inside a Ping-Pong ball.

"Ping-Pong ball?" Wylie recalls Beglinger saying. "You Canadian guides, what the hell does the ACMG teach you anyhow? There was no whiteout yesterday." Wylie held his ground and said he'd done the best he could considering the situation. He went on to chastise Beglinger for cursing on the radio, saying it had been "inappropriate" and could have "easily unsettled the guests." This didn't sit well with Beglinger, who, according to Wylie, snapped back, "You have not heard me use bad language yet!"

Bullock could not recall specifics, but he does remember "sitting on the sidelines and feeling a little bit uncomfortable." It's impossible to know how Craig felt during this exchange, but it likely helped him understand what Paul Norrie meant when he'd said, "You're going to get some hard debriefs, but you're going to learn more there than anywhere else." Craig was most certainly learning, and noting what he might later delete or adopt for his own business model and guiding style. That was, after all, the point of this practicum.

After a moment of silence, they discussed and rated the previous day's snow and avalanche conditions as good in the subalpine, the lower alpine, and higher alpine—with partial wind slabs in isolated areas. Wylie felt the rating was generous, but since they hadn't observed any avalanches for the past two weeks, he did not disagree.

Beglinger concluded the meeting with the day's plan: to ski down from the chalet to Twin Falls on Carnes Creek, skin up Swiss Meadows on the way to Fronalp Peak, and loop back and do La Traviata on the way back to the chalet. After pointing out the objectives on a map, Beglinger, Bullock, and Craig headed back to the chalet. Wylie loitered, studying the ascent and descent routes inked out on the area topo map, and tucked a few "run photographs" of Fronalp and La Traviata into his pocket. If weather moved in, Wylie could reference them while navigating what for him would be unfamiliar territory.

Wylie had to admit to himself that he still wanted to please Beglinger. He wanted to prove to him that he was a competent guide, yet here he was on yet another morning not at all fired up to get out into the mountains and thinking to himself: *I'm not good enough to work here.*

ONCE HE HAD a pretty good idea of the terrain, Wylie walked down to the chalet, packed his lunch, and joined the others for breakfast.

Generally, the assistant guides sat with the guests, but this morning Wylie joined Craig and Bullock, who were chatting about ice climbing. This was something Wylie excelled at; as an Alpine Guide, he led clients and had even scored a midfield finish in the X Games a few years earlier. "You do any ice climbing?" Bullock asked Craig. "No way," he replied. "Too dangerous for my stage in life. You're stuck right there in an avalanche path the whole time, no thanks. Not for me."

Around 7:30 a.m., as the meal was ending, Beglinger announced the day's objectives to the guests and told them, "We will ski down from the chalet to start, so no skins. Be sure they are in your pack." He emphasized the point: "That's very important. You don't want to get down to Carnes Creek and remember they're up here in the chalet."

CHAPTER 23

THERE FOR
THE STORM

KATHY KESSLER, THE REALTOR FROM Truckee, had been keeping pace with Beglinger's fast-moving Group 1 for two days, despite a bad sinus infection, but this morning she was contemplating giving herself a break, which wasn't an easy decision. She didn't give up easily; just ask the Tahoe locals who had dubbed her "the Erin Brockovich of Donner Lake" after winning a two-year legal battle that forced a private water company to update her town's antiquated, bacteria-ridden water system.

Staying in the chalet was not an option, but dropping a gear to a slightly more human pace was, so after breakfast she volunteered to shift to Wylie's Group 2, telling Beglinger, "I don't want to slow you guys down." At the same time, three other guests (Laura Jameson, Dan DiMaria, and Erik Brentwood) told Beglinger they were going to take a rest day and hang at the chalet.

With his total head count for the day at twenty (including himself and Wylie) Beglinger called out the groups at precisely 8 a.m. The guys from the Truckee crew, who had told him the night before that they all wanted to ski with Group 1 today, were surprised and a little miffed when he put them once again in Group 2. It turned out that Beglinger had misinterpreted Kessler's individual request after breakfast as a group consensus.

Next came the transceiver check at the helipad, where Beglinger suggested three-turns spacing between skiers. "As we get lower in the trees, there may be some crust, so be ready for that," he said, and then he dropped in. One after the next, the ten members of Group 1 followed, fanning out per his instructions with plenty of untouched snow for all in the sanctuary of the trees. Wylie next led the eight members of Group 2 and found himself grinning as he listened to his group whooping it up. With each turn, his spirits lifted, his confidence grew, and by the time the trees gave way to some fun open bumpy gullies toward the valley floor, he almost felt like a guide again. *I can do this*, he thought to himself.

Ah, the trees, the magical trees. They are sanctuary in a storm, providing context and vision in a whiteout, the go-to place where the snow is better anchored when avalanche conditions get dicey. Today these steep forested glades were simply their commute to the southwestern quadrant on the SME "trail map." There the mountaintops were start gates for long and speedy multi-pitched downhills beginning on summits like Fronalp and Glarona Peaks and ending far below the treeline via deep and gloriously steep forested runs like Top Gun and Parachute, which Beglinger had named in the eighties. When conditions were right, these "peak to creek" experiences were *the* hallmark of Selkirk Mountain Experience.

Rick Reynolds was tightening up his boots, having watched most of the guests push off the helipad, their powder hoots drifting back from the woods. He edged his ski tips over the steep drop that would carry him across a mellow, sparsely treed incline before the terrain stair-stepped down again into the steeper, forested line toward Twin Falls. He was among the last to go, straight-lining it to gather some speed before dropping his knee and lunging into a long, soulful tele turn. A former internationally ranked (seventieth in the world) ski racer and then coach, Reynolds was the guy you'd watch from the chairlift ripping up a mogul field, then realize, "Wait a minute, that dude's on—holy crap, he's on tele skis." And he hadn't fallen in years until that second turn of the day, when "Bam!" he went ass over teakettle, headfirst into the snowdrift he'd been geared up to rebound off.

"You all good?" was the first thing he heard as he pulled his head out of the snow.

"I had just face-planted," recalls Reynolds, "and there was Craig. He sorta glided to a half stop beside me and I just couldn't believe I fell, so I say, 'Yeah. I'm fine,' but I'm thinking, *Goddammit, did that have to happen? And right in front of a snowboarder.*"

As Reynolds stood up, he watched Craig continue down the mountain, laying down a beautiful carve just as he dropped over the next steep pitch and disappeared.

One can only imagine the turns that followed for Craig in the next eight-hundred-something vertical feet. It was gray and snowing, and riding storm trees was something that always reminded Craig of Mount Baker, so it's a fair bet that this steeply gladed run felt a little like home. If he rode it like he always did, he slashed every snowdrift with style, and aired every powder pillow, probably casually head-dipped a branch or two, all while scanning the surrounding trees for fallen guests. Completely in tune with his board, he would have felt the snow changing as he dropped elevation, triggering a response—as reptilian as it was powder hound—to pressure the tail, lift the nose, and lean it back, just a little. Simultaneously, he'd loosen up his shock absorbers—his knees—and bleed off some speed, just in time for the crust Beglinger had predicted toward the bottom of the valley.

There the contours of the terrain funneled his and all the other tracks to one single, distinctly wider traverse that Beglinger had set toward Twin Falls. A glance over his right shoulder would have had him see Reynolds not far upslope, on the right trajectory to intersect with him on this mini high-way. A glance downhill over his left shoulder would prompt the sheepdog in him—engrained after an entire winter of herding guests at Baldface—checking to see if any tracks had strayed below the traverse and thus indicating somebody had lost their way.

There were no lost sheep, so he maintained his speed on that mellow little traverse where, as anybody who'd ridden with Craig knows, he milked every dip and ollied every hip, because if gravity held out there was fun to be had right down to the last foot of vertical.

Reynolds slid in right behind Craig to a chorus of climbing-skin adhesive being ripped apart, a befitting accompaniment to the carefree and happy banter of new friends and old who had just ripped up nearly a thousand vertical feet of powder. And it wasn't even 8:15 a.m.

During this transition break from going downhill to up, Joe Pojar saw the Truckee crew gathered around Beglinger. Listening in, he got the gist they weren't stoked to be in Group 2 again today. Pojar was happy in either group; in fact, he sometimes found on these trips at SME that the slower group could be a little more fun and a little less aggro, so he volunteered to join Group 2, as did Paula Couturier to even out the numbers a little.

Skiing away from the Truckee crew, Beglinger gathered his group beside a snow bridge that spanned the creek a few meters from the falls. "Durrand Glacier Chalet," he spoke into his radio, "this is Ruedi. We are leaving Twin Falls, heading toward Swiss Meadows then Fronalp."

Beglinger then sidestepped the bridge and instructed his Group 1 guests— Jeff Bullock, Bruce Stewart, Rick Reynolds, Keith Lindsay, Rick Martin, Craig, Evan Weselake, Naomi Heffler, Jean-Luc Schwendener, Heidi Biber, Age Fluitman, and Charles Bieler—to do the same.

Wylie's Group 2 now numbered six and included Vern Lunsford, Kathy Kessler, Joe Pojar, Paula Couturier, Dennis Yates, and John Seibert. They would be ascending and traversing a lot of steep, mostly open terrain including one major avalanche path—Tumbledown Gully—so just before he'd crossed the bridge, Beglinger had instructed Wylie to follow a hundred meters behind. Just a minute or two later, Wylie recalls, Beglinger got on the radio and told him to be sure his guests sidestepped the narrow bridge on their skis, versus skiing straight across. "You don't want anybody in the creek." Wylie was offended. He was, after all, a certified assistant guide, and Beglinger's directive was like reminding a grown man to look both ways before leading some children across a street. Roughly fifteen minutes later, while contouring a semi-steep slope, Wylie made a slight detour—went offroading—above and around where the downhill side of Beglinger's track had washed out, to provide a better platform for their skis. Wylie recalls Beglinger got on the radio and told him, "Ken. Stay exactly in my track." Wylie perceived the comment as another insult, a slight that he chose not to acknowledge over the radio. Instead he obsessed over it, an inner monologue in which he defended his actions. The reason he'd made the detour was that some of Beglinger's Group 1 guests had slipped down out of his track and created a dangerous section on a fairly steep side hill for the Group 2 guests. To repair the track with his shovel would have been time-consuming and, in an avalanche path, unwise, so he'd kept the line moving by touring a couple of feet into the soft surface snow above and then merged back onto the main track a few meters beyond.

He kept his frustrations to himself, because defending his actions on the radio would have been argumentative in front of the guests and pointless besides. Wylie was convinced Beglinger had no interest in his opinion anyway. Even if he brought it up at that night's guide meeting, it would be dismissed. It was maddening to Wylie, who became more and more resentful by the minute as he continued the traverse toward Tumbledown Gully in silence, ascending toward the alpine but descending into "the bitter, angry depths of myself," recalls Wylie.

"I am one hundred percent certain Ruedi had no idea how distraught Ken was," says "Bill," a guide who had worked with Beglinger and was a professional acquaintance of Wylie.

Bill was not there that day but says "Ruedi was mentoring Ken as he'd mentored all his assistant guides, which had been how he himself had been mentored." As a young apprentice guide in Switzerland, Beglinger had learned by observing and then doing exactly what his teachers told him. There had been no room for interpretation. His mentor had expected questions at the end of the day—not topics to be discussed as an equal but questions to be answered.

Over time, as Beglinger's own confidence grew, those nightly debriefs in the Swiss Alps evolved into something resembling discussions, "but that took time," says Bill. "Ken had only been up there, not even two weeks. His training had been Canadian, and his work experience in the outdoors had been Island Lake Lodge and Outward Bound, where you don't only discuss the conditions, you discuss your feelings—they were from different worlds. My take on it is that Ken didn't feel like he had a voice up there and, after just two weeks on the job, Ruedi didn't think he'd earned it."

Beglinger's approach to mentoring is unique because "he is very much like the mountains himself," says a former SME guide. "The mountains don't nurture you, they teach you. You watch the mountains, you spend time with the mountains and you learn, but you're always kind of on edge because you're not entirely sure when that storm's going to hit, that rockfall is going to crash down on you, or, in Ruedi's case, when he's going to jump on your ass about something. He can go off. He can be unpredictable, but so are the mountains, right? And you know this about the mountains; otherwise you wouldn't be there. And anybody who has spent time with Ruedi knows there are times when he'll pat you on the back, give you a beer, or a shot of Jägermeister or even a Ruedi hug. He'll wrap you up just like some sunshine after a storm. There is warmth in the man . . . but that's not why you're there in those unforgiving Selkirks with Ruedi fucking Beglinger. That's not what you signed up for as an apprentice or assistant guide. The clients, *they're* there for the powder. *You're* there for the storm."

JEFF BULLOCK WAS right behind Beglinger as they climbed up and away from Carnes Creek. This was prime placement for a practicum student, a front-row seat to what Dave Nettle, a well-regarded Tahoe, California–based guide, calls "poetry in motion." Nettle skied more than one hundred days at SME and credits Beglinger as his inspiration to guide. "Ruedi taught me more about alpine touring, navigating terrain, and reading the contours of the land than anybody I've ever skied with," says Nettle. "How he anticipates what's coming, whether it's a low rise or where to cut a convex slope, the way he moves through the mountains. Watching him helped me to refine and up my game especially in big terrain."

Bullock was close enough to ask questions but mainly he just followed and observed Beglinger's westerly traverse. "That's big country, west of Carnes Creek," says SME guide Joey Vosburgh. "I didn't fully appreciate the magnitude of Tumbledown's south face until it was looming over me. You get that sense of urgency, where you want to go fast because it's all avalanche runout. There are little islands, where you know you're safe, but they're separated by big slopes, and a couple gullies where you're right in the line of fire if anything big comes down."

Beglinger's traverse soon intersected with Tumbledown Gully. As a terrain feature, a gully is heaven to ski or ride, but in the event of an avalanche, a gully both confines and accelerates the snow coming down from, in this case, thousands of feet. "It's not like one of these little gullies that you just get pushed into a creek," continues Vosburgh. "If you're in the gully, and that south face cuts loose with a big avy the air blast alone will send you hundreds of feet into the air. It's direct action. Nothing's going to slow it down until you're pummeled all the way to the valley floor, which is why Ruedi is selective about when he passes through this area, and how he does it."

In this case, Beglinger skied directly into the gully, took a rounded right turn, and climbed directly up the side, weaving a serpentine track through the remains of a naturally triggered class 2 avalanche Beglinger had observed and recorded three weeks earlier, on December 31, the hardened debris sticking up at odd angles like miniature icebergs jutting out from the smooth, snowy surface. What was going to come down had come down in the last big storm cycle, and the minimal snow fallen atop and around the debris showed it hadn't snowed much since then, maybe fifteen centimeters (six inches). Much of that had blown away and/or been scoured by moderate to strong winds, as evidenced from that ice-scraper-on-windshield sound their ski edges made while ascending this treeless swath.

Once above the debris, he turned left, crossed over to the opposite side of the gully, and skied up and into a little forest of fragrant alpine balsam fir. Here Beglinger's skis sank into powder that remained deep and protected in this grove of trees, which was a waypoint in an ascending westerly traverse toward Lower Swiss Meadows. The intact branches and overall size showed that this stand of old growth rarely saw avalanches. It was an island of safety and a good place to rest if Beglinger had any intention of doing so.

Which he didn't. He did, however, glance back down and see Wylie striding into the gully, while the rear third of Beglinger's Group 1 was still working its way up and across the avalanche debris. There was no immediate danger—the debris showed this slope had already avalanched during the last major storm cycle, and it was cold—but, according to Beglinger, he flipped on his radio nonetheless to tell Wylie to tap the brakes.

Beglinger doesn't recall telling Wylie to stay exactly in his tracks that morning, and as for sidestepping the bridge, that was the direction he gave all his assistant guides the first time he took them across Carnes Creek. What he does recall at that point, roughly forty-five minutes into their tour, was telling Wylie, "Ken. You need to give me more space."

"I already told Ken he was too close at least three times," says Beglinger. "I didn't want more than one group in exposed terrain regardless if it's safe or not safe."

While none of the guests within earshot of either guide can recall exactly what was said—"When you're climbing, you kind of zone out," says Bruce

Stewart—several recall there was the "standard going back and forth, on the radio."

Beglinger continued to break trail out of the trees, setting a gently weaving ascent track through Lower Swiss Meadows into the subalpine, where he paused while traversing across a steep south-facing slope near Tumbledown Lake at six thousand feet elevation, to probe down several times with the upturned handle of his ski pole—a guide's antenna of sorts—feeling for signs of any weakness that would signal an alarm.

Dave Finnerty caught up to Group 2 just as Wylie halted for a break in the forested island of safety just west of Tumbledown Gully. Downshifting just long enough for a quick hello, Finnerty had finished his morning chores and was all smiles as he shuffled past them, on a mission to catch up with Group 1 so he could ride with his idol, Craig.

Looking up and to the right, Wylie could not see the outlines of Tumbledown Mountain through slow-moving storm clouds, but he could feel its presence.

With Beglinger's group far ahead, he would move his group quickly, and encouraged his guests to grab a drink and a quick snack.

"I remember being under that same exposure," Vosburgh describes the daunting nature of this route. "You've got this massive south face looming over you, and the only way you can mitigate the hazard above you is to get out from underneath it. So, you stop and tell your group, 'Okay, guys, get a sip. Take your time right now. We're safe here in these trees, but when we move out onto these open slopes, for the next thirty minutes we're moving. We're not going to stop to powder our noses. We're not going to stop for selfies. We're not going to stop to take a piss. We're just going to hammer.'"

CHAPTER 24

TO SKI OR
NOT TO SKI

BEGLINGER PAUSED FOR LESS THAN a minute on the short and steep south-facing slope in Lower Swiss Meadows and probed roughly four feet down with his upturned ski pole. He couldn't reach any hard layers and found the snowpack to be consistently "stiff and strong."

Bullock followed suit, probing down himself, as did Craig and Evan Weselake, who had taken Beglinger's advanced mountaineering leadership course a couple of years before. An ultra-endurance athlete, Weselake had a favorite spot in line: right where Bullock currently was, on Beglinger's tail because of the challenge of the pace and "to ask questions," says Weselake, "to get an idea of what's going on in his mountaineering guide's computer brain."

Into the subalpine they climbed—systematically probing as they gained elevation—higher still, to where nothing with needles or bark stood between them and the headwall of Tumbledown Mountain. It was the first time this winter that Beglinger had traversed the lower flanks of this old friend that dominated the skyline every time he stepped out his front door. He set his track parallel to the massive slope to their right where he saw up close the remains of several class 3 avalanches that he had observed from afar two weeks earlier on January 6.

For context, and a peek inside what Beglinger's brain was processing as he passed through this exposed terrain, consider the following:

These quite large, class 3 slab avalanches had been triggered "by direct sun impact," he'd written in his logbook, "between 11 a.m. and 2 p.m." on the first clear and sunny day, just two days after an eleven-day storm cycle that dropped roughly two and a half to three feet of snow. On that same sunny day, he had observed nine additional natural and skier-remote-triggered (when a skier's weight or motion triggers an avalanche from a distance) avalanches on other nearby peaks. Beglinger had noted that all these January 6 avalanches had started at elevations above 8,000 feet, except for one that had been triggered at 6,800 feet.

As of today, January 20, Beglinger had not witnessed any avalanches or warning signs such as "whumpfing" or "cracking" in fourteen days, during which he had performed numerous stability tests on various (north-, east-, south-, and west-facing) aspects, and elevations throughout the SME tenure. These included three rutschblock tests, which all scored 7 (highest score for stability), and nine shovel and hand shear tests. The shovel tests scored "hard" or "very hard" (thus very stable) results at the deeper 50- and 120-centimeter layers. The most recent was just yesterday, January 19, at 3:00 p.m. on Mount Durrand's west face. He had paused at 8,500 feet on the 35-degree run called Gendarme, and performed a hand shear test down to the 120-centimeter layer, "to see how that suspected layer behaved," says Beglinger, "and it didn't even shear, that layer. And that is something I noticed already a week earlier, that the layer started to bond, and was not reactive." For this test, Beglinger recorded "No result" in his logbook.

These same tests executed at similar elevations earlier in the season had scored 4 and 5 on the rutschblock, moderate stability, while the shovel shears had scored "easy to moderate."

The more recent results told Beglinger that the snowpack was strengthening. In addition, he had tested slopes by aggressively ski-cutting ridges, convex rollovers, rocky points—areas that were historically common start points for avalanches. In the earlier season, he'd been able to trigger multiple slabs, including some that started on that Christmas layer, then stepped down to the deeper November 20 layer, but for the past two weeks he had been unable to get any of those deep layers to react, that is, slide, not even a crack, which told him, again, that the snowpack was settling and bonding.

His baseline for understanding the overall winter snowpack had been three snow pits dug to the ground and recorded in his logbook during the past twenty-four days: two full snow profiles were dug (by Ken Wylie) on

December 29 and another (by Beglinger) on January 5 at 6,360 feet on Chalet Hill. The third pit was not a profile, but rather a hasty "check on ground layer, visual of whole profile" that Beglinger dug at 7,300 feet on the Goat Face as Wylie had looked on five days before, on January 16.

Beglinger also considered the most recent avalanche report from the Canadian Avalanche Association for the northern Selkirks, posted three days earlier, on January 17.* This CAA bulletin stated: "Several size 1 to 1.5 natural and human triggered avalanches, at treeline and in the alpine, were reported as recent as Wednesday [January 15]. These occurrences are now becoming isolated as the recent storm snow continues to bond. A few remotely triggered size 2.5 avalanches failed in the Eastern Selkirks, some triggered from over 100 metres away. Widespread whumpfing continues to be observed in all areas."

The bulletin's forecast for avalanche danger in effect up until that evening (January 20) was "considerable" in the alpine, "considerable" at treeline, and "moderate" below treeline. Clair Israelson, the managing director of the Canadian Avalanche Association, described "considerable [as] our middle-range avalanche reading, not an unusually dangerous time at the present."

The "Travel Advisory" for this bulletin stated: "It is important to remember that this El Nino year is producing a complex and unusual snowpack for the mountains of BC. We have two deeply buried problem layers that are slow to heal and need our continued attention. Be alert for remote triggering and continue to be vigilant about avoiding those tempting big steep alpine faces. Any avalanche triggered on the older weaknesses may propagate extensively into a large and dangerous avalanche event. Be aware of how stresses penetrate deeper into the snowpack as you group up."

What it boiled down to was those deeply buried layers were there, and they weren't going anywhere. So, Beglinger did as he always had during winters with persistent weak layers in the snowpack: he monitored them, chose his routes carefully, and took his guests skiing while continuing to monitor.

---

* Due to government funding, these public avalanche bulletins were posted every three days, the most recent being the one released three days earlier on the evening of January 17. There was no computer or fax machine at the Durrand Glacier Chalet, so the avalanche bulletin was listened to, via satellite phone, every three days.

"Always, I'm probing," he says, "and doing routine stability tests en route. If I feel some weakness, then of course, I make a decision."

During the past three weeks, he'd led dozens of skiers and snowboarders up and down dozens of runs in the alpine, subalpine, and trees on runs ranging from 30 to upwards of 40 degrees. Beglinger knew this was the perfect pitch for avalanches as well the perfect incline for skiing and snowboarding at the level he advertised. "That's just how it is," says Beglinger. "People try to cheat themselves around this, but every good ski run is an avalanche path."

What gave him confidence to traverse these exposed slopes within range of any large avalanches that might come down Tumbledown's south face? First, he considered this to be an early season and early morning route because the sun is less intense, and therefore less likely to trigger surface sloughs that could build into avalanches. Case in point: the series of avalanches that came down this face most recently had been triggered by solar radiation on the slope between 11 a.m. and 2 p.m. on a clear day following a large storm.

Cold and overcast early season mornings like this—with no recent snow, strong winds, or avalanche activity—didn't concern Beglinger. Still, he maintained his brisk pace and told Bullock, who was a meter behind him, to give him a little more space for this section directly below the south face. Beglinger was ready to tell Bullock to pass that instruction down the line, but a quick glance revealed his group was already spread out. Toward the back third of the line, Jean-Luc Schwendener's slightly slower pace created an even wider gap, further minimizing Group 1's exposure to the slope above as they passed perpendicularly beneath it.

Beglinger had lived in these mountains for eighteen years. In the summer, he'd climbed their rock faces with ropes. In winter, he'd toured these routes and skied their slopes. He'd learned their seasonal nuances and knew what lay beneath the snow. The indicators—the extent of exposed rock peppering the white landscape, and the probing he'd done up to this point—gave him an idea of the snow depth on surrounding slopes, and what was going on within the snowpack beneath his feet. The size and age of the surviving trees gave him an idea of the avalanche history of this slope dating back centuries. He understood that his past eighteen years here were but a blink of an eye in the evolving chronology of these peaks, but still he had learned a lot about their habits.

He was always learning, and thus far his routes and intuition had served him well; however, he had no delusions that what he was doing was without risk.

ROUGHLY NINETY MILES to the northwest, Don Schwartz had started the day chatting with his boss, Bob Sayer, on the way to the morning guides' meeting at Mike Wiegele Helicopter Skiing. The week before, both Schwartz and Sayer had guided their old friend and surfing icon Gerry Lopez, who had learned to ride there with Ken Achenbach, Schwartz, and Craig in the early 1990s. Known for his mellow demeanor, Lopez had asked almost apologetically why they weren't hitting any of his favorite runs. This was, after all, the man known for his masterful but relaxed style deep in the tube at the notorious Banzai Pipeline on Oahu's North Shore.

He had wanted it deep, and preferably steep, which according to Sayer "wasn't happening" on this, Lopez's annual weeklong trip. "We've got a nasty layer down deep," Sayer told Lopez. "It's not just us. It's across the province from the southern Selkirks all the way up to the northern Monashees. Company policy—we aren't doing anything steeper than thirty degrees, no avalanche terrain. We've told all our guides, 'If you take your guests on anything steeper than that, you can come in and clean out your locker.'"

Lopez was "totally cool with the policy," recalls Sayer, which in ski resort terms would be like showing up at Whistler Blackcomb and finding all the black diamond runs you love roped off and closed for the season.

Schwartz recalls this risk-averse policy was born the first week in January, when veteran guide Erich Schadinger sat down at the morning meeting and opened a book. "It was a fishing book," says Schwartz, "and he was just sitting there reading, not seeming to pay attention, while we were going through the avalanche forecast and discussing which runs we'd open up. The forecaster leading the meeting kind of called him out, like 'Oh, Erich, do you have any thoughts?' Erich calmly put his book down, looked around the room, and said, 'Thoughts on what?'

"Everybody gave him the blank stare and he said, 'Well . . . I looked at the forecast board and noticed the [snow] profile that's up there still has that layer. Has that layer disappeared overnight that I don't know about? No? Still there? Okay, that's what I thought. We're not into a new season, it hasn't melted out on us. Still there, right? Look, this is the layer that kills professionals. This is the layer that is deadly, untrustworthy, unpredictable. Until you can show me a profile where that layer no longer exists, all my decisions for the year are made. I know where I'm skiing. We don't need to have this meeting. We should be having coffee with our guests. This is a giant waste of time.'

"I thought, *Oh my God, that is the most profound thing I've heard about that layer.* We were trying to push that line, but in Erich's mind, if you're making a decision based on how stable that layer is, or isn't, then you've already made your choice."

That meeting was a revelation for Sayer, and for Mike Wiegele himself, who said, "There's no sense trying to outthink this. We're not smart enough to figure this out. Nobody is. You can't take it out of the mountains, so let's change how we're guiding."

The policy, according to Sayer, was "If it can avalanche, don't go there. You can ski steeper in the trees in some spots if it's good-supported terrain, but nothing with a steep break-over. Nothing that goes into a creek, a hole, any type of terrain trap. Nothing that's going to sweep you into the forest. Nothing over thirty degrees."

WIEGELE'S EXPANSIVE TERRAIN options and helicopter access were, in part, what made this policy possible.[†] Smaller areas with terrain accessed in a snowcat or on foot made avoiding avalanche terrain even more difficult, if not impossible, whereas skiers using helicopters are only exposed while actually skiing down. As such, Wiegele's extreme risk-averse policy was unique across the province. Most if not all the other operators continued to monitor,

---

[†]   Mike Wiegele Helicopter Skiing terrain tenure was 1.5 million total acres, though "about half isn't skiable because it's too steep, flat, or heavily forested," says Sayer. "Cutting out all avalanche terrain took away roughly 65 percent of our 750,000 skiable acres, leaving around 265,000 acres to service 100 skiers per day." In comparison, the terrain John Buffery guides at Baldface Lodge cat-skiing is 32,000 total acres. Selkirk Mountain Experience is 24,000 total acres.

and cautiously ski much of their terrain. "Guides are inherently problem solvers and want to show their clients a good time," says Sayer. "We believe that we can keep people safe out there—otherwise, we wouldn't be guides."

Down south at Baldface Lodge, "every night, we'd scour the InfoEx," recalls John Buffery, "and it was like 'uh oh, here we go.' We'd see reports all over the place, with sizable avalanches, like size three—that's big—occurring at random geographic areas, latitudes, longitudes, elevation, it was random. So you knew it [that layer] was everywhere, and the triggers were mostly skier remote—[the avalanche] wasn't happening directly on the bottom of your skis, directly underneath where you're standing or skiing. They were something we call 'traveling collapses,' which made it even trickier to move people through."

Imagine tracks of dominoes spiderwebbing out in all directions beneath the snow. If you're standing at point A and knock over a domino it initiates a "traveling collapse" of dominoes. If you're at a place where there is no tension on the snow—it's not steep enough to slide downhill—the snow just collapses with a "whumpf" sound. You'll feel the snow literally drop beneath your feet. You're fine, but the collapse keeps traveling outward, and if it hits a point on a slope where it's steeper, and thus the tension is greater, that slope will avalanche. Thus a skier (or helicopter landing) could trigger the "dominoes." Nothing will avalanche until the collapse hits a slope, likely 30 degrees or steeper. Shape of slope, ground cover, and other variables also apply, but taking tension-filled, 30-degree slopes out of the equation exponentially reduces risk.

So province-wide, guides continued to ski and ride, not so much "on eggshells" but around them, monitoring that buried crust layer and avoiding shallow spots where a skier's weight or movement might trigger the dominoes. "At some point in the season," says Buffery, "when you see a layer and you monitor it, at some point, you kind of take it off your radar because it's so deep that you don't penetrate to it.

"Or, it's not reactive metamorphically, meaning it has bonded to the adjacent layers. But this November 20 layer seemed to be preserved for numerous reasons. First, it was a significantly large surface hoar; and two, it was surrounded by cold snow [that remained below freezing temperatures] on a prominent crust." The cold snow on top was like the lid on a Yeti cooler, and the crust was the cooler itself, insulating and preserving the dominoes/facets in a fragile deep freeze. Instead of melting, and bonding together with the crust, the facets persisted from late November through December, and here it was the end of January, and it was still firmly on Buffery's radar, in great part because the InfoEx kept reporting significant avalanches running on that layer.

"Every morning at the guides meeting," says Buffery, "it was a struggle to find terrain within our tenure that challenged our guests' abilities within a safe experience."

Brad Harrison was part owner of Golden Alpine Holidays, a group of three smaller touring operations located "just on the other side of the Selkirks, so next-door to Ruedi," says Harrison. "That November rain crust was on my mind all winter, but at that point in the season, it just wasn't that reactive for us. Was it there in the snowpack? Yeah. Why wasn't it reactive? Who knows. I knew lots of people trying everything they could to get it to react without success." One of them was Diny Harrison, a guide with Canadian Mountain Holidays (CMH), the biggest helicopter skiing company in the world. She recalls coming out of guide training in the southern Selkirks in late November and everybody was talking about "the November rain crust, look out . . . warning bells, warning bells, this rain crust is going to be around to haunt us, we've got to be careful." Then the season progressed into December. The crust had been covered with snow and Diny Harrison went to help set up CMH Gothics in the northern Selkirks. "Sure enough," she says, "everywhere you went you'd trigger it relatively easily and there's avalanches getting triggered from fifty meters away, or whatever. This is north from Ruedi." But then Harrison returned to CMH's Revelstoke, which operates in the Monashees. She was assisting in the production of an avalanche training video and when she "went out bombing to create an avalanche, I threw twenty-four shots [similar to sticks of dynamite] all over the place and couldn't trigger it. I'm thinking, *What the hell, why don't we have it here?* We just couldn't make it react. I could have jumped up and down on it, and it wasn't moving."

"It just had to be the absolute perfect circumstances to get it to react," says Harrison. "It was a sleeping giant."

CHAPTER 25

LA TRAVIATA

AROUND 9:30 A.M. BEGLINGER CONTINUED to climb into the alpine, traversing beneath the looming south face of Tumbledown Mountain's west ridge, skiing briskly toward a knoll on the snowy horizon. Beyond the reach of avalanches, he stopped atop this high ground and unshouldered his pack for the first time since crossing the Twin Falls snow bridge, roughly two thousand vertical feet below. One by one, Bullock, the Truckee crew guys, and the others glided up. "We'll have some tea here," he said. "Eat a snack." He pulled out his thermos, had a drink, and then radioed their position to the chalet.

Nicoline had been bouncing back and forth between their residence, over-seeing Charlotte and Florina's homeschooling, and the chalet, tending to the guest rooms and helping Kim Lomas prep for dinner, when she heard the radio come to life. Though it wasn't something she dwelled upon, in the back of her mind Nicoline knew that every time her husband skied away from this little haven they'd carved out of the wilderness, it could be the last she saw him. It's the reality of the mountains, so she welcomed the squelch of the radio on the kitchen counter just before 10 a.m. when Beglinger reported they had arrived at Upper Swiss Meadows above Tumbledown Lake and were "having some tea."

"Copy that, Ruedi," returned Lomas. "Enjoy your tea."

Nicoline was focused on her job running the chalet, and she left the guiding to her husband. She would listen in on the radio sometimes, when they called in to hear the avalanche reports, and knew the ABCs of av-alanche safety, avoiding certain slopes for several days after a storm. She knew the runs he stuck to during volatile periods—such as the last big storm cycle three weeks earlier, when it had warmed up and "everything came down." It had taken an entire column in their logbook to record the avalanches observed that day.

But today was "pretty ordinary." It had been weeks since it had snowed. There had been some wind, but nothing beyond moderate. They hadn't gotten the InfoEx yet. In fact none of the smaller touring companies like Selkirk Mountain Experience subscribed to that daily service. They were working on getting their satellite linked up so they could get on the internet for several reasons, but she was more interested in being able to email grocery lists to the office in Revelstoke than following the daily reports. The reports Beglinger did listen to came in every three days and were like the CliffsNotes, summarizing the much more detailed InfoEx reports versus listing, for example, eight separate avalanches, including the size of the avalanche, the elevation it occurred at, the trigger, etc. The public report might say "widespread avalanches, some triggered remotely." Some of the impact is lost, and certainly the details, but Beglinger was still mitigating risks as he always had, based upon his own observations and monitoring of his local snowpack. One thing is clear: Beglinger was not privy to the detailed reporting that operations like Baldface, Mike Wiegele Helicopter Skiing, CMH, Island Lake Lodge, and others were getting.

UP ON THE knoll, it was snowing a centimeter-plus per hour, as Craig wrote in his guide's book at 10 a.m. Checking his altimeter, he noted the elevation was 7,500 feet, temperature 18 degrees Fahrenheit, wind light from the southeast, and the sky was overcast.

It was a slate-gray but glorious day in the Selkirk Mountains for him and all the ski and snowboard mountaineers scattered atop this beautiful knoll, an island of trampled snow surrounded by miles of velvety, untracked powder as far as the eye could see. They sipped tea from thermoses and chomped down pastries and sandwiches while recovering from the climb they'd just completed from Twin Falls, some two thousand vertical feet below, fueling up for the next leg.

When they'd flown into this remote wilderness on Saturday morning, most of them had been strangers, but two days of hard work crossing glaciers, summiting peaks, and that euphoric weightless high while flying down pristine slopes quickly forged a backcountry esprit de corps, a comradeship that was strengthened each evening as they shared stories, adventures, and bottles of wine in the warmth of the chalet. Only a few were aware that the quiet apprentice guide who had carried in their baggage two days earlier was a four-time world champion who had once been the most famous snowboarder on the planet. He was simply Craig—the guy who helped shovel snow around the chalet and who was an understudy of the man most of them revered as the legend in their midst, Ruedi Beglinger.

With a few words and hand gestures, Beglinger pointed out their objective to the group around him: Fronalp Peak was within striking distance— a short tour would take them up gently rolling terrain to a classic, pointed peak visible in the distance. The wide-open alpine slope below Fronalp is a nearly 1,500-vertical-foot dreamland of bumps and gullies all the way back to treeline, where, because of that lower-elevation crust, they'd stay high and circle back to their current location. "Then we will do La Traviata," said Beglinger, pointing diagonally up and across the expansive open slope to their right, toward a south-southwest-facing broad and shallow gully that ran steeply off Tumbledown Mountain's west ridge.

The 180-meter-high couloir resembles a 350-meter-long snow-filled slide that is 65 meters wide at the top and fans out to a width of 160 meters at the bottom. Roughly the height of a sixty-story building, the upper half of the "slide" is bound on the climber's left by a rocky cliff face, while the climber's right is bound by what in summer is a rocky knoll, but in winter becomes a snowy wave, upon which prevailing winds had formed small overhanging cornices. For Craig it was a backside wall that was begging to be slashed and bottom-turned repeatedly for several hundred vertical feet, a snow-surfer's playground.

Named after the opera *La Traviata*, which Beglinger loved, not only for its sweeping natural beauty, but because of its utility as a historically stable route up or down the avalanche-prone south face of Tumbledown Mountain's west ridge. In fact, some of the largest avalanches Beglinger had witnessed in the past eighteen years had ripped down that south face. Many had been triggered from cornice-falls, others from storm wind and/or sheer weight of snow, and some he'd triggered himself purposely when coming in from the top with aggressive ski cutting. He'd once seen the debris of a massive cornice that fell directly onto the bench—a sort of step down below the west ridge—that spans the top of La Traviata's entrance and continues east for several hundred meters. That cornice fall had triggered the adjacent south slope, but the snow within La Traviata couloir had remained solid, and unmoved. "The reason for this is it's always a very deep, strong snowpack in there," says Beglinger. "Even if the wind-scour down the ridge might be a little more shallow, I've seen big avalanches falling off the cliffs down the ridge, but never has it propagated onto that slope itself. Many times I came from Tumbledown Peak, we get caught in a big storm up there, and a group does not want to go down the north side, they ski down the ridge, all the way down, and we take La Traviata—the gully, with the cliff for visibility, that's the safe route, then down to the trees, and we come back to the chalet that way.

"In eighteen-years history, I can't remember that slope ever avalanched," he says. Nor had he seen the remains of a single avalanche that had either started atop or propagated into La Traviata's west couloir. The only thing Beglinger had seen come down this gully aside from harmless surface sloughs were skiers and snowboarders, and that was his plan for later that day if conditions allowed.

For now, as the final members of his group rolled in, he probed around the knoll and its perimeter, searching but finding nothing but deep, well-settled snow with roughly one foot of dry Selkirk powder on top. *This will make for some very nice skiing*, he thought to himself. Looking back at his group, he saw Jean-Luc Schwendener passing out chunks of Toblerone, the Truckee crew bantering, and Evan Weselake and his friend Naomi Heffler laughing as she licked every last smudge of chocolate off the plastic wrap that held her brownie. "You can't waste a single calorie up here," she'd said with a shrug. Heffler's father, Harold, had been one of Beglinger's very first hiking guests in the summer of 1986. After that trip, he had been "infatuated with mountaineering" and returned to ski with Beglinger in 1987, then brought along his wife Lyn, Naomi (then ten), and her younger sister, Laura (eight), in the summer of 1989—the same ages Beglinger's daughters Charlotte and Florina were now.

That really put things in perspective for Beglinger. He'd had two other hiking clients booked that week with Harold in 1986, but they'd canceled—

which was telling of the early years, when bookings were scant, and Beglinger was just building his clientele. Had it really been fifteen years since he'd guided the Heffler family? That ten-year-old girl was now a twenty-five-year-old woman who had conveyed a warm hello from her mother and father when she'd stepped off the helicopter two days earlier, but her presence said more than any handshake or hug. It was a given: the Hefflers had entrusted him with the safety and care of their daughter, and that was, without a doubt, the highest praise Beglinger could receive from a former client.

WYLIE HEARD THE radio exchange between Beglinger and the chalet around the same time he broke above treeline. He was wary of his ability to detect inconsistencies as he probed into the snowpack, and nervous about navigating back down this very slope if, like yesterday, the weather moved in and whited everything out.

Beglinger's track was deep and distinct, but as they continued higher up, all it would take was some blowing snow, and a wind-scoured ridge, and the track would be gone.

For now, it was snowing lightly and visibility was good—he could see Finnerty joining Group 1, gathered in the distance. They appeared like colorful specks against the rolling canvas of white. Usually Wylie was energized by big nature, savored feeling small in the immensity of the wild, but today everything felt ominous. The group ahead appeared like tiny ants lounging not in the shade of a majestic Selkirk peak but rather in the looming shadow of a fixed tidal wave, threatening to crest simply because it could.

Now that Finnerty had caught up, Beglinger might head out with his group at any moment. While Wylie always felt flustered, if not intimidated, around the man, he still found perverse comfort in his presence. Any assistant guide will attest that keeping the lead guide in view while navigating unfamiliar terrain inspires confidence, and that was something Wylie just couldn't seem to muster. He felt anxious about everything—the terrain, his own abilities—and the thought crossed his mind, if he were there alone he would pull the plug and return to the chalet.

It wasn't the first time in Wylie's budding career as a guide that he'd had an uneasy feeling. On day four of his fourteen-day Assistant Alpine Guide exam in 1999, he'd had a bad feeling about a climbing route his examiner had chosen off the summit of Castle Mountain, a short-roping descent the examiner stated would be "easier" after the long day he'd experienced on Mount Louis on day three. With a little research to back up his trepidation, he told the examiner his concerns, which were disregarded. During the descent, a three-foot-square ledge Wylie was standing on spontaneously collapsed. He fell ten feet before his rope came tight and left him hanging there in space, while "microwave-sized" blocks of limestone and a shower of stones echoed down the face of the wall and smashed into the ground far below.

The exam shifted from rock to glacial on the Columbia Icefields, and on day twelve, while roped up on the upper Victoria Glacier, Wylie had another uneasy, what he described as a "strange," feeling. The group was fatigued, and he anticipated somebody was going to make a mistake. He made an executive decision—without the approval of the examiner—and turned the group around, which he was told later by the course leader was "not your call to make." The ACMG technical board reviewed his insubordination, and as punishment added a day to the course, which he then passed, with high marks for "Mountain Sense."

He left the course with the prestigious Alpine Guide certificate but also a scolding reminder that changing a route, pulling the plug, anything that affects the group is "exclusively the responsibility of the supervising guide."

The examiners, collectively, had felt some of Wylie's "strange feelings" of unease came out of left field. "We [the examiners] think you need to work on differentiating between real risk and perceived risk."

Up ahead, on the "anthill," the mood was light and laughter easy when Dave Finnerty strode into an already primed and jovial crowd with a pocketful of jokes to keep the party going.

Beglinger was zipping up his backpack and preparing to move on when he looked to the west and saw "the fog starting to roll in, in front of Fronalp," he recalls. "And I thought, *Ah, not again!* It's nicer with blue sky. . . . It's a little bit gully-shaped terrain and bumpy so in flat light it's more difficult to ski in." And, in a whiteout, much easier to get lost in, but visibility here at La

Traviata—some fifteen minutes into their tea break—was good. Even with some very light snow, he could see clearly to the ridgeline, "Durrand Glacier Chalet, this is Ruedi," he said. "We are leaving Upper Swiss Meadows. Change of plan, Fronalp is in fog. We will do La Traviata first, over."

"Copy that," replied Kim.

Jeff Bullock was near Beglinger and recalls thinking to himself, *Sure, whatever. I don't know what that is.* He didn't know the names of the runs; that was Wylie and Beglinger's job. Shortly after Beglinger announced the change of plans, Wylie arrived. He skied in among the Group 1 skiers scattered atop the knoll, unshouldered his backpack and dug into it for his thermos and a snack. (Beglinger recalls Wylie stopped "right next to me"—no more than a few feet away—in contrast to Wylie's recollection that he was "across the group" which spanned ten, maybe fifteen feet.) Vern Lunsford and Dennis Yates arrived right after Wylie. Next, Joe Pojar and Kathy Kessler shuffled in with Paula Couturier following. John Seibert, who had stopped to take a pee, brought up the rear several minutes later.

Wylie counted them off as they arrived. It felt safe there, clearly beyond the reach of avalanches, but the knoll was only a Band-Aid for his nerves, a temporary rest stop off a scenic route he'd had no part in choosing, which was how it worked—full guides lead, assistant guides follow. Upon arrival, he told his guests to have a drink and a snack, and then pointed out Fronalp Peak, still visible to the west among clouds and fog. Tracing the long ridgeline back with his finger, he pointed up at the rocky nub of La Traviata peak above them to their right, and to its left and below the ridge he pointed out La Traviata west couloir.

Wylie, believing that their next leg was the mellow approach to Fronalp Peak, was grateful he was not facing La Traviata just yet, but still, his tension was building. At the same time, he was completely unaware that he had missed Beglinger's radio call. Perhaps he had inadvertently turned the volume down on his own radio, which he kept in a holster on his chest; or maybe he'd zoned out during the transmittal. He had definitely been experiencing some distress. "A fog descends on me" is how Wylie describes it, "I see the people in my group, but I am barely able to speak. They seem far away, yet I am standing right beside them." On the knoll, Wylie observed everybody having a good time, but he couldn't get out of his funk. When he looked at Beglinger, he saw "... only a man I despise ... I am in a bubble ... Anxiety paralyzes me; halting conversation or connection with anyone in any way."*

ACCORDING TO BEGLINGER, "everybody was smiling, talking, telling jokes" when he focused his attention on Wylie and gave him some brief directions— when to follow, spacing, and the like—just before he shouldered his backpack and prepared to head out. "There was that buzz of excitement, when you're ready to push off," says Heidi Biber, who remembers leaving shortly after her friend Kathy Kessler arrived. "How are you feeling?" she asked, and Kessler replied with a smile and a nod; the slower pace was apparently doing her well. "There wasn't time to chat," says Biber, so I said, "See you later. Have fun." After speaking to Wylie, Beglinger turned to his group, gathered around him on the western side of the knoll. "Craig," he said, "you want to come up front and lead with me?"

There are no notes in Craig's guidebook to document what he was thinking, but La Traviata would have been both aesthetically pleasing as a line and not even remotely sketchy in comparison to lines he had ridden hundreds of times. To ascend it, though, was another matter altogether. How would they approach the couloir? Where would Beglinger set his track? It wasn't gnarly, but it was a big feature, and fairly steep. The opportunity to lead with Beglinger would have been a golden opportunity as a practicum student.

But just a moment before, one of Schwendener's climbing skins had fallen off, probably because some snow had worked its way between the adhesive and ski bottom.

"I'm going to hang back here and help Jean-Luc," Craig told Beglinger. "He's having some issues with his skins. I've got duct tape if he needs it."

Beglinger caught the eye of Finnerty, who flashed a big smile and gave two thumbs up. SME staff usually brought up the rear while touring up. In this case that was perfect because he was ecstatic to hang back near Craig. He leaned in and told Beglinger, "I'm so happy to be here." Beglinger then turned his skis uphill and started breaking trail at a fast clip across the low-angle

---

* Quotations in this paragraph are from Wylie, *Buried*.

terrain. Age Fluitman fell in directly behind him, then Rick Martin, Keith Lindsay, and Heidi Biber, who had been toward the back of the line. Touring skiers are creatures of habit, often staying in the same place in line, following the same person for entire days and sometimes for entire trips. Biber had been behind Schwendener, who had maintained a steady comfortable pace to this point, but it was slightly slower than those in the front half of Beglinger's group, which had created a gap. She wasn't sure what prompted her—perhaps the carbs from her snack or the excitement—but Biber felt a surge of energy and decided in a split second that she wanted to be farther ahead in the middle of her Truckee pals. Bruce Stewart fell in line behind her, then Rick Reynolds.

Evan Weselake watched them head out and was champing at the bit—battling his endurance-athlete, type-A-competitor personality, which didn't relinquish the lead easily—to get moving. He reminded himself that this wasn't a day to train and push. This wasn't a race. He was there having a good time with his friend Naomi Heffler, who was just finishing up a snack. "No rush," he told her as she shoved the last bite in her mouth, then took a swig of water and hoisted her backpack on just as Schwendener stood—his climbing skin now affixed, thanks to Craig—and pushed forward. Weselake followed Schwendener, then Heffler jumped in line, while Charles Bieler stood casually by waiting for Finnerty and Craig to move forward so he could be the caboose on this line.

It was one of those "no, no, I insist, after you" moments, and uncharacteristic for Bieler, who, like Weselake, was an endurance athlete, and had been a competitive Nordic skier. In past trips here, he'd locked into whatever pace Beglinger set at or near the front of the line. On this trip, however, he was dealing with some intestinal issues. The first two days, he'd powered through with barely any food or water, opting for dehydration over dealing with the awkward and embarrassing challenges of having to squat along the trail. Thus far the antidiarrheal he'd taken early that morning had worked its magic, but on the off-chance nature did call, he strategically waited so he could bring up the rear of the lead group. Now that they were in the alpine, ducking behind a tree wasn't going to be an option.

Finnerty, however, insisted that he as staff should bring up the rear and waved him forward, so he reluctantly jumped in before too much of a gap was created. Then Craig and Finnerty followed as numbers twelve and thirteen at the end of Beglinger's line.

Jeff Bullock, who had been right behind Beglinger up to this point, was still standing there on the knoll facing west, inexplicably loitering as his group, Group 1, moved onward and upward without him. As they left, he just hadn't followed, and Bullock himself couldn't put his finger on why.

He just couldn't bring himself to move forward. He was glued to the spot.

CHAPTER 26

UP

BEGLINGER'S BRISK TRAIL-BREAKING STRIDES CUT through the feather-light surface snow, leaving behind a trench that his guests locked in their skis and followed. As they pushed farther away from the knoll, the shooshing of synthetic climbing skins sliding on snow replaced friendly banter, becoming the cadence to their westerly march.

Weselake was pumped for this run. The second that Beglinger had pointed it out, he'd thought, *Oh my god, we get to ski this?* Now, as they approached the cliff face, he got a better perspective of the steepness. *This is going to be so good.*

Had Beglinger continued on this angled trajectory across the bench that spanned the base of the La Traviata west couloir, he could have meandered west up the valley, but as they approached the rocky cliff face, he made his first hard-right turn of the day and headed eastward back toward La Traviata. Fourth in line behind him, Heidi Biber saw that clouds and fog had completely obscured Fronalp Peak to the west as she shuffled her skis around the turn. The cliff face was only a meter or so to her left, and with that dark rock beside her, it was as if somebody had flipped a switch and sharpened her vision. She looked up the craggy, broken walls, happy to be snug next to them versus continuing into an alpine void of flat light and low visibility. Tiny snowflakes swirled and danced with the wind against the cliff, which she skied beside for another hundred meters or so before stopping in the track behind Rick Martin and Age Fluitman, whom Beglinger had instructed to wait at the "corner" where granite face met couloir. The remainder of the group stacked up—ski tips to tails—behind Biber.

Tucked behind the protective rocks, they watched Beglinger angling up and across thirty or forty meters of the midslope expanse of La Traviata, prob ing into the snowpack as he went. Those in the front of the line could look up and left around the "corner," all the way to where this gully topped out onto a low-angle bench—a sort of stairstep—just below the rock-studded, snowcapped west ridge. They could also see, a football field and a half away, the sweeping, feathery details of the long vertical wave on the far side of the gully. Beyond the wave was Tumbledown Mountain, its south face appearing steeper from this side-hill perspective—as did this gully they were poised to enter.

Heidi Biber used her ski pole to flick up the heel risers on her bindings, compensating for the angle of the track that Beglinger had increased a few degrees in order to minimize the number of kick turns required to switch back and forth up this slope. "I don't think we'd be climbing something this steep at home," Keith Lindsay told her. She shrugged in response, thinking, *Ruedi knows what he's doing.*

Farther back in the line, Craig would have understood precisely what Beg linger was doing, having narrated this probing protocol to Ari Marcopoulos a few weeks earlier. "The best thing you can do is feel it with a probe," he'd said. "The variability of how deep the snow is a huge factor. . . . You dig your pit . . . but you never know what it's like another twenty or thirty feet over. . . . We have to be more intuitive." Craig was certainly assessing the snow with his upturned ski pole himself, most likely finding it just as consol idated, what Beglinger described as "fantastic, superstrong. You could drive a truck on it."

And so Beglinger trusted this slope "one hundred percent" when he mo tioned Fluitman forward. "Let's spread out some," Martin said to the group, allowing Fluitman two to four meters spacing before he followed. At the first kick turn on the far side of the gully, where the uptrack switched back to the west, there were a few moments when the skiers at the front of the line were above the skiers trailing on the lower switchback. Craig was known for being hypervigilant about not being above somebody else on a slope, lest he kick an avalanche down upon them—not unlike walking in front of a loaded gun.

However, Craig had learned this past year that there were exceptions—

and indeed more risk—while moving larger groups through the mountains, when the terrain might dictate a route that exposes skiers, albeit as briefly as possible to limit exposure time. And Beglinger, who had deemed this snow too strong for a skier to trigger, stopped probing after the second switchback because he could not reach any problem layers. He'd felt no inconsistencies or weaknesses, and there were no indications of wind or surface slabs. "If you can't get a probe down," he says, "there's no point every twenty steps to push a probe down. After a few times, it comes to a point where you just have to trust."

Each of Beglinger's five switchbacks was also long enough to accommodate thirteen skiers with at least five meters spacing between them, more than enough distance to distribute their weight across. As long as the line kept moving, they would only be above each other at the switchback transitions, whereas in a narrow gully they would have been stacked up two, three, maybe four times.

Although Beglinger was comfortable having a handful of skiers from the *same* group on a lower switchback, he never condoned a *separate* group with a *separate* guide to climb, regroup, ski, or do anything beneath another. It had been his standard safety protocol for as long as he could remember.

Both Colin Zacharias and Buffery had encouraged Craig to spend as much time as possible with more senior guides—either in practicum or training—as practice for the coming exam. "Even if you're following, imagine you're in the driver's seat," Buffery had told him. "Look ahead at the terrain and the objective and ask yourself: 'Is this where I would lead this group? Do I have enough information to assess this slope? Will this run give my clients the best experience considering their skills and current conditions?' And then be prepared to defend your decisions."

These would have been some of the questions Craig was asking himself as he entered the gully, knowing that once all thirteen of them were in, they were committed. Once they started climbing, the only way out was getting to the top.

SEVERAL MINUTES BEFORE, Wylie had been shocked to see Beglinger approach the cliff face and turn right, back toward La Traviata, and not left toward

Fronalp Peak, which had been both the plan and what he'd psyched himself up to do. *Did I miss something?* he thought.

Trying to remain calm, he got on the radio and casually asked Beglinger, "Ummm, where are we going?"

"We're going to La Traviata," Beglinger shot back. "I radioed that into the chalet at the break."

This was news to Wylie, who had zero recollection of the radio call or anything else regarding this unexpected turn of events. "There was no discussion of a change of plans," he says. "The last direction I'd heard from Beglinger was to stay one hundred meters apart during the climb from Carnes Creek." In the split second Wylie had to respond, there was no time to piece together exactly what had happened, and so, even though every fiber in his being told him not to, his response to Beglinger was a short and affirmative "Okay, copy that."

If this exchange hinted that there had been another breakdown in communication between Beglinger and Wylie, neither of them voiced it.

When Bullock saw Beglinger lead his group back toward what he describes as " a pretty big feature, big slopes, steep slopes," he thought, not judgmentally, but more puzzled, like *That doesn't make sense to me.* He had no reason to think it was a bad idea or a good idea because he didn't know the terrain or understand the snowpack there. He didn't really know Beglinger either; but he trusted him.

WYLIE STOOD ON the west end of the knoll several hundred meters away and watched, even "marveled" at Beglinger's confidence and technique as he probed aggressively into the snow ahead of his skis, while moving forward incrementally, leaving in his wake a perfectly inclined track upon which his clients and then Wylie and his group would follow.

Now that the decision was made, Wylie did everything he could to psych himself up and go. This was his moment to shut down those demons, to get on that stage and perform. The more time he had to sit there and think about it, the more likely he would be to freeze up and freak out. But the guide in him was still looking after his group, stalling so that John Seibert, who had been the last to arrive, could have a few minutes to catch his breath and get a drink. Vern Lunsford, the forty-nine-year-old aerospace engineer from Colorado, was standing in the track right on the tails of Wylie's skis. An avid ice climber, backcountry skier, and mountaineer, Lunsford had come here to be challenged and wasn't too happy about being in the slower Group 2 for the third day in a row. He'd told Wylie as much earlier in the day, and conveyed it again now as he stood, pack on, skis pointing west, practically revving his engine.

According to Seibert, the break was short, at most five minutes to have a quick bite before he skied forward to Wylie and Lunsford, who moved out a couple meters apart. Seibert stepped in behind Lunsford and was followed by Dennis Yates, the laid-back ski instructor from Southern California who had been talking with the SME office manager, Paula Couturier, about what a nice perk it must be to come spend a week up here. Seibert glanced back and nodded at Yates as they kicked and glided forward, almost immediately in rhythm. Seibert had skied La Traviata just the year before—though they'd come in from the other side and scored one of the longest, most scenic peak-to-creek runs from the summit of Tumbledown Mountain, down the west ridge, into La Traviata and then across this bench where they dove back into the trees, and by the time they'd hit the creek at the bottom of Powder Mania they'd skied more than five thousand vertical feet of powder. That was the kind of skiing that kept Seibert coming back, that and the people who were drawn to it, like Yates, who had set the mood the evening before, strumming a guitar in the reading room. Seibert could hear Yates now, humming a melodic something that he can't exactly recall, except that it set the perfect pace.

Kathy Kessler jumped in line behind Yates. Even with her cold, she'd had everybody doing the polka the night before, and if somebody was humming, and she knew the tune, she was going to join in.

Next in line was Joe Pojar, on the third day of his second week, so he was acclimated, feeling strong and just happy to be there. He'd been taking care of his ailing mother for several months, and these two weeks were an opportunity to decompress and "just be in nature." Working hard and skiing hard was his own form of meditation. Once he was in a ski track and climbing, he didn't have a care in the world. On this morning he was particularly enthused to knock off La Traviata, which he had "almost skied" a few years earlier, before being turned away during their approach.

Couturier got in line behind Pojar. Everybody seemed cheery and content when they left the knoll. It was calm, a little snowy, and just a perfect morning to have a ski. Meanwhile, Jeff Bullock had still not moved an inch, and remained glued to the knoll as he watched Couturier ski away. He was the last person on the knoll, even though he had been first to arrive with Beglinger at least thirty minutes earlier.

He waited until he was the last person in Group 2, on an intuition, a gut feeling he could not explain. When there was nobody else to go, Bullock had two choices: turn around and ski back to the chalet by himself, or follow.

He followed.

CHAPTER 27

WE'LL BE FINE

It was, in all likelihood, a glorious moment in the mountains for Craig Kelly as he approached the top of La Traviata and was heading back toward the snowy wave that was peaking on the far side of the gully. In surfing terms, he was paddling for the horizon—the top of this gully—where Group 1 and Group 2 would regroup before he would get his turn to spin around and drop in, catch that wave, and ride its clean and glassy face back down this mountain.

Life had come full circle for Craig. Here he was with a group of companions who had bonded over the hard work of climbing up mountains and the pure joy of sliding back down them. That was how this story had begun for Craig twenty years earlier, hiking backcountry gullies with the Mount Baker Hard Core. He was a stone's throw from the top of this gully, chatting with his new friend Dave Finnerty, who, as a fellow snowboarder, had likely noted the surflike possibilities of the terrain feature they were staring at.

Years before, Finnerty had road-tripped down to Mount Baker, which was a pilgrimage for most snowboarders. He'd ambled into the Mt. Baker Snowboard Shop and picked up a jacket and one of the shop's coveted red and white stickers, which he slapped on his board. He stared at the photos on the wall, signed by all the pros who'd put down roots there, and those who had simply passed through. There were legends on the wall like Sims, Carpenter, and of course Craig Kelly, who was now just a couple meters ahead of him on this skin track, talking to him like a brother he'd known his entire life.

The evening before, Craig and Finnerty had joined in on the Truckee crew's impromptu polka dance party in the chalet, had a couple beers, then shared stories and a bottle of wine, which affirmed to Finnerty that heroes—at least this hero—could live up to and even surpass the hype. Yet Finnerty still had not asked Craig to sign the issue of *Snowboard Life* sitting on his bedside table. He'd studied every photo and read every word of that magazine, including those that Craig had written in the opening pages, wherein he'd paid homage to the type of rider he most respected. Craig had written those words three years earlier, in the summer of 1999, just a year after snowboarding's debut in the Olympics and about the time the X Games were heating up, halfpipes were getting huge, and everything about snowboarding was next level—bigger, higher, and faster. With all those rock stars and riding styles to choose from, Craig had written: "While I will always have the utmost respect for the superhuman out-of-bounds freestyle and extreme stunts that seem to continually progress beyond our imaginable limits, my highest appreciation goes out to the simple rider who's out there just for the experience."

A rider just like Finnerty.

BEGLINGER HAD ALREADY crossed over to the far side of the gully, made his kick turn, and was coming back toward the center where he'd make the final turn that would take him up and over the slightly convex roll at the top. The conversation that he could see—and almost hear—going on between Craig and Finnerty made him smile.

Scanning his surroundings as he always did, Beglinger was surprised to see Wylie's group gathered at the corner beneath the cliff far below. They were poised to follow Wylie, who was already in the center of the gully.

"Ruedi," said Rick Martin, "the other group is coming in beneath us."

"Yes, I see this," Beglinger muttered back.

SOME FIVE METERS behind Martin, Biber had been blissfully climbing, step after step, noticing occasional snowflakes drifting down, but otherwise focused on her ski tips. When she got to the kick turn, she stopped and stood tall to fill her lungs with air, before attacking the next switchback. She turned her head to take in the view—and caught a glimpse, far below, of Wylie and his line of skiers, like a string of colorful beads, stretched across the gully bottom.

"Heidi!"

It was Keith Lindsay, who was right behind her. "Don't stop. Keep going."

"That was the first time I realized, yeah, this is steep, there's a group below us, this is not someplace I want to be hanging out," recalls Biber. She pushed off, and with a surge of adrenaline, kicked forward with eyes set on the track ahead of her.

Charles Bieler, who had attempted to bring up the rear of Group 1 due to intestinal issues, was approaching halfway up when he became acutely aware of his surroundings. That's where La Traviata is at its steepest—roughly 38 degrees—so one might reason that's what raised the prickles on the back of his neck; that's where the climbing flipped like a switch, from awesome to ominous. But he'd climbed and skied steeper and had never been bothered. In tune with his body, he self-diagnosed: *Okay, I'm sick, I took those pills this morning, I'm dehydrated, just keep moving, it will pass.*

But it didn't pass; it intensified and within seconds he felt an overwhelming sense of dread, being there exposed on this steep slope. The otherwise pedestrian nature of gravity—the force of it above him and below him—was now suddenly terrifying. He didn't know what the trigger was; all he knew was that something felt terrible. Something told him to get the fuck out of there as fast as he could. He was a fucking maniac. As far as he was concerned, he was in a race. His head was down, he was breathing hard.

Bieler was just ahead of Craig near the back of the line in Beglinger's group when he kicked it into high gear and started sprinting toward the top. He passed Heffler, then Weselake and Schwendener, who stepped aside[*] as he raced forward to escape the claustrophobic panic induced by this ceiling

---

[*]   The order of these events are blurred in the memories of survivors. Some don't recall anybody passing Weselake on these steep switchbacks, while another is certain Bieler passed two or three people. Bieler started out near the end of the line, just ahead of Craig at the bottom, and he ended up just ahead of Schwendener at the very top. It is assumed Bieler asked Heffler, Weselake, and Schwendener to step aside and then, in the chaos that followed, survivors could not recall.

of gravity. If he could just get on top of it, just get to a place where only the sky was above. Then they would ski down. And everything would be fine.

FINNERTY WAS AT the end of the line with Craig, Heffler, Bieler, Schwendener, and Weselake (six skiers) still climbing and visible on the final two switchbacks near the top of the gully. Beglinger and the others were out of sight, having already made it over the summit crux.

No one can say what Craig was thinking as he watched Bieler tear past skier after skier on his sprint toward the top, but his friend and mentor John Buffery can guess.

"Somewhere on that climb," says Buffery, "I think he sensed he shouldn't be there, maybe when he was up high and saw that convex rollover at the top of the gully, which is always a red flag. He was incredibly fit, he could have sprinted to the top, but he was in tailgunner mode; making sure everybody ahead of him got up. This is speculation, let that be clear, but I've gone over it in my mind and I believe anybody who spent time with Craig would agree, on that slope, on that day, knowing about that deep layer, he was pushing the edge of what he would do himself and deferring to Beglinger, who knew the terrain and the snowpack.

"His intuition was dialed in, so yeah, I'm confident he was feeling those Spidey senses and was gripped, probably equally for himself and for the group he saw coming below him. I'd been with Craig many times when he got to that point where the top was right there, and I could hear him. He'd start breathing harder, you know his adrenaline's going, his heart's pumping. He's exposed, probably a little bit scared, but focused on the snow, watching for cracks, listening for settlements. There is no doubt in my mind that Craig wanted to get up and off that slope so he could strap into his snowboard— that's when he felt the safest and most in control."

WYLIE HAD LED his group across the bottom of the couloir, then turned right and ascended the track along the bottom of the cliff. According to Beglinger, this type of high-side approach beneath the rocks was a tactic that limited a group's exposure to any snow that might come down from above—in this case, from the gully itself.

It was at the corner—the final "island" of safety—that Wylie paused, allowing his clients to regroup before he committed to entering the gully.

"I was extremely conflicted, standing at the edge of that slope," says Wylie. "Everything in my being told me I shouldn't be there. I reasoned, or justified, that Ruedi knew better than me, so I brushed off my own judgment and ignored my inner voice."

Then Wylie heard another voice that came from the line of skiers behind him. Vern Lunsford, probably the most gung-ho skier in his group, had edged up close to Wylie and was now in no rush to push forward as he watched Beglinger and his entire group of twelve spread out across the upper reaches of the gully.

"I don't like it," Lunsford told Wylie, "being below the other group."

"Neither do I," replied Wylie.

They weren't the only ones.

Joe Pojar had followed Beglinger to this exact spot just a few years before. He remembered being tucked beneath the cliff, watching Beglinger probe ahead of his skis as he entered the slope. He'd only gone ten, maybe twenty meters when he'd stopped and yelled back to his assistant ski guide to come forward and join him.

Coincidentally, that assistant ski guide had been Paul Norrie, who at the time was in his second or third winter working under Beglinger. Norrie had shuffled past the guests, then followed the ski track out to where Beglinger stood waiting in the throat of the gully. Without a word of explanation, Beglinger gestured to Norrie's ski pole, then took it in hand, turned it upside down, handed it back, pointed at the snow, and said, "Tell me what you feel."

Norrie pushed the upturned pole down steadily into the upper layer of snow and felt a firm resistance followed by almost no resistance, an airy feeling that dropped more than a foot before hitting a harder, more consolidated layer. He interpreted this as a significant surface slab that had formed from a wind event several days before. He probed again to confirm, feeling pressure from both the snow he was trying to assess and from being tested there on the spot by Beglinger in front of the clients.

"Feels like a wind slab," he said.

Beglinger had grinned and nodded. "Ya, that's what I felt too."

"We go someplace else," Beglinger called down to the rest of the group. "La Traviata is no good today. We find something better."

Norrie and Beglinger had walked back under the cliff, ripped off their climbing skins, then skied down back across the lower bench, but from there Pojar couldn't remember if they continued farther up toward Fronalp or over to the trees. All he knew for sure was that Beglinger had decided the slope they were about to ski didn't feel right, and he'd turned around.

This was one of the reasons that Pojar now felt utterly relaxed, like he could check out mentally regarding the snow, the route, whatever, because he knew that Beglinger was on it. If Beglinger thought this slope was good to go, it was good to go.

Edging closer toward the front of his group, Pojar could see up past the cliff into the upper gully where Beglinger's group was still ascending. Pojar also saw Wylie ski out onto the open slope of the gully, probing as he went.

For years Pojar had followed Beglinger around these mountains, sometimes in Beglinger's group, sometimes with the assistant guides. Sometimes the groups were separated, on different peaks or objectives. Other times— like this—the groups remained together, following the same routes, but not this close. Never this close. This wasn't the norm Pojar recalled from years past.

Something didn't feel right.

He watched Wylie kick and glide forward a few strides, before stopping to dig down into the snow and perform a hand shear stability test. At least half of Beglinger's group was still in sight far above. *Should I say something?* Pojar frantically thought. *We shouldn't be under the other group. What can I do?* He didn't want to be *that* client, the guy who gives the guide advice on guiding, but at the same time, his mind was racing. *How can I stop this, how can I make the group stop?*

Looking down at his boots and his bindings, he got an idea. *I'll fake an equipment malfunction, to pause the group, buy some time.* At that same instant, Wylie waved the group forward. *Too late.*

Things went swiftly into motion. John Seibert asked Vern Lunsford, "Does he want us to cross this slope one at a time?" Pushing forward, Lunsford replied, "Ken said, three meters spacing." Seibert following around ten feet, several strides behind. Dennis Yates followed, then Kathleen Kessler, then it was Pojar's turn.

Okay, here we go, he thought. *We'll be fine.*

With a deep breath, he edged his skis out onto the open slope. With the heel risers up, climbing is more robotic than graceful; you're not gliding, you're moving forward, but your stride is shorter—you feel like you're being held back. Pojar tried to find his rhythm. Paula Couturier was just easing into the slope some four meters behind Pojar, and Bullock was right at the corner, still bringing up the rear, and still feeling or sensing tension in the air.

Climbing steadily well ahead of the group, Wylie got to the first switchback, performed a kick turn, and was coming back across on the second switchback, above and approaching Lunsford. They would converge toward the center of the gully. He saw his group was well spaced out as he'd instructed, moving toward him from the cliff, but all now committed in the gully. Glancing up, Wylie could see a skier (it was Charles Bieler) reach the sanctuary of the milky skyline and disappear over the top, leaving five skiers still on the slope several hundred feet above them. He glanced down in time to do a quick count of his group—all seven were committed to the slope and ascending toward him.

"That's when I heard it," he says.

CHAPTER 28

MUTE TERROR

THERE IS A DEEP, HOLLOW, percussive "whumpf!" when a snow layer collapses. Then there is a silent "hope-filled" pause that might be followed by nothing more than the realization that a snow layer has collapsed. This can occur on flat ground, often on frozen lakes, with zero consequences, but on a slope—particularly a steep slope you're standing on—the pause hangs like mute terror. Because in that split second, the snow crystals are conspiring, trying to decide if they will hold together the collapsing layer like Velcro, or let it rip down the mountain.

Up this high, with the wind blowing into the gully, that upper layer of snow could be five, ten feet deep. A slab that immense is going to rip down the mountain like a runaway freight train, taking anything and everything with it.

During that brief moment of purgatory, fully exposed at the bottom of the gully, Wylie had time to think, *Maybe we'll get lucky here.*

Then a voice from above cried out, "Avalanche!"

WHEN BEGLINGER HAD topped La Traviata several minutes earlier, he skied immediately east—setting a traverse to the right, away from the top of the gully upon the gently sloping bench beneath Tumbledown Mountain's west ridge. This was standard operating procedure for Beglinger, who didn't stop until he was some hundred meters east of the gully, his standard regrouping area, not far from the ski route he used when coming down off the west ridge. It was a nice, protected area to have a sip of tea, enjoy the view, and wait for the other group to arrive.

The first to join Beglinger was Age Fluitman, with Rick Martin roughly fifteen meters behind him, then Heidi Biber, Keith Lindsay, and Bruce Stewart similarly distanced—the line stretched back toward the top of the gully. As was his custom, Beglinger ripped his climbing skins off, with Fluitman following his example. That was when Beglinger felt the snow drop beneath him, a massive settlement accompanied by that dreadful "whumpf!"

At that moment Charles Bieler was just below the cresting summit of the gully, still sprinting upward, still uncertain of why he'd been spooked, but not letting up. He knew he was close when Rick Reynolds, the skier just ahead of him, disappeared over the summit. Bieler had passed Jean-Luc Schwendener thirty seconds before, Evan Weselake a minute before that, and Naomi Heffler he'd passed on a lower switchback after first feeling that sense of dread, but now, as he was within spitting distance from the summit, the entire group, including Craig and Finnerty bringing up the very rear of Beglinger's group, were only three minutes from the top. Wylie's group was approximately twenty minutes from the top, so well below.

Some two meters behind Schwendener, Weselake saw a crack shoot across the snow above the ski track. At first he thought it was a bit of surface slough cracking off and sliding into the track, but then another crack opened up between his ski tips, and Schwendener and the snow began to move down the mountain. Something was off: the snow wasn't spilling down into the ski track. The track itself and Schwendener were moving, Weselake was moving, the entire slope was moving and he was on top of it. It was like the sensation when you can't tell if the train or the train platform is the thing in motion. Only this time, he soon realized, it was somehow the platform that was moving—and he was on it.

On his side now, Weselake tried to reach for his bindings, knowing that it was key to release his skis, at this point only anchors that would drag him into the depths. It was instinct. He'd thrown his poles away, the slab was breaking up around him, all of this in a matter of seconds. Rule number one from his training kicked in and, as he kicked violently, trying to jettison his skis, he screamed the loudest warning he could: "Avalanche!"

Bieler had just managed to finish his primal sprint, crest the summit, and get his first glimpse of Rick Reynolds when the concussive burst went off directly beneath the tails of his skis. "It sounded like the loudest clap of thunder you've ever heard in your life," he says. "An explosion. I didn't look back. I just rocketed forward, away from the downhill, and just kept going. I was in shock, just skiing for my life."

Rick Reynolds shuddered when he heard what was, to him, a shotgun blast. He glanced back to see Bieler in full stride flying toward him. He could see the snow cracking behind Bieler, and farther down he could see just the top of Schwendener's head, his body still beneath the crest of the terrain. Then both Reynolds and Bieler were thrust forward in a violent jolt that nearly knocked them off their feet. "I went down to my knees, had to put my hand out on the snow to steady myself," says Reynolds. "I knew what happened immediately. I've seen big avalanche at Squaw Valley, there was so much cohesion in the snow. The snowpack, it's like a rubber band that was under so much tension, getting stretched, or pulled down the mountain, that once it released [cracked] the upper slope that we were on rebounded like a rubber band that had been stretched out to the max, and then cut or just snapped. It recoiled, sprung back, while the slab below slid down the mountain in the opposite direction. That rebound knocked us off our feet."

Still in fight-or-flight mode, Bieler was scrambling on pure adrenaline trying to regain his footing and not certain if he was getting sucked down the mountain. Reynolds pushed himself back upright and came face-to-face with Bieler, who was breathing hard, wide-eyed and shaking.

"We just stared at each other for a second," says Bieler. "I didn't say anything—I was in shock. I heard people screaming 'avalanche' behind me and I realized I hadn't said a word. Not that it would have mattered, but I wish I had."

The acoustics in the mountains and the energy from the collapse were heard and felt differently depending on location. The skiers closest to Beglinger only felt the collapse and heard the "whumpf!" while those closer to the gully heard the concussive thunderclap when the snow cracked.

Yelling "Avalanche!" Reynolds waved his hands toward Beglinger, roughly a hundred meters away. Not sure if Beglinger was getting the picture, he became more vocal: "There's a fucking avalanche! The whole thing went! It's big!"

..

BEGLINGER BEGAN MOVING their way almost immediately. Reynolds crept forward to the fracture line. Once there, he peered over the edge, which was no less than a small vertical snow cliff, five feet tall where he stood. He looked to the right, saw that it spanned across the entire gully, getting shallower, but still had to be three feet deep, and to the left, right up to where that wave had shot down the slope, the fracture line was even deeper— maybe a six- or seven-foot drop to the avalanche bed surface, where several "blocks of snow the size of Volkswagen Bugs were sitting there on this polished surface, this icy surface the whole slab slid on." He scanned the flanks, thinking maybe somebody had been able to ski to the side, but there was nothing but white between him and a massive field of rubble he could see thrust out from the bottom of the gully far below. The depth and width of the fracture line, the size of these automobile-sized chunks, and the silence, the utter silence told him: this is a catastrophe.

"The only thing I could see were two little dots in the debris field," recalls Reynolds, who stepped back and ripped the climbing skins off his skis so he could get down there and help, but steeled himself for what he knew was coming: *There are too many people buried*, he thought to himself. *We aren't going to get them all. There isn't going to be enough time.*

THE AVALANCHE THAT day at La Traviata didn't care that Craig was a father, son, husband, brother, or one of the most beloved snowboarders in the world. It didn't matter that he and nineteen other souls had been led to this pristine gully by a renowned mountain guide with an exemplary safety record.

It hit them all violently with cold, hard indifference at approximately 10:45 a.m. and within seconds had dragged thirteen of them beneath its surface and into the darkness.

Craig had studied the beast—probably more intensely than anybody else on the mountain that day besides Beglinger. And he feared it. He knew survival versus death in an avalanche is influenced by several factors, including the length of time buried, depth of burial, and injuries sustained. Other variables include whether the victim's airway is open or filled with snow; position under the snow (face up or down); the compaction of the snow; and if the victim is able to create an air pocket during the final moments when the avalanche comes to a stop and the snow compacts around the body. As Beglinger had described it in avalanche safety school, "This is the worst part, when the snow comes down." The majority (approximately 75 percent) of avalanche fatalities occur due to asphyxia (lack of oxygen); almost 25 percent occur from traumatic injuries; only a very small number of victims succumb to hypothermia.

Asphyxia is caused by inhaled snow blocking the airway, the prolonged rebreathing of exhaled air, or when an ice mask forms over the face, blocking the airway after burial. Given that a lack of oxygen causes such a great number of fatalities, efficient extrication is key to the victim's survival. The more buried victims, the slower the process of extrication, which is why common avalanche-safety practice is to expose as few people as possible while crossing, ascending, or descending an avalanche-prone slope. Statistics vary, but broadly speaking, if a buried person is extricated within fifteen minutes, the chance of survival is greater than 90 percent. If the time of extrication extends to thirty minutes, the chance of survival plummets to 30 percent. There have been cases, though rare, in which victims survived for an hour or more.

Nobody will ever know with certainty the final thoughts and experiences of some of those who were swept down La Traviata that morning. Craig had little to no time to eject himself from his splitboard skis when the snow cracked and the snow started moving. Had he been on his snowboard, his instincts would have been to either race down the slope and angle out to the left or right at the gully beneath the cliff band, but he was skiing uphill, and while he had become quite adept with his split skis, his heel risers were up. To ski downhill, with heal risers up, would be like trying to run down a very steep hill on your tiptoes. Almost impossible. Whether skiing or "swimming," he would have fought desperately to stay on top of the surface as the snow came to life around him like a river rushing down the mountain.

During Craig's training, he'd read several survival accounts, like that of ski mountaineer Lou Dawson, who recounted the avalanche that nearly killed him in 1982:

The snow picked up speed. For an instant I saw the snow boiling around me in a terrifying vortex . . . a maelstrom like the break of a tsunami. Spun and flipped over, I felt my arms and legs thrown like a ragdoll's. All was darkness and violence as I tumbled faster and faster, losing all control. With a bone-jarring explosion my left femur broke as it surrendered to impossible force. I hadn't hit anything—bone had sheared in cross currents of snow. As I flew through the air, still engulfed in the powder cloud, I had a brief respite of unearthly quiet . . . A flash of light. [Then] the snow slowed down quickly, I felt G-force like a car screeching to a panic stop. Fear engulfed me. I was to be entombed. A panting breath, then all was still.[*]

When Craig felt that deceleration he would have known, from his training, that there were only seconds for him to attempt to make an air pocket with his hands around his face before the snow compressed around him like cement. He came to a stop, not knowing immediately the depth in which he was buried. Even several feet deep, light filters through the snow in ethereal shades of blue. That is if he was facing upward or even sideways. If he'd come to a halt facedown, there were perhaps deep hues of midnight but mainly there was darkness, the only sound his heartbeat, his breathing, and his eyelashes as they brushed against the snow pressed up against his face—a moment described by avalanche forecaster Bruce Tremper in his account of his own snow burial:

> Snow went everywhere: down my neck, up my sleeves, down my underwear—even under my eyelids. With every breath, I sucked in a mixture of snow and air that instantly formed a plug in my mouth and down into my throat. I coughed it out, but the next breath rammed my throat full of snow again. Just when I needed to breathe the most, I couldn't—I was drowning, high in the mountains, in the middle of winter, and miles from the nearest body of water.[†]

Craig likely felt the rush of panic as the snow crushed in on every inch of his body. A moment certainly came when he wanted to scream with all

---

[*]   Lou Dawson's avalanche survival articles were published in both the *Denver Post* and *Couloir* Volume 5 #2 (as told to Ted Kerasote). See Dawson's memoir, *Avalanche Dreams*, for the full account.

[†]   Tremper's account appears in his book *Staying Alive in Avalanche Terrain* (Mountaineers Books, 2001).

his might for help, but his avalanche survival training had taught him that this would only exhaust precious oxygen and wouldn't be heard through the sound-insulating snow regardless. His discipline would have demanded silence. He knew he had to slow his breathing and heart rate to prolong his life, which, he also understood, was no longer in his hands.

It was now in the hands of those on the surface.

CHAPTER 29

THIRTEEN DOWN

BEGLINGER WAS IN A SPRINT on his split skis, counting his guests while he raced back down his up-track toward the crown of the avalanche. Mountain guides always count heads—like camp counselors watching children swimming at the pool or lake. If anybody goes under, there isn't much time.

One . . . two, three . . . four . . . five . . .

"Durrand Glacier Chalet from Ruedi," he shouted into his radio as he ran by Heidi Biber. "We have a terrible accident!"

He rushed past Charles Bieler. Six. He was standing a few meters back from the edge, and stopped beside Rick Reynolds, seven, who was still standing just behind the fracture line. During his roughly hundred-meter sprint over little more than a minute, Beglinger had sounded the alarm at the chalet on the open channel, and gotten no response from Wylie, when the voice of Kim Lomas, the cook at the chalet, crackled back on the radio.

"I'm here, Ruedi," she replied.

It was just past 10:45 a.m.* when he peered into the wide, sweeping—and now completely quiet and empty—contours of La Traviata. The elegant lines of that surfy-white wave on the left, the downy-soft powdery surface, the zig-zagging up-track had all been erased from the mountain, leaving nothing but

---

* This was the time noted for the first radio call at the chalet, and since it was less than a minute after the avalanche occurred, it became the accepted start time.

an icy-still gullet that had swallowed eight of his guests, his assistant guide, two apprentice guides, and two employees.

He was looking down into his worst nightmare, on mute. There were no cries for help, no signs of life, nothing but a silence whose force compounded by the second. Of the twenty living and breathing humans he was responsible for, thirteen had disappeared.

"It's huge!" he returned to Lomas at the chalet. "Everybody's down. We need all help there is. Nobody on standby, everybody coming up here. Selkirk Tangiers [Heli Skiing], CMH [Canadian Mountain Holidays heli-ski], Department of Highways, avalanche-dog masters, paramedics, and everything you can find—bring it up."

To his remaining guests Beglinger shouted "Let's go!" over his shoulder as he clicked out of his split skis. He sat on the edge of the approximately five-foot ledge and dropped onto the hard bed surface, where he rocketed down the slope on his bum, glissade-style, jamming his boot heels down to brake speed while continuing to relay information to the chalet with one hand on the radio. Reaching into his jacket with his other hand, he switched his avalanche beacon to "receive," all while scanning the fast-approaching debris for visual clues: a hand thrust through the snow, a ski pole, a boot. Anything.

BACK AT THE top, Reynolds and the swiftly gathered group of Bieler, Stewart, Martin, Lindsay, and Fluitman ripped off their climbing skins, skied to the edge, and launched themselves into the void. "One after the other, like paratroopers, they were gone," says Biber, who edged forward to watch them high-speed side-slip, hip-check, ski, and in some cases tumble down. Dropping to her knees and feeling "otherworldly," she shoved the pile of climbing skins into her pack, then shuffled her skis forward, and there she froze, her mind racing faster than her heart. She would never air off something like this skiing at home. Should she ski over to the edge, where it wasn't such a drop? Could that trigger the rest of this snow to come down? No, she had to drop off right here where the others had. But she didn't trust her legs to stick the landing, or her tele turns on the steep boilerplate ice. *You're a nurse, Heidi!* she chastised herself. *You're not helping anybody up here. Get down there! Go!*

Beglinger's transceiver came to life the second he hit the avalanche debris, shrieking a cacophony of high-pitched electronic beeps that indicated multiple burials. He ran into the massive debris field, almost double the width and length of two football fields. This wasn't a smooth blanket of white. Rather, it was like exploded wreckage from a collapsed skyscraper made of snow and ice that he had to pick through and climb over in places as he focused on the transceiver signals. *There.* Some specks of color caught his eye.

The snow was compacted and there was little to no boot penetration. Looking out from the bottom some ninety meters to the moraine—where there was usually a slight dip in the terrain—the debris field was predominantly flat. That shallow, bowl-like depression directly beneath La Traviata, where in eighteen years he'd never seen a single avalanche deposit, was filled with deep dense snow.

Some twenty meters in, off to the right, he saw that the specks of color were John Seibert, and then Paula Couturier another twenty-five meters farther out from him. Both were partially buried with their heads exposed, moving and conscious, so he ignored them for the moment.

Eight. Nine.

Vectoring in on the strongest signal, he located the position of someone who was fully buried and flagged the spot with his probe. He picked up another close-by signal and marked a second buried victim with his ski pole.

Reynolds arrived next and ran directly toward Couturier, reaching her about the same time that Beglinger marked the location of a third buried victim with his other ski pole. To Reynolds, it was a time warp, a furious adrenaline rush where he knew everything was happening fast but felt oddly slow, and there was nothing he could do to speed up.

Couturier's arms and chest were loose, and she appeared to be struggling to free herself, digging into the snow at her left side. Moving closer, Reynolds realized that she was desperately trying to uncover somebody buried beside her.

It was Joe Pojar. That made ten.

JUST BEFORE THE avalanche, Pojar had warily followed Dennis Yates and Kathy Kessler away from the protective cliff and out into the open gully. Eyeing the upper group still ascending far above him, he had thought, *Okay, where's my escape route? My escape route is to kick-turn and head back under the cliff.*

Farther out on the slope, Yates and Kessler caught up to John Seibert, and Pojar slowed down, trying to maintain spacing so as not to bunch up together. Some twenty-five feet higher up the slope, Ken Wylie was coming back toward him on the next switchback; he was not yet to the center of the gully when the whumpf occurred and Pojar felt the entire slope drop, "like eight inches beneath me," he says.

As the snow began to move beneath him, Pojar kick-turned and headed for the safety of the cliff, just as he planned. He caught a glimpse of Jeff Bullock and Couturier when he was slammed forward into a raging river of snow. Attempting to spin himself around, while also trying to kick out of his bindings, he was unable to jettison the skis that pulled him down. The torrent tumbled and flipped him, whipped him around and pummeled him as he fought to stay on top, but he kept going under and losing the sky. Using all his strength, he pushed with his legs and pulled with his arms and "made this giant burst with everything I had and found the surface," he says. "There was light, and it just stopped in an instant—like the river I was in froze solid. My arms were behind me, like at the end of that stroke, and I was frozen. I was sort of on my back and could not move a muscle, but my face was above the surface and I'm thinking, *All right, I can breathe*."

Then the second wave hit. It could have been a secondary avalanche, perhaps hanging snow that let loose higher in the gully, but more likely there was a brief pause when the lower part of the avalanche hit bottom and slammed into the bermlike moraine. The upper, and likely deepest, part of the avalanche crested like a wave and rumbled across the first layer of debris. Depending on location, this secondary wall of snow either fanned out shallow or piled up, burying some of those caught in the maelstrom deeper and cycling others toward the surface as the snow came to an instantaneous and crushing halt.

For Couturier, this final moment during the second wave occurred when she was being propelled vertically and facing downhill. Her lower body was stuck as if in concrete, but her arms and head were free. It was difficult for her to see past the surrounding snow chunks and icy boulders, but through a gap between slabs of snow to her left, she could make out devastation that spanned hundreds of meters. The silence was absolute.

Everything came back to her in a flash: the collapse, the "thunder," seeing Pojar's frantic kick-turn that alerted her to do the same. She'd barely gotten turned around before the avalanche slammed into her like a powerful shore break at the beach. Unable to kick off her skis, she'd fought against the currents of bucking, cresting, wild snow, right up to the sudden halt. Then the second wave hit and left her mercifully still on the surface. Now the pressure of the frozen snow squeezed her body from the chest down, a heavy, constricting sensation like a fully pumped blood-pressure cuff.

"Avalanche!" she screamed, and realized it was pointless. It was over, and there was nobody to warn. She was alone, it seemed for a minute, maybe two— her heart racing. Then something came out of the sea of silence around her, a jolt in the snow, some energy, maybe a grunt—startling her like a shark bumping a swimmer from beneath. What was that? Who had been closest to her?

"Jeff! Joe!" she yelled, twisting around, studying the snow. "Jeff! Joe!"

On this right flank of the avalanche, the second wave had seemingly washed over Pojar, who was on his back, his arms pinned behind him, his body angling deeper to where his boots were roughly five feet beneath the surface. His eye sockets, ears, nose, and mouth had filled with snow, limiting his oxygen. He was fading fast, his last conscious thought being, *Well, I'm not too deep. I hope someone finds me.*

"I heard somebody yelling my name. 'Joe! Joe! Where are you!?' I had no idea how long I'd been under. I tried to yell but all that came out was this garbled, choking, grunting noise . . . and then I heard digging and scraping and suddenly there's a hand pulling snow up and away from my head and mouth and brushing off my face, and there's my ski tips just in front of my face in this widening hole. All I could see was the sky, my ski tips, and Paula's face."

"Oh my god, Joe!" she said, shocked yet elated to see him looking up at her.

"Thank you!" he gasped. "Thank you, Paula."

Locked tight in snow, unable to reach back into her pack for her shovel, she used her gloved hands to pound at and try to dig through the rock-hard snow to reach Pojar's pack and his shovel. Not long after Paula uncovered Pojar, Rick Reynolds was upon them.

"We had a terrible accident. You guys got to dig yourselves out and help!"

Reynolds reached into Couturier's pack, handed over her shovel, and hurried away, eyes focused on his transceiver, but he only got a few meters before the strongest signals pulled him back toward Pojar and Couturier.

Rule number one after necessary first aid: when you find someone in a multiple burial, you switch that person's transceiver to "receive" so that it doesn't confuse the search for others still under the snow. "Shit!" Reynolds said, frustrated with himself. He ran back and quickly broke up the snow around Pojar's chest with his shovel, reached down into his jacket, and switched the transceiver to receive. Couturier was switching her own transceiver when Reynolds heard Keith Lindsay call out for a probe. He sprang up and ran diagonally some twenty to twenty-five meters northeast toward Lindsay, who knelt on the surface above somebody who, according to his transceiver, was buried 2.8 meters deep.

"The beacon is the guide for the probe and the probe is the guide for the shovel" was drilled into them at transceiver practice. All guests were required to carry a shovel and probe that was either their own or provided by SME. Their probes were 240 centimeters, or 2.4 meters. Beglinger wasn't right there—he was busy searching—and they had to dig. Fast! They'd probe again once they got down a couple of feet.

Lindsay dove into the digging. Reynolds scanned the scene and saw Seibert buried up to his neck and realized, *I gotta turn off John's transceiver.*

BIELER HAD ARRIVED on scene following an ugly, at times tumbling, descent. His entire body—especially his legs—was shaking as he switched his transceiver to receive.

"It was chaos, trying to pick up and hold a consistent signal. There were burials all over the place, pulling you. It was overwhelming. I just looked for Ruedi and took a breath. He was a maniac in an incredible way on the debris field. He was just marching around, not frantic, but high-speed, crisscrossing. He'd pick up a strong signal, drop his hat, then moved on, drop something else, come back around." He ran to one of Beglinger's markers as a starting point, and still the signals seemed almost impossible, probably because of the close proximity, with at least three burials within three meters of each other. He knew his strength lay in digging. Was he wasting precious time searching when he should be throwing snow?

Somebody cried out, "Shovel!" and he spun around.

••

When Bruce Stewart made it to the debris field, he beelined it straight to a shock of color that ended up being a ski tip jutting from an area where larger blocks of snow had seemingly been pushed by the surge into a haphazard row. Wedged down within a crack, between the slabs, was Evan Weselake. Eleven.

Along with Jean-Luc Schwendener, Weselake had been the highest up in the gully—only a few strides from the top—when the snow had cracked between them, and they'd been hurled down the 37-degree slope.

"It was like getting sucked toward a waterfall in Class Five rapids," recalls Weselake. "You're in it, you're going over, clawing, kicking, swimming—there's nothing you can do about it." At one point he felt weightless, surrounded by white, a flash of gray sky, not knowing how far it was to the bottom but thinking, *Oh shit, this is gonna hurt.*

He had no idea how long the turbulent 250- to 300-meter ride took, maybe fifteen seconds. But it was plenty of time for him to prepare for that anticipated moment of deceleration, when he'd thrust his hands up and make an air pocket before the snow solidified around him. But like the others, there was no warning before his 60- to 80-mph plummet stopped with a jolt, like he'd had a head-on collision with the bottom of the mountain. Pressure crushed in on him like a vise. There was light, and there was oxygen. His lungs screamed for it, but he could only take tiny sips because of the pressure on his chest. His mind raced and his heart pounded in his ears, beating as fast, it seemed, as his panting breathing.

When Weselake was a kid, his mother had introduced him to muscle-relaxing and calming exercises that had evolved into yoga and breathing regimens as an adult. These routines, which had helped him conserve energy during endurance races, now kicked in to help him slow his breathing and stave off the panic. As he systematically relaxed his muscles, starting with his toes, he realized that he was on his left side, with the leg and arm on that side of his body down in the snow while his right leg was tweaked in the other direction facing the sky, its ski still attached and wedged straight up against a block of snow. He had ended up wedged down in a crack—a random gap between broken slabs of snow—with his face pressed up against the sidewall of what seemed like a shallow trench. There was no second wave, an indication that Weselake and the others caught at the top, as opposed to those in Wylie's group, had ridden this disintegrating hard-slab avalanche top to bottom in one massive push. Though loose snow did spill in around his face, adding to the claustrophobic terror, he knew how lucky he was to be trapped in the rubble, and not beneath it.

His mind shifted from self-preservation to Naomi Heffler.

Where's Naomi? he thought. *How bad is this?*

His muscles relaxed, his breathing slowed, and he found that if he sort of twisted his leg, he could wiggle his ski, and that motion, however slight, was more likely to attract the eye of a searcher, so he could join the search himself.

Two minutes of utter silence answered his question, and he thought to himself, *It's gotta be really bad.*

The sounds of footsteps crunching on snow was like a second burst of adrenaline, and before he could think to shout, he heard Bruce Stewart yelling, "I'm here! I've got you!"

Stewart saw that Weselake was breathing, wedged in tightly among the slabs on his side with one arm and one leg in. There were so many people buried, Stewart thought, *if I get him out, he can help. Shouldn't take but a minute or two.*

This was no easy task, taking closer to ten minutes to break up the slabs and push them aside. "It wasn't just digging, it was excavating," says Stewart. Then, with the rest of his body free, Weselake remained stuck from the elbow down, as if his forearm and hand were frozen in a giant ice cube. It took dozens of blows from Stewart's shovel blade before the compacted snow released its grip and Weselake was able to pull his arm free.

He pushed up from his hands and knees and stood shakily testing his legs for injury. Though battered and bruised, he was okay. He switched his transceiver to receive, as Stewart concentrated on his transceiver and followed the signal somewhat toward Seibert, who now had a shovel and was digging himself out.[†]

Weselake paused just long enough to reach into his pack and grab the spare gloves he'd thrown in that morning. His had been ripped off, and the hand that had been buried was frozen. He smacked it repeatedly against his thigh

---

[†]   Rick Reynolds had dug down to Seibert's chest, uncovering his arms, and then was able to reach into his pack so Seibert could dig himself out.

to bring back some circulation, while focusing on his transceiver in the other. He wasn't sure how long it had been—he guessed maybe ten minutes—since he'd screamed "Avalanche!" at the top, just after he had paused and looked down and thought, *Wow*, when he saw "Dave, and Craig, and Naomi— she had this fun green jacket—coming across the lower switchback." He had thought that if he'd had a camera, he would have snapped a photo. He looked across the rubble for that familiar green, expecting that he'd turn around and she'd be right there and he'd say, "Thank God you're alive!"

That was what flashed in Weselake's mind when, just a couple of steps away from where he'd been buried, a strong signal from his transceiver indicated somebody buried only 2.6 meters away. He moved slowly and steadily following the signal, and it struck him, "This must be Jean-Luc."

He homed in on the strongest signal and got down on the ground, where his transceiver indicated that the person was 1.2 meters deep. After probing straight down two meters and hitting nothing, he moved outward six inches, probing in a ring until on his third try he hit the distinct resistance of a body. "Shovel!" he shouted out.

By this time Stewart had also vectored in on a burial and was squinting at the transceiver's display panel in disbelief. "It read two-point-three meters, and I thought, *That can't be right*." But the numbers didn't lie: the person was indeed almost eight feet down. He took his first swing at the surface with his shovel. "It bounced back like I'd hit a concrete wall," he says. "That's how hard it was, but you just keep going. You'd hit big chunks of snow you'd have to move by hand, push aside, dig some more."

Couturier had freed herself to her waist when Joe asked her through chattering teeth, "Ca-ca-can you d-d-d dig me out first so I can ga-ga-go help?"

She had a more immediate reason to get him out. "Joe's lips were purple. He's shaking uncontrollably, and he wanted me to dig him out first so he could go help, and I realized, I better get him out first too, because he was going hypothermic."

Chipping away around his backpack, Couturier passed his shovel blade and handle to him, figuring that if he could also dig, perhaps he'd warm up some, but he had a hard time grasping and dropped the handle several times as he tried to put it together. It wasn't just that his hands were frozen; he was also confused, disoriented, and frantic to free himself. All the while, voices he couldn't recognize called out, "Help! I need a shoveler here! Help, I need a probe!"

FINALLY UPRIGHT, POJAR walked unsteadily northeast in the direction where he saw people digging, and heard shouts for help. While walking, he focused on his transceiver and got turned around by a signal that led him back, not more than five meters from where he had been buried. Then he saw a bit of fabric beneath the surface, and remembered the last person he'd seen before being taken by the avalanche.

"Jeff!"

JEFF BULLOCK HAD been closest to the cliff and, like Pojar and Couturier, had attempted to kick-turn and ski to the side after he'd felt the settlement. He was trending toward the right, was just about to reach the cliff when the avalanche hit him, throwing him down the mountain for fifty or so meters in a disorienting tumble—flashes of light alternating with darkness—that stopped as suddenly as it began. He came to rest on his back, head downhill, arms stretched out overhead and one leg contorted to the side. Opening his eyes, he could see light filtering through the snow. *I'm not too deep*, he thought, and quickly tried to pull his hand toward his face. The snow had some give to it, and he could wiggle his fingers a little. Then he heard a muffled rumble— the second wave—and the weight of the snow instantly increased, squeezing him tighter and tighter as the light dimmed to gray.

"I had a few moments to think," he says. "The first thing I thought was, *Well, I'm alive. I'm not injured.* And there was some light, it wasn't that dark, so I knew I wasn't superdeep. And the second thought was, *I'm running out of air very quickly.* There was a little bit of air in the snowpack, but I couldn't expand my chest to get enough. It's a losing battle. You're trying to get a little more oxygen, but you can't open up your lungs to get it in. And then the ice mask. Your body heat and the little bit of breathing that you're trying to do warms up the snow around you, and then it refreezes.

"Whatever was going on, I could feel the oxygen decreasing and the panic coming. I had to calm down. I knew passing out would help me because I wasn't injured. I wasn't in pain, like I hit a tree or something and was bleeding out. Losing consciousness would slow everything down and give me a fighting chance, so I just let myself fade, but right before I passed out I remember thinking, *I'm going to die. What are my parents going to think!?* And I was like, *Shit!* You have that thought. You're like, *It's too soon! Shit. I'm going to die.* But you're also holding on to hope—you know they're looking for you. You know there's a chance.

"And then, I just blacked out."

CHAPTER 30

NOBODY ON STANDBY

NICOLINE BEGLINGER GLANCED OUT THE window from the SME residence and "knew instantly something terrible had happened." All she needed to see was the expression on Kim Lomas's face as the cook ran up the hill from the chalet, radio in hand.

"There's been an avalanche!" Lomas told Nicoline at the door, then quickly recapped Ruedi's emergency call. Ushering her in, Nicoline gestured toward Charlotte and Florina, who were seated behind her at their school table. "Put on *Mary Poppins* for the girls," she said, then bolted back down the hill. Seconds later, she was relaying the distress call to the Selkirk Mountain Helicopters radio dispatcher, triggering Beglinger's request: all possible assistance, nobody on standby.

SELKIRK MOUNTAIN HELICOPTERS pilot Paul Maloney was already in the air, heading away from the SMH base in Revelstoke on an unrelated flight, when he aborted that mission, changed course, dropped the nose of his A-Star, Rescue One,* and raced toward La Traviata, some twenty-eight miles away. SMH owner/pilot Gerry Richard ran to his A-Star, Rescue Two, powered up, and was in the air little more than five minutes later, flying low under the blanket of fog and weather that clung to the higher elevations. He was approaching Carnes Creek—the standard route by which he flew clients

---

* Not the actual call signs used, Rescue One, Two, and Three and so on are used within this narrative to reflect the chronological order in which the helicopters responded.

in and out of the Durrand Glacier Chalet—at 11:05 when Peter Schlunegger, owner of the Beglingers' neighboring heli-ski operation, Selkirk Tangiers, called Richard and told him he had "three guides working nearby doing snow studies and they are ready to respond immediately."

At roughly the same time, Maloney reported heavy fog above the treeline. He was forced to land at the Durrand Glacier Chalet helipad and now was on standby, waiting for visibility to improve at La Traviata. Hearing this, Richard asked Schlunegger to alert his guides to locate and prep a landing zone[†]—he was heading their way.

Meanwhile, the SMH dispatcher had called in pilot Troy Kirwan to fly a third response helicopter. Mountain guide Bernie Wiatzka was about to walk out the door of his house in Revelstoke to play hockey when a mechanic from Canadian Mountain Holidays called him and said, "Hey, there's been an avalanche somewhere, they might need your help." Wiatzka's wife had just returned from skiing and told him, "Yeah, I just saw Troy Kirwan on the road, he looked like he was in a hurry." Grabbing his gear, Wiatzka jumped in his car and sped to SMH, arriving in time to see Kirwan wheeling his bird out of the hangar.

By the time Kirwan, Rescue Three, lifted off at 11:15, the SMH dispatcher, along with SME office employee Ingrid Boaz, had alerted Canadian Mountain Holidays, Kicking Horse Mountain Resort, and an emergency medical response unit, all of whom mobilized avalanche rescue dogs, paramedics, and additional guides.

Once Richard found a hole in the cloud cover, he flew at top speed into the neighboring Selkirk Tangiers Heli Skiing tenure and at 11:23 picked up STHS guides Ruedi Niffeler, Ron McAllister, and Eriks Suchovs, who were crouched down and huddled together in what appeared to be a large flat meadow.

For Suchovs, news of the avalanche at Selkirk Mountain Experience summoned a dark memory—and the chance to return a favor. During a spring-skiing session fifteen years earlier, Suchovs had been guiding a group of three heli-skiers at Selkirk Tangiers when they were hit by an avalanche and he was buried. A secondary slide pushed him down deeper to 1.2 meters, buried

---

†   One must ensure that a generally flat area (preferably with an approach into the wind) one hundred feet wide by one hundred feet long is clear of trees, debris, or sloped terrain that might impact the helicopter rotor.

one client 2 meters, and partially buried the other two. Guided clients had not been required to carry shovels and probes in 1988, and the partially buried skiers were desperately trying to extricate themselves by hand when their heli-pilot—who had "parked" at a prearranged pickup zone—failed to reach Suchovs on his radio and took flight to investigate after fifteen minutes. He located the avalanche debris roughly five minutes later, and identified the two partial burials and radioed the Ministry of Transportation and Highways in Revelstoke for rescue assistance.

Having been buried three and a half feet under the snow and unable to move for at least twenty minutes, Suchovs assumed the worst, that his clients were also buried and—as he faded in and out of consciousness—he was overcome by sadness and remorse, while coming to grips with the fact that this was the end. Then he heard the pilot attempting to reach him over his radio, which was secured—unreachable—in a chest holster. Suchovs was able to listen to his own rescue unfold, the pilot calling out to anybody nearby to assist, and then over the radio there was the unmistakable Swiss-German accent of his friend Ruedi Beglinger, who directed the pilot to come straight to him at the Durrand Glacier. He was ready for pickup.

Suchovs had known Beglinger since shortly after he'd moved to Revelstoke in the early 1980s. He'd helped Beglinger with projects at the Durrand. They'd built a mountain hut together, skied their asses off, and he was Beglinger's best man at his wedding. But perhaps most relevant was that Beglinger was his guiding mentor, and in a mountain rescue, Suchovs knew of no one better to answer the call.

Over thirty years later, Suchovs still breaks down when recounting those long, dark, suffocating minutes under the snow, as cold and scared as he'd ever been, "and once I heard 'Ruedi.' In my mind, I heard 'Ruedi's coming to get me, I've got to wait. I've got to stay alive until Ruedi gets me.'" The acceptance of his impending death was replaced by hope and resolve until, trusting that he would be rescued, Suchovs at some point passed out.

Beglinger dug Suchovs out twelve minutes after he'd jumped from the helicopter. He was blue, hypothermic, in shock—and had been buried for over an hour.

Beglinger then ran over and helped uncover the other burial eight minutes later. She had been buried the same amount of time, but almost twice as deep as Suchovs. CPR and oxygen delivered by the Highways rescue team that arrived just a few minutes later were not successful in reviving her. The deceased had not just been a client; she had been one of Suchovs's best friends.

Now, fifteen years later, as he sped toward La Traviata, Suchovs knew better than anyone the darkness that those under the snow were experiencing. Still, having beaten the odds of a very long burial himself, he also had hope and faith. "If anybody could get them out fast, it was Ruedi."

No AMOUNT OF meticulously executed transceiver-training drills could have prepared Beglinger, or any of his guests, for the horrifying number of burials they faced that morning. Yet there was no time for emotion. "You take that one, you take that one, you take this one here," Beglinger had said in assigning the burials he'd flagged to different diggers the moment they arrived. According to Beglinger, "I was moving fast. We still had to pinpoint the last meter, the fine search, and probe, and the problem was there were so many deep burials, we had to be very careful pinpointing." At that depth, there was no time for mistakes; you had to get to the victim's airway as quickly as possible. Every second counted.

When Age Fluitman first entered the debris field, Beglinger yelled to him, "Search straight down, that way!" Beglinger pointed toward the left of center—opposite from where he was covering the right side. Roughly a minute later, Fluitman was onto a signal, and a minute after that he had vectored in, and was digging.

Heidi Biber entered the debris. *Disaster* was the only word she could muster. "Everybody was just shoveling, shoveling, shoveling. Either digging themselves out or digging for somebody else."

Charles Bieler was attacking the snow when Biber arrived and started digging next to him. He slammed his shovel down, and the snow was so hard the blade sheared off at the handle, and then he went ballistic with the handle, trying to chisel away at the hard snow.

Weselake yelled out, "Shovel!" after he'd confirmed his transceiver was correct by probing down and hitting a body at 1.2 meters. *This isn't too deep*, Beglinger thought when he ran up. "I have an avalanche shovel which is like [an] ax," he says. "You can hit hard without breaking it, and I was going full steam against that stuff, and it was bouncing back." Beside him, Weselake threw aside the surface chunks that Beglinger was able to cut up

Bruce Stewart was chest-deep in another hole, throwing out shovelfuls of heavy, dense snow, when he felt the ground beneath him drop. With it, another terrifying "whumpf!"

"I rocketed up and out of that hole like a gopher," he says. "Terrified." He looked toward the gully ready to scream "Avalanche!" and run, then realized nothing was coming down, and everybody was still working.[‡] Sliding back into the hole, he resumed his mad digging, too spooked and too frantic to have noticed that the west ridge had vanished into the dense fog that had moved in and settled over them.

Roughly ten minutes into this time-warped nightmare, Fluitman uncovered a green jacket some three feet beneath the surface and called out the first, "I have somebody!" He and Rick Martin dug frantically to Naomi Heffler's head. She was unresponsive as they shouted her name, while using their hands to uncover her face and clear her airway.

With Heffler's head exposed, Martin worked fast to clear the snow around her torso so that her chest could expand while Fluitman attempted mouth-to-mouth, but it didn't seem like any air was going in. She was semi-horizontal, face up, and when Martin had chiseled enough hard snow away from her chest, Fluitman squeezed one fist, with his hand on top, in the space to start compressions.

BIELER HAD BEEN rotating from hole to hole, moving snow like a machine, and he jumped in beside Fluitman as Martin jumped out to get Biber, who he knew was a nurse. The same panicked drive that Bieler had felt during his ascent of La Traviata now powered his shovel and he jackhammered into the wall above Heffler, dislodging larger chunks that crumbled and fell past her while Fluitman continued to give her breaths.

Biber was just a few meters away, digging, when she heard Martin boom, "Heidi! We need you here now!"

---

‡   A few others, including Charles Bieler and Heidi Biber, felt the same settlement, likely caused when air pockets or debris shifted, triggered from the weight and movement of the people digging on top.

"It doesn't seem like air is going in," Fluitman told Biber as she slid down into the hole with him. She swiped her finger deep into Heffler's mouth to make sure her throat was clear, unzipped her jacket, then gave her two solid breaths followed by chest compressions.

"Naomi was like three feet or four feet deep and had been under for about ten minutes," says Biber. "It was fifteen chest compressions, two breaths, fifteen, two, fifteen, two. I kept going and going for at least ten minutes, but there was just no response, nothing. She was gone. It was horrible, but you couldn't think about it. I put my hand on her and said, 'I'm sorry.' I think Age kept going when I climbed out of the hole. It was a shit show, total chaos, but everybody was in their own world. Like in the hole, you're focused, it's focused chaos, but when you stop, that's when it hits you, and that's when I was suddenly frantic again. I remember clearly saying out loud, 'Where's Kathy?!'"

WHILE BIBER HAD been performing CPR on Heffler, Pojar and Couturier were roughly twenty to twenty-five meters south near the moraine, screaming "Jeff! Jeff!" After eighty centimeters (a little over two and a half feet) of clawing and digging, they uncovered Bullock's face. His skin was blue; his eyes were closed. Pojar felt and probed for a pulse, anything. And then Bullock's eyes simply popped open.

For thirty seconds, Bullock stared forward, just breathing, and then he focused, looked at them. "Thank you! Thank you!"

Bullock had been under the snow for about fifteen minutes and unconscious for most of it. "Holy shit, I'm alive." *Twelve.*

Adrenaline surged through his body like fuel and his head spun, likely from all his training, those intense hours of first aid, the daily transceiver practice, the endless scenarios he'd been taught, and now, where could he be the most helpful? *What do I do? Where do I start? How can I help?*

Couturier had continued digging down to Bullock's pack. "Here's your shovel," she told him. "Can you dig yourself out?"

Pojar was already gone. "The whole time we were digging, you could hear people yelling for help over, like twenty or thirty meters," he says. "So I went running over there, which was a mistake. I should have turned off Bulluck's transceiver and checked my own, but these guys are yelling, so I just ran to help." At this—the fifteen- to twenty-minute post-avalanche mark—chaos expanded and overlapped as more people were reached and names were added to the cries for help. "This is Jean-Luc!" shouted Weselake. "I've got Vern!" yelled Stewart. Both yelled, "I need help!"

When somebody called for help, Beglinger would jump in, but as the incident commander he was also counting heads, noting who was there searching and who was missing. Everybody was engaged, digging, probing—was there somebody digging on each of the signals he had already marked with a pole or glove? Time was of the essence. It was twenty minutes in, a critical time, not the time for anybody to stop digging. His intuition told him, do another sweep with the transceiver. There was no time to question the impulse; there was only time to search.

Reaching Stewart's hole, Pojar saw him digging around Vern Lundgren's head and shoulders. He ran over to Bieler, who had called out for a probe while digging with Lindsay. The hole was roughly two meters deep, and as he assembled his probe, Weselake popped his head up a few meters away and yelled, "Joe! I've got Jean-Luc. I need somebody to help dig."

Pojar left his probe with Bieler, and he and Weselake reached Schwendener's head just a couple of minutes later. Pojar cleared his mouth of snow, then asked Weselake if he knew CPR. "Got it," affirmed Weselake as Pojar crawled out, agitated. Kathy and Dennis had been right near him going up. He cursed himself for not checking his transceiver before making the run to Schwendener.

He ran back toward the moraine, where his transceiver led him about ten meters to the left of where he and Couturier had been buried. "It was no more than a meter deep," he says. "I don't think it was even that." He started digging.

BIBER'S AND POJAR'S nightmares converged as she looked desperately for her best friend and saw Pojar digging furiously and screaming, "I've got someone!" She dropped to her knees beside him, and a few minutes later, "we came to a blue jacket and a long brown braid," she says.

"Oh my god," she said. "This can't be Kathy."

"Yes, it is," Pojar said. "I'm so sorry."

Kessler was face down and twisted sideways toward Pojar, who reached in and quickly dug out the snow packed tightly in her mouth. Says Biber, "We dug her out together. Like Naomi, she was not traumatized or anything. She actually looked beautiful as usual. We were able to pull her out so I could try CPR, and I worked and worked and worked and worked on her."

Pojar turned off Kessler's transceiver, and the second Biber started CPR, he pulled his transceiver out of his pocket and followed it slowly away. Behind him he could hear Biber crying, "Wake up, Kathy! Wake up, Kathy!"

You've got to shut that out, Pojar told himself. *You've got to find Dennis.*

In the minutes leading up to this, Beglinger had helped Weselake with CPR on Schwendener, and then continued the search, sweeping the area, hoping to identify a shallow burial. An incident commander's most difficult job is to pull a digger off of one burial, to focus on a shallower one, but he was prepared to do it. With the sheer number of burials in close proximity and several of the deep burials still transmitting while the searcher's transceivers intermittently reverted to transmit,[§] it was extremely difficult to account for everybody. During his sweep, Beglinger had identified another very deep 2.8-meter burial nearer La Traviata's base, and he was heading back across the debris toward the moraine when he picked up another signal. Both he and Pojar converged on it together, probed, and dug down furiously into another section of hard, compact snow until they reached the unresponsive body of the laid-back ski instructor from California, whose humming on the skin track set the groove as much as it did the pace.

His complexion told Pojar—even before they considered CPR and found that his airway had been blocked—that Dennis Yates was sadly beyond help.

Several meters over, Biber stopped chest compressions on her best friend.

"I started to lose it at that point," she says. "Ruedi came up to me right beside Kathy and put his arms around me. He was very emotional, and started crying as well, but just for a moment, like he turned a switch on and off, and he looked at me. I was a wreck and he squeezed my shoulders, and said something like, 'You have to be strong, there's still a chance' or 'We have to keep going, there is still hope.' It was a blur, because right then, somebody was calling for me. I just heard 'Heidi!' and I ran."

[§]   A built-in safety feature in the event a secondary avalanche buries somebody in search mode, their transceiver will revert back to transmit after eight minutes unless a button is pushed. Once a button is pushed, the timer resets for another eight minutes.

CHAPTER 31

ALL BUT
THE DEAD

Heidi Biber ran to Rick Reynolds, who was calling her while shoveling, pushing, pulling, throwing, whatever he could do to quickly move snow and enlarge the opening of the deepest, darkest pit she'd seen that day.

Looking down into this vertical, cylindrical shaft, she saw Keith Lindsay standing at the bottom, straddling while digging around someone's head that was protruding up. "It's Dave," said Reynolds, breathing hard as heaved a chunk of snow aside. He, Charles Bieler, Rick Martin, and Paula Couturier had teamed up and were digging into the shaft from the side, creating a ramp and widening the hole because as it was, there was no way anybody could bend over in the tight confines of the chasm to perform CPR. Biber had arrived less than a minute after Lindsay had reached Finnerty, staring down helpless at the tussled, snow-encrusted dark hair, around which Lindsay was working frantically with his shovel and hands. Her mind was racing and recalled, *This is the snow shoveler who told the joke, Ruedi's nanny.* And, she thought, *this ramp is going to take too long.*

"Hold my boots," she instructed Reynolds before going headfirst into the two-meters-deep hole, where she hung upside down and tried to breathe life back into Dave Finnerty.

At the same time, Lindsay continued to clear snow from Finnerty's shoulders and down around his chest to create more space between his torso and the snow so that Biber could perform chest compressions. He'd jackhammered through much of this concrete on his own, and after a few more minutes, he climbed out, and Bieler slid down to relieve him. "I need some more space over here," she told him. "Is his chest rising?" It was—her breaths were getting in—but she could not feel a pulse. Balling her fist like a hammer, she got her arm down in the foot or so of space and pounded his chest, trying to jump-start his heart.

When Pojar had followed Biber and Beglinger away from the bodies of Dennis Yates and Kathy Kessler, he'd felt like a "zombie." Just an hour before, he'd been chatting with Kessler as they ascended toward the tea-break knoll. It was cold, the sun was in and out of the clouds, and he remembered thinking, *What a beautiful day!*

Part of what kept Pojar coming back to SME all these years was the people he'd met and the comradeship that was established during long climbs. He'd told Kessler he was especially grateful to be here because it relieved some of the stress about his ailing mother, and she shared that she could relate. Her husband, Scott, who was supposed to be on this trip but had to cancel last-minute, was in remission from colon cancer, and they planned to "stop chasing money and do some traveling. More adventures like this."

He'd also connected on this trip with Finnerty, who told him he was living his childhood dream. Pojar had noted that Finnerty's endearing good spirits seemed to rub off on pretty much everybody in his presence—Ruedi, Nicoline, the guests, and especially the Beglinger girls. Pojar had watched Finnerty pull Charlotte and Florina around in the upturned scoop of the snow shovel, "training" for the high-speed toboggan-like sledding run he'd built for them behind the house. According to Pojar, Finnerty was "the grease that kept everything going smooth" and he'd told him as much: "I'm not sure what you're doing, Dave, but keep on doing it because things are looking good around here."

Now, as Biber—hanging upside down in the hole above which Finnerty was buried—attempted resuscitation, Pojar found himself looking away. That was when he noticed how dark the sky had become. *What a shitty, gloomy day.*

JOHN SEIBERT, WHO had been buried to his neck, shuffled his stiff legs as quickly as he could away from the hole he'd finally dug himself out of. Cold, shaky, and off-balance, he navigated through the debris to see what he could do to help. For some twenty-plus minutes he'd been hearing the rescue efforts in progress, but with his face at ground level amid the debris, he was shielded from the visual scope of the catastrophe. This was his first real look.

"It was as bad as you can imagine," he says. "Frankly, I was surprised nobody had broken down. These were friends, and their friends—some of them had passed, and they stuffed that somewhere and kept going. It was heroic. The only people not helping were the dead."

The first thing he heard—words anyway—that penetrated the shock of it all was Charles Bieler yelling, "Has anyone seen Ken!?"

"And Craig!" It was Beglinger, in his unmistakable Swiss German. The queries telegraphed outward: "Has anybody seen Craig, or Ken?" There was a volley of negative responses.

A few moments before, Bruce Stewart had made the hard call to stop CPR on Vern Lunsford, the aerospace engineer from Colorado, whose last words—just before Wylie pushed forward away from the protective cliff onto the open slope of La Traviata—had been, "I don't like it . . . being below the other group." Likewise, Beglinger had also made the call to stop CPR on Schwendener, but Weselake had continued—just in case there was a chance—as he dug him out completely. "He's gone," Beglinger told Weselake for a second time, putting a hand on his shoulder. "It's okay to stop."

As Beglinger moved away, Weselake stood upright for the first time since he'd started digging and was hit by a wave of nausea. He kneeled, took a few slow, deep breaths, and thought he heard the dull "thwap, thwap, thwap" of a helicopter. He leaned over to throw up, then forced himself to stop, literally swallowing it back down. *Don't puke*, he told himself. *It will confuse the rescue dogs.*

AT THE SAME moment, Fluitman and Bieler were running toward "a hat or a glove" they'd seen some twenty meters from the main central burial area, though it was unclear whether it had been placed there by Beglinger as a marker or simply churned up by the avalanche.* They immediately picked up

---

* This "hat" or "glove" recollection became a source of phantom guilt for several survivors who, in the initial and then expanding chaos of the search, had passed by a "marker" while vectoring in on a signal; or had been directed to one pointed out by Beglinger, but left it to answer a call for help, thus delaying the digging. They later questioned if these final markers for Craig and Wylie had been those they had, for whatever reason, been unable to dig for immediately as they rushed elsewhere.

a strong signal, probed, hit a body, and began digging. It was around 11:10, and Wylie and Craig had been under the snow for some twenty-five minutes.

Jeff Bullock had dug himself out and joined Beglinger, who was attacking the snow at the final marker, another "hat or glove"—nobody specifically recalls. What they do remember was the exact depth on the transceiver: 2.8 meters, or more than nine feet, of abominably hard snow.

The two final burials were only fifteen or twenty meters apart, but Fluitman, Bieler, Seibert, and Stewart, digging in the one to the east—more downslope toward the chalet—encountered some softer, more variable snow. This made for quicker progress than the other group.

They were about a meter down when Bieler, Fluitman, all of them, heard a crackling sound beneath the snow. As they dug deeper, the crackling was joined by walkie-talkie static and then some "horrible, inhuman, deep guttural sounds," according to Bieler. Realizing that their weight on the snowpack was forcing the air out of the lungs of whoever was beneath them, Fluitman and Bieler kicked into overdrive and less than a minute later, at about 11:20 a.m., Bieler was brushing the snow from Ken Wylie's face.

Even as they'd remained hopeful through their frantic digging, both had been steeling themselves for what they'd already witnessed too much of this morning. But Wylie, who was buried in a semi-upright, seated position, had the coloration of a rosy-cheeked newborn, breathing and alive—"a gift," according to Fluitman. "We've got Ken!" they shouted out with a collective cheer. Thirteen.

Hearing this, Beglinger, Bullock, Weselake, and the others at the other burial realized at this point the only transceiver signal they were digging for was Craig. Flying on adrenaline, they leaned into their shovels. It didn't matter how hard the snow, or how deep—Ken Wylie had just proven that there was still a chance and none of them was giving up.

Still upside down in the hole and trying to revive Finnerty, Biber heard the muffled cheer. This kept her going for another five minutes, but she knew even before pressing her fingers against his carotid artery for the fourth or fifth time that this was a losing battle. Biber had worked as a hospice nurse and had a keen sense of knowing, usually the moment she walked in, if a patient's room was "empty." She felt that now. Finnerty's spirit was gone—she was alone in the hole.

"I can't do anything else," she called out to Reynolds. "Dave's gone."

Reynolds pulled her up and then ran to join the others. Exhausted, Biber rolled over on her side in the snow, catching her breath, defeated.

But she stood up almost as quickly as she had lain down, hurrying over toward the two remaining burials. "I didn't want to stop. I didn't want to think. I didn't want to go to that place to realize what happened," she says. "I wanted to keep moving because I knew I'd break apart. I knew I'd just totally break apart. To say goodbye to my friend Kathy, while she was laying there, and all of the bodies, it was a really hard thing to see."

Although Biber had seen death come slowly and sometimes painfully, she had never experienced "death in this capacity," she says. "It was unbelievable. . . . Unbelievable. To have just spent, two hours before that, with all these folks. Laughing, having a good time, to all this was . . . outrageous."

Determined to keep her emotions at bay, she found herself central to both groups. Having learned from their efforts to reach Finnerty and Lunsford, some of the diggers were going straight down, while others were coming in diagonally from the side so the second they reached him, they would have room to perform CPR. Paula Couturier was standing beside her, making notes in a notepad, double-checking Beglinger's count, making sure everybody was accounted for.

To Biber's right, there was sudden commotion. Wylie's eyes rolled back, his head slumped forward, and his complexion turned ashen. "He's not getting oxygen," someone said, and Fluitman gave him a big breath of air, then a second, while the others removed more snow from his torso. Jumping into the hole, Pojar grasped Wylie by the shoulders and shook him. As Seibert yelled, "Ken! Wake up!" from above, Pojar slapped Wylie hard on his cheek with the open palm of his right hand. "Ken!" he said. "Wake up! Let's go home!" With this, Wylie's head stopped bobbling, his eyes seemed to focus and track, and he mumbled something. The color that had so quickly drained away returned, Pojar's handprint clearly visible on his once-again very red left cheek.

To Biber's left, Bullock, Beglinger, Lindsay, Stewart, Martin, and others were "working like crazy, shoveling as fast as they could," hammering their way down into the depths.

CHAPTER 32

FLY

HELP FROM THE AIR WAS coming from three directions.

Determined to find a way through the dense cloud cover, pilot Paul Maloney of Selkirk Mountain Helicopters was airborne in the first response helicopter, Rescue One—inbound from the east after being grounded at the Durrand Glacier Chalet for some thirty minutes—along with Dan DiMaria, a guest who had stayed back at the chalet that day. Rescue Two, piloted by Gerry Richard (also SMH), came from the west, where he'd picked up the three STHS guides: Niffeler, McAllister, and Ruedi Beglinger's best man, Eriks Suchovs. Piloted by Troy Kirwan, Rescue Three was inbound from the southeast, flying low and fast over the Columbia River and Big Bend Highway and nearing Carnes Creek, where he'd ascend the drainage. Guide Bernie Wiatzka sat in the seat beside him.

The rescue plan in effect at Selkirk Mountain Experience (SME) had called for Rescue One, the closest available helicopter, to fly directly to the avalanche site fully fueled and without passengers. There the incident commander—in this case, Beglinger—would direct Maloney to pick up the guide from the second group—in this case, Wylie—who, if not already on scene, would be close by. Maloney would then shuttle the second group's guide and clients to the site, where they would assist the rescue in process. This assumed both groups were not involved, but in that rare instance, the plan called for Maloney to land directly at the avalanche site to prep landing zones for the other helicopters and to be on standby to fly casualties to Queen Victoria Hospital in Revelstoke.

But first he had to get there, and visibility was still "sporty" at best.

On a clear day, the flight from the chalet to La Traviata would have been two minutes, but the poor visibility compounded by the innate challenges of mountain flying made the two locations a world away. All systems on a helicopter suffer performance penalties at altitude, and the clouds didn't just limit visibility, they signaled a wind battle in progress that Maloney knew could and would buck around his A-Star as it battled the turbulent air. Mountain helicopter pilots are a different breed. Determined and calm, they control an oversize tin can that flies not by glide, but by beating the wind into submission. And they do it with a soft touch, finessing turbine power, anti-torque foot pedals, the cyclic control stick, and the collective like a one-man band in rhythm with the impossible.

Maloney tilted the nose and descended from the chalet, dropping down a few hundred vertical feet to the upper reaches of Carnes Creek. From there he ascended over Twin Falls, flying low and extra slow between the breaking clouds using treetops, rocky outcrops, and ridgelines for reference in the flat light. When the clouds converged and visibility became nil ahead, he hovered* in place for long periods above these dark reference points on the snowy landscape until a passage presented itself and he throttled forward through the rolling fog. In this manner, he leapfrogged forward from landmark to landmark, following roughly the same trajectory the skiers had traversed that morning as they climbed toward Swiss Meadows. In fact, their skin track might have been visible below the nose of the aircraft if Maloney hadn't been so hyperfocused on the treetops and rock beneath and ahead of him, while maintaining distance from the predominantly white, wind-battered headwall of Tumbledown Mountain to his right periphery.

Helicopter pilots strive to maintain visual reference with the ground and horizon, lest they experience spatial disorientation and "go vertigo" and fly into the mountainside, the ground, the trees. As such, visual flight rules require pilots have one-half-mile visibility horizontally and maintain five-hundred-feet distance from fog or clouds—luxuries not always afforded in a rescue situation. It was "tense flying," says DiMaria, who trusted Maloney "completely" as they inched forward. "He'd sat there on the helipad at the chalet

---

* Hovering is the most challenging aspect of flying because a helicopter generates its own gusty air while in a hover, which acts against the fuselage and flight control surfaces.

for, I'm guessing a half hour, and when it started to clear, I think he knew that was our shot to get in there, so we powered up and went."

Some ten minutes after leaving the helipad, when the prominent rocky cliff of La Traviata suddenly became clearly visible far ahead, Maloney punched forward from the last island of trees—probably just below the knoll where Beglinger had stopped his clients for a tea break. As the helicopter banked over the rubble, DiMaria could see skiers clumped in groups and digging, and a few other lone figures lying on the snow, but it didn't register. He had no idea there'd been any deaths.

At 11:41 a.m.—six minutes shy of an hour after the avalanche had occurred—Maloney in Rescue One landed upon a flat section of snow to the downhill eastern side of the rubble. DiMaria immediately exited with two sturdy lodge shovels, crouched low beneath the spinning blades of the aircraft, then ran thirty or forty meters toward the two groups of survivors, while Maloney jumped out to prep a landing zone—find a flat spot large enough to accommodate the skids of the helicopter, and free of any debris within range of the rotors—for Gerry Richard in Rescue Two, who was "coming in hot."

Richard had picked his way over from neighboring Selkirk Tangiers Heli Skiing, leapfrogging from peak to peak, and accessed the SME tenure by following the rocky west ridge from the opposite direction, via Fronalp Peak. Before reaching Tumbledown Mountain, he went into a holding pattern above the overcast. Patience ultimately revealed a hole in the drifting cloud-scape wherein he dipped his nose and swooped down to the avalanche site. It was a "stomach in your throat" roller-coaster nosedive for guides Niffeler, McAllister, and Suchovs, the latter of whom couldn't recall the way they'd made it in through the clouds, only that it was "absolutely not the standard route" he usually flew to SME.

Maloney waved his arms overhead and marshaled Richard into a land-ing zone not far from his aircraft. Richard flared, and settled the skids right beside Maloney, who had crouched down to mark the spot. Jumping out of Rescue Two, the three guides ran forward: Niffeler and Suchovs toward the group still digging for Craig, and McAllister toward Wylie. Around them the dead were scattered, lying near the holes they'd been dug from. The scene was still frantic as the new guides took over with new strength, digging the final feet to where Craig lay more than nine feet below the surface. With the arrival of the new guides, many of the guests dropped, exhausted. Some broke down as the adrenaline ebbed and the horror of it all sank in.

But there remained hope, very real hope, that Craig might be alive.

In Rescue Three, Troy Kirwan was now ascending Carnes Creek, a route he'd flown dozens of times while shuttling guests. Having never been to SME, this was all new country for mountain guide Wiatzka, who'd planned to play hockey on his day off. He wasn't sure where the "event" was or where they were in relation to getting there, and he wasn't about to ask Kirwan, because he was on the controls and visibility was, according to Wiatzka, "shit." They'd been flying treetop to treetop for some ten minutes when Kirwan slowed and then hovered above the last trees to contemplate a white void ahead.

"Troy," Wiatzka spoke over his headset radio, "we don't have to fucking do this, buddy. We're going to help people; we don't need to be adding to the situation."

But Kirwan knew the terrain. Just beyond this milky abyss was La Traviata, and he was determined to get in there.

Per protocol, nobody was talking over the radio about specifics. No details about numbers of people involved, injuries, deaths, survivors, and certainly no names were mentioned, so Kirwan had no idea if his wife, Kim, the SME cook, had gone out skiing with the groups that day, or stayed at the chalet. Regardless of her whereabouts, Kirwan's resolve would have been the same. This was a "plan Charlie"—plan C—it was "a big wreck," and he was both a mountain pilot and a mountain guide. "He was on a mission," says Wiatzka. "Unless somebody called us off, he knew they still needed help. He wasn't going to turn around."

WHILE JOE POJAR'S and Jeff Bullock's journey back from full burial to the land of the living was accompanied by gratitude, euphoria, and joy, Ken Wylie's awakening was marked by confusion and a dark foreboding. The world came into focus framed by walls of white, and the faces that peered down upon him were alien before slowly materializing into familiarity. These were his clients. They had names . . . and shovels. He'd woken not *from*, but rather *in* a nightmare, and though he couldn't see the scope of it, he could feel the loss. And with that knowing came an overwhelming sense of "anger, shame, and guilt."

Wylie had been buried for roughly thirty-five minutes before they reached his face, but it had taken another fifteen or twenty to fully free him from the snow. While they'd continued to dig his legs out, they pulled his down jacket out of his pack, put it on him, and wrapped him from the waist up in an emergency solar blanket. He remained confused, shivering, moderately hypothermic with a core temperature of 93.2. "Fly Ken to Revelstoke, quick!" Beglinger directed Bieler just as the first two helicopters landed in quick succession.

DiMaria had been on the ground little more than two or three minutes when he got on the other side of Wylie, and he and Bieler helped him out of the pit that had been shielding him from the carnage. He couldn't bring himself to look as he hobbled to Rescue Two with DiMaria and Bieler assisting him. He recognized Richard in the pilot seat, who was speaking into his radio headset while he climbed into the back seat with DiMaria beside him. Bieler leaned into the helicopter and informed Richard that Wylie had been buried for more than a half hour, was hypothermic, and should go "straight to hospital."

After a glance over his shoulder to see that Wylie and DiMaria were buckled up, Richard powered up Rescue Two into a hover while continuing to speak with Kirwan in Rescue Three, who was himself in a stationary hover at treeline some distance downslope. Once Rescue Two's hover was high enough—the two pilots could see each other.

Using each other as points of reference in the flat white void separating them, Kirwan flew upslope toward the landing zone that had been marked with brightly colored flags, while Richard flew downslope toward the trees Kirwan had been hovering above. They crossed paths some fifty feet apart in the center of the void.

As SOON AS Rescue Three landed, Wiatzka rushed to join McAllister and Niffeler, who had jumped into the massive crater marking Craig's burial to dig. At the ramp leading down into the crater, Beglinger, Bullock, and several others stood poised with shovels in hand, ready to jump in the second anyone showed any sign of tiring.

Suchovs had joined Couturier and they were confirming numbers, accounting for everybody one more time. He performed another sweep of the debris with his transceiver, just in case.

In the distance, Weselake was seated beside his longtime friend Naomi Heffler, zipping up her jacket, talking to her. Even though her family had a long history with SME, he felt sick knowing that he'd been the one to invite her on this trip. "I'm sorry," he told her. "I'm sorry I wasn't there for you. I'm here now. I love you. I'll miss you. I'm sorry, I'm sorry, I'm sorry."

Noticing Weselake with Heffler's body, Stewart went to check on him. "Her whole life was still ahead of her," says Stewart, who had a teenage daughter at home. "I followed her down through the trees that morning from the lodge—she was a really, really good skier, a chemical engineer, graduated straight A's. I think I associated her with my daughter, and those paternal instincts kicked in. The father in me wanted to do *something*."

He hugged Weselake, who said almost exactly what Stewart was thinking: "I just feel like I need to do something, and there's nothing."

"We could carry her," said Stewart.

Together they lifted her up—Stewart under her legs and Weselake under her shoulders—and carried her across the rubble, then set her down gently beside one of the helicopters.

Biber was sitting with her back against a slab of snow, watching Stewart and Weselake, when several paramedics from a newly arrived helicopter—Rescue Four—charged into the debris carrying oxygen tanks. "It's too late," she told them as they approached. "I checked them all—they're all gone."

JUST SEVEN WEEKS earlier, Jeff Bullock had sat beside Craig at the ACMG Mechanized course at Monashee Powder Adventures, nervous and excited for all that was to come, both in the training program they'd worked so hard to get accepted into, and for the life they'd chosen—to become mountain guides. "There is always that question," Dwayne Congdon had said during one class lecture. "How will I perform in a real emergency? How will I react? You never really know, but what you can do is train and practice."

When Niffeler said, "I've got him!" at roughly 11:45 a.m., Bullock did not hesitate. He was headfirst into the hole.

LIKE THE OTHERS, Craig bore no sign of traumatic injuries. He looked to be sleeping as Bullock checked his airway and began to blow breaths into his mouth, and Niffeler continued to dig deeper, freeing his chest, allowing the oxygen to fill Craig's lungs,

While asphyxiation is never instantaneous, it can be assumed that Craig was unconscious long before the 11 a.m. "time of death" that would be noted in the coroner's report. That fifteen minutes would be imagined as an eternity by loved ones who agonized over what he must have gone through during his final minutes of consciousness, buried nine feet under the snow, awaiting rescue.

That time reported by the coroner was, in reality, little more than a guess based upon the survivors' inability to revive Naomi Heffler, whose airway was cleared fifteen to twenty minutes after she was buried.

Based on how quickly Bullock and Wylie had lost consciousness (they both estimate two to three minutes, tops), it can also be assumed with a high level of certainty that Craig and the others had lost consciousness within two or three minutes and, likely, much faster depending on depth and snow compaction.

As for those final moments . . .

Researchers with Hadassah Hebrew University Medical Center in Jerusalem conducted a study wherein they analyzed detailed accounts of nearly three hundred legitimate near-death experiences and found that your life really can, and often does, flash before your eyes when you die, "with the parts of the brain that store memories last to be affected as other functions fail." Previous studies have found that the so-called "life review experience" (LRE) is more common among those with a high concentration of carbon dioxide in the breath and arteries, consistent with cardiac arrest, but also prevalent in avalanche burial victims who rebreathe their own expelled carbon dioxide as it saturates the snow around their faces.

At some point soon thereafter, the oxygen-starved brain kick-starts the cerebral cortex into an involuntary—and studies suggest "welcome"—flood of "exceptionally vivid and emotional" memories that span an individual's—in Craig's case, thirty-six years—life history. A common theme among these near-death survivors who have experienced these vivid flashes is the recall of emotional moments with loved ones.

One would like to assume that in his final moments, Craig too went to the ones he loved, especially Savina and Olivia, perhaps even a moment not long after Olivia was born. He was in the hospital room at Puerto Montt, Chile, in April 2001, after a full year on the road—the longest he'd ever gone without seeing his parents, siblings, uncles, aunts, and grandparents. Savina was asleep, recovering from the birth, and Olivia was dozing in the crib beside her bed.

He was looking out the hospital window over the expansive blue of the ocean when Olivia began to stir. Picking her up gently, he settled into the recliner beside the bed, kicked off his shoes, and, when Olivia faded back to sleep, opened his journal.

"Sav is sleeping," he wrote. "My feet are propped next to her and Oli fills my lap with quiet, snoozy love. Thank you God, Namaste. I am a grateful and happy man."

PART IV

LEGEND

CHAPTER 33

THE AFTERMATH AND MEMORIAL

BRUCE STEWART WAS WANDERING THE debris field, trying to remember where he'd left his skis, when he felt a chill and realized he was soaked. "Literally like I'd jumped in a lake," he says. "That's how much I sweated out, and being down in the snow, everybody was drenched.

"It was like a war zone. Helicopters coming and going, bodies, and in the middle of it all I watched Ruedi drop down to his knees and onto his rear. He was just sitting there crying. I'll never forget that."

The survivors were helicoptered back to the chalet. Shell-shocked, the guys from the Truckee crew went upstairs to their room and passed around a bottle of whiskey, listening as Heidi Biber wailed in an adjacent room. She'd just called Scott Kessler on the satellite phone and told him that Kathy—his wife, her best friend—was dead, killed in an avalanche, that she'd tried CPR but couldn't save her. "Listening to Heidi crying, we were incredulous," says Reynolds, "passing the bottle around thinking, *Did that really just fucking happen?*"

Beglinger was among the last of the survivors to leave La Traviata, only doing so after he'd spent a private moment with each of the seven bodies, and a paramedic had told him they would be well taken care of. Upon boarding the helicopter, he asked the pilot to fly the fracture line in order to see the avalanche as a whole, and begin to process the chain of events and understand what went wrong. From the ground, Eriks Suchovs watched Beglinger's helicopter head up along the face, hovering near the fracture line before turning toward the chalet. "Hey guys," said a voice, one of the responders, whom Suchovs cannot recall. "Let's just take a moment here, we're not in a rush. Let's really look after these people in a respectful and careful way."

The responders zipped up the jackets of the victims, checked their pockets for hats or gloves to put on them, then in some cases used their own emergency sleeping bags as body bags. Ceremoniously, they loaded them into the helicopters, which flew to Selkirk Mountain Helicopters, where the hangar doubled as temporary morgue.

At 4 p.m., after a day of guiding guests, Buffery returned to Baldface Lodge—too far south to have helped with the response—and learned that there had been "an incident near Rogers Pass." Each emerging detail delivered via the radio in the guides' office—a "commercial touring operation" involving a "large number, thirteen people" had been "caught in an avalanche" with "multiple burials"—intensified his sickening worry. Says Buffery, "The location, size of the group, and all I'd heard from my own clients who skied with him, I thought what commercial guide might have that many people exposed in avy terrain." Once he confirmed it wasn't at Rogers Pass itself, he was left with only one option: Ruedi Beglinger.

There was no helicopter flight back to Nelson until the next morning, so Buffery called several friends to tell them that he had a weird feeling, and to "start rallying near Craig and Savina's house; be ready to support her if we do hear the worst." Meanwhile, vans topped with satellite dishes, camera crews, photographers, and reporters representing most U.S. and Canadian news outlets crowded the streets and reported, "Breaking news from Revelstoke, BC, Canada—one of the deadliest avalanches in the history of North American backcountry skiing, with seven confirmed fatalities including both American and Canadian citizens."

Pat and Brian got into their car and were driving north toward Nelson when they received the terrible news from Savina that Craig had been killed. Pat then called Janet, who was at home with Jessica and Josh telling herself they hadn't heard from Craig because he "just didn't have cell coverage." She screamed into the phone "No! No! No!" and Josh—three days shy of his fifteenth birthday—put his head down on the computer desk where he'd been following the avalanche and quietly sobbed.

Buffery was with Mark Fawcett at Baldface Lodge when Paula Pensiero came through on the sat phone, her voice shaking as she said, "Craig didn't make it." Away from the guests, Buffery, Turcott, and a couple of other guides told stories and drank Scotch. Feeling suffocated by their grief within the walls of the lodge, they constructed a cross using two-by-four scraps salvaged from a woodpile and took turns carrying it on their shoulders up the mountain. Heads down, boots sinking into the snow, they followed a trail they'd often seen Craig break in order to get to a point of cell coverage so he could check in with Savina and let her know all was well. They used no splitboard or snowshoes because they wanted it to be hard. "We stomped out of the trees onto that barren, corniced ridge," says Buffery, "and a crisp wind woke me up, and I looked up at all the stars. Craig was with us, and we each talked to him in turn. I don't know why I plunged the cross near those rocks on Moshi Moshi—the welcome ridge that Craig had named—but there it lived in balance with the soft Kootenay snow dumps and scouring winds for the remaining winter."

The following afternoon, January 21, Royal Canadian Mounted Police (RCMP) Sergeant Randy Brown provided the public with an updated summary: "Twenty-one backcountry ski mountaineers . . . split into two groups, an upper group and a lower group, were traversing a thirty- to thirty-five-degree slope when the avalanche occurred. Part of the upper group and all of the lower group were struck by the avalanche which initially buried eleven people and partially covered two. The avalanche path had been . . . approximately 75 to 100 feet in width and 300 feet in length. . . ."

Then he read the names of the seven confirmed fatalities.

Devastated survivors, families, and friends mourned their losses and searched for answers while an entire generation of snowboarders stumbled around in disbelief, "feeling like their world had lost a dimension," says snowboard writer Colin Whyte. It was virtually impossible to fathom that of all people, Craig Kelly had been snuffed out by an avalanche that was described as "a fluke of nature" by John Seibert, who spoke at the press conference on behalf of the survivors. Craig's closest friends were the most floored. "He was too cautious, too smart," says Jason Ford. Renowned snowboarding mountaineer Jim Zellers couldn't understand it. "Craig just didn't push it in fatal terrain or exposure," he says. "And with that many people? It didn't add up."

That same afternoon, a trio of avalanche professionals led by Larry Stanier, who had taught Craig's Level 1 and 2 avalanche courses, began an investigation at La Traviata on behalf of the BC coroner in Revelstoke, Chuck Purse. Two consultants hired by Beglinger were also on scene performing their own investigation, which included measuring the avalanche's dimensions and mapping the burial locations and depths, as well as digging snow profiles and performing stability tests to evaluate the snowpack and determine the cause of the slide.

While four of the survivors remained at the chalet for the duration of their planned week, the rest returned to SME's Revelstoke lodging, the Wintergreen Inn, where a grief-counseling session was set for 1 p.m. Wylie had been released from the hospital after a few hours of observation during which he was interviewed by an RCMP constable collecting statements from survivors. Wylie explained that he was an assistant guide still learning the area and had been following Beglinger's directives and routes, but then, perhaps fearing accountability, glossed over the internal fears and doubts he'd harbored that day, with no mention of his trepidations regarding La Traviata. "From my judgment the slope appeared safe," he told the constable, who left shortly thereafter. Alone, he pondered, "How I can avoid responsibility for any of it—the truth too scary to face, my mind continues to construct defenses."

During his medevac ride, Wylie had learned Dave Finnerty was killed, but it wasn't until he nonchalantly walked past the media assembled at the front door of the inn to reunite with the other survivors that he learned the names of the other six. Each was heartbreaking, but hearing Kathy Kessler, Dennis Yates, and Vern Lunsford was especially devastating because he had failed them, especially Lunsford, who had told him he didn't like the idea of being beneath the other group. This haunted him nearly as much as his own response to Lunsford: "Neither do I." Then he had gone anyway.

As the survivors discussed how they considered the rescue of Wylie, Jeff Bullock, and Joe Pojar (all of whom had been fully buried) to be cherished victories, Wylie wished he could rewind the clock and heed the words of Lunsford, who at least had had the courage to speak up. Wylie wasn't the only survivor to wrestle with guilt and second thoughts that they hadn't dug fast enough, performed CPR well enough, checked transceivers when they should have; they also reflected upon fate and how or why their chosen positions in line had ultimately determined life and death.

Once the hour-plus session had ended, some of the survivors agreed to speak to the media out front; others escaped to their rooms. For his part Wylie squeezed through a window leading to the inn's backyard, jumped down into the snow, and followed an alley to where his car was parked a few blocks away.

On January 22, Pat, Brian, and Savina flew to the Durrand Glacier Chalet with questions, all of which Beglinger answered while Nicoline served them lunch. Brian was wary to outright accept Beglinger's assessment of the avalanche, but both he and Pat agreed that the Beglingers expressed absolute remorse and sorrow—even as Ruedi was stoic in his explanations and Nicoline could not hold back tears. After picking at their lunch, they boarded the helicopter and, with Beglinger, flew past La Traviata on their flight back to Revelstoke. While shock and grief fog all their memories of that day, Savina was firm in her belief that "Craig was an adult who made decisions and was responsible for his own decisions as well. And he was not a soft-spoken person who wouldn't voice his opinion." She was heartbroken but did not hold Beglinger accountable.

That same afternoon, RCMP Sergeant Brown announced that the preliminary investigation was complete and there was "nothing to make us believe this was anything other than an accident." Responding to a *Globe and Mail* report that investigators had "played down suggestions" that the upper group of "fourteen skiers traversing a ridge caused the first fracture, dumping a fast-moving slab on a group of seven skiers just below," Brown said, "At this particular time it doesn't look like that's the case." The Canadian Broadcasting Corporation (CBC) reported the next day, "The investigation is entering a second phase which coroner Chuck Purse emphasized would be focusing on finding facts, not fault. . . ."

On January 23, Beglinger made his first public appearance at the RCMP headquarters, saying that his heart went out to the victims and their families and how, during his sleepless night after the avalanche, "It was like a movie. I probably pushed the rewind button two hundred times and looked over it again and again. I asked myself the question, 'Did I really do everything right?' I kept answering myself, 'I did everything right as far as I know. I'm certain I have not made a mistake.' . . . The snow felt super, super positive. Very firm underneath my feet. The pole testing on the way up was strong. I couldn't find a single weakness in it."

When a reporter asked him if he felt responsible, Beglinger responded, "I don't think I'm responsible for that accident. . . . I think that was a pure accident, which nobody could have said, 'This will happen.' Of course, now [in hindsight] it's easy to talk."

Twelve days after the La Traviata avalanche, a second catastrophic slide occurred at Rogers Pass, just a few miles east of Selkirk Mountain Experience. A group of seventeen students and adults on an annual school trip was ascending a popular ski-touring route when a massive avalanche released from the upper slopes of Mount Cheops and thundered down 3,000 vertical feet in seconds. Two guides heard the loud crack and watched helplessly from a nearby slope as the 1,500-foot-wide avalanche swept away the group, all of whom were equipped with transceivers, shovels, and probes. Although they immediately facilitated a search and rescue, seven teenagers lost their lives.

This tragedy occurred the day before family and a few hundred friends gathered at the Bellingham, Washington, Cruise Terminal to celebrate Craig's life. Wearing duct tape armbands in tribute, they wandered the lobby and mezzanine, which had been transformed into a Craig Kelly photo exhibit, before settling into the auditorium that overlooked Puget Sound.

Pat began his son's memorial service "as Craig would have wanted it," he says, honoring the other six who died on the mountain that day by reading their names:

Ralph Lunsford from Littleton, Colorado

Dave Finnerty from New Westminster, British Columbia

Kathleen Kessler from Truckee, California

Naomi Heffler from Calgary, Alberta

Jean-Luc Schwendener from Canmore, Alberta

Dennis Yates from Los Angeles, California

and Craig

There was a full minute of silence interrupted only by the cry of seagulls taking flight over the sound, then Janet shared a poetic tribute she had written from mother to son. She spoke of the mountains and the snow and the oceans and waves and how Craig had enhanced their beauty with his gentle spirit. She talked about rainbows, which had become Craig's special connection to his mom and his sister Jessica: "Whenever you see a rainbow, please think of Craig. He will be our guardian angel in the snow forever."

Story after story from Craig's various tribes followed. Marty Brown on Craig's wheelie ride introduction to the South Twenty-First Street gang; Jeff Fulton on Craig's first life-changing ride on a snowboard; Delta Upsilon fraternity brother Mark Thomas on providing Craig legal counsel regarding his original Sims contract: "He was seventeen, wasn't he? I told him to sign it. 'You're a minor, it won't hold up in court.' I think Jake is here somewhere, and I apologize. That probably cost you a lot of money."

"Worth every penny," Carpenter said as he walked to the stage for an emotional recounting of "happier times," like presenting Craig his lifetime achievement Tranny Award the previous spring. Mike Ranquet followed, looking out over a sea of mourners that included Shaun Palmer, Mark Heingartner, Jason Ford, all of the MBHC, and a lengthy list of pros past and present, as he thanked Craig for saving him from himself that night at Ski Acres, introducing him to all these great people, and giving him a path in life as a successful pro snowboarder himself. He also shared a recent revelation from his mom: that when he was a kid, Craig had always asked her permission for Ranquet to ride Mount Baker before extending the invitation to him. "I never knew," he told the audience.

Others sat quietly, unable to bring themselves to speak but awash in their own memories.

Savina listened intently, holding Olivia in her lap as she held on to each story. She was especially taken by the sheer number of people who referenced Craig as "my best friend."

CRAIG'S LIFE WAS celebrated by many in many different ways. Competition was canceled on day one of the European Open, and competitors were told to go freeriding. Craig's fraternity brothers gathered for a night of reflection and storytelling, while hordes of local riders and wandering travelers gathered around a bonfire in the Mount Baker parking lot. Following the memorial, several of Craig's friends encircled Mark Gallup outside as he lit woven strands of sweet grass and waved the smoke among them. "This ceremony honors our ancestors and opens us up to their wisdom," he said. "Native spirituality and beliefs say that your ancestors will help you along your path in life after they've moved on. Craig has become our ancestor, our grandfather, and yes, he is our guide. Our job is to keep his spirit alive by passing along his stories to each other and to future generations."

Beglinger was in the audience at the Bellingham terminal. In the previous week, either he or Nicoline had attended several of the memorial services, met with families of the deceased, and handwritten dozens of condolence letters. While Beglinger's attorney had counseled him not to speak to the media after the initial press conference, he agreed to an interview for *Outside*, with writer Ted Kerasote. "A Thin White Line" ran in *Outside*'s April 2003 issue, the same month *National Geographic Adventure* published an overview of the two Selkirk avalanches and *Men's Journal* featured survivor Evan Weselake's first-person account of his partial burial. In the absence of the-yet-to-be-released coroner's report, such stories became additional fodder for internet chat rumor mills.

Kerasote, who had previously been guided by Beglinger as a guest at SME and as a client in Europe, noted that

> the two accidents represented the deadliest fortnight in the history
> of North American alpine touring, prompting deep questions about
> ethics, risk, and the business of skiing the backcountry. Despite the ee-
> rie similarities, these disasters involved very different circumstances.
> In the second incident, an inexperienced and young group passing
> through a high-traffic area was blindsided by a more-or-less random
> event. In the January 20 avalanche, however, expert skiers who had
> signed on expressly to seek downhill thrills on exposed terrain. . . .
> Both avalanches left devastated family, friends, and survivors in their

wake. But the fate that befell Beglinger's SME group seemed less purely accidental, and more subtly problematic because it involved the judgment and decisions of a renowned backcountry guide.

Kerasote gave the best overall account of the avalanche yet published, wherein he quoted Beglinger's sadness and regret via a statement that seemed contradictory to many. "'My guests are my friends, and I take care of my guests, . . . But on the 20th of January, at 10:45 a.m., I failed. And I failed not because I made a mistake. I think I failed because nature wanted to hit us.'"

John Buffery followed the aftermath and was enraged by the lack of accountability. Not wanting to add pain to Craig's family or Savina, he bit his tongue, reminding himself that he had not been there, he did not know the nuances of the day or Beglinger's season. Still, he and like-minded guides were all but certain mistakes had been made. "We'd close the door and say, 'You pompous prick, you're not taking responsibility for *any* of it.' No ownership whatsoever. I'm a compassionate guy. I might give him an inch and there might be a crack in the door to have a discussion with him, because I knew it must have been the worst day of his life, but to my knowledge, he never once admitted a mistake."

THE DAY AFTER the avalanche, a raven landed upon the roof of the Durrand Glacier Chalet. Having never seen a raven in the area before, Beglinger's daughters felt it was Dave Finnerty's spirit returning to the home where he had been their beloved nanny. That summer the entire family had a hand in building a walking path to La Traviata that was named Seven Ravens Trail.

In late August, Beglinger guided Scott Kessler, Jean-Luc Schwendener's father, and Janet and Jessica up the trail to add their own rocks to a mountain cairn honoring the victims. Snow from the avalanche still remained, and Beglinger had scoured the area for weeks beforehand to make sure that as it melted, an uncovered personal item would not lead to a traumatic discovery.

As they built up the cairn, said prayers, and told stories, Janet asked Beglinger where Craig had been found. With trepidation she walked across the sun-cupped snow to the general area where a dark speck against the white caught her eye: the tip of a ski pole. Beglinger chipped away at the snow until one of Craig's telescopic hiking poles was revealed, bent from the force of the avalanche. Janet wrapped her fingers around the grip, overwhelmed by the realization that he had been using it on the ascent as the avalanche struck.

The last thing her son had held at the very end of his life calmed Janet's nerves on the way back down the trail, steadying her on the loose rocks and narrow pathway—Craig helping her return to the chalet.

EPILOGUE

On September 23, 2003, the coroner's report was finally released, confirming that the failure plane had been the November rain crust. Measuring depth of snow above that crust, probing, and using snow pit profiles and compression test analysis, all five investigators on scene concluded that the snow within the La Traviata couloir/gully had been "mostly strong deep snowpack" and therefore the skiers within or at the top of the gully did not trigger the avalanche.

Some seventy meters east of the couloir at the high point of Beglinger's up-track, investigators found a "very weak shallow snowpack" and deduced that the weight of the first skiers grouping up around Beglinger triggered a failure on the November rain crust that propagated southeast and started the first of three separate avalanches where the terrain steepened to 30 degrees.

The first large, class 3 avalanche was 50 meters wide, averaged 50 centimeters deep, and ran approximately 400 meters downslope.

A second, small class 1 avalanche then released in rocky "unskiable" terrain directly below the rounded ridge—aka "wave"—which separated the first avalanche from the La Traviata gully/skier's ascent route.

"The third, main, fatal avalanche," the report stated, "then released on the group's ascent route. It is not possible to know exactly what the mechanism was that caused the second and third avalanches to release. They either released sympathetically by the vibration of the first avalanche, or the failure propagated [dominoes] around the lower slope."

The coroner determined the cause of death for all victims was "asphyxiation," classified all as "accidental," and made three recommendations: one, "that all operations concerned with avalanche hazard evaluation in western Canada subscribe or gain access to the InfoEx; two, "that backcountry ski touring lodge and hut operators form an association to promote standards of safety, client care and operating methods"; and three, "that the guides of Selkirk Mountain Experience and all backcountry ski operations continue their professional development."

The report concluded, "Backcountry ski operations will never be able to provide excellent skiing without exposing their guests to some degree of avalanche danger. All these operations need to become more cognizant of the possibility of remotely triggering avalanches from shallow snowpack areas, especially in times of widespread weaknesses."

In the April 2003 *National Geographic Adventure* article "After the Slides," writer McKenzie Funk simplified the findings: "Beglinger (and possibly one or more of the skiers behind him) stepped on a hidden weak spot while traversing out of the couloir, setting off a large avalanche to the east. The energy from that slide radiated back west," ultimately triggering the fatal avalanche—a result of classic "spatial variability," the same thing Craig had identified as the "biggest issue" he would face as a guide.

Craig had learned that intuition, terrain choice, probing, and deep, stable snow were the best defense, and that the old-school stability tests on a slope weren't just unreliable, they were deceiving. Several incident reports Craig had read were cautionary, detailing individuals who had trusted results of a stability test regarding the slope that then killed them.

Just six weeks earlier, Craig had both identified his future killer and predicted the circumstances. "I'm learning more and more that the errors, which are made in snowpack judgement, are due to spatial variability," he'd told Ari Marcopoulos. "In light of that . . . most avalanches occur in the presence of trained people [who] knew the dangers were there. They knew it was possible for a place to slide, but . . . went anyway. It could be they forgot, but most commonly it's social pressure, or human factors within the situation that causes the trouble."

WHEN ANNIE POLUCHA saw Selkirk Mountain Experience described as "a world-renowned hut-based wilderness ski touring lodge" on page 1 of the judgment of inquiry into the death of her sister Kathy Kessler, she was all but certain it would be biased and stopped reading. Her husband at the time, Peter Millar, however, scoured the entire report and learned that the sport of ski touring is unregulated. There are no guidelines to say what is an acceptable risk, how many people should be on a slope at the same time, how many people should be in each party, or any of the other questions which arise after a tragic event. An individual skier can choose not to follow his guide into an area that appears to present a level of risk greater than that he or she is willing to accept. [Clients] rely on the decisions made by their guide to give them the best skiing experience possible, balanced against their expectations and the risk involved to meet that objective . . . The higher the skill level of the client, the more challenging the terrain they want to ski, which leads to a higher level of risk. Ski touring is inherently dangerous. People who ski at this level are aware of the risk. Release of Liability / Waiver of claims documents are routinely signed before skiing begins.

The coroner's findings failed to answer questions that Polucha and Millar—both strong backcountry skiers and alpinists—had about the avalanche. When Beglinger traveled to Truckee to meet with them (along with Kathy's widower, Scott Kessler, and several other family and friends) the meeting turned "contentious" when Millar did not accept Beglinger's explanation of events or, in particular, of the snowpack at La Traviata. At one point, Beglinger told Millar, "You don't know snow." Says Millar, who did have real experience in avalanche and snow science, "I wanted to throttle him."

Believing that Beglinger was criminally negligent, Millar considered taking legal action against SME (as did the widows of Yates and Lunsford). He abandoned that in favor of spearheading an independent investigation with two experts in the field of geology, snow science, and safety: Dick Penniman and Frank Baumann. Neither Scott Kessler nor the surviving members of the Truckee group wished to be part of the investigation, but Annie Polucha still had questions. "Why were 13 [sic] skiers spread over a 100 foot wide path instead of crossing from safety island to safety island, one at a time, which we have all been taught in basic Avy training?" wrote Polucha on the Telemarktips.com discussion board. "I will have to defer to the experts that the technical analysis of the slope was flawless, however, I seriously question the client management on the day in which the Durrand Glacier Avalanche occurred. If these questions are not addressed . . . then 50 percent of the safety equation has been ignored, and the backcountry community is cheated of potentially life-saving information."

This independent report came to several conclusions that were different from the coroner's; in fact, it seemed that the only thing the two agreed upon was the failure plane for the La Traviata accident. Scathing observations included:

It is clear from the data that the La Traviata couloir presented high-risk terrain to the SME touring group. Considering the public bulletins that warned of one or more lingering weak layers in the snowpack at isolated locations throughout the Selkirk Mountains, the wisdom of deciding to ascend the La Traviata couloir must be examined critically so as to avoid, if possible, tragedies of this magnitude in the future.

Clearly the SME guides did not heed the warning signs or at the very least, did not feel that they were applicable to their group. Neither did they feel the need to follow long established precepts in safe winter travel. Placing the weight of as many as 21 closely spaced people on such a slope seems a flagrant violation of the most basic of safe winter travel precepts.

Two DECADES LATER the avalanche, backcountry skiing, snowboarding, and guiding communities remain divided about that day. One camp believes that the La Traviata Avalanche was simply an unpredictable, unavoidable, and at some basic level not-expected tragic accident in the mountains. The other camp maintains it was completely avoidable, a direct result of human error and the arrogance of a ruthless, egocentric guide.

In April 2019, when Beglinger said to me, "After we ski, we talk," my biggest question following years of reporting remained why two groups, each led by a certified guide, were on top of each other in the same gully. The coroner's report, the independent investigation, the magazine articles, chat rooms, a documentary, a National Geographic Explorer television special: none of them ever addressed *why* that had happened.

I had anticipated that this would be answered in 2014, when Ken Wylie broke his silence and published a memoir, *Buried*. On page 55, I reached the crux of all my questions and found myself holding my breath as I read about

Wylie's anxiety filled, fearful steps into La Traviata after the admission that his doomed client Lunsford had expressed his concern about the seven skiers directly above. It was heartbreaking to read Lunsford's final words.

But I finished the book not knowing the reason Wylie had ignored Lunsford's fear, his own extensive training, and his own inner voice. The answer he provided in *Buried* was oblique. I kept coming back to the unsatisfying line again and again on page 55: "I tell myself, I have no choice."

A few pages later, Wylie was buried by the avalanche, and then the book shifted to different parts of his life, lessons learned, and people he'd encountered, that he believed influenced his actions or inaction at La Traviata. Those chapters taught me a lot about Wylie and provided excellent context, but I was mainly interested in the first third of the book leading up to and including the avalanche. Therein, he portrays Beglinger an "abusive" boss who, during nine days of employment, speaks "angrily" and "snaps" regularly. When Wylie himself talks to Beglinger, he has to "muster up" his "courage" and speaks "tentatively." All very effective verbs, adjectives, and anecdotes to describe a tyrant.

I occasionally returned to Wylie's book, trying to piece together the puzzle. There were two points in the story where things went sideways; both coincided with Wylie's very brief mention of the radio. While climbing up from Fang Creek on day two, he attempted to reach Beglinger but heard a low-battery "squelch" and abandoned his efforts. While climbing up toward La Traviata, and at the tea break, he "decides" to "stay off the radio" and then when he missed the directions, realized the radio had been in the top of his backpack. He also gave very clear and candid descriptions of being overwhelmed—more than just normal anxiety. I speculated that after losing Beglinger's tracks during the "whiteout" on Durrand Glacier on day two, Wylie was compelled to follow Beglinger too closely on day three.

In the spring of 2018, I decided it was time to tell Craig's story, as well as a full account of the avalanche that had taken him. Once I had received support from members of Craig's family and close friends to move forward, I reached out to Wylie directly and Beglinger indirectly. Wylie responded to my email within two hours; Beglinger took nearly a year.

..

FROM THE MOMENT I landed at SME, listened to the welcome orientation, and went through the avalanche-beacon training school, I was learning important nuances to the story that included the sheer scope of the terrain, how the groups worked, how quickly they moved, and how a guest can listen to guides converse all day long on the radio yet be unable to recall anything specific unless making a conscientious effort to commit it to memory or actually write it down. But certain moments stick. I remember clearly the seriousness of the avalanche beacon training, especially the "team shoveling" drill while digging for a mock victim, and how utterly blind I was shuffling over Forbidden Pass in a whiteout; how it took all my concentration to follow the etchings of ski edges on a wind-scoured section where the track had mostly disappeared. I remember the comfort in having a guide up ahead and the psychological push of somebody behind you, but mostly I remember it was snowing when I walked up the hill from the chalet the day Beglinger invited me into his residence. Settling into the couch, still uncertain how I would start the conversation, I was relieved of the duty when Beglinger said, "So, Eric, what do you want to know?"

"Well, I know Craig came here to learn from you and—"

"Things didn't turn out so good, did they?" Beglinger cut me off, his pale blue eyes narrowing as if he was probing for my angle, but then they softened and he leaned back in his chair. "You know, everybody is so damn opinionated; they already make their mind before they even ask the question. Maybe you're different."

I told him I wanted to hear the story from all sides, and he replied with a scoff. "All sides. You know what I said when I heard you wanted to talk to me last year? I said, 'You can go to hell.' But now, I meet you, you meet me—you see what we do up here. I look in your eyes. You look in my eyes. Face-to-face. What do you want to know?"

"I want to know the truth, Ruedi. You're a mountain guide, that's what you do. I'm a journalist, but I'm also a snowboarder and I know something about avalanches. I'm going to talk to everyone involved; it wouldn't be fair if I didn't. It might take me years, but I owe it to Craig to find out. I've studied what is out there, and I feel there is more to the story. If there's anything you can share to help me understand exactly what happened that day, please don't hold back."

"That day?" he said. "What happened started *before* that day, you have to understand . . ."

So maybe there *was* something to my theory, but I kept it to myself while Beglinger recounted chronologically the events on what he called "the worst day of my life."

Arriving at his own version of Wylie's crucial "page 55" of the story, Beglinger explained that just before leaving the knoll he'd told Wylie to give his own group a break here, and wait until he neared the top of La Traviata—specifically "twenty minutes"—before Wylie followed.

This directive Beglinger claimed he gave Wylie was a monumental detail. It's not in Wylie's book, which had been out for nearly four years—nor is it in any report or article I'd read. I wondered, could this late addition to his narrative be retribution for Wylie's scathing account? An attempt to somewhat exonerate himself? I asked Beglinger if he was certain about this detail and he confirmed, adding "I would never take two groups up any slope like that at the same time, no matter how safe I think it is."

If Wylie had left the knoll at the time Beglinger claims he specified, and no avalanche had occurred, Group 1 would have been—theoretically—up and out of the gully and far to the right of La Traviata when Group 2 was on the side approach under the cliff. If there had been an avalanche while Group 1 was ascending, Group 2 would have been out of harm's way—a quick reaction force with a guide in case of emergency.

I asked when Wylie had left the tea break knoll. Beglinger wasn't sure, but he searched for a photograph on his computer and showed me on the screen the route they'd taken up La Traviata, tapping his finger at the top, marking the spot where he had been when he had expected Wylie to leave the knoll. I then asked him where Wylie actually was, and he pointed to midway down the slope, exposed in the gully, across from the protective cliff.

"You saw him there?"

He confirmed he had, and also that Rick Martin informed him right then that Wylie's group was coming in under them, something Beglinger had already seen. "If somebody the whole day, every time you say give me more space, and next thing it happens again, eventually you just say well . . . Which now, you look back and you say that was the biggest mistake. You know, I should have said [on the radio], 'Okay, Ken, I'm in charge here. You need to wait until I'm up here, or you give me more space—we don't do it like this here.' . . . This is where I should have clamped down."

I was shocked, after all I'd been told, that Beglinger had just admitted a mistake, and I wanted to know why he'd kept these revelations under wraps for sixteen years, but I also didn't want to do anything to interrupt his flow. He continued talking, and some three hours after I'd walked in the door, we ended our conversation minutes before dinner with a shot of Jägermeister. "To Craig," I said.

As we clinked glasses, I saw his eyes were glassy, and welling up with tears.

He replied, "To all of them."

MANY SAY NICOLINE Beglinger is the secret to SME's success because she is the yin to Ruedi's yang. As she finished tidying up after dinner that night, I sat at the table nearest the kitchen, the same spot—she informed me—where Craig had chatted with Dave Finnerty the evening before the avalanche. We talked for some time, during which she told me she was glad Ruedi had decided to speak with me, and then I asked her why Ruedi had never said anything about what he told Ken.

She smiled. "What did Ruedi tell Ken?"

"To wait twenty minutes," I responded.

Her surprise seemed genuine when she replied, "He told you. Hmmm. You should ask Ruedi, but he didn't want to throw Ken under the bus." In her husband's line of thinking, she continued, he had been the lead guide, so ultimately the avalanche was his responsibility alone.

In my bedroom later, I tested myself. On day one, our two groups came together for a short break after skiing Moon Hill, midway down a tree run called Excalibur. Beglinger and the assistant guide had been talking, and when my group split off for the rest of the day, they maintained radio contact at the top and bottom of each run. Yet I could not recall a single word of what they had said to each other. I realized it would most likely be the same scenario for the survivors—if I couldn't recall a specific conversation from a few days before, how would they be able to from sixteen years before, and therefore corroborate Beglinger's claim. I thought about Vern Lunsford, who had been closest to Wylie at the front of his line when they'd arrived on the knoll. Had he heard Beglinger's directive? Might that have been what prompted him to speak up when he told Wylie he didn't like being beneath the other group? Sadly, there was no way to know.

NEAR THE HELIPAD on the day I left the Selkirks, I thanked Beglinger for the week and squeezed in one last question: What had prompted him to open up with those details? "You said you wanted to know everything," he replied. "Now you know."

Back home, I continued my research, interviewing Jacques Russo, who shared with me dozens of hours of raw interview transcripts from *Let It Ride*, a documentary he'd produced about Craig. I found that cinematographer Christian Begin had interviewed Beglinger the last week in March, 2005, roughly two years after the avalanche. While recounting the avalanche to Begin, Beglinger said, ". . . as I started to walk away, I told him [Wylie], make sure you have twenty minutes space, that's just normal, I don't want the groups together regardless of if it's steep or if it's flat . . ." That interview took place nine years before Wylie's book was published, and aligned with what Beglinger told me fourteen years later.

During the summer of 2019, I called Beglinger with more questions, hoping to understand *why* he had not said anything to Wylie when he'd seen him coming up too quickly—a disclosure that could potentially be a big deal once published. He reiterated what he'd told me about the slope (he'd felt it was absolutely deep, safe snow), and his claims that he'd told Wylie not to follow too closely several times that day. He also still believed Wylie had been insubordinate the day before, so in essence he believed that Wylie was going to do what he was going to do, regardless of Beglinger's directives.

Seeing Wylie on the lower slope broke with Beglinger's protocol to keep the groups separate, but since he believed the slope was safe, he had not called him off over the radio.

I posed for him a theoretical scenario: If Wylie's eight-person group had not been on the lower switchback at mid-slope on La Traviata, did he think the energy from the first avalanche would have still caused the fatal avalanche? (Note: I would later ask several experts the same thing; all acknowledged that there was only a very slim chance that the absence of Wylie and his eight skiers adding weight and tension to the slope might have prevented the third and fatal slide.) Even though I had inadvertently offered Beglinger a sliver of an out with this question, he responded with "We cannot speculate this. All that we know is the avalanche did happen."

While Beglinger believed Wylie was being insubordinate, it seemed entirely plausible—even likely—that Wylie had rushed up La Traviata because he feared a repeat of the previous day. I theorized when Wylie saw Beglinger going to La Traviata versus Fronalp Peak, he had panicked. It had been snowing lightly and he could see the gathering storm to the west and how La Traviata headed up toward a no doubt wind-scoured ridge where tracks would be easy to lose in a whiteout, and so he had chosen to follow Beglinger too close and fast. In fact, Wylie told the constable just hours after the avalanche that the weather had just cleared up as they approached the slope, "It was actually high visibility, you could see the slope quite well." In 2021, I learned that Rick Reynolds from Group 1 and John Seibert from Group 2 had come to the same conclusion, independently, even before they'd read Wylie's book. Using similar language, they told me "the biggest screwup" and "biggest tragedy" of the day was Wylie coming in under the other group. Annie Polucha, Heidi Biber, Bruce Stewart, and Scott Kessler had all wondered why that had occurred. Nearly every survivor, most of whom I'd interviewed by mid-2021, reiterated this point, with one expressing the hope that I would be able to get to the bottom of it because "It's been long enough; we deserve to know the truth."

I interviewed previous SME clients and guides, including those who were not fans of Beglinger. Every one confirmed that he always kept his groups spaced out, especially while a second group was exposed beneath the other.

Around this time I sent Wylie an email asking again why he had decided to enter the gully when he did, telling him "I want to get it right. . . . You'd lost Ruedi's tracks the day before . . . it was starting to snow a bit more . . . do you think there was that worry? It isn't clear in *Buried* . . . you say you felt like you didn't have a choice . . . while you didn't have a choice as to route you did have a choice as to how close you were following." Wylie's response read, in part, "My intuition was screaming at me to not go. My intellect rationalized the decision. . . . The situation was electric and most of us sensed doom, but we all followed. It was vague, and didn't really address the question. Still, Wylie was adamant when he told me that he had no discussions with Beglinger on the knoll during the tea break, and none of the survivors I interviewed could recall one way or the other, nor could they remember if they had been right next to each other as Beglinger remembers it, or "across the group of 21 people" as Wylie describes in *Buried*. In addition, his book gave me the impression that he had been experiencing some sort of breakdown or panic attack right before reaching the knoll, which may have affected his perception. Beglinger, however, told me that Wylie had absolutely made eye contact with him and affirmed—though he couldn't recall if this was with a nod or verbally. Wylie maintains no such conversation occurred. While trying to reconcile these two inconsistent accounts, I wondered if it was possible that Wylie had missed Beglinger's words just as he had missed the route change.

From the moment I informed Wylie about this project in the summer of 2018, he had been helpful and open about his story and how he had struggled with his own guilt and the trauma of being buried for some thirty-five minutes. But one thing Wylie had not experienced was being vilified the way Beglinger had. In fact, Wylie recognized this in a way by writing in *Buried* how convenient it was during conversations to say he'd merely followed the lead guide. "I find myself in conversations casting blame on Ruedi," he wrote. "I cannot stop doing this because it feels good, but it is also hollow. There is no shortage of people willing to listen to my tirade and to take sides."

Based upon my previous research, the chat rooms, articles, Wylie's book, conversations with people I knew and respected, I came into this story almost certain that Beglinger was the villain he had been made out by so many to be. But then, slowly, I found some views of Beglinger to be misinformed at times and perhaps biased by grief, anger, or dislike. When I asked Ken Achenbach—who was so crushed by Craig's death that it took him twelve years before he could drive the Mount Baker Highway without crying—what he thought of Beglinger and what he had heard about the avalanche, he answered with "I have such a fucking grudge, I can't even tell you. That someone could hate snowboarding so fucking much . . . the first thing you learn in the backcountry is not to hike above somebody. The fact that that fucker forgot everything he learned because of his hatred for a fucking snowboarder, that was keeping up with this great fucking Swiss mountain guide. Fuck you, buddy. That he forgot everything he learned and killed seven people. Fuck you, buddy. That's all I have to say about that one." But Beglinger himself is a snowboarder and none of his actions or comments suggested that he disliked Craig or was competing in some way with him. Achenbach had merely picked up on these comments from others and took them as truth. They certainly fit a narrative that had been perpetuated, including a fallacy that Beglinger guided on instinct alone and charged up anything, which didn't match my findings.

In the epilogue of *Buried*, Wylie wrote that "hubris was a contributing factor in this tragic event. It seemed as though the presence of Craig Kelly affected the tone of the week, which had an audacious feel to me." However, the five return guests I interviewed told me that that week seemed very much in line with every other week they'd spent at SME. Evan Weselake described it as "Situation normal—most of the group didn't even know who Craig was."

A review of *Buried* in *Powder Canada* in September 2014 states, "The autocratic behaviour and arrogance of Rudi [*sic*] Beglinger is very accurate. . . . Rudi's clients . . . are not decision makers or experienced, rather followers who entrust their guide. Ken Wylie . . . too was a follower—waiting for the next command from his boss, Rudi the autocrat.—Editor."

To be honest, I was primed to hate Beglinger in the same vein, but the more I learned about him, and the more I spoke to people who had worked with him or been guided by him, the more the man I thought was a monster seemed actually human. As one of Beglinger's longtime clients told me, "Ruedi can be a very abrasive individual. That doesn't make him a villain."

I KEPT GOING back to the very last line of Wylie's author's note: "My ultimate aim is to take responsibility for my actions and learn from their consequences." But I still did not have clarity on these critical events. So, I followed up with Wylie again. I needed to understand how he had missed that Beglinger announced a change of plans to go up La Traviata while others had not. According to my reconstruction of events, this "change of plans" had occurred just a few minutes before Beglinger recalls giving Wylie the "twenty-minute directive," and just a minute or two before Beglinger shoved off. All of this was sandwiched within the period of time Wylie describes himself forthrightly in his book, "Anxiety paralyzes me, halting conversation or connection with anyone in any way." I explained to Wylie how there were other guests, including Jeff Bullock and Rick Reynolds, who had confirmed "they had heard the change of plans, knew they were going to La Traviata before they left, so that's where I'm trying to figure out a disconnect somewhere, if they knew about it. . . ."

"Oh, totally the disconnect was in me," Wylie responded. "I was totally shut down, like completely and entirely shut down. Chiefly because of stress and stress of disempowerment. Totally and completely shut down. And I don't wish that on anybody. If anybody finds themself in that place that's the time to pull the ripcord."

Despite this admission, Wylie remained adamant that he had had no conversation with Beglinger. My feeling, however, is that Beglinger did speak to him, and Wylie did not register for the reason above and therefore believes it did not happen. At the same time, Beglinger believes Wylie did register, which, tragically, caused Beglinger not be more proactive when he saw Wylie coming up La Traviata early, because he thought Wylie was willfully disobeying, insubordinate once again, as he believed Wylie had been the day before when he'd lost his track in the fog.

DURING THIS SAME phone conversation, I asked Wylie one last time if he had rushed up under the other group because he feared losing the track as he had the day before.

"It would be lovely if things were that simple," he replied. "*Yes*, that's part of it, but there's a whole second-soup stuff." The "second soup" in this case was Wylie not having a say in where they went, not having a voice in the decision-making process. "The bottom line is that Ruedi's the lead guide and supposedly offering an apprenticeship.* He could see where I was. He could see what I was doing." Wylie described what he was doing—placing himself under the other group—as "the stupidest thing ever. You teach that in your basic avalanche course. The situation was totally fucked."

---

* Technically, only Craig and Bullock were on apprenticeships. Wylie was a certified assistant ski guide, though of course still working under Beglinger's direction.

He went on to say, "If you're going to believe in a hierarchy then you've got to believe in the hierarchy all the way through to the end and take responsibility at the end. But he never has. There was no dialogue, no exchange, no strategy. I didn't understand where we were going or what we were doing."

I asked Wylie, "Is there any chance that you were in such a fog that if he did tell you anything that you wouldn't have gotten it?"

"Oh, you can throw me under the bus even more if you want," Wylie said. "Here's the thing . . . I didn't have a voice in that situation and it's profoundly unethical. It's profoundly unethical to put somebody in that position and not give them a voice. If they experience consequences and he's been a total dick and he continues to be a total dick. Put that in your fucking book. He was responsible. He was responsible to give me a safe and solid apprenticeship. And he didn't. He fucked my career. He totally fucked me."

While I listened to Wylie—truly I felt sorry for him and the tragedy he had undergone, and, from what I had heard, Beglinger could at times be a "dick"—I still recognized from my research that Beglinger did not in any way encourage Wylie to enter the La Traviata west couloir with his Group 2 while Beglinger's Group 1 was still ascending the gully. Tragically, the only person who put himself and his group in that dangerous situation was Ken Wylie himself.

Still, when Beglinger looked down and saw Wylie coming up, that *would* have been the time to call him off, which Beglinger acknowledged when he told me that was *his* biggest mistake right there. But Beglinger had felt that the deep, consolidated snow in La Traviata was strong enough to support both the tail end of his group about to exit La Traviata as well as Wylie's group, which was just entering the bottom switchback. He also remained convinced that Wylie was being insubordinate and disregarding his directions, just as he believed Wylie had been insubordinate the day before versus the radio miscommunication that seems more likely to have occurred: that Wylie simply misheard a garbled, spotty, and/or Swiss-German accented Forbidden "peak" instead of Forbidden "pass."

This resonates with Craig's prophetic words that "most avalanches occur iñ the presence of trained people" and how "most commonly it's social pressure or human factors within the situation that causes the trouble."

THE CRAIG KELLY Memorial Scholarship Fund at the Avalanche Canada Foundation [avalanche.ca] supports snowboarders endeavoring to earn certifications as avalanche professionals and/or guides. To date, more than thirty snowboarders have been awarded the scholarship. Since Craig broke down the walls in 2002, dozens of snowboard guides have been certified by the ACMG and CSGA, all of whom have studied the story of the Durrand Glacier Avalanche as part of their curriculum.

AT A CEREMONY in Vail, Colorado, on April 13, 2013, Craig was inducted posthumously into the U.S. Ski and Snowboard Hall of Fame.

OLIVIA AND SAVINA Kelly still live in British Columbia, where they often ride together. Olivia is forging her own path in life, having recently completed an internship in Burton's engineering department—with a focus on prosthetics and adaptive snowboarding—while attending university. Although she's not sure where that will lead, one thing is certain: snowboarding—and in a way, her dad—has been a guiding force in her life.

In fact, many of the long days of her internship were spent at a state-of-the-art research-and-development prototype facility at Burton's Burlington, Vermont, headquarters. It's considered the world's premier snowboarding equipment laboratory, and is respected and coveted by the snowboarding industry as setting the standards for innovation.

The ten-thousand-square-foot facility has a one-word name: Craig's.

A NOTE ON SOURCES AND ACKNOWLEDGMENTS

In the mid-1980s, I spent a lot of time at my mom's bedside, often in the hospital. She had battled cancer for nearly four years, and when the pain got bad, the nurse would start a morphine drip and she would fade off to sleep as I escaped into the latest issue of *International Snowboard Magazine*, following the exploits of Craig Kelly and the other radical riders of the era. I'd study every photo, read every word, and then do it again while plotting the next chance I would get to practice the tricks and turns of the new sport I'd fallen in love with.

I was seventeen when my mom passed away in 1986, and one of the last things she told me was, "If there's anything you want to do in life, do it now, because you never know about tomorrow." Well, I wanted to move to Breckenridge, Colorado, and snowboard every day. The short version of the story is: I did. That leap of faith later led me to a degree in journalism, so instead of gracing the covers of snowboarding magazines, I wrote for them and eventually became the editor of one. I still got to ride powder and see the world—on the magazine's dime—and like Craig, I was drawn to the backcountry. That's where our paths often intersected. I think what ultimately connected us as friends, though, wasn't snowboarding but rather books—neither of us ever traveled without one.

Fifteen years after Craig passed away, I was standing in a lift line at a little ski area in Utah when a twenty-something snowboarder pointed at the Craig Kelly Is My CoPilot sticker on the nose of my board and asked, "Who's Craig Kelly?" I couldn't believe there was a snowboarder on the planet who hadn't heard of Craig, but then again, I couldn't believe I was fifty years old, a father of three, and had required a hot shower, 600 milligrams of Advil, and twenty minutes of stretching before I could even put on my boots that morning.

Back home after that trip, I dug my way to the corner of my family's storage unit and found the cardboard box I'd buried there more than a decade before—the one with *Craig* scrawled in black marker on its sides. Inside were stacks of printed papers, articles, newspapers, magazines, microcassettes, mini disks, VHS tapes, a press pass from the Islamic Republic of Iran, some photographs, and a carefully folded silver duct tape arm band that I'd worn during Craig's memorial gathering. On top were the last two items I'd added before sealing the box: the charred remains of a braid of woven sweet grass and a paperback copy of John Long's *Long on Adventure*, which I'd bought at Village Books in Bellingham, Washington, the weekend of the service. Craig had introduced me to Long's writings nearly a decade before, and in a way the introduction of any great author to a fellow reader is a gift. I sat on the cold concrete of my storage unit, surrounded by vintage snowboards and archived bins of snowboarding magazines, and began to read it again.

Craig once also shared with me his copy of James Clavell's *Whirlwind*— a 1,216-page epic adventure story set in revolutionary Iran—when we were snowboarding in the Alborz mountains outside of Tehran on assignment for *Snowboard Life* in February of 2000. Craig had been rapt by the historical novel, and when I expressed interest in it, he looked at me and tore it in half right down the spine. "Here," he said, "I've already read this part. I'll give you the rest before the end of the trip."

Over dinner that evening, Craig asked if I thought the world was ready for a book about a snowboarder.

"You want to write a memoir?!"

"Maybe," he said. "I've been journaling and thinking maybe it's time to tell some of my stories." I told him that I'd be honored to help out when he was ready. He said he'd dream about it that night.

The following morning, he grilled me about present tense versus past tense, publishers, and literary agents, and then he confirmed that although he'd had plenty of adventures, he wasn't sure if there would be enough interest in a snowboarder's life to warrant a book. "Timing," he said, "is everything."

As we walked down to the dining room of our hotel, he continued musing: "The problem with memoirs and biographies is that you have to die before anybody wants to read about you." He paused and lifted his chin—that classic Craig mannerism—and said, "Fuck that." And we laughed. The morbidity of that statement didn't unsettle me at the time because the thought of snowboarding's superhero dying really was incomprehensible.

I BROUGHT CRAIG's cardboard box and several plastic bins of my treasured snowboarding magazines home from the storage facility that day and set myself on a journey. This led me to my notes from that first avalanche course, where I'd scribbled down the instructor's quote that "every storm tells a story if you dig deep enough." It had taken me sixteen years to pull the metaphorical shovel from my pack and start digging, but even before I broke the surface, I knew that the hardest layers to get through would become the final pages of this book. Still, I had to go there, to the day of the avalanche. I kept digging, sensing that somewhere down there beyond the dark hues of midnight, past the fear of the unknown, there was light.

As I cycled through my memories of Craig, I eventually landed on our final day in Iran at Dizin resort. My last-ever run with Craig was following his and Tom Burt's tracks down a snakelike gully run, top to bottom. I'll never forget it.

The next day, while we were packing our bags, he tossed me the second half of *Whirlwind*.

I held the two book halves together while Craig duct-taped the spine. The cover was missing, pages were torn, and it looked like something you couldn't get a quarter for at a garage sale. "Consider it a gift," he said with a grin.

This attempt at duplicating the book's original stature was the best we could hope for considering the circumstances, but it preserved the story and, as Craig put it, that's what really matters.

"You gotta see what happens," he said.

••

THE DARKEST WHITE is the result of more than 350 interviews with some 120-plus individuals over the course of more than five years. Many of these sources have been quoted or cited within the text; some preferred to remain unnamed. I conducted most interviews face-to-face or by telephone, though several individuals corresponded with me via email.

In addition, dozens provided me with their archived audio recordings, film, videos, letters, legal transcripts, notes, memories, and photographs of Craig and relative to their involvement with the Durrand Glacier avalanche. Especially helpful were the raw interview footage and audio recordings concerning the avalanche or direct interviews with or about Craig provided by Wiley Asher (*ISM*); Louise Balma (*TWS*); Christian Begin and Jacques Russo (AdventureScopeFilms); Jeremy Jones (Teton Gravity Research/Jones Snowboards); Ewan Morrison (*Snowboard Life*); Greg Stump (Greg Stump Productions).

Snowboarding historians David Alden, Pat Bridges, Trent Bush, Mike Chantry, Brian Knight, Burton historian Todd Kohlman, former Sims employee Jim Veltman, and others dug into their archival collections of snowboarding media, contest result sheets, photos, videos, and the like, all of which helped me track Craig's contest winnings, historical moments in snowboarding, and his and other pros' career highlights.

Regarding the avalanche, several survivors were interviewed just one year after the event for National Geographic Ultimate Explorer television, which provided me the raw film footage and/or transcripts from their interviews. Other survivors provided me with their personal notes and journals—some written in detail the very evening of the avalanche. Still others gave me copies of their interviews or memories of their interviews with the RCMP conducted the night of the avalanche or the day after. Ken Wylie published his complete RCMP interview (occurring just hours after the avalanche) in his book, *Buried*. I was also privy to a couple of interview transcripts shared by journalists who tape-recorded survivors just days after the avalanche. I utilized all of this material to help verify the memories of survivors and piece together what I believe is the most accurate account of the chaos that ensued.

A heartfelt thanks to all those who spent hours—in some cases, days—recounting stories, including: members of Craig's family, friends, fellow pro riders, survivors of the avalanche, first responders, photographers, writers, editors, publishers, cinematographers, mountain guides, and fans. A special thanks to every single person who ever contributed to a snowboarding magamine or produced a snowboarding video or movie and unknowingly helped document history, when all they really wanted to do was ride pow.

Before naming (and hopefully not forgetting) any of the sources I worked with directly, I want to thank my entire family, above all my wife and in-house editor, Lorien. She continues to make me look good on paper and beyond, as do our creative and talented brood, Merrick, McKinley, and Callia. I love you all. Thanks also to my sister, Lori, and Rick Hennessy for their continued support as well as "office" space at various intervals. Thank you to my longtime friend and agent, Christy Fletcher, and co-agent Eric Lupfer, who far exceeded the role of agent while helping me craft Craig's story. Thank you also to everyone at HarperCollins who believed in Craig and his story, particularly my editor, Noah Eaker.

Thank you to all the snowboarding historians who directly contributed to this book in words, photos, interviews, or otherwise. In addition to those already mentioned above: Larry Balma, Eric Berger, Andy Blumberg, Adam Cozens, Peggy Cozens, Tom Cozens, Lee Crane, Jeff Curtes, Lou Dawson, Craig Dostie, Dave Downing, Chris Doyle, Annie Fast, Bud Fawcett, Jon Foster, Jeff Galbraith, Mark Gallup, Trevor Graves, Mike Hatchet, Marc Hostetter, Kurt Hoy, Tom Hsieh, Kevin Kinnear, Ace MacKay, Ari Marcopoulos, Jamie Meiselman, Billy Miller, Warren Miller (RIP), Ewan Morrison, Guy Motil, Dano Pendygrasse, Fran Richards, Shem Roose, Jacques Russo, Brian Sellstrom, Dave Seoane, Beat Steiner, John Stouffer, Greg Stump, Mark Sullivan, Sean Sullivan, Erik Traulsen, Colin Whyte, Tim Wrisley, Scott Yorko, and Drew Zieff.

And to Craig's family, friends, industry folks, and fellow riders including Ken Achenbach, Paul Alden, Brett Angelosi, Becky Aramayo-Biltz, Jason Basarich (quoting Craig: "Go medium and ride forever."), Tina Basich, Bruce Benedict, Marty Brown, John Buffery, Tom Burt, Lizzy Campillo, Donna Carpenter, Jake Burton Carpenter (RIP), Jeana Clark, Chris Copley, Joe Curtes, Mike "Tex" Davenport, Dave Downing, Chris Doyle, Barry Dugan, Shannon Dunn, Sheri Farber, Mark Fawcett, Evan Feen, Jason Ford, Isabella Franca, Jeff Fulton, John Gerndt, Lori Gibbs, Matt Goodman, Terje Haakonsen, Michael Hanlon, Mark Heingartner, Andy Hetzel, Oliver Holzman, Dan Hudson, Bryan Iguchi, Michael Jager, Victoria Jealous, Dennis Jensen, Shawn Johnson, Jeremy Jones, Brian Kelly, Gillian Kelly, Olivia

Kelly, Pat Kelly, Savina Kelly, Terry Kidwell, Bob Klein, Jeff Krueger, Bert LaMar, Kelly Jo Legaz, Javas Lehn, Bret Livingston, Gerry Lopez, Chris Mask, Steve Matthews, Janet Moore, Jessica Moore, Josh Moore, Hiroyuki Nitta, Shaun Palmer, Amber Palson, Jeff Pensiero, Sherman Poppen (RIP), Mike Ranquet, Harold Rishovd, Scott Rowley, Dave Schmidt, Steve Shipsey, Tom Sims (RIP), Brad Steward, Mark Thomas, Quinn Thompson, Carter Turk, Jack Turner, Circe Wallace, Keith Wallace, Dave Weaver, Ste'en Webster, Tony Welch, Hiroyuki Yamada, Abby Young, Jon Yousko, Jim Zellers, and Keri Zudis-Paulsen.

To everyone who helped me understand and document Craig's journey to become a guide, including those who shared from the heart and allowed me access to dark places in their memories of January 20, 2003: Florina Beglinger, Nicoline Beglinger, Ruedi Beglinger, Marty Benson, Heidi Biber, Charles Bieler, Jeff Bullock, Dwayne Congdon, Paula Couturier, Alison Dakin, Dan DiMaria, Lyle Fast, Age Fluitman, Colin Garritty, Emily Grady, Laura Heffler-Stiells, Nick Holmes, Greg Johnson, Mark Karlstrom, Reto Keller, Robert Kennedy, Ted Kerasote, Scott Kessler, Karl Klassen, Rudi Kranabitter, Steve Kuijt, Corinna Laemmerzahl, Heath Lockhurst, Dave Lussier, Megan Michelson, Peter Millar, Dave Nettle, Scott Newsome, Paul Norrie, Terry Palechuk, Joe Pavelich, Joe Pojar, Annie Polucha, Rick Reynolds, Todd Richards, Bob Sayer, Scott Schmidt, Matt Scholl, Don Schwartz, Chic Scott, John Seibert, Lisa Simon, Johann Slam, Larry Stanier, Bruce Stewart, Eriks Suchovs, Timothy Tate, Lee Usher, Mark Vesely, Joey Vosburgh, Evan Weselake, Bernie Wiatzka, Jason Wishlow, Ken Wylie, Colin Zacharias, and many unnamed former guides and avalanche professionals who lent their time and memories of the winter of 2003. As well as various employees, volunteers, and members of the Association of Canadian Mountain Guides, Avalanche Canada Foundation, Backcountry Lodges of BC Association, Canadian Avalanche Association, Canadian Ski Guide Association, and Thompson Rivers University.

Thanks to the professional members of the NCWA, original Don Julio Crew members, and esteemed inhabitants of the SAC. All of you played a role in seeing this story through to completion, as did select critical readers, story consultants, and friends including the Blakeborough, Cupp, McAfee, and Warner families. Also, Natalie Alderton, Jason Amerine, Matt Baglio,

Ali Margo, Larry Beck, Andy Blumberg, Jon Boyer, Craig Cupp, Brian Drennen, Steve Duff, Daniel Dustin, Paige Clay Goodman, Scooter Leonard, Adam Makos, Alden Nash, Chris Noonan, Chris Parker, Matt Pivetti, Greg Saladino, and Rita Samols.

Finally, thank you to all the individuals who have been recipients of Avalanche Canada's Craig Kelly Memorial Scholarship Fund: Dylan Berger, Jeremy Birse, Anna Victoria Bourelle, Craig Browne, Aaron Chance, Robert Chmelyk, Brittney Dickson, Chiara Dürfeld, Christine Feleki, Jake Foster, Colin Garritty, Jennifer Godbout, Sebastien Grondin, Justin Lamoureux, Eric Layton, Heath Lockhurst, Julien Malette, Mitchel McCambly, Cara McGlashan, Angus McLean-Wilson, Daniel Morton, Michael Packham, Markus Perttunen, Bernie Tomaszewski, Joey Vosburgh, Melanie Weise, Jason White, and Michael Wigley.

You are living Craig's legacy.

ABOUT THE AUTHOR

ERIC BLEHM is the award-winning author of the *New York Times* bestsellers *Fearless* and *The Only Thing Worth Dying For*. His first book, *The Last Season*, was the winner of the National Outdoor Book Award and was named by *Outside* magazine as one of the "greatest adventure biographies ever written."